GRAPPLING
WITH
LEGACY

GRAPPLING WITH LEGACY

Rhode Island's Brown Family and
the American Philanthropic Impulse

SYLVIA BROWN

ARCHWAY
PUBLISHING

Archway Publishing books may be ordered through booksellers or by contacting:

Archway Publishing
1663 Liberty Drive
Bloomington, IN 47403
www.archwaypublishing.com
1 (888) 242-5904

ISBN: 978-1-4808-4417-9 (sc)
ISBN: 978-1-4808-4416-2 (hc)
ISBN: 978-1-4808-4418-6 (e)

Library of Congress Control Number: 2017905472

Print information available on the last page.

Archway Publishing rev. date: 10/31/2017

In tribute to all the Nicholas Browns who came before me,
And with high hopes for those who will follow.

CONTENTS

Acknowledgments

When a manuscript takes twelve years to research and write, the names of all those who have contributed along the way are inevitably too numerous to list. Since history was not my academic discipline, I would nevertheless like to recognize the historians who advised me with such generosity. Early on, I was fortunate to speak with the great author of popular history John Julius Norwich, who told me to read every secondary source and commentary, then make up my own mind. I have tried to follow this counsel, guided by accredited historians, notably Dr. D. K. Abbass, Dr. Patrick Conley, Dr. Robert Emlen, Dr. Caroline Frank, Dr. C. Morgan Grefe, Dr. David Kertzner, Dr. Albert Klyberg, Dr. Jane Lancaster, Dr. J. Stanley Lemons, Dr. Elyssa Tardiff, Kimberly Nusco, Dr. Edward Widmer, Dr. Gordon Wood, as well as fine amateur historians, including Henry Brown, Eric Doeschler, experienced authors, including Ellen Brown, and especially my husband, Andrew West, who also happens to be a wonderful copy editor. Any errors of fact and all opinions expressed are, of course, entirely my own.

The size and scope of the Brown family papers (housed at the John Carter Brown Library and the John Hay Library on Brown University campus, as well as at the Rhode Island Historical Society) are both a curse and blessing. It was only thanks to the detective work of my many researchers, notably Dr. Christopher Bickford and Dr. Elizabeth Cooke Stevens, that the manuscripts were found to support the points I sought to make. I was also fortunate that several family members shared with me letters and diaries, which are not as yet available to the public.

I am also grateful to all those who have assisted me with copy editing and proof-reading.

Finally, my years of research in Rhode Island would not have been possible without the hospitality of Ted and Amanda Fischer, as well as that of Garry and Angela Fischer.

PROLOGUE

I looked up with a start as auctioneer Christopher Burge rapped his gavel on the podium. "We now move effortlessly to lot one hundred," the President of Christie's New York called out loudly, then paused to add with impeccable smoothness, ". . . and I wonder why there are so many people in the room?"

Burge continued: "The magnificent Nicholas Brown Chippendale mahogany block-and-shell desk showing on the screen, and for so many months in the room next door. Lot 100."

Even the television crews at the back of the room fell silent.

"Two million–anyone to start?"

Within three minutes, the bidding climbed to $10,750,000. Only two paddles continued to rise. Then it hit eleven million. Burge leaned forward, gripping the front of the podium.

Silence. The hammer went down. "Sold in front then. All done for eleven million. Eleven million."

I had just witnessed the sale of the most expensive piece of furniture[1] in the world.

My father's desk.

---

[1] The $12.1 million paid, with the buyer's premium, was actually the highest price ever achieved at auction for a piece of decorative art. The highest sum to date for a piece of furniture had been $2.97 million in November 1988 at Sotheby's for a Louis XVI console table that once belonged to Marie Antoinette. The highest amount to date for any piece of decorative art had been $11.8 million in 1983 for an illuminated medieval manuscript.

To many experts, it is the most majestic and spectacularly beautiful piece of furniture ever made in America, a nine-and-a-half-foot masterpiece from its scrolling Chinese ogee feet to the tip of its corkscrew flamed finials. "One more inch, and it would have been a freak," commented the great American furniture collector Maxim Karolik. It was made in the 1760s from Cuban mahogany in the Townsend-Goddard workshop of Newport, Rhode Island. In this American colony where merchants were kings, such desk-bookcases evoked their complex lives and were considered the ultimate status symbol. A few remain today in museum collections. In 1989, my father's desk was the last in private hands: the tallest, almost the narrowest, and certainly the most intricately carved of them all.

I did my homework at that desk.

Four years earlier, in 1985, after both my grandparents had died, our family home in Providence, Rhode Island, was discovered to be about to collapse from dry rot and termites. The 1792 Nightingale-Brown House is not only the largest eighteenth century wooden frame house still standing in the United States, but also one of its most graceful and harmonious Georgian-style buildings. My father, along with his brother and sister, felt strongly that this historic landmark should be saved and turned into a center for scholarship, one providing a congenial environment for visiting researchers. Since the family was unable to raise sufficient cash to restore the house, my father decided to sell his most valuable possession, the desk-bookcase which had come down to him through five generations.

It was valued for insurance purposes at $2 million, just about the initial estimate to renovate the house. So, in 1988, my father donated the desk to the "John Nicholas Brown Center for the Study of American Civilization," named after my grandfather. The Center's new director, Rob Emlen, was charged with selecting an auction house for the *Americana* sales the following May. But before he could finalize an agreement, Emlen was contacted by the pre-eminent New York antiques dealer, Harold Sack, who had a private client willing to pay $11 million for the desk.

Few could have resisted such an offer. That enormous sum was enough to restore the house, pay capital gains taxes, and still allow my father to keep some of the money for himself. "No," he responded, "I have given my word. If the desk is attracting this kind of interest, so much the better for the Center. One icon is saving the other." He also insisted that the auction should proceed. Christie's won the mandate by offering $50,000 to have a copy made[2], and by endowing a lecture series at the Center.

Amazingly, when the hammer fell on June 3rd, 1989, the high bid came from the same collector, Texas tycoon Robert Bass, who had instructed Sack to make the private offer. With the additional auction house commission, the desk finally cost him $12.1 million dollars. The under-bidder was Doris Duke, the tobacco heiress who had done so much to restore Newport's colonial houses and build the collections of the Samuel Whitehorne House Museum. She had even requested a cardboard mock-up of the desk to ensure it would fit in that space. But she set herself a bid limit of $10.5 million; Harold Sack's budget was $18 million.

Six years later, in 1995, following a renovation which in the end cost over $9 million, my father presented the house, along with its furniture, family archives and an endowment, to Brown University.

As one of Rhode Island's founding families, his ancestors had been instrumental in bringing a Baptist university, The College of Rhode Island, to Providence in 1770. Many years later, in 1804, the college was renamed Brown University to honor another gift, one of many made over 250 years by the Brown family. Thus, my father viewed his gesture as no more than the continuation of a family philanthropic tradition. This long-established practice had, in my own perception and (as I then naively believed) in the eyes of the world, actually come to define my family.

MARCH 17TH, 2004

Fifteen years after the record-breaking auction, I was once again sitting in a crowded room, this time for the inaugural symposium of Brown University's Steering Committee on Slavery and Justice. The event was entitled "Unearthing

---

[2] Cabinet-maker Alan Breed of Maine used eighteenth century planes and lathes, and even reproduced the design flaws of the original.

the Past: Brown University, the Brown Family and the Rhode Island Slave Trade." And once again there were international reporters present.

One of the panelists, Dr. Joanne Pope Melish, author of *Disowning Slavery: Gradual Emancipation and Race in New England, 1780-1860*, pulled no punches. As I listened in shock, she condemned each of my eighteenth century ancestors without exception and announced flatly, "There were no good Browns."

By 2004, the highly-charged issue of how slavery and the slave trade were intertwined with the early history of our nation and many of its great institutions had come to the forefront of national consciousness. Two years earlier, a number of companies that could trace their roots to the eighteenth century (including Aetna Insurance, Fleet Boston, and the railway giant CSX) had been named in a class action suit for alleged "conspiracy, unjust enrichment and human rights violations" in the eighteenth and nineteenth centuries, and reparations were sought for the descendants of slaves. Several institutions of higher learning were also mentioned as having benefited from the business of slavery–among them Harvard, Yale and Brown Universities. Although dismissed by the Chicago Federal Court in January 2004, the suit had received substantial press coverage and had galvanized communities. To this day, no consensus exists on how to implement reparations.

Most universities implicated had responded by organizing symposia or publishing articles, such as Yale's 2001 Tercentennial piece, on the connections between their founders and the slave trade. Brown University, however, chose to undertake a bolder and more public endeavor. The university's president, Ruth Simmons, the first African-American female head of an Ivy League institution, announced soon after taking office that she was forming a "University Steering Committee on Slavery and Justice" to organize academic events and activities "that might help the nation and the Brown community think deeply, seriously, and rigorously about the questions raised" by the national debate over slavery and reparations.

A few days before the Steering Committee's inaugural symposium, *The New York Times* printed a front-page story about the Brown University initiative. The response was swift and extensive, focused specifically on the narrow but sensational issue of reparations. Some questioned Brown University's motives: "Is this whole process just a pretentious public relations scam, a way to position the university on the politically correct cutting edge?" asked the *New York Observer*.[3]

The Brown family was placed squarely at the center of the debate. As often happens when issues are highly emotional, nuance and complexity were sacrificed to facilitate a simpler narrative of "heroes and villains." My eighteenth century ancestors were indeed successful merchants in an Atlantic economy underpinned by the slave trade. Since our family archive is on the University's campus, it was expedient for the Steering Committee to focus on the Brown family rather than to conduct laborious research on the more than seven hundred Rhode Island families also involved in the slave trade. The media picked up and amplified the spotlight. In September 2005, a *New Yorker* piece by the Pulitzer-prize winner Frances FitzGerald devoted a third of its pages to the Brown family. In March 2006, the *Providence Journal* published a five-part front-page series on Rhode Island's slave trade, two days of which covered the Browns in the Colonial era. Later that year, Charles Rappleye, a Los Angeles–based journalist, published *Sons of Providence: The Brown Brothers, the Slave Trade and the American Revolution*.

The book you are now reading was born from two seminal events which may seem diametrically opposed: my father's decision to give his inheritance (and mine) to Brown University, and the transformation of the Brown family into the poster child for the evils of the slave trade.

Since that day in 2004 when I sat ignorant and unable to respond, I have tried to understand what fuels our family's enduring compulsion to philanthropy–Self-interest? A feeling of guilt? A sense of genuine altruism? Or simply an odd gene that is baked into our DNA?

---

[3] A month later, President Simmons clarified her position in a Boston Globe op-ed piece: "The committee's work is not about whether or how we should pay reparations ... this is an effort designed to involve the campus community in a discovery of the meaning of our past."

Some might expect that I would produce yet another guilt-ridden apology by a descendant of eighteenth century merchants. Others might relish my attacking Brown University's handling of the complex slavery issue. Instead, my research has led me on a voyage of self-discovery to understand the origins of my deep personal interest in philanthropy.

My entire professional career has been focused on economic development and emerging markets. Ten years ago, a course in strategic philanthropy changed my life and prompted a return to my Rhode Island roots. Now, I engage with a variety of non-profits in strategic planning, governance and donor education. Thus, through the lens of my own vocation, the story of my ancestors became the chronicle of American giving over three hundred years: its evolution from colonial-era charity to the impact-based approaches of today.

Charitable giving is such an intrinsic part of the American ethos that its history deserves to be told. Among the ten generations of Browns that have preceded me in Rhode Island, I have chosen to focus on the man who made the switch from self-interested benevolence to genuine altruism: Nicholas Brown II (1769-1841). He was one of America's earliest philanthropists in the modern sense of the term—someone who seeks to apply science and reason in a proactive manner to make the world a better place (as opposed to charity which is limited to concrete, direct acts of compassion and connection to others). He also was an emotionally complicated individual who lived during fascinating but troubled times when the new nation was defining itself; an interesting parallel with the America of today.

Nicholas Brown II (known to his contemporaries as "Nick") was deeply affected by his childhood during the Revolution and the deaths of nine of his ten siblings. Although he did not reveal his inner thoughts and emotions in diaries or letters, I found a fascinating tension between his yearning for law and order and his concern for those less fortunate; between his resistance to changing times and his promotion of radical new ideas for improving society. His tale still resonates today: that of a tenacious business man, steeped in traditional paternalistic values, who became a humanitarian. He not only pioneered the modern notion that universities can be forces for social good, but also funded one of the country's first insane asylums.

His son and grandson emulated the philanthropists of the "Gilded Age," such as Andrew Carnegie who encouraged successful businessmen to build "the ladders on which the aspiring can rise" —particularly libraries. His twentieth century descendants sought to transform the human experience through great art and architecture. My grandfather, John Nicholas Brown II, called "The richest baby in America . . . maybe the world" when his father died in 1900, was a *Monuments Man* and a founder of the urban historic preservation movement. Following a naval career, my father became the executive director of several non-profit organizations. J. Carter Brown, my uncle, was the visionary director of The National Gallery of Art in Washington, DC, where he conceived the "blockbuster exhibition" and left an indelible mark on America's arts and culture. Angela Brown Fischer, my aunt, has devoted a lifetime to non-profit board service.

Since there exist few well documented case studies of an American family over twelve generations, the story of the Browns may help explain how philanthropy became such an integral part of our national ethos. Indeed, one of the unique aspects of the Brown family legacy is our archive. Alongside the urge to play a civic role there seems to co-exist a compulsion to save every scrap of paper. It was the ready accessibility of this archive on Brown University's campus which made it easy for the Steering Committee's researchers to pick items selectively to support their case. But for somebody seeking to address the family history in greater depth and perspective, over a longer period, the archive perversely presents more of a challenge. For a start, it is truly enormous, spread across three libraries, and even today not entirely catalogued. Much of it is a business archive; the early Browns did not indulge in expressing personal opinions or emotions in private correspondence.

Somewhat surprisingly, Brown University has never commissioned a biography of its namesake (though the paucity of Nicholas Brown II's private correspondence and his evident reticence to express personal feelings make a full-scale conventional biography unfeasible). There also is almost nothing penned by the women of my direct family until the late nineteenth century. Although I am fortunate to have inherited my grandparents' library of Rhode Island books, many privately printed, and to have been shown diaries and manuscripts still in private family collections, I did not set out to fill this biographical gap in a literal sense. Rather, I hope to shine some light on the remarkable scope of Nicholas II's endeavours by describing the forces, beliefs and motivations that moulded him and, in turn, his impact upon the times and society in which he lived. He is the focal point for my family's wider story.

I would like also to make my position clear on the painful issue of slavery that originally catalyzed me to sit down and write, lest it may somehow be perceived as "the elephant in the room." This is not a book about slavery and the slave trade, although both must inevitably feature in the story. It does not seek to defend those eighteenth century ancestors who participated in or advocated for the trade, to whatever degree. The legacy of slavery must be faced and the University Steering Committee on Slavery and Justice made a bold attempt to do so.

However, it is just as fatuous to apply the precepts of the present to the mores of the past as it is to affix the same label to twelve generations of one family. Among my collateral ancestors are both John Brown, an ardent proponent and spokesman for the slave trade, and his younger brother Moses, one of the earliest and most fervent advocates of abolition. Both were intelligent and thoughtful men, each responsible for his own actions. In a much more religious age when people still lived in the expectation of divine judgement, each followed the dictates of his own conscience and was no doubt content to be judged accordingly. To modern perceptions, some of those dictates undoubtedly come across more sympathetically than others; painful topics such as child labor or mental illness offend our modern sensibilities far more than they did two hundred years ago.

Rather than play a sterile blame-game, the best way anyone can seek to atone for the sins of the past is, I believe, to address the very real and continuing problems of the present. Eleven generations after my ancestor Chad Browne arrived in Rhode Island, I relish answering the same irrepressible urge to do my part—in my own way.

CHAPTER 1

SEIZING OPPORTUNITY

"If I Should never Venter nothing I should never have nothing" —Obadiah Brown

The story of the Rhode Island Browns begins on a spring day in 1638 when Chad Browne[4] stepped aboard the ship *Martin,* bound for Boston. A currier (a maker of leather bridles and harnesses for horses) from High Wycombe in Buckinghamshire, Chad epitomized a breed of artisan craftsmen who, by disposition and necessity, embodied the no-nonsense pragmatism of successful pioneers. In the coming months, Chad would meet one of early America's great visionaries, Roger Williams—an early proponent of religious freedom and separation of church and state, which are cornerstones of the United States we know today. As described by Sarah Vowell in *The Wordy Shipmates:*

> Williams might be the most ambitious of all the New England Puritans, but his ambitions are strictly spiritual. He fears no man, only God. He desires heavenly riches, not earthly influence.... His fellow New Englanders find his zeal kind of inspirational but awfully off-putting.

---

[4] The Browns would change the spelling of their name a century later.

Certainly, Williams needed by his side a man who would translate all this spirituality into practical reality. Through a combination of fortuitous timing and sheer strength of character, Chad Browne became the artisan who executed the philosopher Williams's vision. As noted by historian Ted Widmer, "He [Chad] must have been something of a political genius if he could bring consensus to the original settlers, so quick to protest oppression." Thus did the Brown family establish a position of civic leadership from its earliest days in America. It would be bolstered over the coming centuries by extraordinary economic success and possessions far more tangible than Williams's heavenly riches, which in turn would fund extensive philanthropy.

Shortly before boarding the *Martin*, Chad Browne of High Wycombe, his wife Elizabeth and their eight-year old son John had converted to the Baptist faith, one of the Puritan denominations (known as "dissenters") that challenged England's established Anglican Church. Chad and Elizabeth particularly appreciated the Baptists' egalitarian and positive outlook–pastors were unpaid and drawn from the laity. But Archbishop William Laud, a favorite advisor of King Charles I, could not bear such dissent and had launched a brutal campaign against the "non-conformists." Life became so unbearable for the dissenters that over ten thousand migrated to the Massachusetts Bay Colony in America over the course of the 1630s. By following in their wake, Chad knew he was giving up all that was familiar for a dangerous sea voyage and a harsh life in the New World. Who would need his skills as a currier or a maker of bridle leather where there were still so few horses? He did not foresee, however, that Boston's Puritan authorities would be no more tolerant than Archbishop Laud. They prohibited such mundane activities as smoking tobacco or playing cards. Only those individuals whose religious views accorded with their own could become Freemen and vote in the colony. Within six months of their arrival in July 1638, Chad and Elizabeth Browne were thus looking for a way out. Around them, other disillusioned immigrants were leaving for new settlements in the wilderness to the south. Chad and Elizabeth had two options: a settlement on an island with fertile soil and fine harbors (Aquidneck

Island in Narragansett Bay), or a rocky hill at the northern head of the Bay. Chad chose the second option for one main reason: Roger Williams.

The son of a prosperous London tailor, Williams had read law at Cambridge University and was ordained an Anglican priest in 1629 before joining the Puritan movement and immigrating to America in 1631. He preached in Boston and Salem but also supplemented his church earnings as a trader and missionary among the indigenous peoples whose languages and customs he took the trouble to learn. Soon, he began to reproach the Massachusetts Bay authorities for stealing native lands. He also disagreed with the Puritan leaders over the concept of "soul liberty"—an individual's freedom to interpret the Bible and to shape his faith in a secular society, independent of religious or civil authority. Such civil disobedience was not to be tolerated, no matter how admirable the man. In 1635, Williams was put on trial for sedition and sentenced to deportation back to England.

Williams managed to flee south in the dead of winter and lived for three months with the Wampanoag Tribe at the edge of the Seekonk River (now Rehoboth, Massachusetts). Other unhappy immigrants joined him later that spring, only to learn that Plymouth Colony was seeking to arrest them. So twelve "loving friends" packed their goods into a large dugout canoe and paddled across the Seekonk to safety. Williams named the spot in honor of "God's merciful Providence."

Today's Rhode Island is about the size of greater Houston, Texas. A diagonal drawn from its southwest corner on the ocean to the Massachusetts border opposite would be just forty-two miles long. But with over four hundred miles of shoreline, nearly every point in the state is less than twenty miles from the sea. Formed by the melting of glaciers at the end of the last Ice Age, Narragansett Bay eats far north into the rectangle that is Rhode Island. Within the Bay stretches the long, narrow island of Aquidneck. From Providence at the Bay's head to Newport at the southern tip of Aquidneck Island, the distance over water is twenty miles, with another five miles to the open sea.

When the earth's temperatures warmed about eight thousand years ago, spruce forests gave way to pine and later to oak. The handful of indigenous tribes who inhabited the area migrated with the seasons between the coast and the interior, supplementing their diet with domestic crops such as corn, squash, beans and pumpkin. On his quest for a water passage to China, the explorer Giovanni di Verrazzano sailed up the American coast from New York in 1524 and discovered an island "about the bigness of the Island of Rhodes." Based on this observation, early settlers in the seventeenth century named the area Rhode Island.

Verrazzano found the native inhabitants so friendly that he sailed with their guidance up Narragansett Bay. His crew found the inhabitants settled around staked-out fishing areas, cultivated fields, and a number of semi-permanent villages led by sachems. By the seventeenth century, they traded with the occasional Dutch merchants from New Amsterdam, using a system of beads and seashells, called "wampum." When Roger Williams arrived in 1636, the area was home to some twenty thousand indigenous peoples. But their numbers were declining rapidly under the impact of smallpox, alcohol, land skirmishes and enslavement by the Massachusetts Bay Colony to the north. Only the peaceful Narragansett Tribe of about seven thousand, under the leadership of the sachems Canonicus and Miantinomi, remained relatively untouched and thus became the dominant tribe in New England (a smaller tribe of about a thousand, the Wampanoags, also lived nearby).

Sachems Miantomi and Canonicus granted Williams a large plot of land and signed the deed with their bow and arrow. In turn, Williams drafted a simple compact that made the settlers fellow "Proprietors" of these lands. It made no mention of God (as opposed to compacts by Boston's settlers who considered themselves "a model of God's kingdom on earth"). Instead, it noted, "we do promise to subject ourselves . . . to all such orders or agreements as shall be made for the public good of the body in an orderly way by the major consent . . . only in civil things." An unmistakable line was thus drawn between temporal and spiritual power.

Roger Williams dreamed of a utopian colony where each family owned an equal-sized plot and lived in brotherly love; indeed, Chad and two other settlers allocated the land in equal 100-acre lots, sufficient for a home, planting, grazing, and some woodland. Chad, described as a "wise and godly soul," was also among the ten settlers who repudiated their infant baptism in 1639 and re-baptized each other,[5] establishing the First Baptist Church in America. Just four months later, Williams underwent a crisis of conscience over belonging to any established church and withdrew to the wilderness, so Chad took over as lay pastor. Over the remaining twelve years of his life, he would serve as arbitrator to "weigh and consider differences and bring [them] to unity and peace," especially when the early settlers argued that they deserved more land than did new arrivals. Considered "a man of sound judgment" with a "cooler temperament" than that of Williams (who could be irascible and obstinate), Chad helped to draft the 1640 covenant that defined the government of the settlement of "Providence Plantations."

That narrow strip of flat land along a tidal estuary known as the Great Salt Cove soon offered little to boast about. Homes were mostly wattle and daub huts with dirt floors, built along "Towne Street," a path from which the tree stumps had been cleared. Behind it, the rocky ground rose steeply, making farming arduous. Three of the five sons Chad fathered in America sought a better life away from Providence but the eldest, John, followed his father in civic appointments, surveying land and serving as an Elder of the Baptist Church. At a time when boundaries were a central preoccupation, surveyors wielded great power. John Browne did well enough to purchase several of the initial home lots plus land for planting and pastures, as well as livestock.

Life in the little settlement was far from Roger Williams's vision of brotherly love. The rights of proprietors were ill defined and not sanctioned by English courts. Providence was one of five separate settlements around Narragansett Bay (along with Portsmouth, Newport, Warwick and Pawtuxet), which united only occasionally when neighboring colonies tried to grab their land. Williams did his best to build ties of trust with the native peoples; he even published in 1643 the first Native American-English dictionary, *The Key into the Language of America*. But

---

[5] Williams believed that only those capable of confessing their faith and experiencing grace should be baptized.

warfare continually threatened. He had no choice but to return across the Atlantic to secure a patent, a legitimate deed, from England. The Mother Country, however, was in the midst of civil war.

At first, the English Puritan leaders in control of Parliament were impressed with Williams's Algonquin dictionary because it spoke of saving "the souls of the heathen." Accordingly, Williams managed to obtain a patent in 1657. It was quite remarkable that Williams was granted a purely secular patent at the very moment when a bloody civil war was being fought in England with religion a key issue. But while in London, he published another text, *The Bloody Tenent of Persecution,* which declared that "the sovereign, original, and foundation of civil power lies in the People." Parliament was not amused and ordered all copies burned.[6] Fortunately, Williams was already on his way home to Providence.

Thanks to his efforts, the scattered settlements around Narragansett Bay were now united in a colony named *Rhode Island and Providence Plantations.* Rhode Island's first legislative session proclaimed "the form of Government established . . . is democratical, that is to say, a government held by the free and voluntary consent of all." John Browne (Chad's eldest son) was elected to the new General Assembly.

But when monarchy was restored to England fifteen years later, King Charles II immediately nullified all actions taken by the men who had beheaded his father. A new charter was needed urgently to preserve the little colony's hard-won rights. John Clarke, Rhode Island's representative in London, negotiated for three years the document that would guide the government of Rhode Island for the next 180 years (upon its retirement in 1843, it was the oldest constitutional charter in the world). Finally, on July 8th, 1663, a charter was signed by the King which allowed Rhode Island "to hold forth a lively experiment, that a flourishing and civil state may stand, yea and best be maintained . . . with a full liberty in religious commitments." Within this remarkable document were provisions far different from those found in the charters of other colonies: the inhabitants would be free to choose their own leaders and

---

[6] A few survived. One was sold at auction in 2015 for $175,000–it was the copy Nicholas Brown II had given his uncle Moses as a birthday present in 1822.

follow their "personal spiritual instincts" (the laws of England required uniformity in religious belief); it recognized that Native Americans must be compensated for their land; and, it offered democratic freedoms to the colony not found in any other charter. The freemen of Rhode Island could elect their own rulers and make their own laws, as well as control their own military affairs, and trade throughout the American colonies. Every official, from Governor to woodman, would be either elected or chosen in town meetings whose representatives would sit in the General Assembly. Thus, by guaranteeing separation of church and state, as well as freedom of religion, the 1663 Charter established the first enduring republican government in the New World.

Once again, a miracle was achieved . . . perhaps because the "experiment" was at a safe distance across the Atlantic.

Thus, Rhode Island's unique Charter infused its people with both intense pride and the contrarian, sometimes rebellious, spirit that persists to this day. Since church and state were separate, Providence did not physically resemble most typical New England settlements: there was no town green, no church building, and no burial ground. There was no tithing, so the inhabitants could keep more of their spare capital and invest in their own enterprises. But this state of affairs also meant that Rhode Island lacked the communal sense of purpose and the stability that the unity of church and state fostered in other colonies.

By 1663, the number of families in Providence had increased to about fifty, with a total population of three hundred. Activity was centered around the mill and the tavern at the north end of Towne Street. Since farming was almost impossible on the rocky hill, lands on "Weybosset Neck" (on the opposite side of the Great Salt Cove) were set aside as common ground for raising corn, tobacco and food crops, and for grazing livestock. But the local light and sandy soil was poor, yielding just enough for subsistence. The townspeople had few funds to invest in the forests or the sea. Early accounts describe times of great scarcity relieved by occasional "feasts of boiled bass without butter."

In contrast, Aquidneck Island to the south offered some of the richest farmland in New England; its smaller outlying islands provided excellent

pasture, free from wolves. Rather than following Roger Williams's egalitarian utopia, Aquidneck's settlers had been allocated land according to
their wealth and social rank. They invested in livestock; a pound of meat
or wool was more profitable than a pound of wheat since it was easier
to clear pastureland than to plow fields. The wealthy, who were often
familiar with estate management, imported English grass seed to feed
their herds. By 1657, Aquidneck Island was producing enough agricultural surplus to attract traders from Salem, Boston and New Amsterdam
(the future New York). At the island's southern tip, the settlement of
Newport grew up around an excellent harbor, well sheltered and perfectly
positioned at the mouth of Narragansett Bay to take advantage of any
shipping going south from Boston. In the late 1640s, a large wharf was
built and, by 1650, Newporters already had sent cattle to Barbados, rum
to the Guinea coast of Africa, and had served as sales agents for a Dutch
privateer. By the 1680s, they were trading with London. By 1690, the
population was 2,600; over half were engaged in maritime trade. When
the colony's first tax was raised in 1668, Aquidneck Island contributed
£208; Providence only £10.

Much of Newport's growth was spearheaded by the Quakers who
arrived in the 1660s, spreading a message of peace, love and commercial
zeal. With "one foot in the meetinghouse, the other in the counting
house," they also paid careful attention to moral principles of honesty,
thrift, sobriety, hard work in business, and a pious commitment to help
the poor. "Witnessing" for their faith, they became the most successful
evangelists of the seventeenth century; by 1700, half of Rhode Island's
population was Quaker. Although their refusal to swear allegiance to
king or church left Quakers open to persecution elsewhere, this concentration in Rhode Island ensured an element of safety in numbers. The
arrival of Sephardic Jews in the late 1650s and 1660s further enhanced
the scope of Newport's trading network and commercial acumen. They
became prominent merchants and grew to thirty families with names
such as Lopez, Levy, Rivera and Touro.

While Providence struggled with subsistence farming, disaster
loomed. By 1676 there were about seventy thousand Europeans in New

England, insisting on the right to private property and stirring up rivalries among the tribes. Fewer than 1,800 whites had settled around the Narragansett Bay area but even the tribes once friendly to Roger Williams had become estranged from the European colonists. A new Wampanoag chief, Metacomet, known as "King Philip," dreamed of driving them out.

Roger Williams managed to keep the Narragansett Tribe neutral when King Philip's warriors began raiding the Connecticut Valley. Nevertheless, soldiers from the Plymouth Colony attacked the Narragansett's principal village in the "Great Swamp" (modern South Kingston town) on a freezing night in December 1675. Three hundred braves were killed, along with four hundred women and children. Abandoning their neutrality (and believing that Rhode Islanders had been involved in the massacre), the Narragansett regrouped and launched a vengeful offensive the following spring. After killing a company of Englishmen and friendly Native Americans, they advanced on Providence. John Browne and his family fled to Newport. Remaining behind with a handful of townspeople, Roger Williams watched his life's work go up in flames—seventy-two houses were destroyed. By the time famine, disease and wartime casualties finally overcame the Narragansett and their allies, three thousand Indigenous Americans and six hundred Europeans had died. Nearly every farm south of Providence was demolished; only Aquidneck Island remained unscathed.

Yet King Philip's War, the bloodiest per capita ever fought on American soil as a percentage of the population,[7] also proved a turning point for Providence. Out of its ashes grew new opportunities and new attitudes. The refugees returned from Newport inspired by that booming seaport of four hundred houses. New shops appeared in Providence offering farming tools, building materials, food and clothing. Immigrants arrived with the capital, the experience, and the ambition to try new ventures. The rebirth took almost fifteen years, but Providence finally emerged from its slumber.

---

[7] Historian Nathaniel Philbrick estimates that per capita the war was twice as bloody as the Civil War and seven times as deadly as the Revolutionary War.

One of the pioneers who transformed Providence was Pardon
Tillinghast, a former soldier under Oliver Cromwell who emigrated in
1643 as a Baptist "cooper-preacher," combining religion with commerce.
In 1645 he was granted twenty-five acres of land; the deed was signed by
John Browne. In 1680, he petitioned the town for "a little spot of land . . .
for the building himself of a storehouse with the privilege of a wharf
also," the first in Providence. The farmers were extremely upset; how
were they to reach their fields and pastures if the riverbank was built up
with wharves? As his businesses flourished, Pardon Tillinghast became
increasingly involved in the town and in the Baptist Church, serving as
its pastor for thirty-seven years. In 1700, he erected the first permanent
church building "in the form of a haycap with a chimney in the middle."
He fathered twelve children to whom he left an estate of £500 (at the
time, a horse was worth £3 and an ox £4) at his death, at age ninety-six.

Other dynamic newcomers sent the first ship from Providence to
the Caribbean and started building *sloops*, single-mast vessels of fifty to
sixty feet that would become the mainstay of trade with the West Indies.
But maritime commerce was still in its infancy. In his 1680 report to the
Lords of Trade, Rhode Island's governor wrote:

> [Our] chief export is horses and provisions. We import
> a small quantity of Barbados goods to supply our fami-
> lies. Most of our colony lives comfortable by improving
> the wilderness. We have no shipping belonging to our
> colony but only a few sloops. . . . The greatest obstruction
> concerning trade is the want of merchants and men of
> considerable Estates among us.

However, of the fifty-two merchants listed in the Rhode Island land records of 1690, only four were from Providence.

International trade was of no interest to John Browne's son James,
born in 1666. He followed his father on the Town Council, and also
served on special commissions to deal with new highways and bridges.
James Browne tended his land with the help of two slaves and engaged in

minor forms of retailing, principally cider, apple beer and tobacco. His chief interest was the Baptist Church where he served as assistant pastor, then as Elder, until his death in 1732.

Into this pious, dignified family burst another but a very different James.

Born in 1698, this second of Elder James's ten children was fascinated by the sea from childhood. Across from his front door, warehouses were going up, full of exotic goods like molasses, indigo and fine fabrics. Striking up conversations on the wharfs with seamen from Boston, he heard about that maritime powerhouse of seven thousand inhabitants who could afford brick houses. Mariners from Newport told him of fabulous riches to be made as privateers. Young James dreamed of a better future than collecting oysters on the beach or tilling the rocky soil with his back to the sea.

In August 1719, twenty-one-year old James bought a small lot with a gangway to the Salt River for £40 from the prosperous merchant William Crawford. Two months later, he bought himself a "ciphering book" of geometrical and nautical problems in which he proudly inscribed "James Browne His Book Begun October the 24th, 1719." He took its lessons to heart. The first page described navigation "as an art by which the industrious mariner is enabled to conduct a ship the shortest & safest way between two assigned places." James seized every opportunity to sail in Narragansett Bay and along the Atlantic coast. Two years later (and only ten years from the start of shipbuilding in Providence), he and five partners contracted with shipwright John Barnes to construct a 73-ton vessel. By the time the ship was finished, he owned half the shares. Now all he needed was a sponsor to underwrite a voyage to the Caribbean.

Nicholas Power was one of the few men in Providence who understood that maritime commerce was the way of the future; indeed, he was married to Pardon Tillinghast's daughter. He owned a wharf, a warehouse, a cooper shop, a cider mill, and fathered a vivacious daughter, Hope. Power was successful enough to have the first dining room in Providence (furnished with a table, four chairs, a looking glass and a punch bowl). He was also an ideal role model for young James: Power was a third-generation Providence resident who had served on the Town Council, in the Rhode Island General Assembly, and regularly participated in civic projects including a new bridge to the Weybosset side. His daughter Hope carried in her Tilllinghast-Power genes the ideal combination of Baptist piety, commercial acumen, and adventurous spirit. James Browne asked for her hand. They were married in December 1722. Early the following year, he appeared in Newport as "Captain" James Browne of the sloop *Four Bachelors,* ready to "Sayl with the first fair Wind & Weather." In one stroke, Captain James acquired a wife, credibility, contacts and capital to launch a trading enterprise. His new father-in-law signed the instructions on behalf of "myself and the Company owners of the Said Sloop and Cargo on board. . . . And so God send you on a prosperous voyage."

And so it was. Upon his return, Captain James had sufficient funds to purchase three parcels of land on the east side of Towne Street, now "four poles wide," for the substantial sum of £308, together with rights to common lands. He maintained his partnership with his father-in-law until Nicholas Power's death in 1734.

But with his own father, relations were fraught. Elder James disapproved of his son's new vocation as a merchant and his devotion to commercial success rather than Godly favor. Still, despite his misgiving, he gave the young man sixty acres of land on the Seekonk River "Out of love and goodwill" and sold him a small lot on Towne Street for a warehouse and shop. But he feared for his son's soul. In 1731 Elder James wrote a sermon "TRUTH, A chosen description of truth and error"-a poignant effort by an old man to accept that his simple world of preaching and farming was being forever transformed by the advent of maritime commerce. It tells of the "great comfort and consolation as the man of God has," as opposed to the risk and uncertainty faced by the "marchant man." But young Captain James remained unmoved by these words and publicly proclaimed his impatience with "the Ignorance of all ministers who have disputes and debates." To mark the point, he inscribed his children's births in his ledger book rather than in the family Bible.

Captain James realized that commercial success required finding ways to add value to his cargo. But while Virginia and Maryland had tobacco, South Carolina grew rice, and the Mid-Atlantic colonies produced wheat, there existed no staple crop in the North East to barter for English manufactured goods. Rhode Island's best alternative was to import molasses (the bi-product of sugar refining) from the Caribbean and to distill it into rum, which was then re-exported. A gallon of molasses produced an almost equal quantity of rum, but the liquor could be sold for over twice the price of molasses. Nicholas Power was the first to own stills in Providence; Captain James expanded them. By 1760, there would be some thirty distilleries in Rhode Island and molasses was "the engine in the hand of the merchant." In an era when a sip of water could kill, liquor was the common form of drink. Captain James also commissioned ships, opened shops, and built a slaughterhouse—all to grow his trading activities with the Caribbean and other colonies.

Captain James was a tough, impatient man with a strong temper who wasted little time on niceties. To a recently bereaved widow he wrote only "So Shure as we come into the World we must go out" before demanding payment of a debt. He was also deeply pragmatic, a trait that would be inherited by his son Nicholas and his grandson Nicholas II. Intestinal problems plagued him for years. During a severe illness in the spring of 1736, he directed "That if it be the pleasure of the heavens to take the breath out of my mortal body . . . I am quite free and willing that my body may be opened, in order that my fellow creatures and neighbours may see whether my grievance hath been nothing but the spleen or not." He even admitted (uncharacteristically) to his younger brother Obadiah that "Health in this world is better than wealth." But in spring 1739, when a travelling fair came to Providence, he could not resist entering a weight lifting competition to demonstrate his fabled strength. Something ruptured in his weakened abdomen and he died on April 26, age 41.

While her husband was alive, Hope Power Browne was closely involved in Captain James's business, as were many wives in the early colonial era (her account books are the only female business papers in the Brown archives until the late nineteenth century). He frequently entrusted her to carry on trade in his absence; she even had her own clients. Contrary to her non-practicing husband, "Mother Hope" was a lifelong member of the Baptist Church, to which she contributed generously. She was one of her husband's three executors, instructed to sell everything but the homestead and what was needed to support the family. Unless she remarried, Hope would receive one-third of all proceeds, enough to remain in business on her own account. Captain James left her precise directions, anticipating that she would have to carry on the family business without him:

> My Deir, if you follow the following directions whilst I am gon you may do wall: if I naver cum if you should lok on tham once in a while thay will do no harme in your biness…. Trust no man one penny worth of anything. Let them have nothing without money. Take all the cash you can so that your estate is not stolen . . . my deir, if anything is wanting in you it will be cash.

There was little sentimentality in Captain James's letters, in stark contrast with those written by his brother in law, Nicholas Power Jr., who frequently reminded his wife of "that deep bond of affection which has so nerely allied us together."

Captain James's and Hope's six children—James (born in 1724), Mary (born in 1726), Nicholas (born in 1729), Joseph (born in 1733), John (born in 1736) and Moses (born in 1738) —were to receive equal shares of their father's estate when they reached age twenty-one (with an additional £100 to James as the eldest son). Hope Brown "was remarkably amiable in her temper and brought up her boys well; a proof says one, of strength of character and mind."[8] But Captain James's will stipulated that the children should be raised to only a "sensible" level of learning, meaning practical training in business. This task fell to their Uncle Obadiah. Fourteen years Captain James's junior, Obadiah Browne

---

[8] This quote is attributed to the Reverend James Manning.

had started his professional life by helping his brother with accounting duties, then made his first voyage in 1733 on the sloop *Dolphin*. Though Captain James was a demanding task master, Obadiah was devoted to him and wrote to Hope Browne upon his brother's death ". . . he was ye only friend to me." Of his eight children, only his four daughters survived infancy. So Obadiah's nephews became his surrogate sons, particularly Moses whom he officially adopted at the age of twelve.

Thus, nearly a hundred years after Chad Browne's arrival in Providence, his great grandson launched the family on the trajectory that was to be the source of its fortune, fame and influence. Although his own career was curtailed prematurely, Captain James managed before his death to produce the four remarkable sons whose collective mercantile success would far eclipse his own wildest dreams.

Taking over his older brother's business under the name of Obadiah Brown & Co., Uncle Obadiah modernized his surname, dropping the final *e*. He raised his nephews according to John Locke's principles on education: frequent bathing, dancing, swimming and playing in the open air, cheese for breakfast, and no drinking of water. Like other American children of their generation, they thrived on high-protein Native American foods that included baked beans, succotash and corn, as well as occasional treats from the West Indies such as chocolate, sugar, molasses, ginger and dried fruits.

In the Massachusetts Bay Colony, most children received some form of schooling, which the Puritan leaders considered important for a proper relationship with God. Towns were obligated to provide a school. In Rhode Island, however, the Baptists believed that a personal connection with God was inspired by the Holy Spirit and did not require an education. There were only three small fee-charging schools where boys in Providence might learn reading, writing and how to do a sum in three (Mary briefly attended a girl's school whose hours were 6:00 to 7:30 in the morning, and 4:30 to 6:00 in the evening). Fortunately, the Brown boys had a natural aptitude for mathematics. In his cipher book, John Brown noted "John Brown. The Cleverest Boy in Providence

Town." From the age of 16, the boys were apprenticed to their uncle's counting house; in that hive of activity, Captains received ships' papers, supercargoes (who managed the ship's cargo and sales activities) came by for instruction, shopkeepers placed wholesale orders and signed complex barter transactions, and clerks drafted letters and kept the ledgers. Apprentices like the Brown boys ran errands, carried messages to ships at the wharfs, copied letters and accounts, and even made deliveries to Newport. Uncle Obadiah made his nephews study, in his well-worn copy of *A Guide to Book Keepers According to the Italian Method,* the principles of double-entry accounting which he practiced assiduously. Most apprenticeships continued to the age of twenty-one or twenty-two, but Uncle Obadiah allowed his nephews to transact business in their own name from the age of eighteen.

The brothers also found time to enjoy themselves with "turtle frolicks" along the river and pleasant evenings in Luke Thurston's tavern by the Great Bridge (that linked Providence to Weybosset Neck) or in one of the town's thirty-one other taverns. Nicholas's account book includes a fine for a broken window at Joseph Olney's tavern in addition to a substantial bill for punch. John often referred in his day book (personal ledger) to his "club" at which he drank punch, played cards, and "entertained young ladies." When caught breaking a meetinghouse window at fifteen, he managed to have twelve-year old Moses hauled up in his place. John's first run-in with the British occurred at age twenty when his ship, the *Charming Mary,* was stopped on the Delaware River by a twenty-gun man o'war seeking to impress (kidnap) American sailors. Four years later, he enlisted a group of friends in commandeering a cannon to protect a travelling theater which the good citizens of Providence wanted to shut down because they believed public entertainment fostered loose morals.

Nicholas, Joseph, John and Moses—all destined to make such a mark upon their age—were from their earliest years very different but complimentary figures. Nicholas's life was transformed on the eve of his twenty-first birthday when his older brother James took ill and died at sea off the coast of York, Virginia in 1750. With a heavy heart, Nicholas

completed the last entry in James's sea journal. He took his new responsibility as the *de facto* eldest son very seriously. Under colonial laws,
he was allowed a double portion of his brother's estate but instead, he
divided the inheritance equally among his siblings. While they each in
turn married and settled down, Nicholas focused solely on his business
activities, spending his rare moments of free time reading books on
political science and history which he ordered from England. One of his
most treasured books was Samuel Sewall's *Some Few Lines Towards A
Description Of The New Heaven As It Makes Those Who Stand Upon The
New Earth*, a celebrated 1727 pamphlet by an early American opponent
of slavery.

Nicholas did not marry until May 2nd 1762, age almost 33. His
wife-to-be Rhoda Jenckes was his second cousin, also descended from
Chad Browne. She was the fifth daughter of Judge Daniel Jenckes who
had been Chief Justice of the Superior Court for thirty years, a deputy
of the General Assembly for forty years, an active member of the Baptist
Church, and one of the richest men in town. Her grandfather, Joseph
Jenckes—who stood seven feet tall in his stocking feet—was the first non-
Quaker and non-Newporter to be elected Governor of Rhode Island. At
age twenty-one Rhoda had both the youth and connections to make the
ideal wife, and was well suited to her tall husband. The wedding was a
simple civil affair blessed by the Reverend Samuel Winson, Elder of the
First Baptist Church. The couple set up home in a large new house next
door to John's on Towne Street.

Mary, the only girl and two years younger than Nicholas, had married a Dutch Doctor, David Vanderlight, a graduate of the University
of Leyden and the principal druggist in Providence. He brought from
Europe expertise in producing candles from sperm whale "head matter."
Sadly, their only son died in infancy and Dr. Vanderlight followed him to
an early grave in 1755. Mary never remarried and lived with her mother.

The second brother was Joseph, whose passion lay not in commerce
but in the sciences, particularly "natural philosophy" —electricity, astronomy and architecture—all of which he taught himself from books and
scientific apparatus ordered from England. He even kept a thermometer

outside his parlor window. A fine amateur architect, Joseph designed the three major community buildings that embellished Providence in the years leading to the Revolutionary War: the Market House, University Hall and the First Baptist Church. His family home on Towne Street is still notable for its lovely scrolled roofline. One of his greatest achievements was organizing the citizens of Providence to observe the Transit of Venus in 1769, a seminal moment in the town's history both for the communal effort required and for the importance of findings that allowed the first scientific calculation of the size of the solar system. Described by his brothers as "a man with a speculative mind" who was little concerned with money, Joseph often seemed uneasy in their company. His lack of commercial acumen was a source of frustration to his brothers; his younger brother Moses noted that he found Joseph "something wanting respecting the necessary business of his life that sometimes is trying to my patience." In 1759, Joseph married his first cousin, Elizabeth Power, who became closely involved in his business affairs and often drafted correspondence in her husband's name (Joseph's difficulty in writing did not preclude him from assembling an impressive library). Only three of their five children survived to adulthood. His son, born in 1762 and named Obadiah, was known as "somewhat of a free thinker" (a polite euphemism for odd behavior).

John, the third brother, had announced as a youth that he would be a millionaire before the age of 30. By his early 20s, he was already a seasoned supercargo on Obadiah Brown & Co. ships, bound for New York, Philadelphia, Newport, Boston and Nantucket. Soon, he was making loans to friends. He found business stimulating and enjoyed the commercial process as much as the final result. At age 24, John proposed to Sarah Smith whose wealthy Quaker family's extensive lands in the northwest corner of Rhode Island supplied much of the wood to the Brown family's iron foundry near Scituate. They married in a lavish wedding on November 27th, 1760 attended by "all the ladies and gentlemen of the town," and moved to a large brick house on Towne Street with its own lot, wharf and warehouses. Despite her husband's flamboyant lifestyle, Sarah remained reserved and close to her family with whom she continued to attend Quaker meetings.

The youngest of the four brothers, Moses, displayed such a keen intelligence that his uncle and adopted father Obadiah started his apprenticeship early. In 1742, the forteen-year old could be found testing barrels of molasses at the docks—which earned him the nickname of "little molasses-faced Moses." By age sixteen, he was travelling to Newport and keeping records for his brother Joseph at the family's spermaceti candle works. By age eighteen, he was transacting business in his own name. In 1760, age twenty-two, Moses inherited a 145-acre farm from his father's estate at the rear of the settled part of town. That year, Uncle Obadiah made him a full partner of Obadiah Brown & Co. At his adopted father's death, Moses was left an inheritance equal to that of each of Obadiah's four daughters. He spent the rest of 1762 assiduously collecting his uncle's debts, earning a new title—"that damn little Moses." Though a great admirer of pretty girls, he ended up choosing the one he knew best, his first cousin, Uncle Obadiah's nineteen-year old daughter Anna (known as Nancy).[9] On January 7th, 1764, the *Providence Gazette* announced, "Last evening Mr Moses Brown of this Place, Merchant, was married to Miss Nancy Brown (Daughter of the late Obadiah Brown, esq) an agreeable young lady with a handsome Fortune." The couple purchased the first coach in Providence and built a large farmhouse just outside town. When it was ready, only Mother Hope, Mary Vanderlight (Obadiah's unmarried daughter Mary), and "five Negro slaves" were left in the old family home.

On June 15th, 1762, John and Moses were conducting business in Newport when an urgent message arrived that Uncle Obadiah lay dying. He had been on his way from Providence to his country seat in Glocester, Rhode Island, when he took ill "with a stoppage of the surculation of the fluids and somewhat like a bilious colick." Moses rushed back to Providence, arriving to speak one last time with his adopted father. John, true to character, remained behind to "compleat sum business of importance." The four brothers inscribed Obadiah's tombstone with these words: "He had strong mental powers guided with exquisite judgment/ Was honest, industrious, frugal, temperate, affable, benevolent."

---

[9] Thus, three of the four brothers married cousins (two of whom were first cousins). A common practice in colonial America, it reinforced the sense of clan.

Nicholas took over as senior partner of the family firm, now re-named Nicholas Brown & Co. For a decade, until 1771, this was the banner under which the four surviving brothers would remain united and realize their ascendancy within Providence's merchant community. Their success was no accident. It was not simply that four heads were better than one, although it is indisputable that collectively they encompassed an extraordinary range of talent and competence. They also had a singular approach to the whole function of being merchants, one which set them apart from most of their contemporaries (certainly in Providence) and which was a tribute to those early lessons inculcated by their Uncle Obadiah.

Successful colonial merchants needed to be innovative with a high appetite for risk. Faced with a highly cyclical business of constant boom-bust cycles and wildly fluctuating prices, and constantly short of hard cash, knowing how to mitigate that risk was the key to success. Shipping schedules depended entirely on wind and waves that could wreak havoc with a merchant's best-laid plans. One hurricane could sink a cargo or destroy all the crops on a Caribbean island. But for the lucky trader who showed up with foodstuffs and lumber just after a storm, there were enormous profits to be reaped. Maritime commerce left little time for leisurely, "disinterested" pursuits. Opportunism was a way of life; some-times, this meant subordinating conscience to convenience–a theme to which we shall return in later chapters.

Uncle Obadiah used to say "If I Should never Venter nothing I should never have nothing," and taught his nephews to seize opportunity and to manage risk. The four brothers learned early about transforming raw material into higher value products. To Captain James's distillery, shops and slaughterhouse, Uncle Obadiah had added shipbuilding, marine insurance, a rope walk (one of the few enterprises that employed women who stretched and twisted locally-grown hemp fibers), and a chocolate mill that used waterpower to grind cocoa beans. Since rum was not a growth industry (annual consumption was already a huge twenty gal-lons per adult), he looked to new opportunities. One was to invest in the most essential of consumer products: candles. Light was needed in every household but the commonly used tallow, beeswax, and bayberry candles all had disadvantages. Crystallized sperm whale oil, in contrast, resisted summer heat and burned with a very bright light. It could be molded, allowing standardized production. Most important, whale bones, fins, oil and by-products were among the very few products Britain allowed the colonies to export and exchange for manufactured goods.

Uncle Obadiah built his candle works on eleven acres of land at Tockwotton, a thirty-minute walk from the center of Providence. Few colonial ventures required as long and arduous a production schedule and such high capital outlays as spermaceti candle works. Workers' salaries and board were Obadiah Brown & Co.'s largest expense after shipbuilding (including a £1,400 annual salary for Joseph to lend his technical expertise, ten times a farm laborer's wage). Charged with marketing the finished products, Nicholas and John developed the first product label in America and a premium line of candles wrapped in blue tissue paper. They obtained contracts to supply whale oil for the street lamps of New York and Philadelphia. Moses was the purchasing agent and salesman, traveling regularly to Nantucket for tough negotiations with the whalers who demanded cash payment. The Brown brothers' chief concern was obtaining hard currency and bills of exchange (promissory notes) to pay the Nantucket whalers. It was a challenging business: while the price of spermaceti "head matter" rose by 200 percent over ten years, the price of candles increased only by a paltry 20 percent. Competition was cutthroat; in the 1770s, there were twenty-two candle works in Rhode Island. In 1771, the Brown brothers invited candle manufacturers from Boston and Newport to form the *United Company of Spermaceti Chandlers* to stabilize competition and prices—the first example of a cartel in America.

When Nicholas took over from his uncle Obadiah, his first priority was to seek out a second product beyond spermaceti candles that could be traded with the Mother Country. Since Britain had insufficient forests left to produce the charcoal required to smelt iron ore in a blast furnace, Americans were allowed to produce iron. Iron ore had been found near Providence but no one in New England was exporting it. So, the Brown brothers joined several other partners to launch the Hope Furnace.

Their initial £10,000 investment was six times the cost of a new vessel. The brothers undertook one of the first known market studies in America by investigating fifteen blast furnaces in Pennsylvania. Once again, Joseph's engineering skills were invaluable. Under his guidance, proper techniques were perfected slowly and painfully through trial and error. One of the major challenges was recruiting and retaining the hundred workmen needed on site; white and black, indentured, slave or freeman, all were paid in barter. Neighboring forges transformed iron from the Hope Furnace into a range of products from nails to the iron fence still standing at New York's Bowling Green.

The Brown brothers differentiated themselves from most other New England traders who simply reinvested their profits into larger cargoes or more ships. Few colonial merchants were tempted to engage in manufacturing enterprises that required heavy capital investment or a permanent workforce such as the spermaceti candle works or the Hope Furnace (the typical crew for a vessel under one hundred tons was no more than ten men; the Hope Furnace needed at least one hundred workers). Most merchants preferred to ply a shuttle path between two ports that required only one type of vessel (80 percent of Philadelphia firms traded with only one market). The Browns initially had specialized in the cheap molasses of Dutch Surinam, off the Northeast coast of South America, but soon diversified their routes. Captain James had used a combination of fifteen coastal and ocean-going vessels; his two-mast schooner *Ann* was the first Providence ship larger than a sloop. Since coastal trade was a vital component of the Browns' conglomerate, multiple ships enabled them to avoid heavy freight costs or to spread valuable cargo across several vessels. By 1760, the Browns owned shares in more than sixty craft, a substantial percentage of Rhode Island's 184 oceangoing and 300 coastal trading vessels.

The Browns were also unusual in that they favored vertical integration. Most traders were unable to afford tying up capital in accounts receivable and "back country" debts, so they avoided involvement in retail sales. But Captain James built up a network of country stores in all parts of Rhode Island, Southern Massachusetts and Eastern Connecticut which his descendants kept supplied with rum, flour, tobacco and British dry goods. Cash was always scarce—the Browns rarely had more than £700 on hand—but a varied inventory ensured better barter terms for transactions. As the population of Rhode Island increased from 33,000 to 58,000 from 1750 to 1770, the Browns gained the latest information on consumer trends through their network of stores. By the late 1760s, Nicholas Brown & Co. could assure customers that they should "depend on being supplied on as Advantageous Terms as by any other Importers in New England and may depend upon their Orders being executed in the best Manner."

Contrary to many merchants who simply counted their debtors to settle accounts, the Browns kept meticulous records. Moses noted, "To leave a transaction unrecorded is to depend entirely on another man's honesty." He inherited Uncle Obadiah's *A Guide to Book Keepers According to the Italian Method* and took its lessons to heart along with those of *Lex Mercatoria Rediviva*, a contemporary guide to merchant law and practice. John's bookkeeping skills had been so proficient in his youth that he had earned extra money working at night for Captain Esek Hopkins whom he had charged high fees. The brothers dealt not only with multiple bills of exchange drawn on European trading companies, but also in the colony's "lawful money" and over twenty-three different other types of coins, including the much-preferred Spanish silver dollars or "pieces of eight" (clipped to form an octagon). Each of their ventures was charged a 6 percent cost of capital, with revenue calculated to the penny.

Back in 1750 Uncle Obadiah had undertaken the first direct trading voyage from Providence to London. Dispatching *Smithfield* "was an epoch-making undertaking . . . in a sense proclaiming the mercantile independence of Providence." London was the sun of the imperial solar system with seven hundred thousand inhabitants and two thousand merchant vessels. Between 1750 and the Revolution's eve, England's exports to North America would increase 120 percent and the Browns would seize this opportunity to its fullest extent.

Thus, in the decade between 1762 and 1772, Nicholas Brown & Co. became a complex web of trading ventures. Produce gathered in coastal trade was sold in the West Indies for both molasses and the bills of exchange demanded by Nantucket whalers, which in turn allowed the

Browns to produce in Rhode Island spermaceti candles and iron; the firm's ultimate objective was to purchase British manufactured goods.

Most of the time, Nicholas took his role at the head of the family firm extremely seriously. He was methodical and cautious, excelling in his strategic ability to identify emerging industries that served growing markets. But, occasionally, the opportunity to "get rich quick" proved irresistible. Two such schemes ended disastrously: a slaving voyage in 1764 and a 1766 attempt to corner the tobacco market in Surinam. War and major political events provided many opportunities for illicit activities, notably contraband. His father Captain James had been adept at circumventing British customs ships when Britain promulgated the Molasses Act in 1733, unloading cargo in hidden coves or onto coastal packets, and forging invoices. Now Nicholas continued these practices, especially during the Seven Years War[10] when he and his Uncle Obadiah tried profiteering by fake "flag of truce" or "victualing the prisoners and mariners" (shipping authorized by an English colonial governor for the ostensible purpose of exchanging prisoners), as well as "trading with the enemy," and privateering.

Privateering was in fact perfectly legal. Since Britain did not have enough naval vessels to conduct maritime wars, it (in common with other European powers) licensed private ships and ordinary mariners to capture enemy vessels in return for a 10 percent fee. Privateering was the first independent entrepreneurial activity undertaken by Nicholas and John at the outbreak of the Seven Years War (known in America as the French and Indian War) in 1756 when they were twenty-seven and twenty. John invested in four successful voyages and the two brothers were designated agents to manage the paperwork and public auction for all captured ships brought into Providence. In their first year, they earned a 10 percent fee on the sale of thirty-two "prizes" —John alone netted £17,600 at a time when a common laborer earned about £30 a year.

---

[10] Actually fought between 1755 and 1764, the Seven Years' War involved most of the great powers of the time and affected Europe, North America, Central America, West Africa, India, and the Philippines. Europe was split into two coalitions, led by Great Britain and France. In some countries, this war is named after its respective combatants, for example, the "French and Indian War" in the United States.

For a decade, the four brothers' partnership flourished under Nicholas's firm but sympathetic leadership. They shared an innate conviction of their role in the world and could at times be haughty.[11] But, perhaps inevitably, their very different personalities and interests led to tensions within the partnership. John, known as "a stormy petrel and bold adventurer," harbored huge ambition and a gambler's mentality, throwing all available funds at an enterprise. In the unfettered eighteenth century economy, his approach paid off and by age 30, he was the richest man in Providence. But he was also the first to chafe under his older brother's conservative management. Nicholas—who was methodical in his approach to business and dignified in his private life—worried that "our brother has a desire to Enlarge his business more than we apprehend the smallness of the Place and the Number of traders at this Juncture will admit." In 1771 John announced he was pulling out.

Had Moses been willing to continue playing a full role, the partnership might have survived. But, for the past three years, he had effectively withdrawn from day-to-day business activities as he battled with melancholia, brought on principally by the lingering illness of his wife Anna (who would die in 1773). With Moses absent, it made little sense for Nicholas to continue with Joseph his sole partner, as the scientific brother was "much engaged at present in other ways."

So, by the Revolution's eve, Nicholas was alone at the head of Nicholas Brown & Co., lamenting "a Break among brothers, who in the eyes of the world have lived in unity." Nevertheless, the partnership had achieved its purpose of elevating the family to a near-unassailable position among the merchants of Providence. The four brothers would never lose their strong sense of family allegiance, continuing to collaborate on specific ventures, on civic projects and, most importantly, to inculcate the next generation with the values they had grown to cherish. Foremost among these was the importance of being admired not just as wealthy merchants but also as "gentlemen" with a sense of "public responsibility."

---

[11] Once, when a blacksmith accused Nicholas of not acting forthrightly, he responded in a biting letter, alluding to the man's social inferiority.

CHAPTER 2

BECOMING GENTLEMEN

*"It is necessary in the execution of all matters
of a public nature, That the undertakers have a
great zeal for promoting it." —Moses Brown*

The matter of who could claim the status of *gentleman* was particularly fraught for Rhode Island's merchants. The conventions of the time dictated that, as John Locke had argued in 1693, "trade is wholly inconsistent with a gentleman's calling since merchants must be considered to be motivated by avarice rather than virtue." Almost a hundred years later, Adam Smith wrote in *The Wealth of Nations*, "It seems as difficult to restrain a Merchant from striking a Gain as to prevent the keen spaniel from springing at Game, that he has been bred to pursue." Important office should be held only by those who had achieved financial independence and were beyond any commercial self-interest. Therefore, the pinnacle of the colonial pyramid—just as in the Mother Country—was managing a landed estate, the only activity befitting a truly "disinterested man." A true Philadelphia aristocrat was born rich; a Virginia landed gentleman had the spare time to focus on politics and civic affairs. Government service was a personal sacrifice required of certain gentlemen who were free from want, from ignorance, and from working with their hands.

Thus, as soon as Benjamin Franklin acquired sufficient wealth no longer to work, he retired from business at the age of forty-two and became a gentleman of leisure. Since there were no titles in the colonies, being considered a gentleman was all the more dependent on demonstrating manners, taste, and character. Rhode Island's future Revolutionary hero, Nathanael Greene, was the son of an ironmonger yet he declared "the great body of the People [are always] contracted, selfish and illiberal and should not be confused with the noble natures of gentlemen." Indeed, ambition was considered exclusively an aristocratic passion; everyone had appetites and interests, but only the great-souled, the extraordinary few, should dare have ambition.

These rules never could apply literally in Rhode Island where no one was exempt from the worries of trade. Foreign markets were perennially insecure. From the colony's founding, its leaders had to be *practical politicians*, with a foot in both the counting house and the colony house. Authority rested in the Town Meeting of merchant-magistrates, an emergent elite who fused economic *and* political power. It was precisely the relative lack of gentility and ease of access to elite circles that made Rhode Island so politically volatile. What the little colony gained in religious and political freedom from separating church and state, it lost in order and stability.

Nevertheless, Providence was becoming a bustling port. The land on either side of newly paved Towne Street was densely built up, with homes appearing against the hillside while wharves, warehouses, shops and public buildings crowded the water side of the street. The Great Salt Cove gradually was filled in and soon a third of the town's 4,300 inhabitants lived across the water in Weybosset, which hummed with mechanics and manufacturers who were looked down upon by the more established families of Towne Street.

This transformation took place in under thirty years. In 1740, Providence "was still, as in the seventeenth century, but a long straggling street by the water front, where on summer evenings the inhabitants sat in the doorways, smoked their clay pipes, and fought the swarms of mosquitoes that rose from the marsh opposite." By the 1750s, as the merchants gained political control, the center of activity moved south towards the wharf area, away from the gristmill around which the old agricultural community had gathered. Despite the farmers' opposition, a second road, "Back Street" (soon renamed "Benefit Street") separated the dwellings from their fields and provided a vivid symbol of the irreconcilable differences between merchants and farmers that would mark Rhode Island politics for a century to come.

Civic amenities were improving, always initiated by private persons—often the Brown family. The first lottery was organized in 1744 to rebuild the bridge to Weybosset. In 1758, Benjamin Franklin's post office established a station in Providence. A brick Colony House finally was erected in 1760, twenty years after Newport's. It was the first municipal building large enough to hold town meetings, as well as exhibitions and lectures on its lower floor. A new prison was built over mud flats on a lot shared with a schoolhouse. A stagecoach left for Boston every Tuesday morning from Richard Olney's Tavern. Many people now purchased necessities such as soap and candles rather than make them at home. Silversmiths, goldsmiths, spectacle makers, milliners and dyers of silk arrived from Europe. In 1762, the weekly *Providence Gazette and Country Journal* was launched by Philadelphian William Goddard. Though Newport still maintained that Providence was a place "fit only to supply her neighbors' tables with pickled oysters," business was flourishing.

Commercial success transformed attitudes towards material possessions. At his death in 1739, only sixteen years after his first voyage, Captain James left an estate comprising the house and lots on Towne Street, five further lots, a substantial farm of 145 acres on the edge of town, rights to a cedar swamp, and personal possessions valued at £5,653 including four male slaves. He was the owner or part owner of half a dozen boats, mainly sloops of between sixty and eighty tons. In 1736, he even had been able to afford a skilled clerk to keep his ledgers and to handle his correspondence. This estate might have been far less than the £100,000 reportedly left by Jahiel Brenton of Newport in 1732, but it was nevertheless one of the largest yet seen in Providence. But it included few material possessions: £92 worth of clothing, two sets of china dishes and bowls, a clock, a looking glass, and two oval tables.

When Obadiah Brown died twenty-three years later in 1762, his estate was valued at £93,000 *Old Tenor*[12] in addition to a house in Providence, a farm in Glocester, nine slaves, and his widow's jewelry. Obadiah was the third richest man in Providence (the wealthiest one was his youngest brother Elisha), but he too did not own many luxury goods—some books, two looking glasses, a silver tankard and ladle, pieces of Delftware, and a China bowl. Soon after his death, Providence was swept by a thirst for refined goods.

As merchants began to accumulate great wealth and to attain social prominence, they quite deliberately started closing ranks. The price of entry to the upper echelon of merchant society rose ever higher. Until the middle of the eighteenth century, it had been relatively easy to accumulate wealth in the colonies; the first settlers were generally yeomen or lesser English gentry with estate management experience. During the early part of the eighteenth century, one-third of all males in New England were involved in trade, either through direct employment or investment in a vessel. It had cost about £500 to set up a trading business in the Americas—as opposed to £3,000 in London—and credit was easily obtainable from European houses. Since it took only two or three years to establish an effective trading network, it was possible to become wealthy in ten to fifteen years. However, with prosperity came economic specialization: bigger and more expensive ships, complicated paper transactions, increasingly sophisticated trading networks. A successful merchant needed the flexibility to juggle credit, currencies, cargoes and remittances while never losing sight of the big picture. He required an effective system of commercial intelligence and shrewd judgement in delegating authority to captains and agents. All this cost money. As a result, investments in maritime ventures became inaccessible to less affluent people. By 1771, only five percent of Boston's population had shares in big shipping enterprises.

---

[12] Establishing the monetary value of anything in colonial America is complex and often inaccurate. In addition to the Spanish, Portuguese and French coins in circulation, cash was denominated in pounds, shillings and pence (whose value varied in value from colony to colony). Notes were introduced periodically by individual colonies, with terms such as "Old Tenor" and "New Tenor" used to differentiate the date of issue and value.

In Europe, the aristocracy needed to display its status by spending; the responsibility of the common people was to produce, not to consume. In the American colonies, successful merchants began to emulate the European elite by purchasing spacious dwellings with servants and fine furnishings. A large house might cost £3,000 to £4,000, a "country seat" another £2,000. The affluent purchased mahogany furniture such as a desk, valued at £40, or a walnut and gilt looking glass for £45. Upholstery and wallpaper appeared; windows and beds were draped with imported cloth. Emblems of wealth and status included slaves, servants, cows, horses, silver plate and, especially, carriages—a phaeton (light carriage) cost £120. Tables were now covered in fine linens, adorned with silver tankards or Chinese punch bowls. English white stoneware replaced the ubiquitous pewter ware of an earlier era. The modes of speech, dress, and manners that composed polite society became grander. Townspeople began using titles, referring to each other as *Esquire, Gentleman* or *Yeoman* (Moses had "Esquire" carved on Uncle Obadiah's tombstone). Education in refined manners was in such demand that an Italian dancing master ran a successful school in Providence for a month in 1768.

The four Brown brothers were no exception. John was the first to decorate his new home on Towne Street, ordering tables, chairs, and looking glasses through his business correspondents Aaron Lopez in Newport and Henry Lloyd in Boston. His 1760 wedding silver included a tankard, several porringers and a teapot in the fashionable inverted pear shape from Boston goldsmith Samuel Minott. For his wedding in 1763, Moses commissioned a fine set of silver from the same Boston goldsmith who had provided wedding silver for Uncle Obadiah's daughter Sarah when she wed Jabez Bowen. Moses instructed that it be engraved with "marks and Arms . . . the same as that Mr. N. Hurd Ingraved on a Seal for me Some time past." This was the crest used by the Brownes of Abbotts Roodinge, a family from the West of England at the time of Henry VIII, whose crest appears in the 1612 heraldic reference book *The Visitation of Essex*. To create their own coat of arms, the four Brown brothers simply changed the chevron between three lion paws from silver to gold.

Nicholas too ordered furniture of substantial value. In a 1764 letter to John Relfe at Philadelphia, he requested "Mahogany fraim Chairs with Leather Bottom & Co[vered] with Greene Herrcteenc Bottoms made and polished in the best Manner" and noted that "the Last you sent us was Very Slightly made." Prices were high: a 1763 invoice listed a "Mahogany Sconce glass with Gilt Edge and Shell" at £9 6s in the days when a mariner's salary was £2 8s per month and a clerk earned about £4.

Large sums were spent by the Brothers with Newport's famed Quaker cabinetmakers, the Townsends and the Goddards. John Brown's first order in 1760 amounted to an enormous £520, to be paid for in two cash instalments plus "1 Firkin of butter" valued at £54. At the time of his engagement in 1763, Moses also ordered Newport furniture and complained that his brothers and his brother-in-law Jabez Bowen were getting preferential treatment from John Goddard.

When the four brothers launched Nicholas Brown & Co. after Uncle Obadiah's death in 1762, each one marked the occasion by commissioning a bookcase-on-desk which cost close to £350–a year's salary for a clerk, and nine times more than the cost of an average desk. Three of the brothers ordered their *secretaries* from the Townsend-Goddard workshops in Newport. The desks took six months to build, using mahogany that had been dried and cured for ten years and brass fitting from England. Joseph Brown, however, chose a Providence cabinetmaker, John Carlile Jr., in order to incorporate his favorite scroll design, similar to the roof of his house on Towne Street.[13] The desks were to be displayed in the front parlors of their houses (patrician merchants rarely spent more than three hours a day in the counting house) where guests could marvel at the workmanship. Only the grandest of Providence houses would have the ceiling height to accommodate Nicholas's nine and half foot masterpiece.

Where did this thirst for gentility arise from? Certainly Newport was an important influence. In 1760 Newport had sixty wharves, twenty-two

---

[13] His desk (now in the John Brown House Museum of the Rhode Island Historical Society) has a more complex pediment and moldings, with nine shells carved directly into the drawers and cabinets, rather than applied onto them, as was the Newport custom.

distilleries, six spermaceti works, one hundred and ten shops, and forty-seven families who owned five or more slaves. While the population of Providence never managed to surpass 4,300, Newport was a commercial and cultural metropolis with 11,000 inhabitants by 1769. Newport had America's first classical building, the 1747 Redwood Library, and in 1728 had hosted America's first professional painter, John Smibert, who accompanied the philosopher Bishop George Berkeley on his way to found a college in Bermuda. Newport was home to a number of outstanding Jewish merchants who traded all the way to the Mediterranean and the Levant. Most notable was Aaron Lopez who owned a fleet of thirty vessels. A major player in the spermaceti candle business, he both traded and competed extensively with the Browns.

On their frequent trips to Newport, the Brown brothers were invited into lavish homes where they heard for the first time of the new ideas that were sweeping through Europe, ideas to which we refer as the Enlightenment. In the eighteenth century scientific investigations based on experiment and reasoning had widened the horizons of knowledge, sometimes disproving but often explaining much that had previously been accepted on faith. The philosophers of the Enlightenment believed that if reason had proved itself in science, then it might produce equally beneficial results for Mankind when applied to government, laws, religion, economics and social customs.

In Providence, however, inquiring minds like those of Joseph and Moses Brown were highly unusual. Just once, in March 1764, two lectures on electricity were given at the Colony House. The organizers were careful to emphasize the useful nature of the presentation which, "Endeavouring to guard against Lightning, in the Manner proposed [should be] shewn not to be chargeable with presumption, nor inconsistent with any of the Principles of natural or reveal'd Religion."

One of the only ways to access the ideas of the Enlightenment was through Freemasonry, fraternal organizations that trace their origins to the local fraternities of stonemasons. Arriving in America in the 1730s from the learned circles of Sir Isaac Newton in England, Freemasonry offered a brotherhood of cosmopolitan men who sought to better society.

Freemasonry taught genteel behavior and encouraged universal love, replacing the divisive forces of ethnicity, religion and nationality with a simple distinction: "gentlemen" and "others." In 1757, eight years after a lodge was founded in Newport, St. John's Lodge was chartered in Providence.[14] Its members were an exclusive group of upwardly mobile young men from leading families including Joseph, John and Moses Brown, the Tillinghasts, Bowens, Hopkins, Angells, Russells, and Pages. Joseph was the Lodge's Second Master and presided over every meeting from 1762 to 1769. From the age of 20, Moses served as the Lodge's Secretary and began a lifelong correspondence with learned men.

Moses, like Benjamin Franklin, was interested not only in scientific inquiry for its own sake but also in turning "scientific investigation to useful purpose." He read voraciously and used his growing resources to order from London advanced texts and scientific instruments including a theodolite (an optical instrument still used today by surveyors). His closest friend in Providence was his brother-in-law Jabez Bowen, son of the town physician and a remarkable intellect who had graduated from Yale and received further degrees from the College of Rhode Island and Dartmouth.

In 1759, while on his way back from Philadelphia where he had celebrated turning 21, Moses stopped at Dr. William Barnett's hospital for smallpox in Eastern New Jersey. After receiving an inoculation, he convinced his brother John to be vaccinated and offered to supervise the "pesthouse" in Providence. Later, he brought Dr. Barnett to Massachusetts and funded the Point Shirley Smallpox Hospital.

Nicholas, however, did not become a Mason. While Moses and Joseph sought out scientists and social thinkers, Nicholas favored the company of clergymen or Bible study. He felt a personal relationship with God, one which he chose to cultivate in private. Each day, he made time to read the Bible and held evening prayers in his home. On Sundays, he attended up to three services in the meetinghouse where he owned several pews. But he refused to become a member of the church since

---

[14] In 1771, the Lodge moved to the top floor of the Market House designed by Joseph and funded by the Browns.

baptism required the public testimony of a *conversion experience*, and Nicholas shunned publicity.

Instead, Nicholas preferred supporting institutions that would advance knowledge. Despite his lack of formal education, he was a voracious reader who had started purchasing books at an early age. In 1754, he joined with five friends to establish the town's first public subscription library, before a bookseller even existed in Providence. More than five hundred books were ordered from London: the standard classics such as Milton, Booker, Bacon, and Locke as well as political science and history. Having spent all their capital on purchasing books, the library partners asked the General Assembly to store their collection in the Colony House. Nicholas was the first librarian, with hours "every Saturday . . . from two to Five of the Clock in the Afternoon." Just four years later, the Colony House and all the books burned to the ground. When the General Assembly rebuilt the Colony House, it earmarked substantial funds to purchase new books. In 1760 Moses was named clerk of the *Meeting of Proprietors of the Providence Library* and continued to expand the collection with scientific books and even a microscope.

In this manner, as wealth not only grew but sought an outward and visible manifestation, colonial governments could enlist the power of private persons to carry out public ends. Though the elite were expected to engage in civic responsibilities, the blurred lines between public and private interest also provided opportunities to enhance one's social and economic clout. The four Brown brothers—just one generation removed from the coarse, hard-driving Captain James Browne—were able to become "gentlemen of publick responsibility" by underwriting the civic development of Providence. Many successful Rhode Island merchants were attempting a similar transformation. One was Simon Potter of Bristol, Rhode Island. In the 1750s, he had announced "I would plow the ocean into pea-porridge to make money." When offered a post in the Royal Navy a few years later, he had replied "When I wish for a bigger ship, I will not ask his Majesty for one; I will build one myself." But then, as he grew rich trading rum and slaves, Potter mellowed; he served in the General Assembly, as a vestryman of the Episcopal Church, and ultimately became a Major General in the state militia.

A true gentleman could involve himself in benevolent activities without compromising his disinterested status. America's first settlers 150 years earlier had viewed the American continent as a vast exercise in benevolence: the natives would be converted to Christianity, poor men would be provided land, the wilderness would be civilized, and an example would be set for the world. The new communities in America would be better, not just different, from the ones at home. While still aboard the *Arabella* in 1630, Massachusetts Bay Colony's first governor John Winthrop wrote an essay on charity describing the obligations of the rich towards the poor, as well as the need to reconcile spiritual equality with economic inequality by balancing the good of the individual with the good of the community. Winthrop justified disparities in wealth and condition as divinely ordained so that men would have more need of each other. From Rhode Island, Roger Williams noted in a letter to Winthrop's son that brotherly love was no easy task due to "the common trinity of the world–Profit, Preferment, Pleasure."

As the colonies developed, so did the need for social intervention. The French and Indian Wars (1754 to 1763) produced disabled soldiers, orphans, widows and displaced persons. Two serious depressions, a number of epidemics, and major fires in Charleston and Boston in 1760 placed a heavy burden on a colonial society poorly equipped to deal with major calamities. Eighty years after John Winthrop, Cotton Mather (1663-1728) reaffirmed this perspective in his 1710 *Essays to do Good*: "Perpetual endeavor[s] to do good in the world" were an honor and an "incomparable pleasure." Pious example, moral leadership, voluntary effort and private charity could harmonize the competitive and conflicting interests of a rapidly changing society. Mather was the first to emphasize that giving wisely was an even greater obligation than giving generously; good was an obligation to God more than a means of salvation. However, Mather recognized that charity was also an effective instrument of social control: "The poor that can't work are objects for your liberality. But for the poor that can work and won't, the best liberality is to make them." Even Benjamin Franklin concurred with Mather: "I think the best way of doing good to the poor is, not making them easy in poverty, but leading or driving them out of it." Franklin foreshadowed the scientific philanthropists and reformers of the nineteenth century in believing that preventing poverty was more sensible than simply relieving it.

The Browns would have agreed with this perspective. Like most Englishmen, they embraced deeply rooted assumptions about the order required of a monarchical society. They could little imagine a civilization as anything but a hierarchy of some kind in which, as described by the influential American theologian Jonathan Edwards, "all have their appointed office, place and station, according to their several capacities and talents, and everyone keeps his place, and continues in his proper business."

A strong sense of civic responsibility and generous contributions to civic projects were therefore essential for the Browns to establish themselves as gentlemen. They were in fact doing no more than to perpetuate a practice of civic engagement started in the days of their ancestor Chad. Obadiah Brown & Co. had taken the lead on projects such as paving Towne Street, improving the Weybosset Bridge and building the Beavertail lighthouse at the entrance to Narragansett Bay. In 1758, when the town's "water engine" failed to prevent the Colony House from burning to the ground, Obadiah Brown and James Angell volunteered to order a new engine from London that could function with salt water. Five boxes of Obadiah Brown & Co. candles were donated to cover the freight cost.

Now, under the emphatic leadership of Nicholas, the Browns would direct their wealth and abilities in pursuit of these "gentlemanly" credentials. But their benevolence was always self-interested, either to benefit commercial ventures or to enhance social status. The sense of altruism that guides much modern philanthropy would have been unintelligible to these men. However, being regarded as pillars of the Baptist Church seemed a most worthy goal to pursue.

From its earliest days, the First Baptist Church in America had debated the concept of equality. A Dissenter with strong Baptist ideals, Roger Williams had introduced to Rhode Island the Calvinist belief that only a "particular" few would be saved. But in 1652, a group of Baptists had begun preaching that Christ died for *all* to be saved. They adopted a ritual of "laying on of hands" (transmission of the spirit) upon new members and called themselves "Six Principle Baptists." Two decades later, another group of Baptists in the colony adopted Saturday as the rightful day of worship and formed the "Seventh Day Baptist Church."

Then in 1732, Elder James Browne had led the more prosperous Baptists in attempting a return to hierarchy among the faithful and in introducing salaries to attract educated ministers. However, most Rhode Island Baptists felt an inner light was sufficient to preach, prophesy and perform baptisms—singing was considered a desecration of worship. They feared that educating or paying pastors would dampen their spirituality. Elder James was roundly defeated and the First Baptist Church remained under the influence of the "Six Principle" denomination.

But over the next thirty years, urbane Baptists all over New England started seeking greater respectability and formality. "People began to feel that piety was not at odds with learning, that people of good social standing should be represented before God by ministers of respectable attainment and degree." Rhode Island had experienced its fill of spiritual zeal in the seventeenth century and now many ambitious colonists were set on improving their earthly lot.

Given their father's distaste for organized religion, none of the four brothers was baptized as a young man. But their growing prosperity brought a thirst for decorum commensurate with their newfound status. While they remained devoted to such fundamental Baptist principles as personal autonomy, a love of law and order, and a preference for simplicity, they too began pressing for educated ministers. They set their sights on James Manning, the brilliant young minister from New Jersey who had come to the colony a few years earlier to run the College of Rhode Island in the small town of Warren. If they could get him to Providence, the First Baptist Church would be transformed.

The rural Baptists of Providence reacted with fear and suspicion; a learned preacher would pollute the pure word of the scriptures. Led by Samuel Winsor (son of the man who had defeated Elder James Browne), these farmers attempted to deny Manning communion when he first preached in Providence in 1770. They failed, but soon left with half the congregation for the town of Johnston, west of Providence, where they established a new Six Principle congregation. With Winsor's faction gone, the small group of remaining church members quickly established Manning as their pastor for an annual salary of £50. Within five years, 110 new members joined the congregation.

Four years after orchestrating the schism within the First Baptist Church, Nicholas and John Brown consolidated their influence on the church by launching a new organization, the Charitable Baptist Society. Ostensibly founded to handle the financial and real estate matters of the First Baptist Church, it actually owned the meetinghouse and paid the minister. Thus the Society was in fact another way to promote exclusivity and respectability. Church membership was not required, but only pew owners could join the Society. In church, women held equal rights to vote or speak; however, the Society excluded not only women but also Native Americans, African-Americans, sailors and laborers. Nicholas was its first moderator.

Attracting an educated pastor to Providence was only half the battle; the town now needed a college to train future generations of young men. From the very start of the colonial era, various denominations had founded colleges to train for the Christian ministry–Harvard (1636), William & Mary (1693), and Yale (1701). More recently, twelve more colleges had been founded; inspired by a religious revival known as the "First Great Awakening," they included the College of New Jersey (Princeton, 1746), King's College (Columbia, 1754) and The University of Pennsylvania (1755). Following in this trend, the Philadelphia Baptist Association floated the idea of a Baptist college at its 1762 annual meeting. With its strong Baptist inheritance and liberal laws, Rhode Island seemed a worthy location to attempt the experiment.

A college charter was drafted in 1763 and submitted to the General Assembly in Newport. Beginning with the statement "Whereas the institutions for liberal education are highly useful to society," the charter was a unique example of liberal, ecumenical thinking for its time and Nicholas was a signatory. The College of Rhode Island was born in March 1764, based in the coastal town of Warren, with James Manning as President and Professor of Modern Languages. By the time the first class of seven had graduated in 1769, the experiment had proved a success and the College needed a permanent location.

Providence and Newport both wanted the College, along with towns on the western side of Narragansett Bay. The Brown brothers seized this opportunity for Providence to assert itself over its rival Newport. Moses took charge of the lobbying effort. Ultimately, the decision came down to a question of funding. The brothers organized a subscription which included contributions from neighboring towns who were told that "building the college here will be the means of bringing great quantities of money into the place, and thereby greatly increasing the markets for all kinds of Country produce, and consequently increasing the value of all estates to which this town is a market." They were also prescient in predicting that a college in Providence would do "much [to] promote the weight and influence of this northern part of the Colony in the scale of government in all times to come." The campaign raised well over £800.

The brothers enlisted James Manning's support by pointing out that, in Newport, the College would be taken over by Congregationalists and Episcopalians. In Providence, although control would rest with the Baptists, the atmosphere of the institution would not be tailored to one denomination and the faculty would represent a number of religious faiths. That argument swayed Manning who noted "You have the good of the college at heart more than They." Knowing that Newport had more money, he suggested that the Browns should offer to build the College edifice themselves. Anticipating that this gesture might be required, John and Moses had purchased land a short time earlier on the hill above Towne Street (coincidentally on the home lot originally allocated to Chad Browne), and had conducted an exhaustive study of building costs. The numbers worked their magic: once Nicholas Brown & Co. offered to pay for the College Edifice and a president's house, it became £575 cheaper to locate the college in Providence.

Still, the February 1770 meeting of the College Corporation was stormy. One eyewitness commented: "Both sides shewed such indecent beats and hard reflections as I never saw before among men of so much sense as they, and hope I never shall again." After two days of deliberations, Providence won, triumphing over a rival that possessed "superiority in numbers, library facilities and general culture." John Brown laid the foundation stone for University Hall (modelled after Nassau Hall at Princeton) and the whole project came in under budget in September 1771. Thereafter, the brothers continued their involvement in the College. Joseph, whom Manning called a "phylosphical genius," and John were awarded honorary degrees in 1770 and 1773, respectively. John became a Trustee in 1774 and College Treasurer in 1775, often contributing from his own pocket.

Following the successful completion of University Hall, the brothers undertook several other large construction projects that would change the face of pre-war Providence. Among the most notable was the Market House. For years, Providence "had been much inconvenienced by the lack of a central exchange. . . . Provisions were almost spoiled by being carried about the streets through wet and heat." After various unsuccessful attempts by private individuals, the General Assembly in 1771 finally authorized a lottery to pay for a structure. Moses Brown was appointed one of the project directors, Joseph designed the building, and Nicholas laid the foundation stone in June 1773. The second floor provided offices for town officials and tenants, with commercial arcades at street level.

The brothers' next major civic endeavor bore even greater symbolic importance: a fine meetinghouse that would make an architectural statement and affirm the preeminence of the new Baptist establishment. It was a source of great irritation to James Manning that only the Congregational Meetinghouse had sufficient space for the College of Rhode Island's commencements. So, in 1774, the Charitable Baptist Society petitioned the General Assembly for the right to raise £2,000 by lottery for the construction of a large new building. Joseph Brown was the principal architect. John was appointed the "Committee man for carrying on the building" (of his twelve-man committee, only one was actually a member of the church). Those who could not give money donated labor, materials, and liquor.

Considered by many architectural historians to be one of the great buildings of Colonial America, the First Baptist Meeting House was a dramatic departure from the extreme simplicity of Baptist churches to date. Joseph travelled to Boston for inspiration and adapted the final working drawings from plans in James Gibbs's 1728 *Book of Architecture*. The Palladian details of the building were dignified but restrained. The 185-foot steeple—the first on a Baptist church—was a copy of one proposed by Gibbs for St. Martin-in-the-Fields in London. Joseph developed an ingenious design to unfold it telescopically without recourse to exterior scaffolding. There were, however, no religious symbols inside the church, not even an altar or a cross.

During the 16-month period between 1774 and 1775, the First Baptist Meeting House was the biggest building project in New England. Since Boston was under British blockade at the time in reprisal for the "Tea Party," carpenters and shipwrights poured into Providence and completed the structure in record time. Once finished, the Meeting House was the largest building in town, seating 1,200 (one-third of the entire population), a tribute to the optimism of its builders despite the gathering clouds of war. Since 1776, it has been the site of all but two University commencements.

The Brown brothers were also concerned about primary education. If Providence were to become a thriving commercial center, it needed clerks, skilled artisans and *mechanics* (precursors to engineers). There was no public education in Rhode Island, in contrast to Massachusetts where every town over fifty inhabitants had a school. Only wealthy inhabitants could afford to send their sons to the few private schools. The *Providence Gazette* often printed essays and editorials stressing the desirability of education in foreign languages and classical literature, but nothing happened until 1767 when John Brown took matters in his own hands and decided to establish a free primary school. "It would be an Easy Matter," he noted, "to Raise Money by subscription from a Very Fue persons to be proprietors to build a School House to their own privit use [but this would] not be of Servis to Hundreds there is in this Town who is not able to Build a House to School their Children in." Both John and Moses Brown joined committees to purchase land and erect a building, as well as to prepare an ordinance for its support and governance. But when the proposal was put to vote at the town meeting, it was rejected, not by the "Gentlemen of Learning," but by "the poorer sort of people" whose fear of higher taxes outweighed their desire for education.

In reaction, all four Brown brothers—along with thirty-eight others—underwrote the cost of a "New Brick Schoolhouse." Moses served as moderator, clerk and then overseer of its *Meeting of the Proprietors* for decades. In 1770, a section of the schoolhouse was made available to Rhode Island College for a "Latin School."

Such prolific and whole-hearted commitment to civic projects, reaching far beyond mere financial contributions, established emphatically the Brown family's reputation for public virtue and moral rectitude. However, in the equally crucial arena of politics, even the Browns could not entirely paper over the inherent tension that existed between the good of the public and the good of the merchant. Much as Nicholas yearned to appear "disinterested," he knew full well that he could not reconcile the selfless charity admonished by the Bible with the realities of life in colonial New England.

Though Nicholas certainly felt the stigma borne by merchants who fused their business interests with civic affairs, he knew the Providence economy depended entirely on maritime trade: merchants provided jobs, apprenticeships, and paid taxes far out of proportion to their numbers. The entire community looked to them for sustenance and direction. Political office was a logical continuation of this authority. From Rhode Island's earliest days, the Brown family always kept a finger on the pulse of politics: Captain James had served in the legislature in 1730 and 1737, and Uncle Obadiah in 1758 and 1759. Nicholas represented Providence for three terms from 1754 to 1756, also joining Uncle Obadiah and his older brother James in 1757 on a defense committee during the Seven Years War. Between 1764 and 1771, Moses served his time in the General Assembly. While a freshman deputy, he was assiduous in attending all the sessions of the lower house. He also was able to look out directly for his family's interests, such as securing legislation to dam the Pawtuxet River for the benefit of the Hope Furnace. The Brown brothers were convinced that political stability required the merchants' social authority to be visible and uncontested.

Colonial society put a premium on patronage and individual relationships since public action depended on private energy and private funds, especially in a colony which always resisted raising tax revenue. Under Rhode Island's Royal Charter of 1663, provincial authority was thoroughly concentrated in the colony's Legislature. Individual towns gave their deputies binding instructions on how to vote in the Legislature. So political power actually rested at a very local level. Indeed, individual municipalities were also responsible for local military defense, highways and poor relief. The Assembly, in turn, appointed all provincial officials—judges, sheriffs, tax collectors—and thus dispensed considerable patronage. Laws passed by the General Assembly could not be vetoed by the governor nor disallowed by the British Crown. To complicate matter, the General Assembly met in five different locations, which further weakened central authority and often caused dysfunction. Rhode Island, for example, was one of the last colonies to introduce a uniform road building code, as well as standard weights and measures.[15]

Such a fractured system favored the rise of factions, especially in the period between 1756 and 1767 when two groups fought bitterly to control the Legislature. For those eleven years, the annual election for Governor was an exercise in corruption and vote buying. Samuel Ward, a farmer, represented the southern part of the colony: the plantation owners of South County as well as Anglicans and Quakers sympathetic to Newport merchants. The Quaker Stephen Hopkins led the faction representing the northern part of the colony, particularly Baptists and Congregationalists sympathetic to the rising merchants of Providence. The Brown brothers were among Hopkins's staunchest supporters.

---

[15] This imbalance between Rhode Island's executive, legislative, and judicial branches persisted until 2010 when reform was finally adopted!

Stephen Hopkins spent his childhood in the wooded northern part of Rhode Island which had no schools. A voracious reader, he depended on a small circulating library to supplement his family's books. Many years later, John Adams would note in admiration, "Governor Hopkins had read Greek, Roman and British history and was familiar with English poetry." Hopkins began a life of public service in 1730 at age twenty-three, culminating in his election as Governor of the colony in 1755—a post he would hold nine times over the next fifteen years—and later in his signing of the Declaration of Independence. In November 1764, the General Assembly published his "The Rights of Colonies Examined," criticizing taxation and Parliament, and his notoriety grew well beyond Rhode Island's borders. At Hopkins's death in 1785, it was said "He was a man of penetrating astutious, Genius, full of Subtlety, deep Cunning, intriguing & enterprizing . . . a man of a Noble fortitude & resolution . . . a glorious Patriot."

But in order to make ends meet, Hopkins needed an income. From the days of Captain James, the Brown family ensured there was always a job for Hopkins whenever he was out of political office (his son Rufus managed the Hope Furnace for forty years). The Brown family also funded his political campaigns. When Hopkins first ran for Governor, Nicholas Brown & Co. acted as his exchequer and figured prominently among the seventeen citizens of Providence who "promise to pay the Sums . . . as may be the most Usefull in procuring the free Votes of the poorer Sort of freemen in this County." An enormous £4,400 was raised to bribe voters. When it became illegal to pay voters at town meetings, people were paid to stay home. During the 1765 campaign, John Brown noted that he supplied Glocester (on the Connecticut border) with "Rum Enough for a Small Guine Cargo, with Severil other Nessessarys, & Brother Moses & Jabez [Bowen] Sat off for that Town Yesterday."

Rhode Island was derided by many for this chaotic state of affairs, and called "Rogues Island" or even "the latrine of America." Its merchants were deemed an unscrupulous and self-serving lot; indeed, by the late 1760s rumors began circulating to the effect that Britain might use the colony's internal discord as an excuse to rescind the Charter and install a royal governor. When Chancellor of the Exchequer George

Grenville began overhauling the creaking British colonial system in 1763, his first measure was to enforce strictly the old Molasses Act—a terrifying warning shot for a colony fueled by molasses and rum. It was time to bury the hatchet and unite to protect Rhode Island's interests.

Everyone was relieved when the "Ward-Hopkins" feud finally climaxed in the campaign of 1767 with an overwhelming victory by Hopkins over Samuel Ward and the southerners. The two factions then established a coalition government which would last until the Revolution's eve in 1775. Much energy and scarce resources were expended on the feud; bitter animosities had permeated the Brown family. Uncle Elisha, Obadiah's younger brother, had achieved great success as owner of a tavern and the town's corn mill, manager of the poor house, and as a trader in land, merchandise, cattle, and slaves. He built the first brick house in the central part of Providence and was the town's largest tax payer. However, he was also a zealous supporter of Samuel Ward in opposition to his cousins' support of Hopkins. When Ward was elected in 1765 and 1766, Uncle Elisha became deputy governor and made North Providence his personal fiefdom. But the Ward campaigns proved too costly for Uncle Elisha. Within a five-year period, he suffered the loss of five ships, three unprofitable trading ventures, the death of four slaves, and the flooding of his corn mill. In 1770, he petitioned the General Assembly for relief under the Insolvent Debtors Act. Relief was granted, but all his possessions were sold.

Without question, the Ward-Hopkins feud damaged the Brown family's reputation, underlining that there was no way to avoid the conflict between public good and private interest. Nicholas, who sought to maintain appearances by avoiding public controversy, was deeply upset by this taint. His brother John, however, cared little for public opinion (and could bluster his way out of almost any situation). He remained confident that in all four key areas of eighteenth century public life—politics, civic society, education, and religion—the four Brown brothers had managed to assert their wealth and prominence to great effect. They had done so as a cohesive force, with order, stability, and respectability as their creed, while maintaining their individual perspectives. This was the legacy they would pass to the next generation. But the next two decades would shake these beliefs to their core.

CHAPTER 3

TURBULENT YEARS

"We hope that we are gradually Emerging
from the various and multiplied Difficulties
which Continually baffled our wishes."
—George Benson to Dickason & Co.

In the early evening of June 9th, 1772, four lawyers lodging at Sabin's Tavern in Providence were startled to hear a loud drumroll outside. Men started pouring into the inn, soon totaling sixty in numbers. Among them were prominent merchants and sea captains—including John and Joseph Brown—lawyers and doctors, many of them members of the Rhode Island General Assembly. Shortly after ten, the men filed out, their faces blackened or wearing Indian headdresses. Some carried guns while others picked up barrel staves and paving stones. They clambered into eight long boats waiting at Fenner's dock across the road, their oars and oar-locks well muffled. An order was shouted by Abraham Whipple, one of the Brown's principal captains, and the party set off into the moonless night. What followed in the next few hours would change the course of American history.

Three months earlier, the British Crown had sent two eight-gun Navy schooners, *Beaver* and *Gaspee,* to patrol Narragansett Bay to stamp out the illegal smuggling that had reached epic proportions in the years since heavy taxes on trade were first imposed in 1764. *Gaspee*'s commander, Lieutenant William Dudinston, an arrogant and energetic young officer, boasted he would make "honest Englishmen" out of Rhode Island's "piratical scum." He stopped and searched all ships in the Bay, impounded legitimate cargo, sent two captains to Boston for trial (in violation of Rhode Island's Charter), and even took supplies from farmers without compensation. When Governor Joseph Wanton protested, he replied with insolence.

Shortly after noon on June 9th, the sloop *Hannah* entered the Bay on her way to Providence from New York. *Gaspee* immediately hoisted sail in pursuit, ordering her to heave to for boarding. But *Hannah*'s captain Benjamin Lindsey tacked back and forth up the Bay, just out of cannon range. Suddenly, she veered sharply westward and cleared a long sandbank by inches in the shallow waters off Namquid Point, seven miles south of Providence. *Gaspee* plowed into the shoals and became firmly grounded, forced to wait until the high tide at 3:00 am. Meanwhile, Lindsey lost no time in reporting the incident to John Brown who ordered the long boats and the town crier.

Gaspee's sentinel did not see the oarsmen until they had closed in. Dudinston appeared on deck in his nightshirt and called out. John Brown replied, "I am the sheriff of the County of Kent. Surrender." A musket shot rang out and Dudinston fell, shot in the groin. The attackers swarmed aboard, ransacked the ship, off-loaded its crew, and set it on fire.

Daylight brought the sobering realization that an act of piracy had been committed; suspects could be sent to England for trial. Worse, the Crown had an excuse to declare martial law and send troops to occupy the colony, even rescind the Charter. John Brown went into hiding, never daring sleep two nights in the same place. But Rhode Island's leaders took swift action to protect the guilty. Deputy Governor Darius Sessions, another former Brown captain, both offered a large reward for information but also obtained affidavits from the *Gaspee* crew that they did not know the assailants' identities.

In fact, George III only appointed a commission to investigate the affair. Governor Wanton blocked several attempts to name the attackers and claim the reward—while publicly condemning the dastardly act and expressing undying love for law and order. Dudinston was terrified of reprisals. In the end, the commission ended its investigation in June 1773. Not one soul betrayed John Brown.

This act of defiance by the smallest colony was an inspiration for all. Sam Adams counseled union: "Since an attack on the liberties of one colony was an attack on the liberties of all." Later in 1773, Virginia proposed establishing committees of correspondence, the first step towards a Colonial Congress.

It took three years for the British to catch up with Uncle John. By the Spring of 1775, a Royal Navy squadron was based at Newport under the command of the haughty James Wallace (whose 20-gun flagship *Rose* could destroy any Rhode Island town). On April 26th, less than a week after the battle of Lexington, John Brown was in Newport harbor aboard a packet boat laden with flour for the Continental Army. Captain Wallace captured the vessel and whisked John off to Boston, intending to forward him across the Atlantic to stand trial in England. Upon hearing the news, his devoted apprentice Elkanah Watson galloped off at breakneck speed in the vain hope of intercepting the British ship at Cape Cod. By April 28th, Moses and Joseph had set off for the three-day overland journey to Boston where George Washington's Continental Army was surrounding the British-occupied town. Moses managed to cross through siege lines to gain an audience with General Thomas Gage, the military governor of Massachusetts. Gage seemed amenable to releasing John as a show of goodwill towards the colonies, but Moses still had to convince "surly old" Vice Admiral Thomas Graves, Captain Wallace's superior. "Through divine as well as human favor," Graves agreed to free John Brown against an explicit (and extraordinary) pledge that the family would exert its influence to halt Rhode Island's efforts toward military preparedness. Clearly, Moses had seized an opportunity to combine his overriding Quaker pacifist agenda with the immediate imperative to save his brother from the hangman. The three Browns returned home together; John wept openly.

John's contrition was short-lived. In keeping with his pledge to

General Graves, he made one intervention before the General Assembly, albeit with no great conviction. But when Captain Wallace in Newport refused to return the confiscated packet boat and its flour (despite General Gage's pledge to the Brown brothers), John attempted to sue the British for £10,000. Moses was furious at being so blatantly blindsided by his brother. Not only was he being stymied in his agenda to avoid an escalation of hostilities, but he feared that his and his Quaker brethren's neutrality now would be viewed as suspect by all parties concerned. He wrote to John "[I will be] thought to be a deciver [sic] and a hypocrite if thy conduct turns out so contrary to what thou engaged and I was a voucher and surety for." He feared that the wrath of royal officials would fall not just on the Brown family but on all its associates. From that point, Moses refused any further involvement–in cooperation with his brothers or otherwise–in war-time activities. He retired to his Elmgrove estate, emerging (motivated partly by humanitarianism, partly by a desire to avoid public condemnation as a non-combatant) only to undertake two relief expeditions in 1775 and 1776 to the beleaguered citizens of the Bay Colony. This episode was only one of many disagreements that would mark the relationship between John and Moses for the rest of their lives.

In the years before Revolution, all New England merchants had depended entirely on Britain to police the seas, to purchase their candles, bar iron, and agricultural commodities, and to provide the colonies with manufactured goods. But as tensions mounted, all four Brown brothers began participating in "committees of correspondence" to coordinate the colonies' response to British affronts and to supervise adherence to non-importation agreements. The "*Gaspee* Affair" proved the defining moment when they became irrevocably opposed to British imperial policy. For the next decade, all their activities would combine patriotism with their commercial ventures. But the old tensions between public good and self-interest soon would assert themselves, as the lure of war-time riches vied uneasily with patriotic intentions. Perhaps inevitably, as noted by the historian Carl Bridenbaugh, "a whiff of brimstone clung to many of their exploits."

Soon after his release, John offered his sloop *Katy* to the Rhode Island General Assembly's Council of War. Renamed the *Providence,* she was commanded by Gaspee raider Abraham Whipple. She immediately set to work clearing Narragansett Bay of British patrols. Within days, Whipple captured one British ship, "liberated" six impounded colonial ships, and become a serious thorn in the side of Captain James Wallace. The exasperated Wallace wrote Whipple: "You, Abraham Whipple, on the 10th of June, 1772, burned His Majesty's vessel, the *Gaspee*, and I will hang you at the yard-arm." Whipple replied, "To Sir James Wallace, Sir: Always catch a man before you hang him."

Sensing an opportunity to turn a handsome profit, John also went into the munitions business, selling powder to the Continental troops at wildly inflated prices. The brothers also were able to stockpile flour from New York and Philadelphia to trade in the Caribbean, as well as to undertake several lucrative ventures to procure salt. In 1776, they used their Philadelphia connections and Stephen Hopkins's influence to obtain contracts for two of the thirteen frigates ordered by the new Continental Navy. Most significantly, thanks to Joseph's technical expertise, the Hope Furnace was transformed into a canon foundry. As he set about designing a new air furnace and America's first steam engine to pump the ore beds, Joseph seemed animated with energy and a new sense of purpose. The Rhode Island General Assembly enthusiastically placed an order for cannon, soon followed by that of the Marine Committee of the Continental Congress. By August 1776, 139 cannon from the Hope Furnace had been distributed to various batteries around the state. Many years later, John would write that during the Revolution, the furnace produced "about 3000 . . . of the best Cannon ever made in the Nation."

When Congress authorized privateers in 1775 to cruise in its name, Rhode Islanders were once again enticed by "the gold rush at sea." Remembering his privateering successes of twenty-three years earlier, Nicholas too returned to this "most profitable business." But as many of Rhode Island's leading merchants—and the Governor himself—hurried to outfit privateers, the needs of the new Continental Navy lost out. Skilled craftsmen and building materials were diverted from the two Continental Navy frigates under construction in Providence. The Hope Furnace favored casting smaller cannon for private ships whose owners paid on time in hard currency or bills of exchange, rather than fast-depreciating Continental money. Seamen far preferred the loose discipline aboard a privateer; there they shared half of all prizes taken and were paid sixteen dollars a month, as compared to the harsh conditions of the Navy which shared only a third of prizes and paid eight dollars a month, and in "Continental script."

One member of the Naval Committee of Congress, John Langdon of New Hampshire, visited Providence three times in 1776 to purchase canon for his state's Navy frigates. On each trip, he accepted the Brown brothers' escalating prices. But finally he had enough. He dashed off an angry letter to the Continental Naval Committee's new chairman John Hancock. In response, Hancock sent the Rhode Island's Maritime Commission a stern letter denouncing the "extravagant demands" made by the Browns: "no consideration shall induce us to submit to such extortion as was attempted with Mr Langdon."

John protested loudly that he was "as Deeply ingauged in the Cause of the United States as any other men on the Continent." Branding his family as "Extertioners" was "Indecent as well as uncharitable." But it was not long before dramatic events would demonstrate just how damaging the Brown family's self-interested decisions turned out to be.

The Continental Navy's first commodore was another of Nicholas Brown & Co.'s trusted captains, Esek Hopkins. He had undertaken some of their most hazardous (and ultimately disastrous) ventures, notably the 1764 slaving voyage aboard the *Sally* and the Brown's 1766 attempt to corner the tobacco market in Surinam. Now Hopkins was frantically trying to recruit sailors for the Continental Navy, but all the able-bodied men were signing on to privateers. He complained to the Naval Committee about the Browns' diverting manpower and materiel to private use; he asked the General Assembly to halt commissions for privateers until he could fill his ships. But John, who sat in the Assembly, led the vote to defeat the proposal.

When the two Continental frigates finally were delivered in early

December 1776, Robert Morris, the great Philadelphia financier who
served on the Marine Committee of Congress, commented that "in
Rhode Island were built the two worse frigates." Barely had Esek Hopkins
stepped aboard his new ships than the British sailed into Narragansett
Bay on December 7th, 1776 with seven men-of-war, seventy other ships
and six thousand British and Hessian troops. Hopkins was trapped in
Providence. Newport surrendered without a shot. Over the next three
years, that once thriving port would be reduced to a hollow shell, with
hundreds of buildings destroyed and its colony house a stable for British
horses. From a population of 9,200 in 1774, less than 4,000 would remain.
A Hessian soldier wrote in his diary, "It appears as if the entire city had
died." Hopkins was suspended from command and dismissed without a
hearing. Public opinion blamed the Browns.

John seemed not to care. In the first seven months of authorized
privateering, thirty-two prizes were brought into Providence with spoils
amounting to £300,000. His own ship *Diamond,* jointly owned with
Nicholas, set sail in July 1777 and was soon joined by *Yankee Ranger,
Hawke, Polly, Favorite, Retaliation* and *Sally.* The brothers often managed to capture vessels laden with sugar, rum, cotton, and oil; Abraham
Whipple once hauled a cargo back to Boston worth over a million dollars.
John even considered building a thousand-ton ship whose sails, rigging,
provisions, guns, powder and other stores would cost a million dollars,
but neither Nicholas nor Joseph would support him.

Despite John's bravado and Rhode Island's privateering successes,
the broader strategic situation was dire. With the British capturing
over half of all cargoes, trade along the Eastern seaboard slowed to a
trickle, and exorbitant insurance rates made long voyages prohibitively
expensive. John, who owned interests in seventy-five vessels before the
Revolution, lost ten ships in 1777 alone. Nicholas Brown & Co.'s invaluable web of correspondents and agents in Newport, Boston, and New
York disintegrated. The island of Nantucket, a vital trans-shipment point
in the War's early years, was paralyzed, its proud whalers on the brink of
starvation. With no head matter or whale oil to supply the candle works,
there was no light for the streets of Philadelphia or for the parlors of

New York. Nicholas and John attempted in 1776 to purchase war stores in France, but the ventures proved disappointing due to delays, endless red tape, and the wrong sort of cargo. Their ship *Live Oak* and its cargo of rice and indigo for France was captured and burned within sight of Charleston. John's apprentice Elkanah Watson travelled South over seventy-five days with $20,000 sewn into his coat lining, but was unable to drum up business.

In Providence, everyone feared a British bombardment or occupation. Hungry refugees flooded into town. Joseph moved his family inland to Grafton, Connecticut. Then in 1778, news arrived of a treaty of alliance with France which now officially recognized the United States as an independent nation. In August, the French fleet was supposed to liberate Newport in order to open Narragansett Bay in its first joint operation with Continental forces. But a great storm blew in; the French retreated to Boston, abandoning the Americans with insufficient men to free Newport. Now Providence was sure to be captured. Miraculously, on August 29th, General Nathanael Greene managed to keep British and Hessian forces pinned on Aquidneck Island. The Battle of Rhode Island—a successful fighting withdrawal—was notable for the role played by the First Rhode Island Regiment of African-Americans and Native Americans. Providence was saved.

Nevertheless, John ill-advisedly fumed to Nathanael Greene that the operation was "the worst concerted and the most disgraceful executed of any during the war." Greene, who was struggling against insurmountable odds as the Continental Army's Quartermaster General, responded acidly:

> I am not surprised to hear the late unsuccessful expeditions against Newport fall under some degree of censure; but I must confess that I am not a little astonished to hear, from such a principal character in society as yourself, illiberal reflections against a gentleman, merely because his measures did not coincide with your opinion. . . . I have been told that your brother Nicholas let

fall some very ungenerous insinuations with regard to
me a few Days before the Action upon the island. These
are the rewards and gracious return I am to expect for
years of hard and dangerous service. . . . I cannot help
feeling mortified that those that have been at home making their fortune, and living in the lap of luxury, and
enjoying all the pleasures of domestic life, should be the
first to sport with the feelings of the officers who have
stood as a barrier between them and ruin.

John later apologized; after the Revolution, he would host a huge dinner
party for Nathanael Greene (the largest ever held in Rhode Island). But
Nicholas was deeply upset at this mark of pubic disproval. In fairness,
the Browns were not the only Rhode Island merchants accused of "exploiting the patriotic self-sacrifice of others." Nonetheless, in an era when
the stability of the political system depended on the incontestable social
authority of its leaders, public denunciations of his private character and
the family's relentless pursuit of personal profit were deeply worrying.
Nicholas had spent a lifetime cultivating the family's reputation, perhaps
on occasion sailing rather close to the wind, but ultimately, he believed,
dedicated to the good of the community. These criticisms were a bitter
pill to swallow. The lesson was not lost on his son, Nick, whose life-long
concern with propriety and rectitude would outweigh even his father's
preoccupation.

The British forces finally pulled out of Narragansett Bay in October
1779, as General Washington's war of attrition moved South. The French
General Jean-Baptiste Donatien de Rochambeau arrived in Newport
with six thousand soldiers to take their place in July 1780. Although
the victory at Yorktown followed in October 1781, it was not until the
end of 1782 that the final French troops left on their homeward journey.
During their period of occupation, the French soldiers consumed vast
amounts of foodstuffs and their largesse trickled through the population. When the troops finally departed, the exhilaration of victory soon

disappeared as the flow of hard currency into the pockets of merchants and farmers ceased almost instantly. Agricultural prices fell sharply; it took greater and greater quantities of goods to pay creditors. With New England's fisheries destroyed, and Rhode Island's whale oil and candle manufacturing businesses ruined, there was little that could be traded for hard currency.

A cash crisis gripped the new nation and Rhode Island in particular. The colonies had issued their own treasury bills to deal with the Revolution's unprecedented financial demands. Inevitably, prices had risen and the paper money depreciated. By the War's end, the situation was perilous. Congress needed a new, steady source of revenue to fund its $42 million war debt, its $12 million foreign debt, and to pay soldiers' certificates. Yet it had neither the power to raise the $1 million needed annually to service foreign and domestic debt, nor the authority to stop British vessels carrying off America's meager supplies of gold and silver. Congress could not even raise cash by selling the Western lands occupied by the Native American tribes still under Britain's protection. In February 1781, a desperate Congress turned to Robert Morris of Philadelphia who suggested a 5 percent "Impost" on all imported goods. Though it would provide only $500,000 out of the $35 million the country needed—"a Tub for the Whale"—the plan attracted broad support. But one group stridently disagreed: the merchants of Rhode Island.

Since Rhode Island was heavily involved in the re-export trade, its merchants needed to be exempt from taxes on any goods that would be immediately shipped out again. However, the Impost suggested by Morris did not allow for this draw-back. The merchants argued that taxes raised in Rhode Island should remain in Rhode Island—indeed that federal officials should not be allowed to operate within the state's borders, uncontrolled by the General Assembly or the people. In the winter of 1781-82, the "Impost Debate" monopolized every conversation. The town printer John Carter complained that letters and editorials were pouring in so quickly to the *Providence Gazette* that he simply could not print them all. Nicholas and John led the merchants in opposing the Impost. "Our State do the most in Coasting according to the Bigness

of any State in the Union, indeed our Navigation for foreign ports far
exceeds any State in proportion," protested Nicholas; why should little
Rhode Island shoulder an inordinate share of the federal burden? Even
Joseph, who generally stayed out of public debates, scoffed at the "ingenious and importunate" pleas of Congress. On November 1ˢᵗ, 1782, the
General Assembly voted unanimously on John's motion to reject the
impost. Since any amendment to the Articles of Confederation needed
to be unanimous, Rhode Island thus singlehandedly blocked the other
twelve colonies from passing the Impost.

Thomas Paine spent a frustrating month in Rhode Island during the
winter of 1782 to 1783, trying to reverse the state's decision. He pleaded
for a union and rebuked, "Be ashamed, gentlemen, to put off the payment
of your just debts, the payment of your suffering army, and the support
of your national honor, upon such illiberal and unbelieved pretenses."
Congress desperately needed the power to regulate interstate commerce.
In 1783, it tried to placate Rhode Island by making several fundamental
concessions, but the state again refused the Impost. By 1784, a motion
was put forward to expel Rhode Island Congressmen from the Federal
Government. In reaction, John refused to serve in Philadelphia when he
was elected to Congress in May of 1784.

While Rhode Island merchants were engrossed in fighting the proposed Impost, its farmers were becoming increasingly discontent. When
the British had occupied Newport and blockaded Narragansett Bay, the
burden of supporting the war effort had fallen on the state's mainland
agricultural towns. So long as demand and foodstuff prices had remained
high, sustained by the presence of foreign troops, the agricultural communities had taken on large amounts of debt. But after the Revolution
farmers faced a bleak future, especially those who depended on exporting
their production. When land taxes surpassed actual agricultural revenue, Rhode Island farmers left in droves for Western Massachusetts and
upstate New York. But the General Assembly was firmly under merchant
control and ignored the farmers' growing fury. This proved a fatal error.

The anger was so deep that a new "Country Party" swept into power
in the election of 1786 under the slogan "To Relieve the Distressed." It

offered a means of meeting its debt obligation without increasing the tax burden on landholders: paper money.

During the Revolution, the state of Rhode Island issued over $1.5 million in notes, which now required $25,000 in annual interest payments. Other states could fill their treasuries from the sale of confiscated loyalist lands, but Rhode Island had only two options: raising taxes on real estate or issuing paper money. Many people felt that paper money, however much it depreciated, was far preferable to having no medium of exchange at all. So once in power, the Country Party authorized £100,000 of paper money emitted through a land bank scheme. Paper bills were considered legal tender in all contracts. To enforce compliance, the Country Party instituted drastic measures including fines, disenfranchisement, or denial of a jury trial for those who refused paper notes.

Rhode Island's merchants were incensed; they considered paper money a cheap and fraudulent panacea, incompatible with their carefully cultivated image as respectable gentlemen. Crippled by debt, they watched foreign ships crowd their harbors and take away the trade that should have been handled by Americans. Coming on the heel of his commercial setbacks, Nicholas was deeply concerned that this artificial currency would deal a fatal blow to his business. He felt that the Country Party's administration bordered on despotism; paper money was a direct assault on private property. Nicholas and John sponsored a propaganda campaign quoting Thomas Paine: "Money is money and paper is paper. All the inventions of man cannot make them otherwise . . . Gold and silver are the emissions of nature, paper is the emission of art." They also ordered their stores closed. Farmers responded by refusing to bring their produce to market. Providence went hungry. An eyewitness reported:

> The condition of the state during these days was deplorable. Merchants shut their shops and repaired to the tavern. Men lounged in the streets or wandered aimlessly about. . . . A French traveler who passed through Newport about this time gave a dismal picture of the place: idle men standing with folded arms at the corners

of the street; houses falling to ruins, miserable shops
offering for sale nothing but a few coarse stuffs, grass
growing in the streets, windows stuffed with rags–everything announcing misery, the triumph of paper
money, and the influence of bad government.

Paper money was not, of itself, unique to Rhode Island. Other states
adopted the expedient. However, both the quantum of paper issued and
the stern measures taken to enforce its acceptance were unprecedented.
As the crisis got into full swing, shop-keepers who would not accept
paper money were taken to court, as happened to Newport butcher John
Weeden whose trial went all the way to the state Supreme Court. The
Court denied having jurisdiction and dismissed the case. Enraged by this
defeat, the Country Party leaders then tried to revise the 1663 Charter
but lost by a single vote. They also failed to force every freeman to take
an oath pledging to accept paper currency. Despite these defeats, the
Country Party was re-elected by a landslide in 1787. Farmers supported
paper money both as a solution to their economic woes and as a way to
insult their merchant antagonists.

College of Rhode Island President James Manning, who had very
reluctantly agreed to represent the state in Congress, found himself
stranded in Philadelphia in January 1787 as his salary was paid in worthless Rhode Island paper money. Exasperated, he wrote:

A more infamous set of men under the character of a
legislature, never, I believe, disgraced the annals of the
world. . . . Rhode Island has not many more strides to
make to complete her disgrace, and ruin too, but that is
not all–she is likely to hold a distinguished rank among
the contributors to the ruin of the federal government.

From Philadelphia, George Washington branded Rhode Island's policies
"scandalous," and James Madison condemned the state for its "wickedness and folly." Neighboring states resurrected all the old criticisms

about Rhode Island being the home of rogues and rascals, heretics and ne'er-do-wells. An article in the *Newport Herald* described Rhode Island as the "quintessence of villainy" and "a State verging into anarchy and ruin from democratic licentiousness, while her Representatives are actuated by the most dangerous sentiments of usurpation and despotism."

As expected, Rhode Island's paper money continued to depreciate dramatically. However, some merchants began looking for compromises. John (who vigorously denied reports that he was paying the workmen on his new house in paper bills) led a bipartisan initiative to allow payment in hard currency for past contracts. Nicholas "reasoned, persuaded, persisted & prevailed" on his debtors to avoid payment in paper, and even accepted title to tracts of land instead of cash. By 1789, Rhode Island paper was worth less than eight cents on the dollar. The pain and disruption of the paper money crisis was making it obvious that state sovereignty was fatally flawed; a strong national government was the only way forward.

Two years earlier, in the summer of 1787, a federal convention had been called to raise revenues for Congress. Participants believed that a strong union could revive the economy since the federal government was better equipped than the individual states to administer taxes, to service war bonds, to increase the money supply, and to field an army powerful enough to defeat both Indians *and* rebellious farmers. But these powers needed to be embodied in a federal constitution.

Rhode Island sent no delegates to the 1787 Constitutional Convention and therefore had no voice in framing the document. Many of the Constitution's Framers thought the state would end up being divided between Massachusetts and Connecticut. But the Country Party was determined that the state should remain outside the Union so long as the paper money program had not run its course.

Furthermore, most Rhode Islanders still feared the encroachment of central government on their long-standing autonomy. They had not fought British trade restrictions simply to hand the same power to a federated congress in which they would have a very small voice. They also believed that Rhode Island could prosper on its own through the duty free sales of cheap foreign goods or even smuggling, if necessary. The

"Free Port of Rhode Island" could be the "wealthiest, happiest, and the most envied State in all the world."

For the state's beleaguered merchants, however, the proposed Constitution offered a way out of the Country Party's paper money policies. On May 28, 1787, the Philadelphia Convention accepted a letter of good wishes from thirteen leading Providence and Newport merchants, including President Manning of Rhode Island College, as well as both Nicholas and John Brown. These gentlemen—who now called themselves "Federalists" in support of the Federal Constitution—wished to prevent "any impressions unfavorable to the Commercial Interest of this State from taking place in our Sister States" as a result of "our being unrepresented" at the Convention. Evidently, the Brown brothers saw no inconsistency between fervently advocating Federation and their earlier passionate opposition to the Impost (here lies just one more instance of public and private interest proving impossible to separate).

New Hampshire became the ninth state to ratify the Constitution in June 1788 and a great celebration was held in Providence by "Pro-Union" supporters. Following a ceremony at the First Baptist Meeting House, a crowd of over five thousand gathered at "Federal Plane" where a table a thousand feet long was loaded with food. Two oxen were roasted along with many hams, washed down with wine and punch. But suddenly a thousand armed farmers appeared, ready to disrupt the festivities. At the last minute, a committee of prominent citizens negotiated a compromise: the planned toast "To the Ninth State" would be substituted with a toast "To the Day."

In April 1789 New York ratified the Constitution, a Bill of Rights was promulgated, and George Washington was inaugurated. Rhode Island's debt was almost liquidated and more of its residents now wanted to join the United States. A May 1789 vote on holding a ratifying convention was defeated only narrowly. That September, Congress temporarily exempted Rhode Island from duties on foreign trade as a further enticement to join the Union.

When North Carolina ratified the Constitution on November 1st, 1789, Rhode Island found itself alone. The effect was electric. James

Madison wrote, "Nothing can exceed the wickedness and folly which continue to rule there." Even George Washington lost patience, warning the General Assembly that it should "consider well" the consequences of refusing to ratify the Constitution. On his New England tour in the Fall of 1789, he pointedly avoided visiting Rhode Island.

Finally, a ratifying convention met in South Kingstown in March 1790—but accomplished nothing. The merchants were embarrassed. A letter was sent to George Washington requesting that he not confuse the actions of the General Assembly with the true character of Rhode Island:

> The majority of the administration is composed of a licentious number of men, destitute of education, and many of them, void of principle. From anarchy and confusion they derive their temporary consequence, and this they endeavor to prolong by debauching the minds of the common people, whose attention is wholly directed to the abolition of debts both public and private. . . . It is fortunate, however, that the wealth and resources of this State are chiefly in possession of the well affected, and that they are entirely devoted to the public good.

The Browns funded another newspaper campaign to blame the postwar depression on Articles of Confederation that had been too weak to guarantee free trade or to protect America from foreign competitors. The seacoast towns were receptive to this argument. Rumors arose that they would join with Providence in seceding from the state, and apply for separate admission to the Union. Then the commercial farming towns also joined the pro-Constitution faction. But it was Alexander Hamilton's proposal that the Federal government assume state debts which finally convinced a majority of voters. In April 1790, just as the U.S. Senate was about to adopt a resolution calling for the severance of relations between the United States and Rhode Island, Arthur Fenner of the Country Party was elected Governor. A skilled politician, later known as "the Great Fence Walker," he pressed for a ratifying convention.

Following twelve separate attempts over a period of three years, the state ratifying convention finally took place on May 25th and a vote taken four days later. Ratification was approved by two votes, the smallest margin of any state. On May 29, 1790, the General Assembly ended its session with the words "God Bless the United States."[16]

Ratification was swiftly rewarded by a special visit to Rhode Island by George Washington who declared, "Since the Bond of Union is now complete and we once more consider ourselves as one family, it is much to be hoped that reproaches will cease and prejudice done away...." On August 16, 1790, Nicholas and other leading gentlemen requested a town meeting:

> ... to consider the most proper Measures to shew the Veneration the Town hath of his Character and the Sentiments of Gratitude the Inhabitants entertain for his rescuing America from the Prospect of Slavery and establishing her Liberty upon the broad Basis of Justice and Equity under a Constitution the Admiration and Envy of the civilized World.

The windows of the Market House were mended, the streets cleaned, candles distributed to the poor, and the statehouse illuminated.

On August 17th, Washington arrived to a rousing welcome in Newport. The next day, he sailed seven hours up the Bay in a packet ship, accompanied by an entourage that included Thomas Jefferson. "... As Washington stepped upon the wharf, he was greeted with a Federal 13-gun salute. Governor Fenner headed the largest and most distinguished procession the town has ever seen." After dinner at the home of merchant John Innes Clark, Washington was about to retire when he learned that the students at the College had organized a spectacle for him. Although it was raining and the President seldom went out in the evening, he

---

[16] Roger Williams's principles of religious liberty and separation of church and state were enshrined in the First Amendment.

walked up the hill with his hosts to view the College Edifice brilliantly alight with a candle in every window. The next day began with heavy rain and a cold, easterly wind, but cleared at 9 am. Washington took a four-hour tour, riding some of the way in John's chariot. He visited the College and climbed to its roof to see the view, boarded *The President,* John's 900-ton ship, drank wine and punch at the houses of John Brown, Governor Fenner, and Deputy Governor Jabez Bowen. Later, a dinner for two hundred was held in the town hall, with toasts, punctuated by cannon, drunk to the French King and National Assembly of France.

Rhode Island could breathe a sigh of relief. It was now back in Washington's good graces.[17] More importantly, the radical paper money scheme had worked. The hated legal tender law now could be repealed and direct taxes could be abolished, since funds were no longer required for interest payments. Paper money had bought time, provided cash to pay taxes, and saved the state from the kind of despair among farmer-veterans that had caused Shay's Rebellion next door in Massachusetts.[18] Now no longer needed, the Country Party was voted out of office and paper bills were burned.

Few men were more relieved at the turn of events than Nicholas and John Brown. Over the course of the 1780s, they had speculated heavily in war bonds and government securities. They now stood to gain spectacularly from Hamilton's assumption plan but for many years, such a happy ending had seemed almost impossible. Over the War years, Nicholas had acquired enough federal and state bonds "to fill a small trunk" —a total of twenty-three different kinds of public paper in various amounts which ultimately came to nearly $200,000. Indeed, Rhode Island had held the nation's highest per capita amount of war debt in 1782 (75 percent of voters owned government securities). But within a few years, these

---

[17] True to form, Uncle John immediately wrote Vice President Adams to submit three names of "gentlemen of good connections" for the federal posts that now would be available. A new nation may have emerged, but the old incestuous interplay between public and private good was as prevalent as ever.

[18] This armed uprising badly frightened Congress and led directly to the Constitutional Convention.

became concentrated in just a few hands; nine men owned almost half of the federal securities in the state.

Nicholas had used some of his war bonds to buy land in New York for resale to speculators, or to make payments to his creditors in London. Once again, Nicholas allowed his commercial ambition to overshadow his moral principles. As in the past, when he had sought to influence the market price of rum, candles or tobacco, Nicholas used his social prominence to spread false rumors to affect the price of these securities. He was not alone in undertaking these dubious activities; most soldiers had no choice but to sell their paper wages to speculators at a mere fraction of face value. In Pennsylvania newspapers, brokers quoted security prices as freely as those of commodities. In Massachusetts, Harvard College bought up paper from eighty individuals. But many people were outraged: an editorial in August 1787 *Virginia Independent Chronicle* noted "By far the greatest part of your military debt is no longer due to your well-deserving soldiery. . . . Pressing necessity has caused these HEROES . . . to become the prey of usurers." In the taverns, a popular ditty ran:

> *In times of war, we fought and bled,*
> *For fine times which they promised;*
> *And since the jewel we did gain,*
> *We'll bleed again, or it sustain.*
> *Stock–jobbers did not fight at all,*
> *Hawkers and sharpers got our all;*
> *And now we'd rather die like men,*
> *Then be slaves to such as them.*

One day, as John Brown rode through town in his fine carriage, an old cooper remarked audibly, "Soldiers blood makes good varnish."

The situation had become so dire during the "critical period" of the mid 1780s that tax collectors, judges, and sheriffs charged with repossessing property had felt sorry for debtors and refused to carry out their duties. Therefore, Nicholas had not been able to obtain the interest payments due to him. The Brown family's predicament grew worse when the Rhode Island General Assembly announced that persons refusing to accept payment in paper bills would forfeit their state securities. Rhode Island merchants risked losing $335,000. At that point, the Brown family owned 20 percent of Rhode Island's war debt–Nicholas's loss would be two-thirds of his personal net worth. James Manning wrote to him from Philadelphia, warning, "I fear the Mercantile Interest will suffer amazingly. You must prepare to sustain the shock in the best manner possible."

Therefore, when Alexander Hamilton announced that state debt would be subsumed into federal debt, few men were more relieved than Nicholas and John Brown. At the stroke of a pen, their massive speculative investment in state bonds was transformed into an asset of great value–rather than the total loss they had so feared. This windfall would enable Nicholas's heirs to pay off a large debt which had become a millstone around the family's necks. It also provided the foundation for the vast wealth that Nicholas's descendants would accumulate in the nineteenth century, which in turn would fuel their philanthropy. Had events turned out differently, Brown University would have a different name and Nicholas's grandson might have been a factory foreman rather than a factory owner.

Throughout the Revolution, Nicholas had never stopped yearning to resume trade with London—especially when his French ventures proved so disappointing. In January 1781, well before the final victory at Yorktown, he had forwarded bills of exchange to John's former apprentice, Elkanah Watson (now established in Nantes, France) for future use in the British market. As soon as hostilities had ended, London merchants had begun eagerly soliciting new American clients. In the spring of 1783, six different English representatives called on Nicholas. He chose the reputed London firm of Champion & Dickason, who already had sold £150,000 worth of goods to Boston merchants. Two large consignments of American goods were prepared. Unfortunately, Champion & Dickason sent the goods in several ships, so Nicholas lost disappointed customers to Boston and New York. To ensure he would always have sufficient capacity in the future, Nicholas commissioned a new ship, the *Hope,* specifically for the London trade. He also led ten Providence trading houses to sign a covenant harmonizing credit terms and mark-ups on imports from Britain.

Problems began within just a few months. At the end of 1783 the British government announced a duty on whale oil—one of Nicholas's prime means of barter. Believing Champion & Dickason's assurances that the tax eventually would be greatly abated or abolished, Nicholas placed another extensive order for English goods to arrive by early spring. Champion & Dickason were alarmed by the rate of American spending and warned, "It does not at this time appear clear to us how America can supply remittances to discharge the astonishing exports, particularly the Northern States."

Yet Nicholas placed a further order in June 1784 for delivery in spring 1785. Less than a month later, devastating news arrived: the British whale oil tariff would remain in place and Connecticut was instituting its own impost, costing Nicholas customers on the state border. That same year, America's credit bubble burst; the nation ran out of cash and plunged into depression.

Many of the goods Nicholas had imported in 1784 remained un-sold; an even greater number remained unpaid. His firm owed £26,144 to Champion & Dickason. Recriminations crisscrossed the Atlantic: Nicholas claimed he had been given faulty advice about the whale oil duty. Champion & Dickason accused him of "conducting business on a shoestring."

That comment must have stung. Yet all Americans were in the same predicament; the entire nation was in the throes of a deep depression, with a trade gap now well over £5 million. Those few shopkeepers with cash bought their inventory from New York or Boston. Nicholas pleaded with customers to settle their debts (he was owed 117 separate notes), but even "the most gentle and conciliatory measures necessary to collect" were often to no avail.

Over the next ten years, the debt to Champion & Dickason would be reimbursed slowly and often painfully. Since the *Hope* could not be sent to England, she was loaded with rice at Charleston to be sold in

Amsterdam, but the cargo was damaged and netted only £1,700. Barrel hoops, beef, and codfish were shipped to the French West Indies; there tobacco was loaded for France, and profits of £2,500 remitted to Champion & Dickason. *Rising Sun* went to Virginia with New England goods to be exchanged for tobacco to be sold in Bordeaux, with profits then sent on to London. None of these measures made more than a dent in the sum owed. It was only when the assumption plan provided what was, in effect, a massive one time liquidity event that the problem loan could finally be extinguished.

The Brown brothers' commercial acumen served them well during the Revolution. Despite moments of acute trepidation when they stared into the abyss, they managed not just to hold onto their wealth, but added to it. The uncomfortable public accusations and insinuations of self-interest notwithstanding, their conjoining of merchant savvy with patriotic zeal had proved highly felicitous. Luck, however, had played no small part. Providence was never occupied, whereas many Newport and Boston merchants were ruined. In different circumstances, the combination of massive speculation and heavy borrowing could have resulted in a dramatically less happy ending.

CHAPTER 4

EARLY LESSONS

"What worries you, masters you." —*John Locke*

Nicholas and Rhoda Brown's much desired son finally arrived April 4th, 1769, as the clouds of insurrection were gathering over the colonies. Named Nicholas after his father and in homage to his Power ancestors (it was, after all, Nicholas Power who had launched Captain James's career), the little boy was known to all as Nick. His childhood would be dominated by the Revolutionary War during which the actions of his father and uncles would cast long shadows on his adult persona. Although he came of age with the new Republic, a period of huge optimism and euphoria, the anxiety of his childhood and adolescent years left an indelible emotional mark. For the rest of life, Nick would support institutions—the church, schools and civic organizations—that gave society stability and offered a moral compass.

Three little girls had come before Nick's birth in 1769: two Hopes who had both died in early childhood (the oldest fell off a dock at age four), and Joanna who was born in 1766. Nick was followed by Chad in 1771, a third Hope in 1773, Moses in 1775, Rhoda in 1777, Jenckes in 1778, Nancy in 1783, and finally John in 1786. Of these ten siblings, only one would survive into adulthood; the "third" Hope.

Such experiences of profound personal loss and sorrow were common at the time, but no less painful. Nick's safe haven through the stormy years of his childhood were his schools—and he would remain forever devoted to them. At the age of eight, he attended Benjamin Stelle's "Latin School" (and would later marry Stelle's daughter, Mary). When Nick reached age ten, his father was advised that the boy should be "sent abroad for a season, [so] he will be separated from the worst boys & habbets . . . get closely attached to his books. . . weaned from habbets of being out evenings & make swifter progress in his studdys."

Having postponed marriage until his younger siblings were first settled, Nicholas was already fifty years old by the time his two eldest children, Joanna and Nick, were thirteen and ten. By 1779, he had lost three children (Chad had died in October 1778, age seven); it must have been hard to send these two away. But Nicholas was determined they should benefit from a "more liberal and finished" education than most children of merchants generally received.

Nick's older sister, the vivacious Joanna, had already joined his Uncle John's daughter Abby under the care of Reverend Samuel Stillman in Newton, Massachusetts. It had been made clear that "Mr & Mrs Brown did not wish to dictate or control her Judgement that they fully approv'd of her Conduct & were not Only willing but even Desireous that She'd Exercise her Own Opinnion." But despite guitar, spinet and dancing classes to supplement her studies, Joanna was miserable. While Abby was regularly receiving packages from home of short cakes, gingerbread and loaf sugar, her cousin received nothing. When Rhoda Brown came to visit her daughter, Joanna burst out "Mamah I hant eat no Appel py since I came here nor cake."[19]

In Nick's case, the choice was between two schools in Connecticut: Mr. Uptick's tutorial at Grafton or Mr. Pemberton's highly regarded Academy at Plainfield. Reverend Stillman also weighed in, arguing that

---

[19] Rhoda Brown immediately sent for fabric, ribbons and two new gowns from Providence. She even asked her husband to secretly supply Joanna with *(word missing?)* but warned "don't let it be known in the family to no one but your self."

Nick might become "awkward" in the countryside where an ignorance of men and manners would hold him back in life. He pushed for yet a third choice, Mr. Moody's Grammar School nearby in Boston. But since Uncle Joseph's family was living in Grafton, Nicholas felt it would be easier for his son to attend Mr. Uptick's Tutorial for a transitional year, then move to Plainfield.

Little Nick was terribly homesick. To make conditions worse, the winter of 1779 was particularly hard; Narragansett Bay started freezing over in November. Nick was not able to come home for Christmas and had to share his turkey with his cousins in Grafton. In early January, his father received the following letter:

> Gennuary 2, 1779
>
> Honour'd Father,
>
> I receivd your kind Letter dated ye 10th of Last Month, and am very glad to here that you are well. I dind at Capt. Power's christmas day. Oliver has had his Turkey coockt at home and I am going to have mine Cook'd at uncle Joseph's and Intend to invite the schollars. Uncle Joseph delivd one My Stock Buckle & turkey from you for wh I now return you thanks & should be very glad if Mamma would send me a pair of Mittens & Some Blue patches for my every day Clothes. I am very much ebige for her truble making me my candles I am glad that you are got better. you muſt tell Joanna to tacke care of my too black Cats you muſt give my love to all my friends and So no more at Preſent.
>
> So I remain your Affectionate Son Nicholas Brown

(On the back is inscribed "Letr. From Our Nick In Grafton, Jany 2nd 1780.")

Much of Nick's schoolwork consisted of Latin and Greek. He also was taught to solve practical problems in mathematics: "A young gentleman being sent abroad, had a certain number of guineas given him to defray his charges; he spent two thirds and one fifth of that number and brought home 36, therefore how many had he at first setting out?"

Nick came home little during his time at boarding school. He was in Plainfield in July 1780 when six thousand French soldiers and ten ships under the command of General Rochambeau arrived in Newport, while British warships patrolled menacingly outside Narragansett Bay. He was also in school when he learned of the victory at Yorktown, the following October 1781. But his rigorous preparation paid off when he passed his entrance examination to the College of Rhode Island in 1782 at the tender age of thirteen. Nick was tested on the accuracy of his reading, the interpretation and parsing of the "Tully" (as the Roman orator Cicero was known), the Greek Testament and Virgil, as well as on his ability to write Latin prose, the rules of Prosody (linguistics) and "vulgar arithmetic." He also had to provide suitable testimony to a "blameless life and conversation." Nick returned to Providence just as his sister, nine-year old Hope, was leaving for Mrs. Wilkinson's School in Newport.

In the fall of 1782, Nick and eleven others began their freshman year at the College of Rhode Island, just as it reopened. The College Edifice had served as a barracks and hospital for the Continental and French armies. French troops were still in Providence waiting for passage across the Atlantic. While the soldiers camped to the north of the College, many local families opened their homes to the officers. Baron de Vioménil, Colonel of the Regiment of Bourbonnais, and two of his aides were quartered with Uncle Joseph on Towne Street (one of the French officers rode his horse through the house). General Rochambeau hosted several balls and assemblies.

The College was in a sorry state, poor and damaged; there was a woeful lack of books and apparatus. Commencements were suspended until 1786. President Manning presented the new United States government with a repair bill for £1,309, but nothing would be paid until 1800. Fortunately, Manning stood ready to lecture, take in boarders, and even build "thirty-two Rods of Stone wall on the College Land" himself since there was no cash to pay for stone masons.

Nicholas could not have picked a better mentor for his son than the Reverend James Manning. Robust and unpretentious (he wore his own hair), Manning was known to be always cheerful—"more disposed to pleasantry than seriousness"—his conversation full of anecdotes. Though he was a powerful orator, his sermons were practical rather than doctrinal. His deepest interests were ethical and religious rather than intellectual, but he was a good all-around scholar, with a gift for languages. Most important, he was an excellent administrator who governed the College with "Persuasive authority," and was respected and beloved by all.

Manning adhered to the College's founding principle of not requiring "religious tests" for admission (as did most other universities). Although deists and atheists were not tolerated, he was careful to honor the "religious scruples" of Jews, Quakers and members of other denominations on such matters as church attendance or removing hats. No sectarian instruction was required; of the seven tutors who served under Manning, four were not Baptist.

When Nick entered the College, it was announced that "The President and Tutors, according to their judgments, shall teach and instruct the several Classes in the learned Languages and in the liberal Arts and Sciences, together with the vernacular Tongues." In addition to the classics in Latin and Greek, first year instruction included vernacular Grammar, Rhetoric, Oratory, Elocution, Geography, Criticism, and Logic. In the third year, Latin and Greek would be replaced with Moral Philosophy, Arithmetic, Algebra, Trigonometry, Surveying, Navigation, Astronomy, and Globes. However, there was no instruction in modern languages nor in natural or social sciences; the scientific apparatus in 1782 consisted of one malfunctioning telescope and a library described by Manning as containing "about five hundred volumes, most of which are both very ancient and very useless, as well as very ragged and unsightly."

Manning lectured in Philosophy and Logic, but the primary method of instructions was recitation from textbooks. Oral examinations were held quarterly, emphasizing English composition and public speaking. Every student had to pronounce an "oration" from memory, often of their own composition, on the first Wednesday of each month; juniors and seniors had to write a weekly "dispute" in Latin.

Nick must have complained to his family about the lack of equipment and instruction in the sciences, for, in his sophomore year, the Corporation named two committees to solicit donations for "philosophical instruments" (science equipment) and books. The Brown family rallied to the cause: Uncle John offered a match fund and, by 1784, sufficient funds were raised to import fourteen hundred volumes from London. Uncle Moses donated a collection of fifty-six books relating to the Society of Friends, and John Tanner of Newport gave 135 volumes.[20] By the end of 1785, the College had a valuable library of two thousand volumes. Uncle Joseph offered his services as professor of experimental philosophy, and Benjamin Waterhouse became a professor of natural history. Both proposed "to give Lectures in their respective Branches, without any Expence to the College while destitute of an Endowment."

While Nick was a student, fees of twenty dollars covered "Commons" (food), tuition, room rent, as well as use of the library and "Scientific Apparatus Privileges" for nine months a year. These were among the lowest fees in America, as befitted the relatively poor Baptist denomination. Students supplied their own firewood. The concept of *in loco parentis* was applied quite literally; indeed, most students probably lived under stricter discipline at college than at home. Approximately ten hours a day were designated study hours, during which they remained alone in their rooms and could read nothing but the classics or books relevant to their recitations. Attendance at morning and evening prayers was mandatory. Professors did not dine with students (though in 1785 a steward was recruited by the Corporation to "Preserve order and Decorum" in the unheated common room).

---

[20] The following year, Dr. Caleb Evans of Bristol, England, announced a gift of 149 volumes for the library by the Education Society of Bristol (founded in 1780 to promote the supply of able Baptist clergy). This was a particularly gracious gesture since the College of Rhode Island was no longer in the British dominions.

Violations such as profane language, misbehavior at prayers, associating in each other's rooms during study hours, or insulting the seniors were punished by fines: "Fairbanks is find [fined] also six shillings for permitting, sometimes since, liquor to be brought into, and to be drunk in his room. . . . How all [are] find [fined] six shillings for . . . [a]t late Hours in the night running through the College, beating against the doors, hallooing and using prophane [sic] language." A student might be temporarily banished to some rural pastor's house, but expulsions were rare.

The number of students increased steadily to fifty in 1786. The College's liberal reputation even attracted the two young sons of Robert Carter of Nomony Hall, Virginia. In February 1786, he asked President Manning to accept them as boarders until old enough for university because he did not want them exposed to slavery.[21]

In September 1786, Nick's class of fifteen was the first to graduate in a proper commencement ceremony, wearing caps and flowing black robes. The event soon became a highlight of the Providence calendar for it offered much "merriment" and "conviviality." The long procession from the College Edifice to the First Baptist Church included the United Company of the Train of Artillery and a choir of singers representing every society in town. Inside the church, each graduate pronounced an oration. Two of Nick's classmates spoke on "Whether it would have been better for America to have remained dependent on Great Britain" and a "Tribute to the Memory of our late departed Friend General Greene"— Nick addressed "The Advantages of Commerce."

Nick's student days should have been joyful and carefree; the Revolutionary War was over and the new nation was filled with optimism. But his college years were marked by a succession of family tragedies. In April 1783, another little brother, Jenckes, died at just four years

---

[21] Carter wrote to Manning: "The prevailing Notion now is, to Continue the most abject State of Slavery in this Common-Wealth–On this Consideration only, I do not intend that these my two Sons shall return to this State till each of them arrive to the Age of 21 years."

old. Baby Nancy was born a few months later in July, but died within a month. Rhoda Brown's health had been declining for some time. Her tenth pregnancy and the loss of these two children were more than she could bear. On December 16th, she breathed her last. Three such tragedies in the same year must have deeply scarred the forteen-year old Nick.

The following year Joanna fell ill. Aunt Mary Vanderlight cared for her at *Poppasquash*, Uncle John's estate near Bristol. Nicholas called on the most reputable doctors he could find, but he knew that she was doomed; "The whole Business of this Life is to Learn to Die well, that is to die in faith of the Memory of Christ Death, being apply'd gives us Hope & a Submission to the will of God," he wrote. By January 1785, radiant eighteen-year old Joanna was gone. Nick was devastated: "I have lost an irreparable Sister, One who would have filled a Mother's Place, which some time since I have been deprived of." He was especially struck by Joanna's regret in her final days at not having obeyed "Pappa, to spend that time which young People commonly spend in reading Novels & Romances in Reading the Bible. She repented she had so often wasted her Time in reading them instead of that HOLY BOOK, which she now experiences the want thereof."

Uncle Joseph suffered a stroke in November 1784 and withdrew from teaching at the College. He was ill throughout the next twelve months and died on December 3rd, 1785, just short of his 52nd birthday, leaving his wife Elizabeth and three children—Mary, known as Polly, Obadiah, and Nick's contemporary, Elizabeth.

But while Nick was coping with so much tragedy, his father found a source of solace.

Three months after little Rhoda's birth in March 1777, Nick's mother had been inoculated against smallpox and gone into quarantine. During her absence, a young woman from Boston, Avis Binney, came to help with the children. She had been introduced by the Reverend Stillman who had invested with Avis's father in Demerara sugar plantations. Following Captain Binney's death in 1774, his wife and three children could no longer afford their large house in Boston. Barnabas Jr., the middle child, had graduated with highest honors from the College of Rhode Island and served with distinction as a surgeon in the Continental Army.[22] Ann, the youngest, was betrothed to Samuel Anthony of Providence. Since the Binney children had been raised by parents of "high intellect," Reverend Stillman thought the Brown household would appreciate Avis's learning and resourcefulness. She stayed for three years.

Avis left the Brown family in 1780 for a small cottage in Newton, Massachusetts, near Reverend Stillman, where she supported herself modestly by carving quills from feathers. She wrote regularly to her Providence benefactors, usually enclosing a note to her sister Ann and a small gift of tea or herbs. She also frequently visited Joanna in Newton, and sent reports to Nicholas and Rhoda on their daughter's wellbeing.

Nicholas, rather than Rhoda, began responding to her missives and supplying her with turkey feathers. Though always decorous, the correspondence grew warmer—Avis allowed her feelings to show: "My heart is so deeply affected with the contents of your truly friendly letter that I want words to express my feelings." The letters continued over the next two years, even though Nicholas and Avis saw each other only once, in November 1783, shortly before Rhoda's death.

Then in May 1784, Avis needed eye surgery. Nicholas dropped all restraint and wrote "I have—the most palpable Tender feelings for you." — would Avis consider a marriage proposal? At first Avis was frightened by Nicholas's eagerness; it was so out of character. He was understanding,"I can't at present think amiss of one I so much adore"—but insistent.[23]

For the courtship to proceed, Avis needed approval from the children. In November 1784, she sent Nick an affectionate letter: "Though you, my dear young friend, may not expect a letter from me, the afflictions of your family and the sincerity with which I wish your Happiness induces me to write you a line or two. I doubt not you will patiently

---

[22] He was credited with unmasking Deborah Sampson, who fought in the Revolution under a man's name, escaping detection until she was wounded. Dr. Binney nursed her in his own home and arranged for General Washington to grant her an honorable discharge and fund her trip home.

[23] Until now, anyone writing about Nicholas Brown has described him as "dour," "plodding" or "stern." They obviously never read his love letters. . . .

attend the well-meant advice of one who was your Mother's friend, and wishes to be the real friend of her Children. . . ." Nick responded politely; he had just lost his sister Joanna. He shared his grief with Avis, assuring her that "I shall always Receive letters & especially those of Advice from my Mamma's Friends with the greatest pleasure."

The greater hurdle was public opinion in Providence where people would question the propriety of the town's most distinguished citizen, now 56, marrying an impoverished spinster two decades younger. Nevertheless, Avis and Nicholas were married on September 9th, 1785. A few weeks later, Avis traveled to Philadelphia with the youngest children, relishing her role as a stepmother: "Our dear little prattling Rhoda [age 8] enjoins me to give her love to you, and the Children all send their duty to you, & all behave very well. . . . Your absence gives me leisure to feel how dear you are to me!" A year later in December, Avis gave birth to a boy who was named John but died two weeks later. Little Rhoda was taken from them in April of 1787.

Fortunately, Nick had the company of a merry band of cousins. In the summer of 1788, young Susan Lear of Philadelphia arrived in the company of Avis's sister-in-law, Mary Woodrow Binney, for an extended stay with the Brown family. Susan Lear's colorful diary depicts a tight-knit family of cousins and siblings who gathered daily to partake in outings, tea parties, and cotillions, in addition to attending church three times on Sundays. Only Uncle Moses's children Sarah (then twenty-four) and Obadiah (then eighteen) remained apart, home schooled and steeped in their Quaker faith.

Susan struck a friendship with Uncle Joseph's daughter Mary, still unmarried at age twenty-eight. She considered Mary's younger sister Elizabeth (known at Betsy, then age nineteen)"mild and amiable in her manner, and I think very pretty." She often went out riding with Nick's sister, fifteen-year old Hope. Uncle John's son James, then age twenty-seven, often took charge of the entertainment and was noted for his "great gift of being welcome wherever he went." His two younger sisters Sarah (age fifteen) and Alice (age eleven) participated in outings, usually accompanied by their mother. They all would drive in carriages and chaises to *Spring Green*, Uncle John's country seat seven miles from Providence for afternoons of "singing, playing, walking, fishing, etc." During her time in Providence, Susan Lear also paid a call on Mary Vanderlight and "Mother" Brown, then age eighty-eight, and found "her countenance and manners so interesting that I loved her the moment I saw her." She viewed the College with Mrs. Manning and grew particularly fond of Governor Bowen's wife (Uncle Obadiah's daughter Sarah).

A highlight of Susan's trip was the month of July that she spent in Boston–the fifty-five mile journey took eleven hours. On the ride back to Providence, she shared her carriage with "an Indian chief educated in Paris" (a member of the Oneida Tribe, sent to France at the Marquis de Lafayette's expense) whom Nicholas Brown invited home to dinner and dancing. "I don't wonder for the ladies of this place are all in love with him and are striving who shall pay him the most attention," commented Susan. The "Indian Prince" also joined the Brown family for the weekly assembly at Mr. Tweedy's "about five miles from town where an entertainment is provided by subscription open to all the people of character in the place."

The Nicholas Brown house on Towne Street was constantly filled with visitors. During the day, important meetings took place in the front parlor (away from the bustle of the counting house), where callers could marvel at the towering mahogany desk. In the evening, dinner was at 5:00, after which the company would often move up the hill for an evening of pianoforte at Uncle John's house. Susan Lear considered it "the most elegant building in America, very large and furnished in the most extravagant manner." All those residing with Nicholas and his family were summoned home by ten p.m. for "rather tedious" prayers.

His formal education complete in 1786, seventeen-year old Nick presented himself at his father's counting house on an autumn morning. The paper money crisis in Rhode Island was at its zenith and trading conditions throughout the former colonies were grim in the extreme. Nick's apprenticeship would be not so much an introduction to the world of commerce as a baptism by fire.

After the Revolution, Nicholas would have welcomed nothing better than a reunification of the four brothers under his aegis. But their aspirations differed too greatly. He and John still collaborated on selected ventures, and their children saw each other almost daily. But Uncle Joseph was quite content teaching "Natural Philosophy" (he would die in 1785) at the College. And Uncle Moses had chosen a very different path. So, in 1783, fifty-four year old Nicholas felt he needed a younger partner to mentor his two remaining sons. (Moses was still alive; he would die nine years later, age sixteen).

George Benson had started at the age of fifteen as an apprentice clerk for Nicholas Brown & Co. in 1767. He then had acted as the firm's agent in Newport, even remaining through the British bombardment of October 1775. A nasty rumor had circulated that he was trading with the enemy. Benson claimed he simply had sold goods on commission, not knowing they were of British origin. So he moved to Boston to again represent Nicholas's interests. While in Boston, Benson kept an eye on Joanna who was attending Reverend Stillman's school in Newton. But again his detractors accused him of slandering a Rhode Island court. In 1781, the General Assembly ordered his arrest if he should set foot in the state.

Nicholas paid little attention to these reports; he was impressed by Benson's Baptist faith and loyalty. The two tightened their business relationship. In 1781, still two months before the American victory at Yorktown, Benson found a source of English goods for Nicholas through the Faro Islands off the coast of Denmark; the voyage never materialized, but Nicholas was further convinced of Benson's resourcefulness. The twenty-nine-year old also negotiated a complex agreement regarding arrears owed to the Hope Furnace by the Cabot family of Boston. Two years later, Nicholas offered Benson a stake in his business. One of his responsibilities would be to oversee the apprenticeship of Nicholas's two sons.

When questioned on the wisdom of his choice, Nicholas responded curtly "From my many years experience of his integrity, I choose him from all the young men of my acquaintance." But there was another reason for Nicholas's interest in George Benson: he was resolutely anti-slavery and not reticent about proclaiming his beliefs. Uncle Moses was by now a leader in the movement to abolish the slave trade. Though Nicholas firmly supported his brother, he recognized that as a prominent merchant who had sponsored a slaving venture and produced rum, barrel hoops and iron shackles for the "Guinea trade," it would be difficult to take a public stance; his reputation was sufficiently tainted at the moment. It was far easier to employ a younger partner with bold opinions to ensure that young Nick and Moses would learn the right values.

The Brown & Benson partnership agreement stipulated that 10,000 Spanish Milled Dollars in solid coin, as well as Nicholas's interest in the Hope Furnace, the spermaceti manufactory, and the sugar refinery would all be held for the "Use and Advantage" of the new partnership. Nicholas would provide funds "necessary and requisite, from his own private Stock or Capital, so far as may be Convenient and Possible," for which he would receive 6 percent interest. He also covenanted all his "credit, Estate and property for the use, benefit and advantage of Brown & Benson." George Benson was to invest whatever he could afford; Nicholas would double that amount. Benson would oversee the firm's day-to-day affairs so that Nicholas "need assume no greater part than what was agreeable to him." Profits would be split with one-third to Benson and two-thirds to Nicholas. The agreement stipulated that the partnership should continue for seven years to cover an adequate apprenticeship for Nick and Moses.

In addition to Benson, there was a teenager in the counting house who awaited Nick's arrival with some trepidation: Thomas Poynton Ives. Born five days after Nick on April 9th, 1769, Tom Ives had grown up in Beverly, Massachusetts, the son of Captain Robert Hale Ives. His mother Sarah Driver Bray was a Baptist but had allowed her four children to be baptized as Anglicans. Tom was just four when his father had died at sea on a passage to the West Indies. He had attended a Boston public school until the age of thirteen when his mother too died. Kindly relatives took the boy in for a few months, but it was decided that an apprenticeship was best. So, in 1782, just as Nick was entering the College of Rhode Island, Tom had stood on the doorstep of Nicholas Brown & Co.

Very quickly, it became apparent that the boy had remarkable talents. Despite his rudimentary education, he had a masterful "command of the English language, writing in the style pure and terse, his arguments clearly ordered no matter how complicated the subject. He was famous for never needing to alter or amend the wording of his original draft." His ability to capture complex details and assemble them into a broader picture, his seriousness and diligence so impressed Nicholas that by his late teens the young man was practically directing the mercantile affairs of the firm.

There is no record of Toms impressions when the boss's son arrived, brimming with classical oratory and flowery declamations, but the two soon became the closest of friends. George Benson, however, did not hide his disdain: "[a] classical education is not worth a copper in the counting house." Nick would have to earn his stripes.

Brown & Benson had been launched in the euphoria of the immediate post-war period. Trade on Narragansett Bay had resumed when the British left Newport in October 1779, far earlier than other ports such as New York, occupied by the British until 1783. However, the two lynchpins of Nicholas Brown & Co.'s business model—candles and iron—soon became moribund. The demise of Nantucket's whale fishing meant that no supplies were available for the spermaceti candle works. Hope Furnace cannons were no longer required for a war effort, nor was low quality Rhode Island iron wanted in London (the Furnace would be sold in 1806). His manufacturing abilities stymied, Nicholas's initial reaction was to turn back the clock to his early days of maritime trading.

The Caribbean seemed the obvious destination to sell the flour and meat he was receiving as payment in these cash-strapped times, in order to obtain much needed bills of exchange. But in July 1783, a British Order in Council stipulated that American products could be transported to the British West Indies only on British ships, thus effectively closing most island ports to American ships. Many merchants were devastated, particularly those from Boston who depended on selling salt fish to the Caribbean. Still, Brown & Benson persisted in finding ways to trade with the old family favorite, Dutch Surinam. Over the course of twenty-six voyages, Brown & Benson's captains used a number of strategies to circumvent the Dutch regulation that all sugar be shipped to Holland.

But what to do with the molasses which their ships were bringing back from Surinam? The obvious answer seemed a return to the family's original business: distilling. Despite dire warnings from his trusted correspondents, Nicholas was determined to build the finest—and certainly the most expensive—rum distillery in America. He forged ahead in a $25,000 joint venture with his fellow merchant Welcome Arnold.

At first the distillery was successful due to the "extreme neatness and good order of the casks and the superior good quality of the liquor." However, Welcome Arnold never managed to supply enough molasses for it to operate at full capacity. The relationship became stormy. To make matters worse, Secretary of the Treasury Alexander Hamilton in 1790 introduced an excise tax on all distilled spirits. The nation reacted in fury; distilling was its third most important domestic product. More and more, cash-poor frontiersmen who could not afford to ship their grain back across the mountains were simply distilling it as whiskey. In Pennsylvania, opposition to the new excise tax grew violent and exploded in the Whiskey Rebellion of 1794. George Washington personally led 13,000 troops to disperse the insurgents. Ultimately, locally sourced whiskey and gin would become exempt in 1801, but rum would remain subject to tax. Distilling rum was not the way forward.

Brown & Benson also attempted a return to coastal trade and in 1784 invested in a packet ship. But *Delaware* began her career just as the nation slipped into depression. It was obvious that something more substantial was needed to replenish the firm's coffers.

When Nick started at the counting house after graduation in 1786, George Benson ensured that his first task would be challenging: the youth was sent to manage Brown & Benson's general store in Grafton, Massachusetts. They hoped customers there would pay in hard cash rather than in worthless Rhode Island paper currency.

As if it were not testing enough for Nick to start his professional life in the thick of the post-war depression and the Rhode Island paper money crisis, the added uncertainty of his family's debt to Britain and the outcome of their war bonds made the situation almost unbearably stressful. Had Nicholas not played such an instrumental role in pressing for Rhode Island's ratification of the Constitution, and had his gamble in securities not succeeded so spectacularly, he might today be remembered primarily for his self-interest rather than his effective leadership. Certainly, his son Nick found the experience so shameful and disturbing that he never again incurred debt.

After five years, Nick was made a partner in Brown & Benson in January 1792; he was twenty-one. The firm still owed a huge debt to *Champion & Dickason* and did not know what would happen to its enormous investment in potentially worthless Revolutionary War securities (Congress had approved Hamilton's assumption plan, but it would take another year to be implemented by the Rhode Island legislature). Then on March 7th, Nick's younger brother Moses died, age only sixteen. He had shown intellectual promise at the College of Rhode Island. His death was wrenching. George Benson witnessed the last moments between the two brothers and reported that the dying Moses had said, "Do not, my dear Brother, trust in Riches but in a good family, or good Education."

Less than three months later, on May 30th, Uncle John dashed a hasty note to his son James in Boston. Never forgetting his priorities, he first spoke of his ship, then wrote:

> On my Return Home [yesterday] by the Back Street [Benefit Street] I was Supprised with the news of my Brother N's Departure. I immediately came to his House & where I am now writing I found my D'r Brother a Corps on the Bed on the Floor with his widow & Two children also on the Floor in the Greatest Agoney of Greaf Stricken on the Sean.

Nicholas's health had been declining for some time; nevertheless, his death at age 61 came as a shock. On May 29th, a Sunday, he had ridden

out to Pawtuxet, then hurried back home to change for a service at the
Baptist Meeting House. Avis saw her husband was unwell and convinced
him not to attend church. Nicholas went instead to his "keeping room,"
sat down at his great desk, and collapsed. Avis immediately sent for the
doctor who arrived just as Nicholas breathed his last. Servants were
dispatched to alert Nick and Hope who were in church, as well as Uncle
John and Uncle Moses. The Reverend Stillman was notified and arrived
from Boston with two of John's children, James and the youngest daughter, Alice (Abby and Sally, however, were in Philadelphia). In his funeral
oration, Reverend Stillman preached that Nicholas had been:

> . . . from sentiment a lover of all mankind, especially of
> good men. He was not ashamed of the Gospel of Christ,
> nor of the poorest of his disciples. His manners were
> plain and sincere. He was a faithful friend and a good
> companion; and combining with his excellent social
> qualities a general knowledge of the world, of books
> & of men, his conversation was always pleasing and
> instructive.

Reverend Stillman also noted that he already had buried nine members
of the family-a wife, six children and a servant.

A few days later, Uncle John's son James commented to his sister
Abby, "Poor Grandmother [Brown] weeps incessantly, indeed she is quite
a child. . . . Hope supports the shock beyond all belief, you may easily per-
ceive that her struggles are great, and that her calmness does not proceed
from insensibility." Closest in age to Hope, Uncle John's second daughter
Sally was particularly concerned and wrote from Philadelphia, "Poor
Hope, my heart aches for her, she most assuredly is the greatest sufferer,
and has real cause for affliction, pray write me directly and inform me
how she is. Heaven I hope has endowed her with fortitude to bear up,
under this severe trial."

As was customary, Nick received the family brick house on Main
Street (the new name for Towne Street), his father's apparel, and rights

to Providence Common Lands, to the Brick School-house, and to the "Proprietor's Library" in the statehouse. Hope inherited the clothing of her deceased mother Rhoda and of her sister Joanna.

But everyone gossiped about the terms of Nicholas's will regarding Avis, now age forty-three. She was to receive $2,000, an annuity of £200 in silver ($910), and use of the "Bowles Estate" on the west or Weybosset side of town. Across the Great Salt Cove from Main Street, this new residential area offered more pleasant surroundings for Avis and eighteen-year old Hope than the crowded and noisy town center. However, it was far from Avis's friends and Hope's merry band of cousins. The two women pleaded that "had the said Testator lived to redraw his will which he proposed . . . and known the Value his estate had come to, he would have further Provision for his said widow."

It so happened that Uncle Moses had bought several plots five years earlier in 1786 from Thomas Angell, on the north side of the First Baptist Church. A young clockmaker, Seril Dodge, had built himself a small house on one plot, then sold the property back to Moses in 1790. This dwelling was perfect for Avis and Hope. It now needed to be "handsomely finished and papered" as would befit "the Widow Brown." The best craftsmen were imported to provide decorative woodwork–elaborate cornices, handrails, chair rails, and balusters richly carved with Chinese fretwork–and two spectacular fireplace mantles with Ionic and Corinthian columns. Watches (clocks), a pianoforte, and a chandelier were ordered from London with the assistance of Thomas Dickason. Avis furnished the house in the latest style, so that each room would serve a function; the southwest parlor was a dining room with a mahogany sideboard and eight matching chairs. Looking glasses, chintz, and andirons were ordered from Boston, as well as bookcases for her large library. She expected to entertain in style; there were enough wineglasses for nineteen and silver teaspoons for twenty-one.

People were amazed to learn that Nick and Hope had been asked to sign a pledge to "faithfully & most affectionately love esteem & in every respect do for her as my respective wife & most deserving in every respect & esteem and one who your worthy deceased mother had the greatest regard for. . . ." Most revealing was Nicholas's explanation of this codicil to his will: "I have known great misunderstandings," so he hoped that everything after his death be done in "love and harmony."

This was not to be. In 1793, two years after Nicholas's death, Avis noted in her diary:

> Ever since the death of my Husband I have been en-
> gaged in a most unhappy altercation with His Executor
> [Moses] & family about Property. I think I have been
> cruelly used, and such deep [*deceit* is crossed out] finesse
> has been blended with the most unfeeling Harshness as
> has distracted & distressed me beyond measure.. . . . O
> what wounds and bruises I have procured myself!

Despite a lavish house and substantial allowance, "The Widow Brown" was deeply upset. Moses could be tough and intransigent; he was "laying the blame on the children."

Indeed, no one in the Nicholas Brown branch of the family was particularly adept at showing emotional warmth. Though deeply concerned about his children's education and welfare, Nicholas had been rather stern and aloof, engrossed in the challenges of the Revolutionary War, the critical period, the paper money crisis, and the ratification debate, not to mention the pleasant distractions of a new wife. In a July 1820 diary entry, thirty years after Nicholas's death, his only surviving daughter Hope was still musing about whether she had provided him with "sufficient comfort and consolation." Nicholas did, however, ensure his children benefitted from the best education available, along with commercial training and a partnership in the family firm for his son. But he did not attend much to his son's broader moral and spiritual development. That task fell to others.

From an early age, Nick's social conscience had been honed by Uncle Moses, with the added influence of ardent abolitionist George Benson. Moses had long since evolved and articulated a very definite moral philosophy. He believed the purpose of trade (as he reminded his brother John in 1770) was to accumulate an estate large enough to make one independent of the "various scenes of fortune incident to trade." Man should only engage in what he could attend to with due care "and leave time to enjoy his family and connections." The real meaning of life was to be found in public service. "When a man has business enough to earn reasonable security for the present and the future, he has an obligation to lay by all his profits where it will be most advantageous to society." Moreover, a man should donate "part of his time in the business of the community without profit so soon as his business brings him any over-plus more than to supply his family."

At the same time, Uncle John's bravado and commercial daring must also have enthralled the young man, even if that uncle's pro-slavery declamations left him deeply uncomfortable. No less a figure than the French Duke de la Rochefoucauld Liancourt, visiting Providence during his exile in America a few years later, would note as follows:

> The richest merchant in Providence is John Brown. . . . In one part of the town he has accomplished things that, even in Europe, would appear considerable. At his own expense he has opened a passage through a hill to the river, and has built wharfs, houses, an extensive distill-ery, and even a bridge, by which the road from Newport to Providence is shortened by at least a mile. . . . At his wharfs are a number of vessels, which are constantly receiving or discharging cargoes.

How much more profound must have been the impact of this larger than life figure upon a young man on the threshold of adulthood? As Nick came into his vast fortune and pondered his life choices, both these un-cles were pioneering new forms of enterprise. Which to emulate?

Nick was of the generation that came of age with the new nation. As explained by the historian Joyce Appleby, "Never forced like their parents to revoke an earlier loyalty to Britain, the men and women of the first generation were much freer to imagine what the United States might become." They would attribute economic progress to the soundness of the revolution they had inherited. Historian Gordon Wood also noted, "The revolutionary generation was very modern: they were optimistic, forward-looking, and utterly convinced that they had the future in their own hands." Nick certainly believed in the connection between democracy and prosperity. At a time of political revolution, commercial expansion and intellectual ferment, he had inherited the capital and ships to turn that promise into profits. As one of the generation who "inherited the Revolution," he had the great wealth and the pre-eminence to pursue any opportunity of his choosing in the New Republic. But he also had grown conscious of the potentially disastrous consequences of speculative dealings and of the general fickleness of fate. These were lessons that would permanently impact upon both his career and his adult persona. As a result, he would never cease to believe that "authority should be exercised through the uncontested leadership of a recognized cadre of families"–including his own. Nick was a child of the eighteenth century and its sense of certainty. The presidential election of Thomas Jefferson that would launch the uncoupling of social and political power was still nine years away. But after that turning point, the tension between Nick's cherished eighteenth century ideals and the realities of American society–transformed by industrialization, urbanization, emigration, political radicalization, and religious revitalization–would be the single most determinant factor in Nick's life.

For the moment, however, poised on the brink of financial autonomy and freedom from supervision, Nick must have felt that the world was his oyster.

CHAPTER 5

A CHOICE OF MENTORS

"Though I am not endowed with the divine light to see the Guinea trade with the same eyes as you do, I respect you as a brother and a friend." —John Brown to Moses Brown

From an early age, Nick was introduced to the important men who constantly visited his father's home, from distinguished theologians to leading politicians. But the two men who most influenced young Nick were his uncles John and Moses. The brothers could not have appeared more dissimilar: Uncle John, age fifty-four in 1791, was of enormous girth—"fleshy and rather unwieldy in movement"—with boundless energy and ceaseless drive. At fifty-two, Uncle Moses was thin and cerebral, a vegetarian, a teetotaler and a Quaker. Having withdrawn from commercial affairs, Moses spent most of his days receiving visitors at his pleasant Elmgrove estate. John, however, "might be observed riding daily in all the business portions of the town in a one-horse sulky driving bargains, and personally superintending all the branches of his affairs at the counting house, at the shipyard, on the wharves, at the bank, and wherever his business operations called." Each man bore great affection for his nephew, and Nick admired them both.

Though he lived some distance from the center of Providence, Uncle

Moses kept himself informed through a steady stream of visitors and abundant correspondence with learned men. He regularly purchased books from London to sell or to distribute, especially pamphlets on the Quaker faith. After the death of his first wife in 1773, he remarried in 1779 to another small, frail woman, Mary Olney, a thirty-five-year old widow, who died in 1798.

Uncle Moses was also spiritually removed from his brothers. While they pushed for the gentrification and greater decorum of the Baptist Church, he had sought a faith more in line with the fundamentalist principles of his forefathers, tinged with the zeal of his newfound Quaker beliefs. Like the early Baptists who relied on an "inner light" for guidance, the Quakers had an anti-authoritarian streak, tempered by a strong social conscience. From his conversion in 1774, Moses spent a lifetime combining spiritual reflection with social enterprise; his ventures sought both a financial and a humanitarian return. He agreed with the Quaker leader William Penn that "mending the world . . . [was the] major business of life." Thus Uncle Moses found a way to resolve the tension between private profit and public good.

Of all the social issues that stirred Moses Brown to action, none exercised him more than slavery and the slave trade. It was also the issue that would strain the fabled bond between the brothers almost to the breaking point, particularly in the period between 1784 and 1796. For Nick who admired his uncles equally, the recurring family tension during his adolescence and young adulthood must have been deeply upsetting.

America was only a minor player in the Transatlantic slave trade compared to Portugal, Britain, Spain or France[24], but Rhode Island dominated that slice of the trade. Throughout the eighteenth century, the colony's ships had carried more than 100,000 enslaved Africans over nearly a thousand voyages. Since almost everyone in Rhode Island was involved in some aspect of West Indian provisioning, the entire colony was entangled, directly or indirectly, in the slave trade. Newport was the principal slave market of the northern colonies.

---

[24] Representing six percent of the total

The first enslaved Africans had arrived in Rhode Island in 1638, the same year as Chad Browne. While most slaves were sold in the West Indies or the Southern colonies, 17 percent of Rhode Island families owned slaves or bound servants of color by the Revolution. They either labored on the large agricultural estates of South County, or were treated like apprentices or white indentured servants, serving as household staff, seaman, dockhands, and laborers in distilleries and candle works. As the Browns had grown prosperous, they had begun owning slaves. Elder James was said to have owned two. Captain James purchased four, two in 1728 through trade with South Carolina, and two from the failed 1736 voyage of the *Mary* to Africa, an ill-advised "get rich quick" scheme to raise cash for his distillery. Uncle Obadiah occasionally included slaves in his transactions, such as the voyage of the *Speedwell*, sent to New Orleans in 1758 with candles, wine, a French flag-of-truce prisoner, and ten slaves. In 1759, in the midst of the Seven Year's war, he also tried his hand at the Transatlantic trade. But his *Wheel of Fortune* and its cargo of slaves were captured by a French privateer. In his will, Uncle Obadiah ordered Adam, one of his nine slaves, to be freed and given twenty acres of land.

By the time Nicholas succeeded his uncle in 1762, he too had bought slaves and been indirectly involved in the triangular trade, producing special hogsheads of rum and candles for fellow merchants to sell in "Guinea." In 1764, the four brothers had needed cash for their new iron foundry. After exhausting all other alternatives, they had decided to attempt another slave trading venture.

The *Sally* expedition was the worst ever undertaken by a Providence trader. Of the 196 Africans acquired by the ship's master Esek Hopkins, at least one hundred and nine perished–some in a failed insurrection, others by suicide, starvation, and disease. The emaciated remainder were sold in Antigua. Following this debacle, Nicholas, Joseph and Moses not only foreswore the trade but began personal journeys of moral reevaluation towards the institution of slavery. But Uncle John was determined to persevere, convinced that a merchant should be free to trade in whatever manner he please. Five years later, he dispatched the *Sultan* to Africa.

When Nick was born that same year, 1769, his father and three

uncles owned fourteen slaves between them. Most worked in the spermaceti candleworks, on Nicholas Brown & Co. ships, or at the Hope
Furnace; two were in his father's household. While more and more New
Englanders were beginning to oppose the slave trade, only a tiny minority contested the institution of slavery. The concept of bondage was
still a cornerstone of society and emancipation was considered heretical
by theologians and political thinkers. Even the "New England Yearly
Meeting" of Quakers condemned only the active buying or selling of
slaves—not the institution of slavery—and simply encouraged owners to
treat their slaves with "tenderness." Most people believed that abolishing
slavery would undermine the entire social order. So, when Uncle Moses
decided to manumit his seven slaves on November 10th, 1773, he caused
quite a sensation.

Many years later, he would say "[Had the *Sally* never sailed] I should
have been preserved from an Evil, which has given me the most uneasiness, and has left the greatest impression and stain upon my own mind
of any, if not all of my other Conduct in life." At first, he had believed
that slavery would wither away naturally once slaving became illegal. But
ultimately he understood "that the holding of negroes in slavery however
kindly treated by their masters has a tendency to encourage the iniqui-
tious practice of importing them from their native country."

Uncle Obadiah's youngest daughter Mary (a Quaker convert) was
the first to free her two slaves. The following week, Moses repeated a
similar ceremony, promising to educate the younger slaves and binding
his family to care for them. Each freed slave was given an acre of land
and a savings account (to be held by Moses), to encourage "sober prudence and industry." They should consider him a friend always ready to
assist them if they used their "liberty wisely." Most continued to work for
the Brown brothers.[25] Though patronizing and ultimately demeaning to
modern perceptions, this behavior was considered unusually benevolent

---

[25] In his memoirs William Brown, great-grandson of a Brown family slave, noted the
family lore: "Mr. Brown [Moses] was very particular that his men should not be overworked, and allowed no punishment on his farm. He was always willing to grant his
men leave of absence whenever they desired."

for the time; indeed, Moses Brown was exceptional in acknowledging African-Americans as his spiritual equals. Paternalism and dependence were inherent in the hierarchical society of colonial America. Colonial bonded servants shared much of the chattel nature of black slaves.[26] 60 percent of youths between the ages of fifteen and twenty-four were in servitude, for much longer periods than in England-they could be bought, sold or rented, and they could not marry or buy property. Slavery was often regarded as merely the basest and most degraded of the numerous lowly stations in society.

Uncle Moses then threw himself into the anti-slavery movement, distributing essays and pamphlets, intervening in court cases, lobbying fellow merchants and even the New England Yearly Meeting. In the heady days before the Declaration of Independence, Nicholas noted that "the present disposition of people in New England [is] against slavery." Uncle Moses used this window of opportunity in 1774 to push a ban on the slave trade through the Rhode Island General Assembly. Though amended to insignificance by a coterie of Newport slaving interests, it was one of America's first anti-slaving laws. The following year, with Nicholas's support, he convinced the Providence Town Council to emancipate an enslaved family whose owner had died intestate. During the Revolution, when few slaving ventures took place, Uncle Moses visited numerous Quakers who were hesitating to manumit their slaves. He must have influenced his elder brother, as Nicholas drafted the following note on November 1st, 1779:

To all whom it may Concern-

This may Sertifie That I Nich.[s] Brown, being the Quarterpart Owner of the Negro man (cooper) Called Tom do upon mature Consideration & by these Lines make it manifest That I do make free the said negro man Tom, that is to say for all my right and tittle to him,

---

[26] British visitors were astonished to see how ruthlessly Americans treated their white servants: "they groaned beneath a worse than Egyptian bondage."

which Freedom is to be in full force on the day that the
news comes of the Settlement of the present dispute between this Country & Grait Britain, and my Heirs &c.
are to take notice & Govern themselves accordingly –
Witness my hand

[signed] Nich Brown"

After the War, Uncle Moses took his personal anti-slavery campaign
public. His objective was a new, far stronger law for Rhode Island. The
Providence Town Meeting approved such a measure in January 1784; but
when the bill reached the General Assembly, it hit a wall of opponents
led by none other than John Brown.

Fresh from his victory against the Impost, John Brown was not about
to allow any further limits on maritime commerce. After much discussion, the economic argument carried the day: what other possibilities
were open to Newport? With whaling, fishing, candle making and iron
smelting defunct, and the West Indies precarious, a return to the slave
trade seemed one of the few available options. Furthermore, argued
Newport merchants, Rhode Island's actions would amount to "the smallest spot on the face of the sun, and would no more stop the trade if we
passed the new act than ye spot would the light." Moses admitted defeat.
But at least the General Assembly passed a manumission measure, "The
Gradual Abolition Act," which freed all children born of slave mothers
after March 1st, 1784 (though they had to serve their mother's owner for
twenty-one years).

As a result of the 1774 prohibition against importing slaves and the
1784 manumission law, Rhode Island's enslaved population began to
drop.[27] Moses wrote to a British correspondent, "The trade is carried on
from these states yet the general voice of the people is against it." Then in

---

[27] The 1790 Federal Census listed 427 free people of color and 48 slaves in Providence
out of a population of 6,400.

November 1786, Uncle Moses learned that his brother John was mounting another slaving voyage.[28]

The two brothers had spent the previous eighteen months avoiding any mention of the General Assembly debates. In April 1785, Nicholas and John had asked Moses to represent Providence in the Rhode Island legislature, but he had declined the offer. It was only when Moses's son, Obadiah, showed up to deliver an abolitionist pamphlet that John realized he was now in his brother's cross-hairs.

Uncle John immediately responded: "[It]has beene permitted by the Supreeme Governour of all things for time Immemorial, and whenever I am Convinced as you are, that its Rong in the Sight of God, I will Immediately Dessist but while its not only allowd by the Supreme Governour of all States but by all the Nations of Europe. . . ." Then he dispatched *Providence* to the Gold Coast to purchase eighty-eight slaves, seventy-two of whom were sold in Hispaniola.

Nevertheless, Uncle John did not want to cause further dissent within the family; times were sufficiently stressful with Rhode Island in the midst of the paper money crisis. He wrote to Moses, "Tho I am not endowed with the divine light to see the Guinea trade with the same as you do, I respect you as a brother and a friend. . . . I respect your children and sincerely wish they might be indulged to be more familiar with mine, I am sure my children has a particular regard for yours," signing "Your affectionate brother."

Uncle Moses seethed but ploughed ahead with his cause. In 1787, he hoped to capitalize on the spirited atmosphere surrounding the Constitution ratification debate to push through a new state law against the trade. Indeed, like many Quakers, Moses criticized the proposed Constitution for failing to address slavery in the Southern states.[29] For once, Uncle John did not intervene and Uncle Moses was successful. America's leading slave trading state became the first to prohibit that

---

[28] John actually had already sent a ship to Africa in January 1786; the voyage was a disaster–half of the seventy slaves died, along with the captain and the first mate.
[29] He only changed his mind at the 11th hour, in early 1790, when Rhode Island risked secession, and agreed to lobby fellow Quakers to support ratification.

trade. Rhode Islanders could not agree on ratifying the Constitution but they united on a law to prohibit any inhabitant of the state to "directly or indirectly import or transport, buy or sell, or receive on board their vessel . . . any of the natives or inhabitants of state or kingdom in that part of the world called Africa, as slaves or without their voluntary consent." Uncle Moses rejoiced that the bill had passed "not upon mere commercial views but the more noble and enlarged principles expressed in the memorial and act."[30] Now he now needed to focus his energies on ensuring that the new law was enforced as slave ships were still setting sail unhindered from Rhode Island.

The time had come to form an abolition society, much like those already formed in Pennsylvania and New York. The "Providence Society for Promoting the Abolition of Slavery, for the relief of Persons unlawfully held in Bondage, and for Improving the Conditions of the African Race" was launched in February 1789, and formally incorporated by the General Assembly in June 1790. By early 1791, it counted 171 members; Moses Brown served as treasurer, Thomas Arnold (married to Uncle Obadiah's daughter) was its secretary. Nick abandoned his father's traditional reserve and announced his true colors by becoming its vice president.

The Providence Abolition Society had not even been formally chartered when an article signed "A Citizen" appeared in the *Providence Gazette*, castigating the abolitionists for their naiveté: since American ships carried only a fraction of the total traffic from Africa, prohibition was pointless and harmed the nation's economic interests. Slavery simply reflected God's will. Everyone knew that "A Citizen" was in fact John Brown.

This public diatribe was distressing to Nicholas and Moses. They let their cousin by marriage and Quaker Thomas Arnold respond with passion in the *United States Chronicle*, under the pseudonym "A Foe to Oppression." The tone grew bitter. Uncle John wrote that the Abolition Society was a plot to deprive citizens of their lawful property; tribal

---

[30] Within five years, all the Northern states would follow in outlawing slave trading.

warfare and slavery were ancient African traditions and the abolitionists were sinners covered in hypocrisy. Eventually, Uncle Moses stepped in to end this unseemly exchange. But the public seemed engrossed; new letters appeared and other newspapers began reprinting the debate. Nicholas and Moses became increasingly alarmed at the lack of family unity just at a time when the Browns were pressing for Rhode Island to join the Union. Indeed, Uncle John picked up on this irony:

> Permit me to remind you that it cannot be long before this state becomes a member of the Union; and I beseech you, in the most friendly manner, not to become the means of dividing the general government against itself, by influencing the northern part, through your mistaken zeal for the abolition of slavery, to create a war between the two extremities of the Confederacy.

Uncle John had the last word when he noted that both Moses and Thomas Arnold's fortunes came from Uncle Obadiah's estate "which was got from the labor of slaves. . . . I condemn your partiality, that you are so unwilling that others should acquire property in the same way yours was got."

Then, everyone's attention turned to the Abolition Society's first case, *Gordon v. Gardner et al.* Caleb Gardner was a prominent Newport merchant who had sent his brig *Hope* on two slaving voyages in 1787. Hoping to escape notice, he had applied to change the ship's name and ownership in Bedford, Massachusetts. When the case finally came to trial in March 1791, the court found the Newport slaver guilty. But Gardner was a Revolutionary War hero and a member of the Legislature's Upper House. He paid only a minor fine and *Hope* returned to Africa four times over the next four years. Then when the Society tried to assist one of Uncle John's black seamen, James Tom (originally captured from a British ship) to gain his freedom, John riposted, "You have as much right to the coat on my back as you do to my Negro."

The quarrel abated on this note, but the matter was far from resolved. Moses would continue to proselytize for abolition and John for the rights of the slave traders. Quite remarkably, the dispute between John and Moses did not lead to their breaking off relations but it did prompt Nicholas to appoint Moses as his sole executor. Nicholas and John had shared a lifetime of business collaborations, but his choice of Moses showed clearly whom he favored not only to extricate his legacy from its precarious financial position but as the better mentor for his children.

Second only to ending the Transatlantic slave trade, Moses's principal concern in the years after the Revolution was to find employment for the women and children left destitute by the War. He soon realized he could advance both aims by sponsoring manufacturing ventures: if "the money'd men of Newport and especially the Guiney Traders who disgracefully Continue in the Beaten Track of that inhuman traffick . . . turn'd their stock to the duk [sailcloth] or other manufactorys," society would be much improved. A factory that offered substantial employment to entire families would benefit everyone: the poor would lead diligent, principled lives and no longer drain the public purse, while slave traders "would be more comfortable and happy for themselves and the Publick to feed the poor by Employing them than doing it . . . by charity." Moreover, an indigenous manufacturing capacity would reduce American dependence on British imports.

To this end, Uncle Moses returned to the commercial arena and began experimenting with a number of revenue producing activities that could revitalize Rhode Island. He found new ways to produce potash and pearlash (the research he sponsored received the first ever US patent in 1790), crop and livestock improvements, and new methods to make cider. But these were all merely stopgaps until he could perfect a spinning frame.

Until the 1780s, linen or wool yarn was spun in private homes, then woven into cloth on home looms—a process that had changed little since the Middle Ages. Shopkeepers bought the raw wool or linen, then put it out successively to pickers, spinners, and weavers, and finally sold the finished cloth in their stores. Cotton was much appreciated for its comfort and hygienic properties, but no one knew how to spin cotton yarn strong enough to be woven into 100 percent cotton cloth. Then in 1769, Richard Arkwright in England invented a water-driven machine, a "jenny," that gave cotton thread a twist, so that it could be woven into the smooth, even cloth that eluded home spinners of wool and linen. The technology remained heavily guarded (industrial espionage was a capital offense in Britain), so the colonies could only stare across the Atlantic with envious eyes while spending their scarce cash on imported British cloth.

From time to time, however, British mechanics managed to escape to set up imitation Arkwright frames in the United States. Beginning in 1785, Uncle Moses seized every opportunity to inspect machines smuggled from England, and to correspond with English mechanics and factory overseers. He knew that a confluence of climatic and geographic realities made Rhode Island well suited to the textile industry. Sheep farming had been widespread since the colony's earliest days, so people knew how to spin and weave wool, as well as linen and flax. The state was blessed with fast-moving rivers that ran in a 150-foot drop from the state's northern borders to Narragansett Bay; these could generate steady sources of waterpower. The water was soft, requiring no treatment to wash yarns and cloth, and dyes took easily. The state's climatic conditions were also perfect for the textile industry, with just the right amount of moisture in the air to keep threads from drying out and breaking on fast-moving machines.

Over the next few years, Uncle Moses installed various imperfect looms and machines in the basements of several Providence houses under the supervision of clock maker Seril Dodge (who would go on to found the silverware industry) and Smithfield native Oziel Wilkinson (whose family had worked on a steam engine pump for the Hope Furnace). He bought supplies of Trinidad cotton from his brother John, since American cotton was short-staple, usually dirty and badly packed. He hired a succession of mechanics. But the improvised "jennies" and carding machines broke down continually and the cloth produced with a cotton weft and a linen warp was too coarse; 100 percent cotton cloth seemed beyond reach. It was particularly galling that he could not overcome these technical challenges at a time when the demand for American-made textiles was growing. At Washington's 1789 inauguration, the President, Vice

President, and several members of Congress appeared at the New York ceremonies dressed from head to toe in homespun clothing. That Fall, a despondent Uncle Moses gave up his experiment and suspended operations until he "could procure a person who had wrought or seen them [Arkwright frames] wrought in Europe."

It was all the more frustrating for Moses that he was coming under mounting financial pressure as his son Obadiah, age 19, was nearing adulthood and his daughter Sarah was about to marry William Almy, "a circumstance which brings on me some exercise to have him settled in some satisfactory way." So he decided to call in loans and to sell large amounts of continental and state securities in order to go into partnership with his new son-in-law as "Almy & Brown." Then, a miracle happened. A letter arrived dated December 2nd, 1789:

> Sir, - A few days ago I was informed that you wanted a manager of cotton spinning, etc. in which business I flatter myself that I can give the greatest satisfaction, in making machinery that produced good yarn, either for stockings or twist, as any that is made in England; as I have had an opportunity, and an oversight, of Sir Richard Arkwright's works.

It was signed Samuel Slater.

Born to a Derbyshire farming family in 1768, Slater had started work at age ten in a new cotton mill launched by Jedidiah Strutt, using the water frame pioneered nearby by Richard Arkwright. By age 21, he had gained a thorough knowledge of cotton spinning. Hearing of the bounties offered in America to mechanics willing to smuggle cotton machinery to the United States, "Slater the Traitor" secretly embarked for New York in September 1789, disguised as a country bumpkin. But within a few weeks, he became dissatisfied with his job at the New York Manufactory Company on Vesey Street, a "jenny workshop," and started looking for a better opportunity.

Uncle Moses immediately offered young Slater a dollar a day to construct for Almy & Brown a spinning frame in Pawtucket, on the Blackstone River, five miles from Providence. But when Slater saw Moses's machinery in January 1791, his heart sank. Fortunately, he fell in love with Oziel Wilkinson's daughter Hannah and so had an incentive to remain in Pawtucket. He also realized that Uncle Moses could purchase the best tools and parts in New England, and attract good mechanics. In less than twelve months, Slater built an Arkwright frame powered by a water wheel. On December 20th, 1791, he cleared ice off the wheel, lifted the sluice, and the American textile industry was born.

Rhode Island, the most liberal and entrepreneurial of the colonies, was particularly suited to be the birthplace of the American industrial revolution. Not only was the entire population involved in some aspect of trade, but farm families had a long tradition of part-time manufacturing and entrepreneurship in order to increase their incomes. They borrowed to finance projects–indeed, Rhode Island had recognized the entrepreneurial character of debt before anyone else and offered very lenient terms for the relief of insolvent debtors.

Within two years, Almy & Brown were turning out more yarn than they could either weave themselves or even sell. Nevertheless, it would take a long time for Almy & Brown to become profitable. The mill was an unpretentious structure, overlooking the Pawtucket Falls. The 24-spindle water frame and two carding machines were operated by nine children, between seven and twelve years of age. The cotton was picked and hand cleaned by industrious housewives. Uncle Moses invested more than $65,000 in this first venture and continued making loans in $20,000 installments.[31] In the meantime, British imports of printed cloth and linen also kept climbing, from 353,762 yards in 1785 to 3.7 million yards in 1800.

William Almy oversaw the manufacturing side of the business, while young Obadiah managed sales. Born in 1770 (a year after Nick) with a

---

[31] Though he earned a handsome income from his numerous investments in agricultural lands, Uncle Moses complained to Slater that his "spinnery" was turning "my farms into yarn."

lame leg, he was educated at home by Quaker tutors. Uncle Moses spent considerable time and effort in raising his boy about whom he wrote, "[he is] a pleasant plant who I have dedicated to the Lord." Obadiah dutifully followed in the path his father traced for him. He also inherited his father's ability "to reconcile commerce and conscience in an age when commerce was too often captured by mere gold and conscience polluted by avarice."

Once William Almy and Obadiah Brown were established in the textile manufacturing business, Uncle Moses—who was already fifty-two in 1790—went back into semi-retirement. For the next forty-six years, he would be a gentleman farmer on the three hundred serene acres at Elmgrove whose good table and comfortable appointments impressed visitors. He remarried a third time in 1799 to Phebe Lockwood, a widow with grown children, who remained by his side for only nine years before dying in 1809 at the age of sixty-one. He never ceased experimenting in agriculture, meteorology, and preventative medicine. When a yellow fever epidemic struck Providence in 1797, Uncle Moses took careful notes and was the first to advance a theory of the disease's domestic origin (though its cause would remain unexplained until 1900). His report to the Town Council served as the basis for a major sanitation program. He introduced smallpox vaccination to Providence and provided cowpox matter without charge throughout New England, dispatching the vaccine in small wooden tubes or sealed between two pieces of glass.

Uncle Moses also continued to invest his time and treasure in civic projects–a theodolite from London for surveying roads, funds for re-paving the streets, even a "mud machine" to dredge the Great Salt Cove. He considered himself an elder statesman, never hesitating to advise Quaker Friends or to reconcile petty conflicts within the New England Yearly Meeting. He mentored many young men, including his nephew Nick. When twenty-one-year old Nick and his sister Hope set off for Philadelphia in May 1790, Uncle Moses wrote a long, affectionate note, advising his nephew to be "attentive to Collect and Treasure up in your minds the Truly Usefull parts [of the journey], which may come within your observation." Commending Nick to "Divine protection," he urged him to "avoid the Evils, the temptations and the snares that may attend" the trip. Reminiscing about his own travels to these cities at the same age, Uncle Moses noted that he had found his "mind Quietly strengthened in a wish of Integrity; that I might Improve so as to be usefull in my Day & generation" despite certain moments of temptation. Uncle Moses hoped that this trip "among strangers in larger cities than thou hast hitherto been acquainted with" would prove of lasting benefit to Nick. He signed the note "thy Thoughtful Unkle & Friend, Moses Brown."

Though Uncle Moses's social conscience could not fail to impress his nephew, it is hardly surprising that twenty-two-year old Nick was enthralled by his flamboyant uncle John. Like his brother Nicholas, John had gone through the post-Revolution decade uncertain about the fate of his Continental securities or his huge debt to Champion & Dickason in London. Yet his precarious finances had not prevented him from purchasing two lovely waterfront properties, *Spring Green* at Warwick, and the 221-acre *Poppasquash* at Point Pleasant, near Bristol. At the height of the Critical Period, he built a grand brick mansion on the hill above Towne Street, which was inaugurated in January 1788. En route to New York in 1789, Abigail Adams (then the Vice President's wife) recounted visiting the house: "Mr. Brown sent his carriage & his son James to conduct me to his House which is one of the grandest I have seen in this Country. Everything in and about it, wore the marks of magnificience & taste. . . . They had collected between twenty-two persons to dine with me though the notice was so short, & gave an elegant entertainment upon a service of plate." In keeping with John Brown's personality, the house was decorated with three oil paintings (no family portraits but two Charles Wilson Peale copies of George and Martha Washington), many English prints, and twenty-four "mirrors and looking glasses, including some large French ones in elaborate gilt and gesso frames."

"I owe an enormous sum of money in Europe," Uncle John admitted, "and am striving in every trade which appears lawful and right to me, to pay as much of that debt as possible"; he embarked on a series of *get-rich-quick* schemes. These included a plan to capture a piece of the cod market dominated by Massachusetts. He ordered fifteen twenty-five ton schooners to be built all at once, driving up the price of labor and materials all around Narragansett Bay. The fleet only made a modest return and ended up selling salt to the West Indies. "Trades that appear right to me" also included two attempts at slaving of 1786; neither was profitable. What he really needed was a spectacular new venture with no local competition.

Uncle John's hero was George Washington, but the businessman he admired most was the Revolution's financier, Robert Morris (the two had exchanged bitter words during the Revolution over the shoddy state of the ship John had sold the Continental Navy, but now all animosity seemed forgotten). During the Revolution, Morris, known as "The Colossus from Philadelphia," had introduced major financial reforms to the new nation, notably competitive bidding for government contracts, and personally had supplied the funds to move the Continental Army from New York to Virginia. In 1783, he had issued $1.4 million in personal notes to pay soldiers.

Uncle John therefore paid close attention in 1784 when Robert Morris sent his *Empress of China* to the Orient, the first American ship to trade with China. Fourteen months later, she returned, laden with tea and porcelain which brought an impressive 30 percent return. A New York newspaper noted that the voyage ushered in "a future happy period [when] burdensome trade with Europe could be replaced with profitable navigation to this new world in the East."

Starting in 1699, when Canton was opened to foreign commerce, the British East India Company had dominated the tea trade, followed by the French and Dutch merchants; Americans were kept out. But once independent, the United States could transact business as it pleased. Robert Morris's 1784 venture was seen as a "national effort" to challenge the British East India Company in its own market: the capital came from Philadelphia and New York, the vessel from Baltimore, and supercargo Samuel Shaw was from Boston.

Uncle John knew that the Atlantic world was mad about tea. "There are few families in our country, however humble their situation, that would not be greatly inconvenienced by a deprivation of this exhilarating beverage," wrote the merchant Robert Waln about America. The Chinese were somewhat bemused at the West's appetite for their products; as Emperor Ch'ien Lung wrote to the British King George III:

> Our Empire produces all that we ourselves need. . . . But since our tea, rhubarb and silk seem to be necessary to the very existence of the barbarous Western peoples, we will, imitating the clemency of Heaven, Who tolerates all sorts of fools on this globe, condescend to allow a limited amount of trading through the port of Canton.

Regarding themselves as uniquely civilized - and all foreigners as barbarians and inferior- the Chinese imposed elaborate regulations on their trade. The port of Canton was created specifically to control commerce with "foreign devils." Foreign supercargoes were allowed to live above the factories of thirteen "Hong" merchants; crews and any foreign women remained aboard their ships in Whampoa, twelve miles below on the Pearl River. The Hong merchants provided interpreters, permits and surety for the ships, and accepted consignments so that the foreign traders could return home in good time—all for a stiff price. The most successful among them, Houqua, was worth over $26 million at his death in 1843, and even invested in American factories and railroads.

In the three years after 1784, the six American ships that sailed for the Orient were true pioneers. No one really knew what mix of cargo the Chinese would want. The Americans initially carried lead, ginseng, camlets (waterproof woolens), and cotton they had stopped to buy in India. But the United States had few goods to barter; the Indians preferred wax candles to spermaceti, coconut oil to whale or fish oil, and disdained American flour, pork or beef. Fortunately, Captain James Cooke had noted on a 1776 voyage that the Chinese were partial to sea otter fur, native to America. Trinkets from Boston thus could be exchanged in the Pacific Northwest for pelts that would then be sold in China. In the end, however, American traders learned that only hard cash or bills of exchange could fill a cargo hold with Chinese tea. Other goods, such as coarse cotton cloth (nankeens), silk, spices, lacquerware, and porcelain, were placed at the bottom of the hold to protect the tea from moisture. Only a small portion of the purchase could be obtained for credit, and that on very hard terms. American supercargoes constantly complained that the Chinese were "crafty and duplicitous."

Uncle John began planning for a China venture of his own early in 1787. He selected his 385-ton, fast sailing *General Washington*, a 20-gun privateer built in 1779.[32] With the paper money restrictions in place, it was almost impossible to find the hard cash necessary to stock her. Stretching his credit to the limit, he assembled a cargo of spirits, ginseng, codfish, ham, anchors, cordage, sailcloth, munitions, copper, rum, brandy, wine, cheese, and candles valued at £17,000 lawful money ($57,000). Uncle John tried unsuccessfully to get his brother Moses to invest in the venture, promising that he would "not to be any More Concerned in the Ginney Trade." Nicholas, however, took a 1/8th share.

On December 27, 1787, at nine o'clock in the evening, *General Washington* weighed anchor at Newport, fired a three-gun salute to John Brown, and headed for the "heither Indies." During her 18-month trip, she traded wine in Madeira, cotton in Pondicherry and returned to Providence not only with 490 whole chests and 66 half chests of tea, but also Chinese goods, fine white sugar, calicoes, muslin, cambric, and chintz from India, all valued at nearly £30,000 ($100,000). This was a far smaller cargo than the $170,000 Uncle John had expected to receive, but he made a profit of $20,000 and considered the experience worth repeating. In December 1789, Brown & Benson and Welcome Arnold joined him in sending *General Washington* straight to India, while another ship went to Madeira with wine. Although the last of fifty-two ships to arrive in Canton that season, *General Washington* was one with Indian cotton to sell. Uncle John's anticipation was palpable through the entire two years it took for his ship to return. This time the voyage was a great

---

[32] Which had brought the clock and bell for the First Baptist Church from London in 1784.

success as the cargo sold for $200,000. Within six months he dispatched the ship again, entirely on his own account.

With sixty wharves now jamming the Great Salt River (now the Providence River), Uncle John's operations needed more space. He moved to the land occupied by the family's idle spermaceti candleworks in Tockwotton where he already owned a wharf and two warehouses. From 1787, he began developing paved roads and gangways, a dock, and a state-of-the-art fireproof warehouse, as well as a number of small manufactories (small, unmechanized factories)—in the hope of attracting artisans and home builders to the tip of Fox Point, the southern end of the Providence Peninsula, which he named "India Point."

Thinking big was paying off. Now Uncle John needed an assured supply of goods to trade with the Orient. Gin, until then only imported from Holland, was increasingly replacing rum in popular taste and finding a ready market abroad. But Uncle John knew that to be successful, he would need to build a distillery that yielded 25 percent more than Dutch distilleries, while maintaining equivalent strength and purity. He built his distillery at India Point; by January 1791 it was working at full capacity, powered by both wind and water. He advertised to farmers that it was their patriotic duty to supply their grain and drink American gin (but grumbled that the distillery's 14 percent return was too low).

In his 1840 *Reminiscences of the Last Sixty Five Years,* Ebenezer S. Thomas wrote:

> Providence carried on a great trade with the East Indies. At the head of this business for a number of years, stood John Brown, who had long been among the most successful and enterprising merchants in the United States. To him, Providence was much more indebted than to any other individual. His improvements in the town, and at India Point, were many and great; the latter establishment, which was very extensive, was his sole property. There were no bounds to his enterprise and his charities were extensive.

Uncle John's success was inspiring. After six voyages to China, he was no longer in debt and had invested in three more ships including the 950-ton copper ship *President Washington*, one of the largest ships in America at the time (the one he showed George Washington on his visit to Providence). There had been great excitement when a wagon carrying $600,000 in hard currency (the price of the *President)* was unloaded at the Providence Bank.

Indeed, Uncle John's Providence Bank was the clearest example of how he wrapped his self-interest with public benefit. He had first floated the idea of a bank in Providence in 1784, but the concept had been premature in the midst of the Critical Period and the paper money crisis. He was full of admiration for the "Bank of North America" that Robert Morris proposed to create soon after the victory at Yorktown in 1781. Alexander Hamilton also promoted a national, for-profit, private monopoly bank modeled on the Bank of England: "the happiest engines that ever were invented for advancing trade." Within three years of its launch, that Bank was considered creditworthy. Soon, The Bank of New York and the Bank of Massachusetts appeared in 1784, and the Bank of Baltimore in 1785. Up north in Providence, John Brown despaired that "Punctuality in business engagements was observed nowhere outside Philadelphia." He wrote of his:

> . . . anxious desire to promote the commercial, mechanical & manufacturing Interest of this town by the Establishment of a Bank which experience has Taught (where this Establishment has taken place) promote Industry & a Rigid Punctuality in the Performance of Contracts–We hope the good Citizens of this Town will be impress'd with the Utility of such an Institution. . . .

Hamilton had "used the rich for a purpose that was greater than their riches," and John Brown was happy to follow. So, when Congress chartered the First Bank of the United States for a twenty-year term in 1791, Uncle John decided to revive the concept of a bank in Rhode Island.

Uncle John urgently needed access to credit in order to assemble cash and bills of exchange to trade with the Orient. He also saw an opportunity to reconcile with Uncle Moses after his fierce public attacks in print just a year earlier. Moses had begun mending fences by purchasing West Indian cotton from John for his new spinning frame. Now John could offer his brother a project with sufficient social value and an intellectual challenge to boot. He wrote to Moses:

> I fulley Join You that this Town must of Course be Insignificant [,] and I may ad Mizarable inpoint of Welth, when Compaird with the Four Towns in the Union who now have Banks Established... but by our Exurtions [and by] Forming a Good & Substantial Foundation for the Commercial Manfactoral & Macanical, Riseing Generation it may in time become no inconsiderable Cappettell but without a pring to promote Our Young Men in Buissiness, hear they must & will Continue to go to such places as will Aid them with the Means of Buissiness & in short all our Welth . . . Must be transferred to those other States. . . .

John guessed right; Moses agreed to assist his brother and set to work analyzing the First Bank's charter, as well as those of other American and British banks. He recommended that small stockholders and out-of-state subscribers be encouraged to invest.

The Providence Bank was launched on October 3rd, 1791 with a heavily oversubscribed capital of $250,000 held by 138 investors.[33] Uncle John pushed Moses to invest "a Considerable part of our Worthy Deceased Brother's estate" in the venture. Nick used his inheritance to purchase stock worth $38,000. Welcome Arnold was the first chairman; Uncle John was named president; Nick and Uncle Moses sat on the board

---

[33] Small shareholders held an unusually strong voice in management; the average holding was only $4,000; only six had more than ten shares.

(directors received no compensation unless net profits exceeded 6 percent).[34] The Browns were united once again.

Early banking in America was a very personal business, based on close ties between bank directors and customers. The loan policy remained conservative: individual loans were limited to $20,000, about 5 percent of the bank's capital funds. In the early years, Uncle Moses often lent money to John, Nick, and the Arnolds to pay off their short-term notes, and even to the bank itself when withdrawals threatened the level of cash reserves. After just six months of operation, the bank paid its first dividend and continued to distribute 6 percent to 10 percent annually well into the twentieth century. As John had hoped, the bank also would prove extremely useful to the Brown family, especially to Nick.

Next, Uncle John lobbied in Philadelphia for the First Bank of the United States to open a branch in Rhode Island. He filled the *Providence Gazette* with editorials extolling the "Great man's blessing on Providence Bank." Instead, Alexander Hamilton sent William Channing, the US customs officer at Newport, to investigate "some Melishus information" that Providence Bank officers were mishandling public money. Uncle John demanded to read Hamilton's instructions; Channing refused. Tempers flared. Finally, John called on Moses, knowing that everyone trusted his impartiality and honesty. Hamilton later acknowledged that he had been incorrect about the "deranged state of the bank," but no branch of the First Bank of the United States was ever opened in Rhode Island.

In 1795, a second bank was founded in Newport. By 1812, the state had fifteen banks—one for every 3,357 inhabitants. Indeed, the first bank failure in America took place in Rhode Island when the Farmers Exchange Bank declare bankruptcy in 1809 to the tune of $800,000 in unsecured loans. Hundreds of families were affected. As a result, the Rhode Island Legislature made bank directors personally responsible

---

[34] Uncle Moses assured Philadelphia Quakers that ethical considerations had prompted him reluctantly to accept a place on the board so he could ascertain that bank funds were not used to finance slave trading activities.

for all debts if liabilities exceeded assets, a limitation soon circumvented by founding even more banks, rather than increasing assets. The social mission of banks did not last for long; by 1810 it was obvious that banks were no longer trustees for the community's business interests and had become primarily a source of gain for their stockholders. (Thus the General Assembly started taxing banks). While many banks succumbed to the lure of speculation, the owners of the Providence Bank continued down the path of conservatism and self-reliance, conscious of their fiduciary responsibility to the community.[35]

Uncle John also played a major role in launching Rhode Island's first insurance company. Since the mid-eighteenth century, Narragansett Bay merchants had been insuring each other's voyages through informal syndicates, a good way to raise supplemental income although maritime insurance was too risky to produce substantial revenues. Obadiah Brown had provided insurance to fellow merchants, charging premiums of 3 percent to 8 percent in peacetime, 10 percent to 30 percent in times of war.

Once again, Uncle John was inspired by Philadelphia where the Insurance Company of North American (1792) and the Insurance Company of the State of Pennsylvania (1794) had been launched. John formed the Providence Insurance Company in 1799 with a capital of $150,000. It was enthusiastically endorsed by the General Assembly which sought to "give encouragement to every institution which promises to advance the interest of commerce." Though 142 individuals subscribed to the stock, the bulk of the holdings was in the hands of the same group that controlled the Providence Bank: the Browns, Lippitts, Butlers, Ives, Halseys, Clarkes, Allens, and Masons. The policies of the two institutions were harmonized. Thus insurance companies earned profits both as underwriters and as lenders of mercantile capital to fund maritime ventures. The Providence Insurance Company's by-laws stipulated "that

---

[35] Of its 140 stockholders, most held only one to five shares (Nick and Tom Ives had sixty-five each), in contrast to the typical bank which had only four stockholders who received dividends in the form of speculative stock notes.

no insurance is to be made on behalf of this company upon any vessel, or property laden therein, for the purposes of carrying on the Slave Trade."[36]

Much to Uncle John's chagrin, it proved impossible to inculcate any enthusiasm for business in his son James. After five years of harangues and rebukes, Uncle John finally gave up on his efforts to persuade James to show more enthusiasm for business after graduation. Feeling the need for a younger partner, he invited John Francis, the amiable and erudite twenty-three-year old son of the Brown family's former Philadelphia correspondent to join him—Brown & Francis was launched in February 1786. It did not take long for the handsome John Francis to catch the eye of Uncle John's eldest daughter Abby. Their courtship lasted over two years; Uncle John was not about to let his eldest daughter go without a struggle. Several parties surrounding their wedding (which took place in the family home on Towne Street) were held in Uncle John's unfinished brick mansion in January 1788—unquestionably the highlights of Providence social life that year.

Cousin James and John Francis got along extremely well and shared an interest in architecture and design which was put to good use as they collaborated in the building and furnishing of Uncle John's lavish new house. But given Uncle John's personality, it was hardly surprising that he would have a stormy relationship with the cosmopolitan John Francis (who thought his father-in-law a "country bumpkin"; Uncle John accused his son-in-law of being an incompetent gold digger). The tension was only exacerbated by the one truly disastrous commercial venture of Uncle John's career.

John Francis suffered "constant and severe" stomach pains which he quelled with alcohol and morphine. His judgment may have been impaired on a fateful New York day in July 1795 when he accepted notes secured by 210,000 acres of wilderness in the Adirondacks as payment for $157,000 worth of Chinese tea. At the time, Uncle John had seemed pleased to invest in the land: "my securing the 210,000 Acres Land will be

---

[36] The Rhode Island General Assembly soon would adopt the same restriction for all future insurance companies.

fixing a certain and handsome fortune to . . . dear John B. Francis [his lit-tle grandson] who is a fine fellar. . . ." It took two years to secure the tract; then John plunged headlong into this grandiose new project, plowing his China trade profits into surveying townships, building roads, bridges, mills, houses and stores, and planting orchards - oblivious to the sterility of the land and its distance from transport routes. When John Francis died prematurely in 1796, Uncle John took over the management himself.

In 1799, he visited the property and gave its eight townships the names Industry, Enterprise, Perseverance, Unanimity, Frugality, Sobriety, Economy, and Regulation. But as the foolishness of this investment be-came increasingly apparent, Uncle John blamed his dead son-in-law for the consequences of his own stubborn and reckless behavior: "John Francis, my late partner, never put any property into the company's stock, and from his almost constant sickness and our bad fortune during the partnership, I do not think my estate was worth as much . . . as at its commencement."

The barren, rocky tract that was valued at $210,000 in Uncle John's will turned into a curse of epic scale for all his descendants; his son-in-law Charles Frederick Herreshoff even committed suicide in 1819, ex-hausted and ruined by the project. For once, Uncle John's fabled business acumen failed him. To this day, the Adirondacks remain a wilderness.

As Nick launched into adult life, flush with a vast inheritance, he therefore had two very different role models to emulate. But maritime commerce was in his blood. Clearly, Nick venerated his Uncle Moses and it was unquestionably from Moses that he inherited his moral com-pass and lack of ostentation. Though Nick must have been impressed by Moses's desire to solve social ills by providing factory jobs,[37] he was well aware that his uncle's industrial venture was not profitable (and in the 1790s seemed far from ever becoming so). Nick lacked the scientific bent of his Uncles Joseph and Moses, so felt little attraction to industrial technology for its own sake. He perpetuated his father's attitude that

---

[37] Uncle Moses was in fact a precursor—albeit in a naïve and primitive way—to the modern concept of social enterprise, a "do good-do well" form of business.

manufacturing was the servant of commerce, not an end in itself. Thus, it was Uncle John's boldness as a merchant that spoke loudest to Nick. Fortunately, he had inherited from his more prudent father the ability to temper grand schemes with a sense of self-preservation. The choice of maritime commerce would prove extremely lucrative for several decades even if, with hindsight, Uncle Moses's bet on industrialization was ultimately the winner.

CHAPTER 6

BROWN & IVES

*"[T]hey had the ability to undertake distant
enterprizes of Magnitude with their own means."*
*—The Providence Bank, writing to the British
Admiralty Court for the return of the John Jay*

Beyond the inestimable advantage of inherited wealth, the key to Nick's commercial success was his forty-year partnership and absolutely trustful relationship with the remarkable Thomas Ives. Despite vastly different upbringings, the two young men had deeply compatible personalities and complimented each other admirably. Tom handled the business correspondence, accounting records and investments. Nick—dealing with the vessels, their maintenance and insurance—often traveled for the firm or could be found at the wharf checking on the ships, their crews, and cargos. Thanks to Nick and Tom's aptitude at managing risk, they would pass enough money down the generations to fund philanthropic endeavors to this day.

The bond between the two young men was reinforced when Nick's teen-aged sister Hope announced that she had fallen in love with Tom Ives. But Nicholas was dismayed that his beloved only daughter had fallen for the penniless young man. Much as he valued his apprentice, family lore claims Nicholas told Hope, "You must marry a gentleman, . . . a man of money, wit and manners." Unruffled, she is reported to have replied, "Mr. Ives has wit and manners and I have money. Is that not sufficient?" Nicholas did not agree and sent Tom to his Baltimore correspondents Sears & Co., hoping that distance would cool the two young people's ardor; but soon he died. According to the terms of Nicholas's will, his two children could not receive their inheritances until Hope turned twenty-one or married, whichever came first. By the end of 1791, her father properly mourned, she had an excellent reason to plead with her brother Nick and George Benson for Tom's return to Providence.

Nick, meanwhile, also set his sights on matrimony. For the past four years, he had courted Ann Carter, eldest child of the town's main printer and the publisher of the *Providence Gazette*. Born in Philadelphia in 1745, John Carter had apprenticed to Benjamin Franklin before arriving in Providence in 1767 to work with the printer William Goddard; the following year, he took over Goddard's business. By 1772, his sign *Shakespeare's Head* was hanging outside a large three-story house on Meeting Street, across from the Friend's Meeting House. On the ground floor were the print shop, the post office (Carter became Providence's first postmaster in 1790), and the bookstore; the family lived on the two floors above. When Carter's brother-in-law, John Updike rented his house next door to a rival printer, the townspeople were treated to regular sparring matches of wit and intellect. John Carter and his wife Amey Crawford had thirteen children, nine of whom reached adulthood. A strong supporter of abolitionist causes, the Carter family would offer their home as an early waystation on the Underground Railroad. A year younger than her betrothed, Ann was therefore raised in an intellectual environment. Her father was one of Providence's leading citizens, with great power to influence public opinion. Though an Episcopalian, John Carter had been part of Nicholas Brown's inner circle–the two shared similar political views and regularly asked favors of each other. Over the years, John Carter had placed the Brown family's editorials and advertisements in the *Providence Gazette;* meanwhile, Nicholas had paid more than $200 in medical bills to Dr. Bowen for attending Ann in the period from 1787 to 1789, while Nick was courting her. Nick married Ann on November

3rd, 1791. He was overjoyed. In a hasty note to his new brother-in-law Benjamin Carter, he exulted:

> Now I shall place myself on the most Intimate footing with you, being perfectly happy by the acquisition of your fair sister's hand. . . . I have taken my abode in your family and feel an entire satisfaction from the friendship of my Ann. Happy mortal, am I not, to be surrounded with such earthly favours. My expectations are more than realized. An unexpected satisfaction results from my connection–health prevails–happiness awaits me.

Hope's path to the altar was somewhat arduous. Once Tom Ives came home, the romance became quite public, so "the people began to talk. While the old folks liked Mr. Ives, they did not desire their daughter to marry so poor a man." The good citizens of Providence felt quite proprietarily about the daughter of their leading citizen. Hope countered the rumors with a campaign to win their approval: she paid to have the interior of the First Baptist Meeting House painted and for a large crystal chandelier to be specially ordered from Waterford in Ireland. When the oceangoing ship arrived at New York, Nick arranged for the coastal sloop *Peggy* to pick up the chandelier in the harbor and rush it to Providence (where it still hangs in the First Baptist Meeting House). The First Baptist Society voted a formal resolution of thanks, noting that the "most affectionate Condolence of this Society be communicated to her upon the death of her worthy Father." Shortly thereafter, a strategically placed editorial appeared in the February 7th, 1792, *Providence Gazette*:

> Blush churlish reas'ners who pretend
> that sordid self commands each breast,
> for DELIA [Hope] views a nobler end. . . .
> And were it not a crime to love,
> soon would the gen'rous bosom burn
> Thrice happy swain, decreed to wear

The bridal charm with DELIA kind
Since every tongue would call her fair,
But fairer still that gen'rous mind.

It was obviously all part of Hope's campaign to win public approval of her betrothal to Tom Ives.

On the evening of March 6th, 1792, nineteen-year old Hope finally married her Tom in the front parlor of her stepmother Avis's new house. The *Providence Gazette* reported that "all 19 candles [of the Waterford chandelier] were lighted in honor of the new couple" and could be seen blazing through the windows of the First Baptist Meeting House just across the road.

Both sets of newlyweds appeared blissfully happy as they set about establishing new homes. Nick and Ann remodeled the family brick house on Towne Street. They ordered new housewares such as a "Sett of Derbyshire [porcelain] ornaments." Tom Ives and Hope placed orders with the Newport silversmith Joseph Anthony, Jr. for "1 Elegant Plated Tea Urn, 2 Mahogany knife cases, 1 Fish Knife, 1 pair of asparagus tongs, 1 Silver Soup Ladle." Craftsmen all down the eastern seaboard were kept busy as Avis and her two stepchildren all furnished their respective houses at the same time. Nick and Tom ordered new carriages from George Harrison of Philadelphia, and looked for matching horses from New Jersey. The carriages were delayed because one of the workmen was "getting drunk," and even "one thousand guineas" could not buy an "elegant pair." Nick must "be contented with plain sober family steeds."

Before the end of 1792, a baby arrived in each family: on October 2nd, a boy named Nicholas, born to Nick and Ann, and on December 18th, a girl named Charlotte Rhoda, born to Tom and Hope. To crown this happy family scene, Tom became a partner in the new Brown, Benson & Ives, now reinvigorated with the proceeds of Hamilton's assumption plan for state debt.

Hamilton's financial stabilization program worked wonders to dispel uncertainties and to provide the impetus needed for the New Republic's economy. In September 1791, an investor who had spent $160 in gold in February 1778 to buy a $1,000 Loan Office Certificate now could sell the bond for $513 of hard money, triple his investment. During the Revolution, army provisioning had fostered enterprises of a larger size and greater complexity than those of colonial days. Many Continental Army purchasing agents became major merchants in the postwar era. They understood the usefulness of commercial networks on a national scale. Now, thanks to Hamilton's assumption plan, they could use war debt and "soldier's pay certificates" to fund novel transportation projects, to experiment in new manufacturing processes, or to settle west of the Appalachians.

Then in April 1792, France declared war on Austria and Prussia, and Europe plunged into a twenty-three-year war. This turn of events, though ultimately a mixed blessing, suddenly offered the United States a golden opportunity to assert itself commercially. Its neutral ships could provide food to France at a time of bad harvests and revolution for, as Thomas Paine once remarked, "America will always have a market while eating is the custom of Europe." American farm income finally began to grow again and old inventories were worked off. Over the next seven years American shipping tonnage would increase by 267 percent.

Maritime commerce in times of war offered great opportunities but also great risk. When Britain entered into war with France in 1793, its powerful navy began imposing rigorous procedures on neutral shipping including American vessels. It declared American grain destined for France to be contraband. The French responded by authorizing the capture of any vessel carrying British goods and closed their ports to any ship that had stopped at a British port. By 1799, the situation had escalated to the point where Britain was blockading the coast of Holland; meanwhile Russia was in league with Denmark, Sweden, and Prussia to counter English interference in neutral shipping. Britain sent its navy into the Baltic to destroy the Danish fleet at the 1801 Battle of Copenhagen. Yet all the while, the United States continued to assert that "free ships make free goods."

American traders also faced a menace that respected no borders:

pirates. For the past 250 years, Barbary (from the tribal name "Berber") pirates had been raiding Mediterranean ports from their bases in North Africa, capturing more than a million European slaves on raids from as far as Iceland and South America. Although the European powers could have ended this practice by force, they all preferred to pay for protection while encouraging the pirates to attack their rivals. While colonial America was under the protection of the Royal Navy, British treaties with the North African states had guarded American ships. But once independent, the United States was forced to pay not only for protection from attack but also to ransom captured crews. In 1793, while France was caught up in its revolution and Portugal ceased guarding the Straits of Gibraltar, pirates came pouring into the Atlantic. By 1800, fully 20 percent of the U.S. government's total annual budget was being spent on ransoms and protection payments to the Barbary States.

Uncle John was incensed; acting "like Quakers" would not guarantee protection. A government's duty was to safeguard its industrious citizens with a strong Navy: "every Doller Laid out in it will make the Nation a Doller the Richer for it." He also saw an opportunity to revive the Hope Furnace. He sent a long letter to Rhode Island Representative Benjamin Bourne, detailing exactly the ships and guns required to build a navy whose $5 million price tag should be covered by a land tax that would cost each American only one dollar. If Congress did not take steps to protect trade against "Little Pickeroone Priveteers & Allgereens," then "Every Man of Spirit ought to Quit the Union and Leave Congress & the Friends to Abollish Slavery and Live without Trade." America also needed a navy of its own "lest France or England or any other of the armed powers should conclude it to be in their interest to capture all vessels under the American flag."

Many Rhode Islanders, including Governor Arthur Fenner, suspected that the merchants who offered to act as contractors for a new Navy simply sought to make a tidy sum. If Britain was so intractable, why not side with France? The Southern states and land speculators also opposed building a strong Navy since a real estate tax to fund the military could wipe out their profits. After much discussion, Congress voted to fund the construction of six frigates in 1794, not by taxing land but by charging an additional impost on merchants.

Uncle John's dire predictions came to pass. In 1793 and 1794, Britain confiscated over 250 neutral American merchant ships. American sailors were continually impressed into British service; meanwhile, British officials in Canada were supporting Native American tribes fighting American settlers in the Ohio Valley. Rhode Island's merchants advocated economic warfare through tariffs. At the eleventh hour, Britain ended the confiscation orders and both countries withdrew from the brink of war.

President Washington dispatched a peace delegation to Britain in 1794 under the leadership of Supreme Court Justice John Jay to normalize trade relations and resolve the many issues still pending from the 1783 Treaty of Paris that had ended the American War of Independence. But Britain was not in a conciliatory mood; Jay had to accept the best package available. American ships were granted limited access to the West Indies in exchange for granting Britain "Most Favored Nation" trading status and supporting its anti-French maritime policies. However, Jay could not halt the impressment of American sailors. The American public was disappointed with the treaty's resolution of war debts, its claims for confiscated ships, Canadian border issues, and compensation for the slaves that British troops had "removed" during the Revolution. But George Washington had few other options: "Europe will always have wars, while Americans must cultivate the arts of peace."

In Rhode Island, most merchants saw the Jay Treaty as an opportunity. In February 1796, the merchant-controlled General Assembly voted to support it. They were vindicated; Rhode Island's exports increased by 30 percent, leading one observer to exclaim "there is more prosperity afloat belonging to the inhabitants than the whole personal property of the town is worth."

Before Nick and Tom could embark seriously upon seizing their share of this bonanza, however, there was the maddening liability of the Brown family's English debt to be resolved. Thomas Dickason & Co., the successor firm to Champion & Dickason, was becoming increasingly insistent about repayments and even sent Thomas Dickason, Jr. to America. It would take him four years to collect debts from his clients in Providence, New Hampshire, and Philadelphia.

Although Nicholas had died in May 1791 without knowing with certainty the outcome of his investments in government securities, by November that year Uncle Moses was able to write Thomas Dickason & Co.:

> The Loss of my Eldist Brother I expect you have [been] made acquainted with, it only remains for me to inform you in respect to Browns & Bensons Affairs, I have no doubt they are good but my Brother's Estate by the Rise of publick Stocks Amts to more than any of us Expected he havg at his Decease upwards of 200,000 Dollars in the Various Publick Securities.

In his capacity as executor of Nicholas's will, Uncle Moses endorsed $30,000 of Continental securities to the English firm. Brown, Benson & Ives sent another $3,000 in cash to Thomas Dickason, Jr. in Boston with a note stressing how difficult it was to obtain hard currency. Even at year's end 1791, the firm was still struggling:

> We have not yet recovered from the embarrassed & detrimental state into which the Paper Money system plunged us [and] We have large sums due to us & a large amount of our old importations on hand but we hope that we are gradually Emerging from the various and multiplied Difficulties which Continually baffled our wishes & endeavours to reduce our Debt.

Over the next three years, Brown, Benson & Ives juggled further reimbursements to Thomas Dickason & Co. with the spending required to expand their business. Finally, on November 14th, 1794, Thomas Dickason & Co. wrote that the account was closed. The repayment process had taken ten painful years but a relationship of trust had been forged.

Contrary to many American establishments, Brown, Benson & Ives reimbursed their debt to the penny and the British firm was patient to the extreme. This meant that Thomas Dickason & Co. could play an instrumental role as the clearinghouse for all of Nick's and Tom's future maritime ventures. However, Nick had learned his lesson; he never again would fund an investment with debt.

As per his original agreement with Nicholas Brown, George Benson was still very much in charge of Brown, Benson & Ives. According to the terms of the previous Brown & Benson partnership, Nick was required to remain under the tutelage of George Benson for another three years. Benson insisted that the firm undertake several freighting voyages which produced disappointing results: in 1793, *Three Friends* was wrecked in a storm (a portent of things to come), and *Rising Sun*, captured by a British privateer while sailing from Baltimore to Bordeaux, returned to Providence in ballast. The following year, *Harmony* was captured twice, first in Santo Domingo-after which her cargo of salt was destroyed by a hurricane–and then by Barbary pirates on her way from Charleston to Bilbao, Spain. After two round-trip freighting journeys to Le Havre, France, her captain vanished with a cargo worth over £10,000, and *Harmony* was sold without authorization. Only *Hope,* carrying freight and sugar from Surinam to Amsterdam, then returning via Lisbon, netted a $10,000 profit. By 1795, European markets were glutted with American exports and Brown, Benson & Ives finally ended their unsuccessful attempt at freighting.

The partners' bad luck continued with speculation in rice and flour. The proposition seemed tempting since war-torn Europe was desperate for foodstuffs. But transporting commodities across the seas was extremely hazardous. Brown, Benson & Ives's first voyage in February 1795 was a success. Dispatched to Bilbao, Spain, the cargo ended up in Bordeaux where money, brandy and cloth could be smuggled out of France, netting a profit of $7,400. But that June, *Rambler* was captured by the British and joined the 150 American vessels detained in Portsmouth Harbor. Shortly thereafter, while sailing to Bordeaux, *Charlotte* was captured and taken to Britain. In both cases, Thomas Dickason (who maintained his relationship with Brown, Benson & Ives despite tensions between Britain and the USA) was able to negotiate compensation, but neither venture returned a profit. Later, while carrying a valuable cargo from Copenhagen to Providence, *Hope* was wrecked off the Orkney Islands; patched up, she limped home in late 1796. *Friendship* was making its way to Hamburg in dire need of repair when she disintegrated at sea and all the cargo was lost. So, of the five voyages to the Continent, only one was profitable; two ships were seized, one wrecked, and one vanished. In fact, far from supplying the French, Brown, Benson & Ives were provisioning the British.

Yet George Benson insisted that the partners persevere and proceeded to plan four voyages in 1796. Competition from cheap Indian rice was intensifying in Europe, while France was growing poorer. Neither *Harriet* nor *Charlotte* could find buyers for their rice in Le Havre or Dunkirk, France, so they tried Copenhagen and St. Petersburg. Both times they obtained paltry returns and the voyages incurred substantial losses.

In Charleston, seamen were demanding outrageous wages of thirty dollars a month. *Elizabeth* sold her cargo in Europe with a $10,000 short-fall, but tried to recoup the loss by purchasing wine in Cadiz for delivery to the island of Guernsey. After endless storms left the ship tossing at sea for seventy days, *Elizabeth* was wrecked off the coast of Ireland. *Hiram*, finding no buyers for flour in Le Havre, France, finally sold the cargo in London at a $5,764 loss. Thus the rice and flour ventures were an absolute disaster, with losses totaling $45,000. Of course, Brown, Benson & Ives were not the only firm to suffer: one Charleston trader lost over $60,000 and another in New York lost $100,000.

The financial losses were, in themselves, less significant than the rift that was growing within the partnership. Nick and Tom complemented each other admirably; both had "clear and direct minds." Benson was the third wheel. The two young men felt increasingly constricted by Benson's reluctance to innovate.

Benson in turn resented having his authority questioned. At the distillery, relations with Welcome Arnold also were turning increasingly bitter, in great part due to an ongoing feud with Benson. An April 1794 letter to Arnold reveals his frustration:

On reflection–I have Concluded to waste a few moments in telling you some plain 'tho perhaps mortify-
ing Truths. You appear to imagine that a great degree
of muscular strength implys merit, but if so how much
more meritorious are Bears, Wolves, Tygers and many
of the Brute Creation. – If you aspire at the ignoble Pre-
eminence of a Bully or a Boxer you may enjoy the Vulgar
distinction as unenvied by me as are the other traits in
your Character. . . .

The letter goes on to admonish Arnold for his disparaging comments
regarding young Nick's piety—"Altho you ridicul'd my worthy Partner's
attention to Publick worship, I wish you was half as exemplary as that
Excellent young man is." Despite standing up for his partner, Benson
felt bullied. Arnold did not respond but rather wrote to Tom Ives that
Benson's position as an outsider was untenable:

A most Scurrilous Insolent & abusive letter from that
narrow Souled, Hypocritical partner of yours G. Benson,
whose Insolence for the Seven years past to those who
have dealt with him has been such as to render him not
worth any mans notice, nor would he have been spoken
to by me the other day had he kept his monkey face a
proper distance off, and come forward when he had been
called by Mr. Brown who was there, as other puppies
do when they are called by their master —Should he
run under my feet again, if I should happen to see him,
perhaps I may Give him a kick as we do other Curs that
dont move when they are spoken to.

The time had come for Nick and Tom to take stock and re-evaluate their
approach. Technically, they were free by 1794 to disband the partnership.
But Benson fell ill, then spent several months in Newport caring for his
brother. Finally, Nick made it clear that Benson's services were no longer

required. Benson stalled. The partners still had a ship in the Orient; he needed to know the voyage's outcome as it represented a substantial investment. He also disagreed on how to divide partnership shares in the new Providence Bank. Tempers flared. In a December 1795 letter Nick noted dryly,

> It appears to Crowd Upon Us & has caused real regret, that we should be addressed in so peremptory a Manner. We wish you had call'd to mind, that you was addressing, the Children of Your best friend, that ever liv'd or ever will appear in your behalf — We hope his memory is not forgotten by You & that it may again occur to you the signal favours rec'd from him.

Negotiations between the partners continued throughout most of 1796. Benson claimed that he was being unfairly compensated due to the partnership's misfortunes:

> I again repeat that I sincerely regret your losses but consider your resources & your Means not only of repairing them, but of a large acquisition of property. . . . I wish you to consider not only what I am to receive but the Magnitude of what I have relinquished.

After months of recriminations, the partnership finally was dissolved at year's end 1796 and the firm became Brown & Ives.[38]

---

[38] George Benson used his partnership profits to build himself a fine house at the crest of Angell Street where he raised nine children. Tensions persisted with Nick's family. In 1799, he was accused by the Charitable Baptist Society of writing a letter "vilifying Mrs [Avis] Brown in the most odious terms, exciting uneasiness in the Family." When interviewed, Benson responded with contempt and "refused to have anything more to do with them. Thereupon he was excluded as a disorderly walker." He nevertheless remained in Providence until 1824 when he bought a 64,000 acre farm in Brooklyn, Connecticut. There, he remained involved with abolitionist causes, including the Underground Railroad and the New England Anti-Slavery Society (and so stayed in touch with Uncle Moses). In 1834, his daughter Helen married the abolitionist leader, William Lloyd Garrison.

In the mid-1790s, Providence docks were humming. On a 1795-99 American tour that took him to Rhode Island, the exiled French Duke de la Rochefoucauld-Liancourt commented that "the trade of Providence employs 142 vessels belonging to the port, and very little of it is shared with foreign ships, even by those of other states." Rhode Island's customs revenues increased six-fold between 1792 and 1806. In addition to manufactured goods, liquor, cheese, salt, and coal were imported from England, France and Holland. From Southern Europe came currants, corks, baskets, and merino sheep. Northern European ports such as Copenhagen, Gothenburg and St. Petersburg supplied Danish hemp, Swedish naval stores, German iron and glass, and Russian duck cloth (canvas). In exchange, while some Rhode Island merchants continued to ship provisions and wooden staves as well as re-exported sugar and rum from the Caribbean, many found success trading the tobacco, rice, and indigo from Virginia and the Carolinas that Europeans craved.

The arrival or departure of the great China trade ships still brought flocks of Providence's inhabitants to the quay-side. A January 1791 article in the *Providence Gazette* describes Uncle John's *President* as it departed for the Orient: "The Weather proved uncommonly fine and she moved majestically from the ships, amidst the plaudits of an immense concourse of Spectators among whom was a brilliant assemblage of the fair Daughters of America."

It was also a time of great adventure. Captain Robert Gray of Tiverton, Rhode Island, pioneered the Pacific fur trade in 1792 when he sailed *Columbia* into the "Great River" (renamed for his ship) and claimed the Pacific Northwest for the United States. The following year, Uncle John's *Hope* was the second American ship to reach Australia.

Before his death in 1791, Nicholas had agreed to participate modestly in his brother's China ventures, more out of brotherly duty than conviction. At the time, Brown & Benson were deeply involved in their rum distillery which absorbed a large amount of capital and heavily committed the firm to the Surinam molasses trade. Had Nicholas been younger and more adaptable, could he have warmed to the novelty of the China trade? Nick and Tom certainly pushed him in that direction, but George

Benson was reticent. However, a few months after Nicholas's death, the young men convinced George Benson to make a substantial investment in a voyage to China. *Rising Sun* departed for India in January 1792 with $36,000 in silver dollars (which had been a huge challenge to raise at a time when interest rates were averaging 2 percent to 3 percent a month).

Uncle John sent his own *George Washington* to China at almost at the same time. Nick and Tom guessed that she would have only enough cash to purchase tea and chinaware, so they decided to compete on nankeens and black satin. They planned to purchase cotton in India to barter for Chinese tea. This first venture was only moderately successful, returning $6,000 by the time all costs had been deducted, including a 6 percent "opportunity cost" on invested capital. However, valuable lessons were learned, principally that American merchants were playing a losing game exporting American goods to India in order to raise funds for China. Cash (principally Spanish silver dollars) and big, fast ships were the key to success since any delay rounding the Cape of Good Hope could lead to scurvy among the crew.

In September 1794, Brown, Benson & Ives took delivery of the 460-ton *John Jay*. The partners practically cleared out the cash reserves of the Providence Bank in preparation for its maiden voyage to the Orient—a December 1794 ledger entry states that no silver dollars should be paid out "until Messrs Brown, Benson & Ives's ship John Jay sails for India." *John Jay* cleared Providence for Bombay that month under the command of Captain Daniel Olney with a new style of cargo that included Russian goods and spirits valued at $34,500, as well as $46,000 Spanish dollars. The voyage to India was fraught with bad weather, steep cotton prices, high operating costs, and insufficient cash for a full cargo home. The Hong merchants gave only 20 months of credit, less time than it took to make a round trip, and charged a twenty percent discount on letters of credit. Despite all these challenges, the *John Jay* sailed into Providence after a two-year voyage with a cargo of tea that sold for $256,000. Rarely had two twenty-five-year olds seen such a return. Uncle John became so nervous at the competition from his nephews that he actually offered to drop out of the distilling business if they would abandon China. They refused.

Free at last to act as they pleased, Tom and Nick commissioned a new ship specifically for the China Trade. A recent losing voyage by the *Hamilton* had confirmed that they required vessels designed for the light airs of the Indian Ocean. Despite all their recent losses, the partners had enough cash (Nicholas's public securities alone had grown to $270,000) to spend $45,000 on a 536-ton vessel which they named after their two wives *Ann & Hope*. She soon earned a reputation as the fastest vessel in America. On her 1798 maiden voyage, the "elegant copper ship" carried a well-paid crew of fifty-seven including Ann's brother Benjamin Carter as surgeon, along with twelve nine-pound guns and a cargo worth $121,000, plus $80,000 in hard cash. Her master was the very experienced Benjamin Page who had taken Uncle John's *Hope* to Australia. Her supercargo Samuel Snow would stay on in Canton as U.S. consul to expedite purchases and obtain Chinese credit.

The eleven-month voyage returned 33 percent. Soon after, *John Jay* made a 78 percent profit on her 1799-1800 voyage. By 1807, the partners were reaping regular profits of 169 percent, sometimes carrying as much as $575,000 aboard in cash. In addition to *John Jay* and *Ann & Hope*, they added in 1804 to their fleet of sixteen ships *Isis* (318 tons) in 1801, *Arthur* (266 tons) in 1802, and *Asia* (340 tons), as well as shares in a variety of other vessels. Although Philadelphia led in ships and volume of trade with China, it was Brown & Ives that obtained the best credit terms from the Chinese.

Other lucrative opportunities beckoned in Indonesia, the Baltic, and South America. Since 1645, when the first coffee house had opened in Italy, the Atlantic world had become addicted to coffee. For a long time, Haiti produced two-thirds of the world's crop, but that trade ended in the slave uprising of 1792. Since the Dutch East India Company was successfully cultivating coffee on the island of Java in the Indonesian archipelago (producing over twelve million pounds annually), Americans could attempt to break into the lucrative "Batavia" trade (the Dutch name for Indonesia).

John Jay was the first Rhode Island ship to sail for Java in 1799 carrying $52,000 in cash and letters of credit. The risks were high: capture by British or French war ships, tropical disease, and Malayan pirates (President Adams even sent the *USS Essex* to Batavia to protect US shipping). Sometimes ships had to wait months for the new coffee crop or accept part of their cargo in sugar. From London, Thomas Dickason & Co. provided invaluable assistance in handling sales and marketing in European ports. As the Napoleonic wars raged on, coffee prices in Amsterdam kept rising: coffee bought at eight cents a pound in Java sold for thirty-five cents in Holland. It made sense to sail directly from Batavia to Amsterdam, then to load up in St. Petersburg or another Baltic port with the iron, hemp or sailcloth needed for shipbuilding back in the United States. After *John Jay*'s first trip to Amsterdam, *Charlotte* followed and made $111,000 on an investment of $60,000. Brown & Ives juggled bills of exchange on Thomas Dickason & Co. with letters of credit from Copenhagen. They deployed fleets of smaller craft to Southern European destinations such as Lisbon to trade fish, wine, brandy, and fruit for the funds needed in the Baltic.

The Napoleonic wars distracted European traders from not just the Far East but also from Spain and Portugal's colonies in South America. It did not take long for Americans to discover that New England codfish commanded $13.15 a quintal (about a hundred kilograms) in Rio compared with three dollars or four dollars in the United States. An ocean-going ship could be sold in Brazil for a 300 percent profit. All over South America, independence movements were seeking closer relations with the United States.

For several decades, Rhode Islanders had traded textiles and flour with South America as an adjunct to their Caribbean trade, bringing back sugar, coffee, cocoa, beef, hides, wool, horsehair, feathers, and copper to Providence[39]. Now, the larger firms could ply between Canton and

---

[39] In 1785, Nicholas Brown had even attempted to open trade with Brazil.

Batavia and the ports of Peru. In 1799, Providence merchants John Innes Clark and Joseph Nightingale pioneered trade with Argentina. Edward Carrington—who started as a supercargo for Brown & Ives, then became a consul in Canton from 1802 to 1811—used the Chilean and Peruvian trade to build himself the largest fleet in Providence.

In 1800, Brown & Ives loaded *Charlotte* with European goods for Rio de Janeiro and Buenos Aires. The trip netted $75,000 in Spanish dollars and $13,000 worth of gold ingots, ox hides and copper. But South America was not to prove a lucrative market for Nick and Tom. In 1800, their *Mary Ann* set out carrying false papers (including a Spanish passport bought from the Consul in Boston) and $80,000 of European goods. When she reached Rio de Janeiro three months late, the captain fell ill and local officials imprisoned the crew, then seized the cargo (now worth $300,000) which, after a dramatic series of twists and turns, was impounded in 1802 by the Spanish Viceroy. Finally released in 1803, the ship and her crew eventually sailed for London in late 1804 with a cargo of hides and tallow, only to be captured by a British cruiser, condemned as Spanish property, and sold at auction in Halifax, Nova Scotia. Brown & Ives claimed $843,264 in losses, including compound interest, but their case was heard in 1823—a full eighteen years later—only to be rejected as the voyage was considered illicit.

Overall, however, Brown & Ives flourished in the first years of the nineteenth century and the partnership's earlier debacles faded into distant memory. Although American merchants commanded fewer funds than the massive British East India Company, they excelled in seamanship, Yankee shrewdness, and the ability to cut costs to the bone. The partners depended not just on the advice of their captains and supercargoes, but also on trusted lieutenants such as Benjamin Tallman who built the *Ann & Hope* and Richard Jackson who insured their ships. In Canton, a succession of Providence men served as American consuls: Samuel Snow (1798-1802), Sullivan Dorr (1798-1803), and Edward Carrington (1802-1811) developed relationships with the powerful Hong merchants, Mouqua and Geoqua. In London, Thomas Dickason received remittances from Brown & Ives's correspondents all over Europe, honored their drafts, gave advice on market condition, and assisted in time of crisis with repairs, seizures and Admiralty Court proceedings. In Amsterdam, the Scotsman Daniel Crommelin made dollars available to Brown & Ives in Gibraltar and Lisbon, remitted funds to Dickason in London, and sold tea, coffee and sugar on the firm's behalf in Northern Europe.

Between 1795 and 1805, American trade with the East Indies was greater than that of all the European nations combined. At the same time, Americans imported manufactured goods from Europe and Britain, re-exporting most of them to the West Indies and South America. In 1807, American imports and exports reached $246 million, 92 percent of which was carried by American ships. The value of American foreign trade increased nearly six-fold between 1793 and 1807, while American tonnage tripled. As stated by the era's famed architect, Benjamin Latrobe, "America's business [was] to make money."

Trade with Europe, the Orient and South America brought a six fold increased in customs revenues to Providence between 1792 and 1806, peaking at $400,000 in 1804. Over $1.5 million worth of goods was re-exported. It was a risky business but as each venture formed a discreet enterprise, losses could be absorbed. Brown & Ives refused to take on debt. Beyond the cost of their ships, Nick and Tom had no other permanent capital outlays, and no permanent workforce to pay. A contemporary observer said of Brown & Ives that the firm was:

> . . . Possessed of a character, a credit and a name that commanded un-limited confidence and respect in every mart of commerce throughout the world . . ., pursued their undeviating way alike through disasters and successe, and, in accordance with an unfailing law of human affairs, they reaped an ample harvest of mercantile wealth.

Even Uncle John benefitted from his nephews' success; he sold them large quantities of gin from his distillery and rented them space on his wharves. But just as it had been with Nicholas, the nephews' relations with John Brown were not always smooth. When in 1800 Uncle John told Tom Ives he was increasing the rent on a brick storehouse to $400, Tom responded icily that "Yr high opinion of the condition and value of yr wharves & Stores with the Prices you have generally fixt for Rent . . . has bin the cause of that part of the loss being [experienced by] others as well as our House."

Great fortunes were being made in a similar fashion in other American ports. In Salem, Elias Hasket Derby, Joseph Peabody, and William Gray were particularly successful among the China Trade merchants. At his apogee in 1807, Gray was worth over $3 million; he reputedly owned 115 vessels, employed 300 seamen and, according to his 1825 obituary, was "probably . . . Engaged in a more extensive commercial enterprise than any man who has lived on this continent in any period of history." John Jacob Astor and Archibald Gracie made their mark in New York; Stephen Girard in Philadelphia accumulated the wealth that would later fund his remarkable bequests.

But no merchant's luck was inexhaustible. Operating at the extreme edge of their capabilities, Nick and Tom's ships regularly tempted fate. And when disaster struck, it hit hard.

On a return voyage from Batavia in December 1805, *Ann & Hope* suffered substantial damage in storms and put in at the Isle of France (now Mauritius in the Indian Ocean) for repairs. At the Cape of Good Hope, she was detained for thirty days by an embargo. Finally, she made landfall at Hampton Heights, Long Island, on the night of January 10th, much later than expected. A course was set to pass Block Island, Rhode Island, on its south side and head for Newport Light. Suddenly, at midnight, a horrific crash reverberated. The *Ann & Hope* had struck a reef. Her captain had misjudged the distance of the snowy shoreline. All hands worked to fend her off as she pounded against the rocks in heavy seas. Only three men were lost, but the graceful *Ann & Hope* broke up, scattering her $300,000 cargo into the sea.

Tom Ives was hosting a dinner when a messenger came to the door.

A servant whispered the devastating news to his ear. Tom blanched but said nothing to his guests. Then, only four days later, news arrived that *John Jay* had been captured by the British and was being held in Bermuda. She had been carrying contraband iron bars with false destination papers for Canton while, in fact, returning from Batavia. For six months, Brown & Ives negotiated with the High Court of the Admiralty in Bermuda and even sent former Governor Samuel Ward as their representative. Uncle Moses interceded in an eloquent letter to the authorities, thus describing Brown & Ives:

> [It is] one of the most Oppulent and Respectable Mercantile Houses in the State, [t]rading on their own Capital in such manner as to have Mannefested as much Integrity & Punctuality in Business as any which I have had an Opportunity of knowing. . . . [N]o Merchants of the Extensive Trade among us do their Business upon their own property [fund themselves] so generally as they do.

The entire capital stock of the Providence Bank was pledged if needed to obtain the ship's release. Uncle Moses gave his personal guarantee of $175,00. But nothing would sway the Court of Admiralty: Brown & Ives lost their case, forfeited the cargo, and had to post a $35,000 bond to retrieve their ship. Following *John Jay's* return to Providence that October, she was sent out again to Batavia and loaded with a cargo of coffee purchased for $131,000–the most expensive cargo Brown & Ives had ever bought. But on August 16th, 1807, she struck a reef and went down. Everything was lost. Had both cargoes returned safely, they could have been sold for half a million dollars. Nick wrote in anguish to his young brother-in-law, Crawford Carter: "You will have heard of the Immense loss in the *John Jay*. I have thought last Summer that you & Amos would go out in her, but she is gone!!!!"

These great calamities occurred just as the winds of war were blowing once again across the Atlantic. The 1802 Peace of Amiens, intended to end hostilities permanently between France and Britain, had lasted only a year. On May 17th, 1803, the Royal Navy captured all the French and Dutch merchant ships stationed in Britain, seizing more than £2 million in commodities. A trade war resumed; the May 1806 "Fox Blockade" closed eight hundred miles of coastline from Germany to France. Napoleon riposted with first the Berlin Decree that created a permanent blockade around the British Islands, then the 1807 Milan Decree that prohibited any European country from trading with Britain. In response, Britain banned neutral ships, including American vessels, from trading with ports from which it was excluded. As a result, 528 American ships were seized by the British and 206 taken by the French in the years between 1803 and 1807.

Once again, the Royal Navy became desperate for more sailors and regularly stopped American vessels to "impress" their crews into British service. Some of these men were indeed Englishmen fleeing the grim conditions of the Royal Navy for the promise of better pay aboard American merchant vessels; others were U.S. citizens. President Thomas Jefferson had successfully overcome the Barbary pirates,[40] but he could not stop French or British seizures of American merchantmen. In December 1805 alone, seventeen Rhode Island seamen were taken by the British. The state's leading merchants gathered in Providence to send Secretary of State James Madison a list of their captured, detained, condemned and plundered ships.

When in June 1807, the *Chesapeake* was fired upon by the *Leopard*, a British vessel searching for deserters, the American government was compelled to take strong action. Despite efforts to remain neutral, the United States could not extricate itself from the conflict. President Jefferson thus explained the young country's predicament:

> Our lot happens to have been cast in an age when two
> nations to whom circumstances have given a temporary

---

[40] President Jefferson refused to pay tribute to the Barbary States and sent the Navy's best ships to fight the pirates between 1802 and 1805–the first foreign military action authorized by Congress.

> superiority over others, the one by land, the other by sea
> [;] degrading themselves thus from the character of law-
> ful societies into lawless bands of robbers and pirates,
> they are abusing their brief ascendancy by desolating
> the world with blood and rapine.

In December 1807, Congress passed the Embargo Act, forbidding trade with Europe. For Brown & Ives–and indeed for all of America's merchants–it was a catastrophe.

Nick and Tom tried to compensate for lost revenue by engaging in the bustling Canadian goods trade up the Maine coast, but remained cautious about venturing into the Atlantic: "It would not be prudent at this moment to hazard much property abroad," they wrote to Daniel Crommelin in Amsterdam; "the hostility of all nations at war to neutral trade would render it very insecure." But they remained optimistic that the situation would improve and ordered two new ships to replace *Ann & Hope* and *John Jay*. The 558-ton *Ann & Hope II*, again commissioned from Benjamin Tallman, was ready in 1807 but lay idle for a year. The 291-ton *Robert Hale*, built by Benjamin Ives Gilman in Marietta, Ohio, was sent, via the falls of the Ohio River at Louisville, down the Mississippi to New Orleans, through the Gulf of Mexico, and eventually arrived in Providence in March 1809.

That same month, during the last sixteen days of Jefferson's presidency, Congress replaced the Embargo Act with the almost unenforceable "Non-Intercourse Act" that allowed American ships to visit all but French and British ports. *Robert Hale* was immediately sent to Europe. But France and Britain simply began seizing American ships all over again. On her second voyage, *Robert Hale* was captured first by the French, then by the English who confiscated the cargo worth $148,000. Brown & Ives hoped, nevertheless, that the combined 2,852 tons of their nine other ships (*Arthur, Asia, Isis, Charlotte, General Hamilton, Ann & Hope II, Robert Hale,* and *Patterson,* joined by *Hope* in 1809) would beat the odds. New records were broken in 1810 when *Ann & Hope II*, having outdistanced all other ships, returned to Providence from the Orient with a cargo worth over $228,000, which then was sold in Hamburg at a 300 percent profit.

When the War of 1812 broke out, the partners sent no further ships to Canton or Batavia but focused on the Baltic, managing to complete nine voyages. Three were extremely successful and returned profits of 100 to 300 percent. However, *Hope* was captured by the Danes on her way to St. Petersburg in 1810, *Asia* became stranded in Copenhagen, and *General Hamilton* in St. Petersburg, for "The Danes take all American ships bound to Sweedland. The Sweeds take all bound to Russia. The Russians stop all in their ports." Amazingly, Brown & Ives lost only one ship, *Isis,* sunk by the French. They also tried smuggling cargo overland from the German North Sea coast to Amsterdam, and sent twenty-five ships to Spain and Portugal during the Peninsula War (using special licenses sold by Britain to neutral ships in order to transport flour, rice, and rye). They even tried gun running along the Peruvian and Chilean coasts to supply the Latin American wars for independence.

Despite these setbacks, Brown & Ives prospered during the golden years of this first decade and half under Nick's and Tom's unfettered control. The partnership succeeded because the brothers-in-law had learned the harsh lessons of their apprentice years and understood the cardinal importance of managing risk. Undeniably, it helped that Nick started out with such massive financial underpinning, but of equal importance was his steadfast refusal to overstretch his resources or resort to borrowing.

Nick had inherited his father's innate sense of caution. Many years earlier, Uncle Moses had thus admonished his brother John: "Who Ever plays a Game the Rubbers, or plays the last for the Value of the whole gain of the Preceding many, will Sooner or Later Loose the Whole at one Throw." That prediction regularly came to pass in Providence. A cousin by marriage, Cyprian Sperry, once Providence's largest slave trader, was forced to petition for bankruptcy in 1798 following repeated losses at sea and saw his assets reduced to two feather beds. Robert Morris, once so admired, failed spectacularly when a Dutch loan—meant to finance the purchase of six million acres in the South—was stymied by Holland's declaring war on revolutionary France. In 1798, Morris, once America's greatest landowner, was arrested and imprisoned.

Though maritime commerce was the most uncertain of businesses, Nick had sufficient reserves and diversified activities to survive calamities such as the simultaneous loss of the *Ann & Hope* and the *John Jay*. His abhorrence of disorder gave him the unflappable discipline needed to deal methodically with pirates and embargoes, duplicitous Chinese traders and hurricanes. With Brown & Ives thriving, it was time to promote civic organizations that instilled decorum and order in a society that was fast becoming unrecognizable.

CHAPTER 7

THE END OF AN ERA

"The means of defense against foreign danger
historically have become the instruments
of tyranny at home." —James Madison

Like his father before him, Nick's spectacular early commercial success was tempered by a full measure of personal tragedy. In July 1794, his second son Moses died before reaching his first birthday. Then on June 16, 1798, just as the new *Ann & Hope* was preparing for her maiden voyage, his beloved wife Ann Carter Brown died, leaving behind three small children: Nicholas III was five, Little Ann was two, and John Carter (known to all as "JCB") was only ten months old. Fortunately, Nick was able to call on his wife's cousin, fifteen-year old Amey-Ann Stelle, who moved into the Brown household to help with the children (her mother, Huldah Crawford Stelle, and Nick's mother-in-law, Amey Crawford Carter, were sisters).

Amey-Ann's father Benjamin Stelle had run the "classical school" which Nick had attended before going to boarding school in Grafton. He also owned a small business selling chocolate out of the Unicorn & Mortar, an apothecary shop near the Baptist Meeting House, and served as clerk to the College trustees. Once, in 1793, Nick mediated a dispute between Stelle and his neighbors, the Metcalfs. Afterwards, Benjamin

Stelle wrote to Uncle Moses, "Your nephew, Mr. Nich's Brown, a Man who wishes Peace & Happiness to all Mankind, has, unsolicited, offered his best Services as a Mediator in the present case & proposed you to assist him, which will meet my most hearty wishes."

And Ann Carter Brown's best friend had been Stelle's eldest daughter Mary.

So when, after a period of mourning, Nick sought a new mother for his children and a hostess for his home, he did not need to look far. Mary Stelle was exactly his age; he had known her all his life. But the Stelles were not merchant princes like the Browns. Remembering all too well the public criticism when his father had married Avis Binney after Rhoda Brown's death, and when Hope married Tom Ives, Nick decided to marry quietly outside Providence on July 22nd, 1801. Cousin Abby Brown Francis, Uncle John's daughter, described the event to her sister Sally:

> Cousin Hope Return'd the next Morn'g [from the Ives farm at Potowomut]. It appears that her Brother [Nick] had determined on taking a journey for his health & Aunt B [Avis] with the aid of Doc'r W. Bowen have been the fortunate Agents in the Business. Old Mr. C [Carter–Nick's father-in-law from his first marriage] was the only of his family who had been made acquainted with it yesterday—when, I suppose, Mrs. Carter wisely thought it was too late for her any longer to oppose the wishes of Nich's best friend [Mary Stelle] & without the least Noise or Ceremony he simply set off with Miss Stelle in a Chaise, her Father, Mr. & Mrs. Ives [Tom and Hope], rode 8 miles when Mr. G [Stephen Gano, Pastor of the First Baptist Church and widower of Uncle Joseph's daughter Mary] met them & the ceremony was performed. Hope hasten'd back in order to entertain her dinner Company & the new couple were to proceed as far as Fishers Tavern & Hope is to return very tranquil and satisfied to the Farm.

Sally responded that she was extremely glad of the news: "it will make a change in both I hope for the better. . . I shall write Hope by this mail to wish her all happiness in her new sister-in-law."

The newlyweds honeymooned in Saratoga Springs for almost two months while the house on South Main Street was repainted and re-papered in preparation for a grand reception. Upon their return, the Providence "season" was at its peak; "We had a very gay commencement the Theatre was open every night through the week, & a number of tea parties among the Ladies," wrote Cousin Sally. The new marriage certainly suited Nick. Uncle John's ten-year old grandson John Brown Francis was able to report a few months later to his Aunt Sally, "Nicholas appears happy--& increases in corpulency." His Carter in-laws all came to meet the new Mrs. Brown—except for Rebecca and Mrs. Carter who "will keep aloof."

Like his father before him, Nick was engrossed in running a com-plex, risky business in difficult times. Although he lacked the advice and support of three brilliant brothers, at least Tom Ives provided a steadying hand and outstanding business acumen. Such rock-like dependability was of immeasurable importance to a man who, as he approached middle age, was beginning to show the signs of the dissatisfaction and disillusion which would become a marked feature of his later years.

Nick's frustrations stemmed not from his business dealings but from his inability to control his external environment. From the tumultuous experiences of his early years, Nick had developed a yearning for law and order. In the 1790s, his views coincided with the prevailing notion that the wealthy, educated elite were best suited to govern. As Alexander Hamilton declared, "The people are turbulent and changing . . . they seldom judge or determine right." He felt the American people needed a "common directing power" for private interests would not regulate themselves. Strong institutions, such as the Bank of the United States, would connect people though hierarchies of patronage and dependency.

Now that Rhode Island had ratified the Constitution, most citizens turned away from political affairs to focus primarily on the pursuit of wealth. Voter turnout fell to 9 percent. The population of Providence grew to 7,614 inhabitants, America's ninth largest town according to the 1800 census. The top 10 percent controlled almost 60 percent of the town's resources; just ten men, all merchants, held nearly a quarter of the wealth (Uncle John paid the most taxes). Merchants dominated the local economy even though new voices were increasingly to be heard. Among them, artisans (known as "mechanics"), shopkeepers, and tradesmen banded together in 1789 to form the "Providence Association of Mechanics & Manufacturers." Its mission was to promote "the mechanic trades . . . so that people of better fortunes may not deem it below their esteemed to be concerned with them." The Association pressed for trade restrictions on "the geegaws of foreigners" to allow fledgling American manufacturing initiatives to grow and flourish.

At first, Nick had few worries on the political front since Alexander Hamilton's Federalists were in power. The Federalist Party governed with the wholehearted support of the Brown family. Both believed that the Constitution gave the Federal Government "implied powers," and that Congress should promulgate all necessary and proper laws required to carry them out. They did not trust ordinary people to have good judgment; elected officials should govern in the people's name.

Uncle John was elected to Congress on a Federalist ticket in 1799. He served his first year in Philadelphia; then on December 1st, 1800, he set sail for the new capital at Washington. Landing at Baltimore, he made his way by stagecoach to the new capital. Washington was in fact nothing more than a handful of buildings in a boggy marsh drained by open sewers. The unfinished Capitol had no dome or marble cladding, and the White House was still being built. The entire government lived in boarding houses. Unlike the previous capital in Philadelphia, there was no social life: "Not a drink of cider to be had for love nor money, so you may judge whether I'd rather be at my own table or here," Congressman John wrote home.

Uncle John's time in federal government was fairly unremarkable, except for the emotional speech he pronounced on the House floor April 26, 1800 to contest a proposed bill banning the slave trade. His views on the subject had not abated one jot. Not only did slave trading provide vital business for New England distilleries, he said, but a ban would only benefit Britain since the United States could not prevent other nations from engaging in the trade. Furthermore, he claimed, slaves in America were better treated than Africans treated each other.

When he rose to address Congress for his first and only time, Uncle John knew perfectly well that he represented a minority view: the ban passed easily, Uncle John being one of only six Congressmen who opposed it. But he cared little for the reaction of his colleagues on the Hill. Rather, he was determined to use this national forum to demonstrate that an American should be free to undertake any endeavor he chose— whether a slaving voyage or a speech to Congress. His was Rhode Island's famous belligerent spirit taken to the extreme.

Uncle John did not remain in Washington for long. Federalist President John Adams neglected to consolidate his political bases or to control his own cabinet which shifted its allegiance to Alexander Hamilton. Following France's declaration of "quasi-war" in reaction to the 1794 Jay Treaty, Adams had raised an unpopular land tax. The public had been further angered by his "Alien and Sedition Acts" of 1798 which empowered him to deport "dangerous aliens" and to forbid criticism of the Federal Government. As the presidential election loomed, Adams's days were numbered.

Americans united one last time to mourn George Washington who died on December 14, 1799. All over the country, orations, prayers, sermons and mock funerals were held. Given the Federalists' precarious position, it was in their interest that the grieving last as long as possible. But on December 3rd, 1800, Thomas Jefferson and his Republican party swept into power on the 36th ballot of the House of Representatives.

Jefferson's arrival in the White House proved a turning point in American history. Before 1801, under the Washington and Adams administrations, people had recognized that the country needed a steadying hand and accepted a government that favored the rich, the able, and the wellborn. But Thomas Jefferson ushered in a new era of participatory politics by promoting free association and limited government. His Republican followers wanted Congressional power limited to an absolute minimum. They believed that democracy and liberty would only be safe if ordinary people played an active part in government. The new President was convinced of the virtue and natural sociability of the American people: "I am not among those who fear the people. They, and not the rich, are our dependence for continued freedom."

Rhode Island's Republican governor was the eminently pragmatic Arthur Fenner who knew "how to trim [his] sails to catch an approaching breeze" and made alliances across party lines. He thereby attempted to reconcile the interests of men whose livelihood depended on free trade (ships' carpenters, sail makers, coopers, cordwainers, as well as artisans such as barbers and tailors) with those of more modest means who did not depend directly on maritime commerce (house carpenters, saddlers, tanners, and stonemasons). Thomas Jefferson also showed that he understood Rhode Island's competing constituencies. He sent a memorandum to Governor Fenner stating:

> I am sensible of the great interest which your state justly feels in the prosperity of commerce. It is of vital interest also to the states more agricultural, whose products, without commerce, could not be exchanged. As the handmaid of agriculture, therefore, commerce will be cherished by me, both by principle and duty.

Jefferson hoped that the Federalists would disappear through attrition and so rewarded those who were willing to work with him, notably former President Adams's son John Quincy Adams.

Other prominent men jumped on the Republican band wagon to champion a specific agenda; especially the DeWolf family of Bristol, Rhode Island. Born in 1764, James DeWolf, the second of five brothers, had served on Uncle John's privateer *Providence*, then launched his own slaving ventures. Though indicted in 1791 by a Newport grand jury for ordering a sick woman thrown overboard, he was never convicted and went on to finance twenty-five more slave trading voyages. In the period between 1784 and 1807, James DeWolf and family undertook eighty-eight slaving voyages, nearly a quarter of all such of Rhode Island's illegal voyages. In order to smuggle slaves into the United States or to hold them off the market when prices were low, the DeWolfs acquired five sugar plantations in Cuba. They founded the Bank of Bristol, run by Charles DeWolf, and the Mount Hope Insurance Company, run by his brother William. The family built the *Mansion House* and *The Mount*: a white three-story home with five chimneys, a deer park, and a glass-enclosed cupola. By 1800, Bristol surpassed Newport as the busiest slave port in America.

When Nick was still young, he had his first unpleasant encounter with James DeWolf in 1795: the start of a lifetime of antagonism between the two men. Brown, Benson & Ives had been short of cash, so Uncle John had advised his nephews to approach the Bristol merchant. Nick and Tom composed a polite letter requesting a loan of five to ten thousand dollars, "if it is convenient for you to do it," for which they proposed to pay interest at six percent. Should he be unable to acquiesce, would James DeWolf kindly refer them to his friends? DeWolf replied the next day that he did not have the funds and that a six percent return was far too low. Then he added, his words dripping with irony:

> Besides, I should be fearful it would hurt the feeling for our Mr. Benson, as a person of his nice sensibility must conclude it smelt rank of inhumanity for it would be money arising from the sale of Negro slaves in the West Indies. . . . I do not know of any of my friends having any money to loan.

DeWolf was attacking both George Benson's strong abolitionist stance and Nick's role in the Providence Abolition Society.

There was one man determined to thwart the DeWolfs: Newport's customs collector William Ellery. This "straight-gazing patriot" regarded smuggling slaves as "nothing short of treason." Although many Newport vessels cleared for Africa in the period between 1798 and 1802, the number would have been much higher without the incorruptible Ellery. In

July 1799, hearing that the DeWolf's *Lucy* had recently returned from Africa, he arranged to have her seized by federal officials and sold at auction. This time, he was determined to prevent the usual outcome: a third-party slave trader managing to re-purchase the confiscated ship at a fraction of its value. The government's Port Surveyor Samuel Bosworth was sent to Bristol with instructions to outbid any competitors. The night before the auction, three of Rhode Island's wealthiest men appeared at Bosworth's home: Charles and James DeWolf were accompanied by Uncle John, who had just been elected to Congress. Though frightened by this "disagreeable business," Bosworth responded that he intended to proceed. On the morning of the auction, Charles DeWolf approached Bosworth once again, warning that if he tried to buy the *Lucy*, he would likely be "insulted if not thrown off the wharf by some of the sailors." Bosworth continued on his way. As he neared the ship, eight men in Indian garb grabbed him and bundled him into a skiff. With Bosworth out of the way, a DeWolf captain bought *Lucy* for $738.

In order to curry favor with the Republican administration, the DeWolf's switched allegiance and became ardent Republicans. From that point, they appeared invincible: Newport courts refused to prosecute them; zealous officials were assaulted. Only William Ellery stood in their way. So they petitioned Congress to place Bristol in a separate customs district. At first, the House "Committee on Commerce and Manufactures" was shocked by the reports it had received of recent events in Bristol. It fully intended to reject the town's petition. But Congressman John Brown lobbied hard on Bristol's behalf and, in the space of two days, managed to convince all six committee members to show support for "enterprising small ports." The bill passed and Charles Collins, former captain of the *Lucy* and James DeWolf's brother-in-law, was appointed Bristol's Customs Collector. As a direct consequence of Uncle John's intervention, Bristol would transport more slaves after 1808, when the Federal government finally banned the sale of slaves, than all other New England ports combined. Once again, it is easy to imagine Nick's embarrassment and chagrin.

Rhode Island Federalists lay low. They did not even protest the 1803

Louisiana Purchase, although Nick and Tom felt that $15 million was far too much money to pay for this vast, ungovernable wilderness. Even banking became politically motivated: the Providence Republican clique launched the Roger Williams Bank in 1803, followed in 1804 by the Farmers Exchange Bank in Glocester, both in a direct affront to the Federalist Browns' Providence Bank. It finally took the "bewildering shock" of the 1807 Embargo Act to wake Rhode Island's merchants from their complacency. Despite high risk, trade during the Napoleonic war years had been yielding huge profits and even the agrarian community was benefitting from the European demand for farm products. Now an embargo spelled disaster.

At first, the Rhode Island Federalists refrained from launching an anti-embargo campaign for fear of uniting the Republicans who, in turn, hid embargo violations from federal officials in hope of softening the law's economic impact on their supporters. But when a second Embargo Enforcement Act was decreed in early 1808, all of Rhode Island rose up in protest: the Federalists issued memorials; Republican Congressmen Elisha Potter of South Kingston and Richard Jackson of Providence called out "Rhode Island expects every man to do his duty"; even Governor James Fenner (who had succeeded his father in 1805) was praised for his anti-embargo stand.

The embargo lasted fifteen months and wrecked business, not only in New England but all across America. Economic stagnation set in and popular discontent grew; voters coalesced behind the Federalist standard. Republican James Madison won the presidential election of 1808, but without New England's vote. Nonetheless, he ended the embargo and opened trade again, hoping to ally himself to whoever would respect American neutrality—France or Britain.

For Nick, the time had come for action despite his discomfort with public appearances; unlike his uncles John and Moses, he much preferred influencing decisions "behind the scenes." Now aged thirty-eight, he decided to run for office and was elected in 1807 to the Rhode Island Senate and would later represent Providence in the Lower House. He concurred with the gloomy conclusion of Joseph Dennie that "the sunlit world of peace and order and prosperity [we] had so recently known under Washington" would not return, but he would try his best to limit the damage.

Through these rocky years, Nick preached moderation. He had a powerful role model in Uncle Moses. When the embargo was declared, Nick had invited his uncle to attend a Providence town meeting to "recommend moderation & that nothing be passed improperly. We both want you to come in Town, & Join us in recommending Prudence, &c." If Uncle Moses attended, Nick explained, his influence would allow the meeting to enact measures "to the credit of our town & not act violently & harshly. . . . However opposed I am to the Embargo, yet it behoves me to get redress in a constitutional way, & not to Encourage people to open Rebellion, or violation of the Law."

In 1811, Nick's name was put forward as a candidate for governor, but the Federalist Party realized it should not be beholden to the Brown family. So William Jones of Providence, who had strong ties to the Newport mercantile community, was selected as a worthy citizen who "goes to church while Fenner only goes on Thanksgiving." With 47 percent of adult males voting in the most heavily contested gubernatorial race to date, Rhode Island elected its first Federalist governor. Nick was finally in the majority.

Washington, DC, however, was dominated by a group of young Republicans known as "War Hawks," led by House of Representatives Speaker Henry Clay of Kentucky and Senator John Calhoun of South Carolina. On June 18th, 1812, the United States thus declared war for the first time in its short history. None of the thirty-nine Federalists in Congress voted in favor of war—which they referred to as "Mr. Madison's War," a ploy to grab the fertile forests of Southern Canada from Britain and the cotton lands of Florida from Spain. They had a point: the United States Army consisted of only seven thousand trained men, five thousand new recruits, and less than a hundred thousand poorly equipped militia, along with a navy of sixteen ships. In contrast, the mighty British Army could call on almost 250,000 soldiers (albeit stretched to commitments in all corners of the globe), two thousand Canadian militia, and three thousand Native American warriors;

after the 1806 Battle of Trafalgar, the Royal Navy controlled the seas unchallenged with five hundred active warships, eighty-five sailing in American waters. Even with Britain engrossed in the Napoleonic wars on the European Continent, the disparity seemed ludicrous.

In Providence, the news of war was received as a national calamity: bells tolled, flags hung at half mast, and men of all rank went to work throwing up breastworks at Fox Point. The Federalists became the peace party. Like its neighbors, the Rhode Island legislature opposed sending its militia to support Congress's "work of darkness."

To compensate for the lack of a strong navy on the high seas, the United States rushed to commission privateers. Over 1000 British ships were sunk or captured; James DeWolf's *Yankee* captured forty-one prizes worth over $3 million. This time, however, the Browns stayed away from privateering. Other Rhode Islanders preferred more conventional heroism: for example, Oliver Hazard Perry's September 1813 victory at the Battle of Put-in Bay on Lake Erie preserved Ohio, Pennsylvania, and Western New York from a British attack.

As a serving legislator, Nick was exempt from military service. Tom meanwhile was appointed with five others in 1813 to a Council of War chaired by Governor William Jones who called the conflict, "a war of conquest, protracted by means ruinous and unnecessary." The War of 1812 devastated American merchant shipping. The coast was fully blockaded and some 1,400 vessels were captured. Between 1811 and 1814, American exports dropped by more than 90 percent—from $61.3 to $6.9 million in 1814. As one editorial lamented in the *Providence Gazette*, "Our ships, rotting by our wharves, remind us that commerce is sacrificed to the ambition of France."

By September 1814, the U.S. Treasury had defaulted on public debt interest payments. In New England, there was talk of secession; indeed, the governor of Massachusetts sent a secret peace mission to England. In December 1814, Rhode Island appointed four delegates to a convention in Hartford, Connecticut, to discuss grievances and suggest constitutional reforms to the Federal Government. The principal objective of the Hartford Convention was to embarrass President Madison (whose administration appeared near collapse) and to force a peace deal. But when the three representatives from Hartford finally arrived in Washington in February 1815, they learned of Andrew Jackson's battle at New Orleans. Suddenly, in the popular imagination, the War of 1812 was transformed from a stalemate to a victory. Their presence in the capital then seemed subversive; they left in haste.

News that a treaty had been signed at Ghent (which actually happened before the Battle of New Orleans) arrived in Rhode Island on March 14, 1815[41] in a letter to Cyrus Butler, president of the Exchange Bank, from the bank's London correspondent. Bells tolled, cannons were fired, and the town was illuminated. Nick threw a large party. Three months later, on June 18, 1815, the Napoleonic wars came to an end with the Battle of Waterloo. Had the United States and Britain not reached a peace settlement at Ghent, the full might of the Royal Navy and the British Army would then have become available to crush the Americans.

Ironically, the War's end—so welcome to the merchant fraternity generally and to Nick personally—precipitated the final demise of the Federalist Party which had discredited itself irremediably by trying to disassociate from the Union. Although the Treaty of Ghent (unanimously ratified on February 28, 1815) left many issues unresolved, public opinion was grateful for a painful chapter closed. Economic opportunity beckoned in manufacturing and Western lands; political opportunity should follow. The United States was becoming a "constant churning of people . . . here, all is circulation, motion, boiling, agitation." Ordinary people ceased to defer to their social superiors; young men appreciated the Republican faith in the capacity of the masses to govern themselves. They would return that party to the presidency seven successive times. For its part, the Republican administration recognized that some of its policies needed reform. A new national bank was essential to raise significant amounts of public debt.[42] Only a strong military could deter foreign powers from ever attempting another invasion. Moving troops and supplies called for good transportation links, especially roads and canals. Supporting fledgling industries meant

---

[41] Possibly the first news of the treaty to arrive in America.
[42] The First Bank of the United States' charter had lapsed in 1811.

tariff protection. In a stunningly short space of time, the Federalists found that they were not only out of office; they had become irrelevant. Shortly before his death in 1813, the last Federalist Speaker of the House Theodore Sedgwick stated dramatically and in terms that Nick no doubt endorsed with a heavy heart, "The aristocracy of virtue is destroyed."

To ensure political calm and to retain the hegemony of the "Democratic-Republican Party" (as the Republicans renamed themselves), President James Monroe, elected in 1816, distributed patronage irrespective of former party allegiances. He acquired Florida from Spain and his "Monroe Doctrine" (which advised European powers not to intervene in their former colonies) ensured that international affairs would not adversely affect the United States. He even toured New England on a goodwill visit in the summer of 1817, and received a cordial welcome in Providence.

One of Monroe's first acts as President was to establish a new national bank. The Second Bank of the United States opened its doors in Philadelphia in January 1817. Its directors then were charged with establishing twenty-five branch offices of discount and deposit throughout the country. Brown & Ives led the lobbying effort to locate a branch in Providence. They soon found themselves in competition with James DeWolf who was using every means possible to attract a branch in Bristol: he purchased a massive $200,000 stake in the new National Bank and travelled in person to Philadelphia to remind the directors of his fidelity to the Republican cause. In order to counter the strong Federalist reputation of Brown & Ives, Nick was advised to prepare an "exhibit to be laid before the directors stating the superior claims of Providence,"[43] to be presented in Philadelphia by "two or three respectable intelligent Inhabitants, . . . the majority in the Republican interest in politics." The partners also purchased 520 shares in the Second Bank of the United States. Nick made sure to point out that James DeWolf had accumulated his vast property through the slave trade "in defiance of the laws of his country & of humanity [and that he still pursued] that trade in an indirect manner even to this day." Despite DeWolf's vehement protests, the

---

[43] Much like the presentation his father had produced a half century earlier in competing for Rhode Island College.

Bank chose Providence. Still, both James DeWolf and his nephew George were made directors.

While keeping a low profile and adopting the new name of "Federal-Republicans," the Federalists continued to run Rhode Island until 1817. In 1818, the Democratic-Republicans took back the Rhode Island Legislature and James DeWolf became Speaker of the House. Only in 1820 did Federalism experience a modest resurgence when North and South debated the admission of Missouri as a "cotton-and-slave state." Nick and his allies seized the opportunity to voice their opposition to the "Missouri Compromise," calling attention to James DeWolf's involvement in the slave trade. When that merchant retorted that it had been "many, many years" since he had trafficked in slaves and that the greater portion of his property had been obtained in honorable employment, the *Providence Gazette* defined those more recent endeavors as the "[m]ore humane, honourable, successful and constitutional business—that of privateering." The deadlock was broken when the District of Maine was paired with Missouri in a compromise to hold the balance of power between free and slave states.

Despite the demise of the Federalist Party, Nick soldiered on in the Legislature because he had found a new cause to defend: free trade. Unfortunately, like Federalism itself, this cause too was rapidly to prove itself a lost one.

Nick passionately agreed with the French eighteenth century philosopher Montesquieu that commerce "enlarges the acquaintance of men, unites distant nations in affections; promotes spirit of peace, and gradually cements the whole world into one family." He believed that industry and commerce should exist within the compass of a moral world that stressed the obligations that merchants, farmers, and artisans have to one another. In the turbulent early nineteenth century, Nick agreed, commerce should be a source of modern virtue because it created "a chain of confidence and friendship throughout the world" by bringing wealth to society, tying the nations together, and even helping to civilize peoples. But these were pious thoughts that stood little chance when faced with harsh economic realities.

Following the 1815 Treaty of Ghent, Britain had dumped its unsold iron and textile stockpile on the United States—with devastating results for Rhode Island's young factories. From London, U.S. Minister John Quincy Adams told of deep hostility in Europe towards the fledgling United States; indeed, Britain's systematic flooding of U.S. markets with superior goods at cut-rate prices was an act of economic aggression. Despite the Rhode Island's rich maritime history, there was a growing feeling that the domestic commerce of the United States was "incalculably more valuable" than its foreign commerce. It was therefore not surprising that the state switched from its traditional antipathy toward federal regulation to one in support of tariffs that would benefit the state's infant industries. In direct opposition to that growing segment of public opinion, however, Nick remained dedicated to maritime commerce and free trade.

In April 1816, Congress passed the "Dallas Tariff" (named after Secretary of the Treasury Alexander Dallas). For the first time, the young country's goal was not revenue generation but protection. The tariff received wholehearted support from the Rhode Island press but, elsewhere in New England, merchants still hoped to restore trade with Britain and other European powers. Represented in Congress by the great orator Daniel Webster, the merchants won some concessions. Within a year, their worst fears came to pass: Britain decided to exclude American flour from its ports and to increase its imports of Brazilian and East Indian cotton. The price of flour fell from fifteen dollars a barrel in 1817 to just six dollars in 1819. The resulting impact on farmers and banks led to the nation's first major financial crisis.

The new National Bank was put to the test. Too many inexperienced banks had been chartered, counterfeit notes issued, credit overextended (to purchase 3.5 million acres of land), and unsustainable investments made. When the Napoleonic wars ended in 1815, demand for American foodstuffs fell sharply while revolutions in Mexico and Peru disrupted the world supply of precious metals. The speculative bubble burst in 1819. Banks called in their loans. President Monroe allowed the suspension of specie payment. All over the country, foreclosures, and bank failures abruptly extinguished America's blithe spirit. In Philadelphia, unemployment reached 75 percent.

Many of the very mills which the tariff was supposed to benefit were forced to close. In Rhode Island, New York, and Pennsylvania, some 60,000 people were thrown out of work. America became divided between two camps: those who supported protective tariffs and those who opposed them.

Mill owners clamored for higher, permanent import duties. They noted that tariff protection was allowing them to invest in high-grade machinery to produce special calicoes and other complex fabrics more cheaply than the equivalent English imports. They even hired lobbyists in Washington to ensure that protection would become enshrined as a principal of national well-being. The industrialists were championed by Henry Clay who sponsored a new tariff in 1824 that funded a specific program of internal improvements through a 35 percent ad valorem duty on iron, woolens, cotton, hemp, as well as wool and cotton bagging. Rhode Island congressmen Dutee Pearce and Tristam Burges emerged as vocal spokesmen for the manufacturing community.

As the arguments developed, Nick found that his vehement opposition to the tariff placed him in the camp of farmers and landholders—once his traditional enemies but now the only allies to support free trade. But foreign markets retaliated, and it became increasingly apparent that the anti-tariff forces were fighting a battle they could not win. Disheartened, Nick decided in 1821 to give up politics. He left the Rhode Island Legislature after a nearly fifteen-year tenure which, it seems fair to surmise, can have afforded him little satisfaction or sense of lasting achievement. For the next twenty years, he would continue to promote free trade, although no longer in a public forum. He did not lack moral courage, but simply did not feel at ease taking a public stance. Rather, he would support politicians who espoused his views and work "behind the scenes" through institutions that could shape values—notably the College on the hill.

When James Manning died of "apoplexy" on July 29, 1791—exactly two months to the day after Nicholas Brown had died, the College of

Rhode Island was left leaderless and bereft. The Corporation turned to the twenty-one-year old pastor of the First Baptist Church Jonathan Maxcy who had graduated a year after Nick in 1787 and been a tutor at the College. After a probationary period of five years, he was confirmed as president, the youngest in the country.

Maxcy was broader in outlook and more liberal than his predecessor. Although he lacked Manning's physical presence, Maxcy's "transcendent powers" of oratory widened the institution's reputation. Commencement ceremonies attracted visitors from far and wide. The alumni started organizing themselves in societies such as the "Federal Adelphi for Improvement in the Arts and Sciences." In 1802, however, Maxcy resigned to become head of Union College in Schenectady, New York[44]. The College again elevated a president from within its ranks, Asa Messer, a Massachusetts contemporary of Nick who already had served as tutor, professor of Learned Languages, of Mathematics and of Natural Philosophy, as well as librarian. More broad than tall, Messer swung his cane far and wide when he walked, gesticulating and impressing with his "powerful and sound moral reasoning." In his first years, he was admired for his even temper, honesty, freedom from prejudice and fatherly interest. The number of graduates increased to twenty-five (most still preparing for the church or the law).

However, the College continued to struggle financially. At its founding in 1764, the initial subscription of £4,000 had been laboriously raised by soliciting all down the Eastern Seaboard (the Brown family had contributed £760). Until the Revolution, America's nine colleges had relied on the generosity of donors in the Mother Country, with Harvard commanding the major share of philanthropic attention. The Englishman Thomas Hollis gave Harvard £5,000 over a fourteen-year period from 1717, the largest gift to an American institution of higher learning until well into the nineteenth century. The fabulously wealthy East India trader Elihu Yale was persuaded by Connecticut's London agent to donate to education in the colonies, his birthplace, rather than to Oxford. And

---

[44] He would become the first president of South Carolina College in 1804, where he would remain until his death in 1820.

the energetic John Witherspoon of the College of New Jersey (the future Princeton) managed to raise more than £7,000 in the five years before the Revolution. But in that same period, Manning collected only £900. He tried showering honorary degrees on English clergymen in the hopes of eliciting similar gifts for the College of Rhode Island. At one point, he thought that a Reverend Thomas Llewelyn would oblige: "We should think ourselves no less happy in the patronage of a Llewelyn. Llewelyn College ap-pears well when written and sounds no less agreeable when spoken . . ."– but Llewelyn died before receiving the solicitation letter.

After the Revolution, Manning again looked for a foreign patron:

> Can you find no Gentleman of Fortune . . . who wishes
> to rear a lasting Monument to his Honour in America?
> If you can direct his attention to the Hill of Providence
> in the State of Rhode Island, where an elegant Edifice is
> already erected, which waits for a Name from Some dis-
> tinguished Benefactor the Corporation are determined
> to do this Honour to its greatest.

He even tried the King of France; Benjamin Franklin and Thomas Jefferson each intercepted a letter. In the meantime, Uncle John offered to pay for half the cost of "a compleat Philosophical Apparatus & Library" if the Corporation could raise the remainder: £700 was secured in a few days. Six years after graduating, Nick gave a law library of 350 volumes, imported for £138 (nearly $700). But a major gift remained elusive; there were now fifteen new colleges in the United States, all competing for funding.

In 1795, President Maxcy wrote to South Carolina Baptists, looking for an eminent wealthy man: "Any person giving to this corporation the sum of Six thousand dollars, or good security therefore, before the next annual commencement, shall have the honour of naming the university." There were no takers. The twelve dollars of annual tuition and five dollars of room rent paid by the forty-one students barely covered running costs; salaries at the College remained among the lowest in the nation (in 1801, tutors received $350, professors were paid $600, and Maxcy $1,000, plus the use of a house and fees from the graduating class). The Corporation tried again in 1797, voting "That the donation of $5,000, if made to this College within one Year from the late Commencement, shall entitle the donor to name the College."

Shortly after President Asa Messer's arrival, Uncle John's health began to decline and he resigned from the Corporation. At the September1803 annual meeting, he made one last request—that a chair be endowed in:

> Oratory and Belles Lettres [as] the most beautiful and handsome mode of speaking was a principal Object, to my certain knowledge, of the first Friends to this College. I do wish that the Honorable the Corporation may find means during their deliberations of this week, to establish a Professorship of English Oratory.

A few days later, he was dead.

One year later, at the September 1804 annual meeting, the Corporation received another letter:

> Gentlemen– It is not unknown to you that I have long had an attachment to this Insti-tution as the place where my deceased Brother Moses and myself received our Education—This attachment derives additional strength from the recollection that my late Hon. Father was among the earliest & most zealous patrons of the College: & is confirmed by my regard to the Cause of Literature in general—Under these impressions I hereby make a Donation of Five Thousand Dollars to Rhode Island College to remain to perpetuity as a fund for the estab-lishment of a Professorship of Oratory & Belles Letters— The Money will be paid next Commencement, and is to be vested in such funds as the Corporation shall direct for its Augmentation to a sufficiency in your judgment to

produce a competent annual Salary for the within mentioned Professorship—I am very respectfully Gentlemen
with my best wishes for the prosperity of the College

Your obedt: friend—Nicho Brown

It is telling that the gift was in honor of Uncle John to promote good
speaking and writing, skills that few would associate with the chronic
misspeller.

Messer responded to Nick with "a heart glowing with gratitude,"
congratulating him for his generosity to the poor, "to these your whole
life testifies that you have been a compassionate, a generous, benefactor." He also commented on "The attachment you express to religion,"
and that "Your temporal prosperity, Sir, will never be diminished by a
generous munificence."

In keeping with the resolution adopted by the Corporation in 1797,
Nick's endowment of a chair in "Oratory & Belles Lettres" to carry out his
uncle's wishes caused the College of Rhode Island to be renamed "Brown
University in Providence in the State of Rhode Island and Providence
Plantations."

So it was, in the heyday of Brown & Ives's success and at a time when
maritime commerce remained the mainstay of Rhode Island's wealth,
that Nick made his first major contribution to the University that would
in his later life, and in a very different economic environment, become
the central focus of his attentions. This was exactly the sort of cause Nick
liked best; one he could manage and fashion to reflect his values. Even
adjusted to allow for inflation, the sum of $5,000—while considerable
at the time—appears to modern eyes a somewhat modest contribution
to secure the right to append one's family name to a seat of learning for
the rest of eternity. Fortunately for the University, this gesture would tie
Nick to the institution for the remainder of his lifetime–and the Brown
family for generations thereafter. Fortunately for Nick, the University
would provide a source of solace and an anchor to windward in what
were destined to become, at least for him, increasingly stormy seas.

CHAPTER 8

A NATION TRANSFORMED

*". . . the variety of opportunities, motives,
and attitudes which created the new species
'Businessman Americanus'" —Daniel Boorstin*

Brown & Ives emerged from the War of 1812 confident that success could be revived, much as Nicholas Brown had assumed he could simply resume his old trading patterns after the Revolution. It was not yet apparent that America was undergoing an ineluctable transformation from an agrarian to an industrial economy. Contemporaries said of Nick, "No man possessed so extensive and accurate a knowledge of the commercial marine of the whole country." Therefore, he felt no reason to question either his dedication to seafaring or his belief that manufacturing should be more than an adjunct of maritime commerce.

In May 1814, even before hostilities had ended, Brown & Ives formed a consortium with Massachusetts traders to invest in the speedy brig *Rambler*. Dodging British frigates, she returned from China a year later, earning a 112 percent profit; Brown & Ives immediately bought out the other owners. *Ann & Hope II* was the first Rhode Island ship to set sail back to Canton, returning directly to Amsterdam in time for the Dutch government's 1815 tea auction. The next six years were as busy as ever. New reciprocity treaties with Britain and Sweden meant more voyages to those countries, rather than the old destinations of Russia, the Hanseatic ports, and France. Gibraltar became a new Brown & Ives favorite. The firm also made twelve trips to South America.

But in Batavia, Brown & Ives's former success eluded them. Java coffee output rose six-fold in the decade after 1815, but so did the number of trading ships—some willing to make purchases at any price. Inevitably, the coffee bubble burst. In 1824, the Dutch government organized the Netherlands Trading Company so that Dutch royal patronage would drive all other countries out of Batavia. *Asia* was sent to Java in 1827 and again in 1831, but by then the Dutch had monopolized the market. In 1828, 110 Dutch ships arrived in Java, compared with only thirteen from the United States. Meanwhile, Brazil was affecting world trading patterns by reorienting its cash crops from sugar and indigo to coffee. Huge shipments of Brazilian coffee started to make their appearance in Providence, supplanting imports from Indonesia.

Nevertheless, in the seven years following the Treaty of Ghent, Brown & Ives sent an average of three ships a year to Canton and Batavia, a total of twenty-one visits by *Ann & Hope II, Patterson, Asia* and *Rambler*. They carried hundreds of thousands of dollars in cash, spread over several vessels. Once, in 1816, *Ann & Hope II* managed the roundtrip Amsterdam-Canton-Amsterdam in a record breaking eight months and seven days.

On a purely financial basis, 1819 (ironically, the very year of America's post-war economic crisis) was the high-water mark of Brown & Ives's entire career as maritime traders. Seven ships arrived in Providence that year from the Orient, rather than the usual three.

Yet only two years later, the firm's maritime fortunes began a gradual, unbroken decline. By 1825, manufacturing dominated Rhode Island's economy; shipbuilding had fallen by 50 percent. Revenues were diminishing steadily and losses were frequent. The high premium on Spanish silver dollars ate into profit margins which now were never more than 63 percent on average; gone were the days of 300 percent returns. The value of re-exported goods from Providence fell from $1.5 million in 1805 to only $72,000 in 1830. At that point, Brown & Ives and Edward

Carrington (whose fleet had surpassed that of Brown & Ives a decade earlier) were the only major players in the Far Eastern trade; there was no longer a resident consul in Canton. Most of the merchants who remained in maritime trade now operated fleets of small coastal vessels that hauled freight: cotton from the South, or flour, corn, and iron from the Mid-Atlantic States. Brown & Ives simply followed this pattern on a larger scale, supplying Britain's great factories with Southern cotton as well as importing wool from Europe and dyes from the tropics for the American textile industry. Indeed, U.S. cotton production soared from 73,000 bales in 1816 to 730,000 bales in 1820, more than that of India. Cotton represented 39 percent of U.S. exports in 1816, and 59 percent in 1836. The new marketability of short-staple cotton also prompted the expansion of slave-plantation agriculture far beyond the areas that would have sustained traditional export crops such as tobacco, rice or indigo.

Nick and Tom could have moved into the opium trade which was booming in China, but they never showed any inclination for this commerce. By 1835, maritime interests in Rhode Island were almost extinct; New York was America's leading port with its rich hinterland, superior harbor facilities, and a population of 270,000. When the last Brown & Ives ship *Hanover* returned to Providence from Canton in 1838, she was immediately sold. Thus ended not only fifty-one years of trade with the East Indies, but also a maritime tradition started when Captain James put to sea on the sloop *Four Bachelors* in 1721. The "golden era"—with all its triumphs and vicissitudes—had lasted barely more than three decades.

In its place, the new industrial era was in the process of fundamentally altering the United States in every imaginable way. When Uncle Moses and Samuel Slater built the first textile mill in 1791, no one anticipated the extraordinary advances American manufacturing would make in one generation. In 1798, the British Consul in the United States had reported to London that "a series of centuries" would have to elapse before a people "possessing [so] strong a natural disposition" to agriculture as the Americans would undertake manufacturing on a large scale. With hindsight, most successful merchants would concur with the great businessman, politician, and philanthropist Abbott Lawrence

who admitted, we "resisted the adoption of the system which we honestly
believed would greatly harm navigation and drive us into a business we
did not understand."

Rhode Island had always harbored a small but active group of middling merchants and artisans on the lookout for new opportunities. The
Far Eastern trade was pumping hundreds of thousands of dollars into
the state's economy but only providing a limited number of jobs. These
entrepreneurs used profits from the China trade as venture capital to
fund the nascent manufacturing sector. When the 1807 Embargo halted
British imports, many skilled craftsmen turned from shipbuilding to
designing manufacturing machinery. In colonial times, they had honed
their mechanical aptitude and ingenuity with sawmills and gristmills,
tanneries, ironworks, and candle works. Now, they made an easy tran-
sition to machine tools. The Embargo also provided a guaranteed home
market for American-made fabric and yarns. Best of all, the price of raw
cotton fell by 50 percent. It was ironic that Thomas Jefferson, who so
opposed the "evil effects" of manufacturing, would cause it to flourish
in New England simply by declaring an embargo.

Until 1799, Almy & Brown was the only firm producing cotton yarn
to make 100 percent cotton cloth. The thread from their Pawtucket factory was woven and finished at home by twenty-three cottage weavers.
The firm marketed the finished cloth and ran all aspects of the business, from setting wages to providing workers' lodgings. They used the
Quaker network to obtain spare parts for their machines and to purchase
high-quality West Indian cotton from Surinam, Cayenne or Hispaniola[45].

Almy & Brown built a second factory in 1792. In addition to aggressive marketing campaigns using newspaper advertisements and direct
mail, the firm sent Uncle Moses's son Obadiah from Boston to South
Carolina to present this new industry as "useful to the country"—the first
known attempt to develop a national market for a domestically-produced

---

[45] It took over a decade after the invention of the cotton gin by young Eli Whitney (while
he was lodging in 1793 at the Georgia Plantation of Rhode Island's Revolutionary War
hero Nathanael Greene) for indigenous American cotton to be of sufficient quality for
use in a spinning jenny.

manufactured product. Obadiah dispatched samples and advised retailers on displaying their wares, on the importance of a female sales force, and on the advantages of saturating dry goods stores in a particular locality. Mrs. Slater obtained a patent for cotton sewing thread while Obadiah suggested that stores offer courses in weaving to potential customers.

Three years later, Almy & Brown had grown to forty employees in three mills. When the first competitors appeared in 1799, Almy & Brown chose to provide better quality and service, rather than simply cut price to maintain its market share. By 1807, Almy & Brown owned five mills out of the thirty in existence in the United States; one-third of American yarn passed through its doors. Hand spinning was finally displaced by machine-spun yarn, and cotton cloth was now more popular than wool fabric.

The state of Rhode Island provided no assistance to budding entrepreneurs,[46] only an unregulated environment where the needs of mill-owners eventually took precedence over those of farmers and river fishermen. Fortunately, Uncle Moses's network of commercial interests, his reputation for honest trading, and most importantly his ability to tap into significant investment capital proved extremely helpful to Almy & Brown. Most industrialists delegated supervision of their mills to hired managers, but Uncle Moses, William Almy and Obadiah participated actively in directing operations. To overcome the limitations of America's immature banking system, they developed their own network of hard-nosed collections agents.

Samuel Slater, however, never quite appreciated the shortcomings of the American economy and how difficult it was for the partners to obtain cash, supplies, and raw materials. He yearned for more autonomy, sighing "I suppose that I gave out the psalm and they have been singing the tune ever since." In 1799, he left Almy & Brown to launch his own ventures with family members. His 1807 Slatersville Mill was for many years the largest and best equipped in America. One of its few competitors was

---

[46] The Pennsylvania legislature, which invested heavily in more than 150 ventures, and Massachusetts provided both funding and tax relief to manufacturers.

DeWolf's Arkwright Mills in Coventry that produced a thousand yards of cloth a day.

When the Embargo was declared in 1807, Rhode Island had been home to a third of all American cotton mills (over twice as many as in Massachusetts, its closest competitor), valued at $3.1 million in total. That number rose to thirty-six mills in 1811 and a hundred in 1815. For his 1817 inauguration, James Monroe wore a suit of cloth from a Pawtucket mill. By then, Almy & Brown had more than doubled their capacity to twenty-one mills and were clearing sales of $1 million with returns of 20 percent to 30 percent. Improvements in cotton cleaning equipment and the power loom were transforming the industry; Rhode Island was consuming 29,000 bales of raw cotton a year. A new link between Southern planters and Northern cotton manufacturers soon would become a potent political force.

Even Brown & Ives conceded it made sense to take "an Interest in this New Establishment." In the Embargo's second year, Nick was forced to admit that "the increasing embarrassments attending Commerce" made it impossible to think of "increasing . . . navigation." Joining with Seth Wheaton and Samuel Butler, Brown & Ives invested $50,000 in the Blackstone Manufacturing Company in Minden, Worcester County, Massachusetts. The partners proceeded slowly and cautiously, in fifty installments of $1,000, paid from 1808 to 1811. The Blackstone Mill was profitable from the start and their investment doubled in six years. By 1821, annual dividends were 13 percent and the original $150,000 outlay was worth $380,000. It would become the most heavily capitalized cotton spinning mill in America, one whose capacity was only exceeded by the mill at Slaterville. The partners emulated Almy & Brown by developing Western markets via wholesale distribution through Philadelphia.

But success was fragile. The windfall for manufacturers of the Embargo and the War of 1812 did not resolve the fundamental weaknesses which still plagued American industry: a lack of skilled labor, poor machinery, scarcity of credit, and high interest rates. Mill owners were very vulnerable to the health of the banking sector: they relied extensively on credit in order to function during the lengthy delays between shipping products to market and receiving proceeds from those sales. Most could not afford large networks of sales or collections agents. Thus, when a monetary crisis occurred in Fall 1814, Rhode Island mills were forced to accept more than $1 million in depreciated currency (Almy & Brown alone was owed $250,000). As soon as hostilities ended, Britain flooded the United States with the cheap goods it had been stockpiling for the past seven years. Mill owners sent over forty memorials to Congress, begging for a new tariff on cotton fabrics.

The economic crisis of 1816-19 caused possibly more harm to the young nation than had the actual War of 1812. Established manufacturers could absorb the setback but inexperienced, undercapitalized entrepreneurs did not stand a chance. Two-fifths of Rhode Island mills closed down. Thirty years earlier, during the post-Revolution "Critical Period," there had been great concern about society's obligation to the poor and unemployed. This time, there were no such concerns. Marked by harsh working conditions, job insecurity, and low pay, Rhode Island's textile industry in the 1820s was to become a far cry from Uncle Moses's early vision of social responsibility and reform.

Crisis notwithstanding, Rhode Island's manufacturing sector was going through a period of great innovation. Modern factories were built; Almy & Brown adopted the water-powered loom, first introduced by William Gilmore in 1815. Despite its complexity and capital cost, it stabilized production, provided a more standardized product, and ultimately reduced weaving costs by 50 percent. Spinning and weaving could take place under the same roof, tended by unskilled women and children who now replaced skilled craftsmen. Samuel Slater was the first to add power looms in his spinning factories where weavers toiled seventy hours a week.

Not everyone kept pace. Until the 1830s, many Rhode Island mills were reluctant to invest in the new technology. Next door in Massachusetts, Francis Cabot Lowell had no such reservations. Just before the War of 1812, he had spent two years in England engaging in industrial espionage. He built a power loom at Waltham in 1814. Then his half-brother Charles Lowell introduced an integrated system of cotton manufacturing which placed the carding, spinning, weaving, bleaching, dyeing, and finishing processes all under one roof. Massachusetts investors were prepared to spend ten times more than the capital required of the early Slater mills. Rhode Island may have introduced the industrial revolution, but Massachusetts would soon transform it into big business.

In 1822, disaster struck at Almy & Brown. Cousin Obadiah —just a year younger than Nick— died at age 52. Since he had no children, Obadiah bequeathed his entire personal estate of $127,000 to various charitable causes, including $100,000 to a Quaker school started by his father. He also set up an annuity of $1,200 for twelve trustees to distribute for benevolent purposes (the forerunner of the modern community foundation). These funds were therefore removed from the partnership. Then, four years later, Almy & Brown's $100,000 Smithfield mill was destroyed by fire; the firm went into debt to rebuild it. Obadiah's place was taken by William Almy's capable and experienced son-in-law William Jenkins, but the partnership never regained its preeminence.

Brown & Ives too suffered setbacks in their manufacturing investments. In 1813, the partners offered to assist the firm of Gilman & Ammidon to establish itself in Philadelphia as an agent for Rhode Island mills (Benjamin Ives Gilman was Tom's cousin). Within a few weeks, the firm attracted eighteen clients. But as middlemen in cash-strapped times, it ran into trouble collecting payments. Brown & Ives was called to the rescue, and advanced the enormous sums of $10,000 to $15,000 at a time to support cash flow. Nick even travelled to Philadelphia to deliver $20,000 in cash himself. By 1821, Brown & Ives was owed a combined total of $140,000 by 138 debtors who had overextended themselves in Ohio, Kentucky, Indiana, Tennessee, Missouri, and Alabama. In the end, the partners wrote off $75,000, a particularly bitter pill for Nick to swallow.

Fortunately for Rhode Island, the American textile industry entered a period of steady growth in the 1820s, greatly assisted by the transportation revolution that linked the industrial hinterland to the cities and towns. Samuel Slater continued leading technological innovation by introducing a steam-powered cotton mill in 1828. Steam-driven machinery operated at more constant and higher speeds than water power; it thus eliminated the constant nuisance of dams, locks, water wheels, and reservoirs. Textile mills no longer needed to be situated on rivers. They now could be built both along the coast where the high humidity was good for cotton fibers and coal could be delivered by boat, and in urban areas where their surplus power could be sold to small enterprises such as jewelry workshops. Indeed, steam power in the 1830's led to the prodigious expansion of the base metal industry, of gold-filled, gold plated, and paste jewelry (pioneered by Jabez Gorham), and of machine tool manufacturing. Later, in 1844, George Corliss from New York would revolutionize the reciprocating steam engine and Col. Steven Jenks would launch the massive screw, nut, and bolt manufacturing business of W.H. Haskell and Company.

The number of textile mills in Rhode Island grew from 100 in 1815 to 226 in 1832,[47] employing 11,273 workers, 12 percent of the state's population. At that time, Rhode Island was manufacturing one-sixth of the nation's cloth and was ranking second in New England as a producer of cotton goods, ahead of much larger states such as New York. The total capital invested in cotton manufacturing approached $5.6 million, more than triple that invested in maritime commerce. The number of woolen mills also began to grow significantly in the 1830s. Even Providence's largest maritime merchant Edward Carrington started to invest in cotton manufacturing in the late 1820s, and within a decade transferred most of his capital to the huge Providence Manufacturing Company at Crompton and to the Hamlet Mill on the outskirts of Woonsocket.

Brown & Ives continued to invest selectively when particularly attractive industrial opportunities presented themselves—probably at the instigation of Tom Ives. In 1818, the partners bought into a Herkimer City Mill located in New York State between Syracuse and Albany. In 1821, they participated in a $65,000 joint venture with Holden Borden in the Massasoit Manufacturing Company in Fall River, Massachusetts. Nick and Tom were in the advantageous position of having a finger in both trade and industry; textiles sold in Kentucky were paid for in

---

[47] The largest mill was the Almy & Brown factory in Smithfield, capitalized at $240,000.

tobacco, then traded in Europe. It felt almost like the days of old. As described by Daniel Boorstin:

> Mastery of the sea, when the sea was highway to the world, meant mastery of sources of raw materials. New England's ability to bring large quantities of cotton from the South or from Egypt, of hides from Argentina or from the Pacific Northwest, enabled her to supply factories making textiles or shoes or almost anything else. And the sea led to all the customers in the world. Lowell's miles of coarse cloth and Lynn's thousands of pairs of cheap shoes would have glutted a local market, but they went profitably thousands of miles overseas to the unclad and unshod in Africa, Asia, and Latin America.

In 1822, Nick and Tom agreed to purchase power looms for their mill in Newport, New York. In 1825, they bought the lands and water-power rights to a 4.5-mile stretch of the Blackstone River just north of Valley Falls, along with their former captain Wilber Kelly[48] and Edward Carrington. The Lonsdale Water Power Company was formed with Kelly as agent (for a salary of $500 a year) to supervise the construction of four large new mills and villages. Lonsdale was one of the first businesses in Rhode Island to incorporate in 1834. By 1846 (five years after Nick's death), it would be one of New England's largest textile firms.

It is understandable that Nick never felt comfortable in the world of manufacturing. Narragansett Bay traders were first and foremost merchant-adventurers who sought out speculative profits. They could create opportunities where none appeared to exist. But this aggressive opportunism lent itself to only the experimental phase of manufacturing. A merchant's sense of place and timing had little value in a factory where the machines must always run. In the world of maritime commerce,

---

[48] Two years earlier, Kelly had taken over the *Smithfield Cotton and Woolen Company*, a small mill of 25,000 spindles known as "Sinking Fund."

where ownership was synonymous with management, merchants rarely supervised more than a handful of clerks, assistants, and supercargoes (who were often from the same socio-economic background as their employers). But the impersonal world of nineteenth century capitalism required professional management of many dozens if not hundreds of workers who had little in common with their employers.

In this unsympathetic new environment, Brown & Ives nonetheless continued to deploy to advantage its two most valuable assets. The firm's tremendous financial resources meant that it never needed to extend itself financially and could afford the periodic losses it was obliged to endure. And Nick's innate, inherited sense of caution ensured that, whatever the temptations from time to time, the firm would never "Loose the Whole at one Throw" as Uncle Moses had cautioned. Thus, as Rhode Island's textile sector inevitably rationalized and consolidated around a small number of strong players, Brown & Ives would be one of the survivors—Nick's own lack of enthusiasm notwithstanding.

Nevertheless, the early success of Rhode Island's industrial sector hid fundamental flaws that eventually would prove too severe to be overcome. One such flaw was the marked reluctance to adopt the concept of limited liability ownership. This was a legacy of the very mercantile values that Nick so cherished. Merchants found that joint-stock partnerships offered the flexibility they required. While senior partners provided capital, expertise, and connections, the junior partners handled routine management; a merchant's word was his bond. Indeed, well into the nineteenth century, many Rhode Islanders thought of limited liability as a means to defraud the public; individual manufacturers should be held personally liable for all the debts of their firm. Courts continued to consider the threat of ruin and imprisonment as the best way to preserve business integrity. Thus it was not until 1829, eighteen years after the first limited liability law was passed in New York, that the partners of the East Greenwich Manufacturing Company were allowed to form a corporation "composed of a great many individuals . . . willing to invest small sums in the experiment." Yet even by 1860, most Rhode Island mills were not incorporated.

Another fundamental Rhode Island weakness was the failure to attain scale. The typical Rhode Island unit remained small, capitalized at less than $40,000, and employing only thirty-five workers; it could not afford sophisticated machinery. Without steam power, the amount of machinery that could be operated in any one place was limited by the river's water supply, so mill owners could only expand by building new mills. Successful manufacturers assembled little empires of a dozen or more small mills scattered throughout Rhode Island and its neighboring states. Often poorly integrated and far beyond the management capacities of their owners, they were also difficult to liquidate in times of economic hardship. A web of complex credit arrangements financed their expansion, so the downfall of one could cause the insolvency of all. Conversely, those industrialists who could build larger and larger steam powered mills were also losing their flexibility to shift into new products or new types of enterprises if times became tough. Thus, Rhode Island's fabled entrepreneurial spirit became subsumed by the routine of simply keeping the economic machine ticking.

Rhode Island's industrialists proudly defended the "Slater system" of hiring entire families, claiming that their small mills offered greater social and moral benefits than the giant operations of Lowell or Waltham which were filled by thousands of young women who worked for a few years before getting married. Thanks to the "Lowell System" of large-scale, completely mechanized and integrated production, as well as its adoption of limited liability, Massachusetts by 1831 had twice as many mills as Rhode Island, spun 50 percent more yarn, and wove twice as much cloth.

It took a banking crisis to bring these flaws into stark relief. Even at the best of times, Rhode Island's banking system was extremely fragile and vulnerable to the dramatic market fluctuations of the nineteenth century. The nation's money supply was largely unregulated, gyrating wildly between extremes of scarcity and plenty. Farmers preferred to loan their money directly to mills rather than to the banks; everyone lacked hard cash. Often, less than a third of a bank's capital was actually paid in. The Farmers' Bank of Glocester, which failed in 1809, nominally had capital of hundred thousand dollars but only about $19,000 was actually on deposit. Yet the General Assembly continued to be inundated with petitions to establish banks. The number of banks in Rhode Island increased from fourteen in 1815 to sixty-eight in 1838. This was a bubble destined to burst.

The "Panic of 1829" happened suddenly and without warning. More than sixty cotton manufacturers collapsed in Providence County alone. As noted by Benjamin Cozzens in 1832, "manufacturing is the most difficult and the most perplexing business that is carried on." Indeed, 90 percent of the industrialists in Rhode Island went bankrupt at least once in the period between 1790 and 1860. Samuel Slater's in-laws, the Wilkinson, who were the leading manufacturers in southern New England, declared bankruptcy and David Wilkinson went to prison. Even Slater lost almost all his investments, saved only by a loan from Uncle Moses.[49]

The crisis eliminated the last "farmer-investors" (thereafter, farmers put their money in savings banks) and "craftsmen-proprietors" who lacked capital, sold on credit, and expanded too rapidly. Those mills that were sufficiently capitalized and well-organized survived while others revived under new ownership. New centers appeared and the march of mills resumed up the Blackstone Valley, especially around Woonsocket, the second largest mill complex in the state. Brown & Ives's own textile holdings flourished.

However, not all the partners' attempts at diversification produced positive results. Success consistently eluded their ventures in real estate and infrastructure. Yet they persisted, often in direct contradiction to their own rules of engagement. This error in judgement led Brown & Ives to its worst debacle, the Blackstone Canal venture.

Nick and Tom could hardly be blamed for wanting to invest in real estate and infrastructure. They shared the Founding Fathers' view that American lands should be developed in an orderly, progressive fashion by industrious farmers who respected boundaries with the indigenous

---

[49] Some historians have commented that the most valuable piece of fabric ever woven by Slater was "Moses Brown's safety net."

tribes. Instead, the opposite happened: there were never enough settlers willing to pay for lands they could grab for nothing. The combination of over-leveraged absentee landlords and lack of government control rapidly transformed Western expansion into a jumble of bankrupt real estate concerns, conflicting claims, and defiant squatters—matters often turned bloody. By 1790, two-thirds of Virginians without property had left the state for Western lands. Tennessee had more than 35,000 settlers, Kentucky had double that number, and pioneers were spilling north of the Ohio River. Congress considered the hundred thousand Native Americans of the Trans-Appalachian West to be a conquered people who should give up their culture and become farmers. By 1802, three-quarters of the tribes along the Mississippi and Missouri rivers had perished from disease. A new approach was then tried to "save the Indians from extinction" by distancing them from white settlers and slowing down the process of assimilation, which in fact culminated in their wholesale removal in the 1830s under Andrew Jackson.

America's expansion seemed limitless. In one generation, its people occupied more territory than they had in the entire 150 years of colonial existence. A treaty with Spain recognized the Florida border and allowed free navigation on the Mississippi River. In 1802, a cash-hungry Napoleon sold "Louisiana," 900,000 square miles of land (more than the entire United States at the time) for $15 million. The Federalists, including the Brown family, immediately decried the Louisiana Purchase for enhancing the slaveholding South at the expense of the North.[50] But Thomas Jefferson believed the United States could only maintain a republican society of independent yeoman farmers by expanding westward, free from the disease and vices of East Coast urban centers. This was his "Empire of Liberty" which he sent Meriwether Lewis and William Clark to explore.

The 1810 census counted a million Americans west of the Appalachians out of a total population of 7.23 million. A decade later, it was 2.4 million out of a total population of 9.6 million. Small farmers

---

[50] Slavery was allowed from 1798 in lands to the west of Georgia

from New England planted corn and wheat (with whiskey as a major by-product). In the milder climate of the Southern Territories, corn and tobacco were supplanted by cotton, which required more acreage and thus a larger numbers of slaves. Thousands rushed to cotton lands, especially following the introduction of steamboats on the Mississippi and Ohio Rivers in 1818. Land sales climbed from $1.3 million in 1820 to over $14.7 million a year in 1835.

Already in 1796, Nick and Tom had made several real estate investments which proved both unprofitable and extremely slow to liquidate. They had been impressed by the returns Nicholas had achieved on a 1786 purchase of 4,494 acres of "loyalist lands" in the fertile Mohawk Valley of New York for $1.30 an acre: ten years later, the land was worth $6.00 to $7.00 an acre. Little did they know that all of Nicholas Brown's other real estate investments would prove unsuccessful.[51] So Brown & Ives bought 13,491 acres in Luzerne County, Pennsylvania at $1.92 an acre, an exceedingly high price for "wild lands." Recruiting settlers to the hilly and thickly forested lands was a struggle; only the hardiest souls survived. Finally, in 1823, they hired a remarkable agent, Parly Coburn, and settlers slowly began to trickle in. These hardy men thanked Brown & Ives for "the lenity with which you have always treated [us]," but it took another fifty-three years to sell the last parcel. Brown & Ives also found themselves embroiled in the infamous case of "Yazoo Lands"—35,000,000 acres (most of the present-day Alabama and Mississippi) fraudulently sold in 1796 to unsuspecting New England investors. It took twenty years, a Supreme Court case, and an Act of Congress for investors to be partially indemnified. Most tellingly, Nick and Tom witnessed firsthand the results of Uncle John's disastrous investment in the Adirondacks. Charles Frederick Herreshoff, Uncle John's son-in-law, frequently borrowed from his cousins (sometimes without permission) in a vain attempt to develop

---

[51] In 1781, he had purchased 7,288 acres at six cents an acre in the township of Random, in the future Vermont. Brown & Ives would only manage to sell the last acre a hundred years later. Nicholas also had led the family's major investment in The Ohio Company which by 1820 totaled 18,000 acres. It also took almost a century to sell off.

the cursed tract. After his suicide in 1819, Brown & Ives watched Uncle John's descendants sell acreage off at a pittance simply to pay taxes.

Once Nick realized that his real estate investments had yielded lack-luster returns, he ceased to show any interest in further real estate development schemes. In his opinion, purchasing land was no better than investing in manufacturing; both were useful if they provided goods to trade. He therefore supported the purchase of tobacco farms in Ohio but not of wild lands to be cleared in Western Pennsylvania. His only truly successful investment was a "Military Tract" (land given to veterans in lieu of cash) of 1,920 acres in western Illinois that he received as settlement for an 1835 lawsuit. Over the next twenty-five years, Brown & Ives would eventually own 14,881 acres of that tract, some of which had cost only three cents an acre, and would receive returns of 187 percent.

Infrastructure ventures seemingly offered much speedier returns than real estate investments. Everyone recognized that the United States urgently needed better infrastructure to supply raw materials to factories, foodstuffs to urban centers, and finished goods to market. The public continually demanded better transportation and communications. But democratically elected state legislatures were reluctant to raise taxes to pay for infrastructure. Thus nearly all the states turned to the traditional mobilization of private power for public ends.

In his 1808 "Report on Roads," Secretary of the Treasury Albert Gallatin wrote, "no other single operation within the power of the Government can more effectually tend to strengthen and perpetuate the Union." Congress set aside revenues from Ohio land sales to build a road from Cumberland, Maryland to Ohio. Construction began in 1811 and finally ended in 1825 in Jefferson City, Missouri; it was funded by the admission to statehood of Ohio, Indiana, Illinois, and Missouri. The road allowed farmers in the Great Lakes and Ohio Valley to ship their produce to Atlantic ports rather than to send it down the Ohio and Mississippi Rivers to French or Spanish markets. Yet despite the road's popularity, Presidents Madison and Monroe both vetoed federal appropriations for its maintenance and repair. Even John Quincy Adams who was enthusiastic about public works felt that the planning and development of infrastructure projects should be left to the states. His successor, Andrew Jackson, firmly opposed federal funding for internal improvements and exercised his veto eight times against public works projects, claiming that roads and canals had only local benefit. His most famous veto in 1830 denied funding for extending the Maysville Road in Kentucky, eventually completed through private funding.

Some states had the means to undertake massive infrastructure projects. The greatest of these was probably the 360-mile long Erie Canal in New York State, inaugurated in 1825 after eight years of construction at a cost of $7 million. It succeeded almost immediately in tying Western grain producers to the port of New York. New England farmers thus lost any remaining competitive edge: many abandoned agriculture for full-time factory jobs, or moved to Western boomtowns like Cleveland or Chicago. In contrast with New York, Massachusetts or Pennsylvania, the government of Rhode Island would not invest in infrastructure projects. The state counted on the private initiative of families like the Browns (who had invested in infrastructure from their first days in Providence when Chad Browne became a surveyor).

Before the Revolution, the only organized form of conveyance was the sailing packet—a speedy maneuverable ship of 75 to 100 tons, small enough to avoid pilotage or docking fees. After independence, a group of Rhode Island merchants adopted the English concept of the chartered "turnpike company" which charged tolls every ten miles to fund the upkeep of a stretch of road. Once shareholders had achieved a 12 percent return, the turnpike would become a public road. In the 1790s, thirty-three turnpike charters were issued throughout New England. The first to radiate from Providence was the Providence & Norwich Turnpike chartered in 1794; John Innes Clark, Uncle John and Nick invested in it; Nick and Tom sat on its board.

Forty-six turnpikes eventually were incorporated in Rhode Island, but profits remained elusive: traffic was often less than anticipated, construction costs ran over budget, farmers resisted subsidizing highways for which they had little use (herds did not require good roads), and local landholders refused to pay for a road they considered theirs by right. When the Rhode Island Legislature became Republican and pro-agrarian in 1801, all turnpike proposals were successfully opposed. In 1803, overland freight was moving so slowly that Almy & Brown was advising consignees just seventy miles away in Hartford that a shipment would arrive "sometime in the course of the winter." The only successful project was the Providence–Pawtucket Turnpike which earned $56,000 on an investment of $7,000 (launched in 1809, it was taken over by the state in 1833).

Nevertheless, roads did improve, starting with the development in the 1780s of the "round road" that allowed water to drain to the sides. Over the next fifty years, journeys became three times as fast and one-third as expensive. In 1820, 250 stagecoaches left Boston each week on sixty different routes. The fare between Boston and Providence was $2.50—two days' wages for a skilled journeyman artisan. From Boston to New York, it was $10.00—approximately eight days' wages for such a worker to travel twenty or thirty miles a day at nine miles an hour. By the 1830s, one hundred stage lines were dispatching six hundred coaches a week, 328 of which ran between Boston and Providence. It even became possible to travel for pleasure: a rarity in the eighteenth century.

Although turnpikes were a doubtful investment, they allowed investors to cast themselves as public benefactors; Uncle Moses owned shares in nine turnpikes. In 1793, both he and Uncle John sponsored bridges over the Seekonk River in competing locations; both were authorized by the General Assembly and inaugurated within three days of each other. Moses's bridge (known as the "Red Bridge") was near his Elmgrove estate, connecting the post road between Rehoboth and Providence. John's "George Washington Bridge" was strategically positioned near his newly redeveloped dockyards at India Point. Tom Ives supported Uncle Moses; Nick invested with Uncle John. Indeed, Tom Ives was especially enthusiastic about infrastructure investment. He usually sat on the boards of the management companies which he funded. One form of transportation that particularly caught his eye was canals.

In 1796, Uncle John had proposed a grandiose plan to build a canal between Providence and Worcester, Massachusetts, similar to the waterways of England, Holland, France, and Italy. He had offered to put up $40,000 towards digging a 45-mile canal to provide cheap transportation for farm produce, lumber, firewood, lime, and stone. Trade from the inland cities of Massachusetts could thus arrive in Providence rather than travel overland to Boston. The Rhode Island General Assembly responded enthusiastically and funds were quickly subscribed. But "the good people of Boston, with no love of Providence" balked and convinced the Massachusetts Legislature to refuse the project. So the venture was delayed by a generation until such time as the merchants of Boston felt a canal would no longer threaten their interests.

By the 1820s, the 540 square miles of the Blackstone River basin covered one of the nation's most important manufacturing centers, encompassing a population of 80,000 in three states. The construction on the Erie Canal had reawakened the nation's interest in waterways, and Uncle John's arguments still rang true. Ordinary laborers who earned less than a dollar a day simply could not pay 12.5 cents in tolls for their wagons to travel ten miles. The often remote location of textile factories along rivers made transportation even more challenging. The only solution was for farmers, artisans, manufacturers, and merchants to band together to build a canal. Indeed, an animal that could pull two tons on a paved road could pull fifty tons on a canal towpath, saving 50 percent in freight costs.

However, two powerful groups opposed a Providence-Worcester canal: mill owners on the Blackstone River who feared that an active canal would divert their water, and Rhode Island farmers who did not want competition from their Massachusetts counterparts. Some of the Providence newspapers voiced doubts about the canal's viability. But investment capital was plentiful in the 1820s and businessmen on both sides of the state border made grand predictions about the venture's success.

The major promoters in Rhode Island were Brown & Ives along with Edward Carrington; together they owned a seventh of Providence's total wealth.

Tom Ives started by raising $400,000 in 1822; the total cost of the canal was anticipated to be $323,319. Public enthusiasm was such that the promoters easily could have obtained a million dollars (a huge missed opportunity as the project ended up costing more than $700,000). Excavations began in 1824 with Moses Brown Ives, Tom's son, in charge of construction management, and Benjamin Wright, a chief engineer of the Erie Canal, overseeing the topographical survey. More than five hundred men from Providence (and by 1827, a thousand men in Massachusetts) toiled from dawn to dusk for twelve dollars a month. Agents in Boston and New York hired Irish immigrants, some veterans of the Erie Canal, and many then settled permanently in the area. At the end of four con-structions seasons, the forty-five mile long, forty-five foot wide canal with its forty-eight granite locks, high dams, warehouses, and wharves was completed in July 1828. On October 7th, the *Lady Carrington,* "a handsome white packet boat with red curtains and cushioned and car-peted interior," drawn by two horses, arrived in Worcester "to a celebra-tion worthy of the 4th of July: incessant cheers, thunders of cannon and peals of bells." At capacity, the Blackstone Canal could accommodate one passenger packet and twenty horse-drawn barges carrying between twenty to thirty tons of freight over three or four days for a round-trip fare of sixty dollars.

Then the problems began. The first full operating season was blighted by an economic depression and fall floods. There were engineering issues as the canal's four-foot depth made it vulnerable to droughts and ice. As construction costs began to soar, shoddy workmanship became the norm. But the greatest headache came from the mill owners who retained joint use with the Canal Company of the river waters that drove the mills' water wheels. The Canal charter contained elaborate mechanisms to guarantee that waters drawn by the Canal from the Blackstone River's natural run "in no way hampered the mill owners' operations." This plan proved im-possible and soon the Canal Company was being attacked in endless law suits. Mill owners tipped rocks into the locks and Canal boatmen threat-ened to set mills on fire. Over the dry summers of 1833 and 1834, mill owners brought 149 writs against the Canal, each leading to a $50 fine.

The enterprise was doomed by lack of foresight, inefficiency, and rapid obsolescence. The founders had vastly underestimated capital requirements. At its peak in 1832, the canal brought in tolls of $18,907 and paid a 2 percent dividend; but over its entire lifetime, it would earn investors a paltry $1.25 per share. A joke circulated around Providence that the company's only profit was from the sale of grass mowed along the canal towpath. In 1827, when the project was running $50,000 over budget, the Canal Company was refused a bank loan of $10,000. Never before had Brown & Ives been turned down in such a manner. So the Canal Company approached forty-nine "men of substance" to guarantee a further $100,000. The Providence Washington Insurance Company, many of whose directors were connected with the Canal Company, offered a $32,000 loan and bought $10,000 in Canal Company notes. Brown & Ives took ten new certificates; Moses Brown Ives and Robert Ives each took two. But most of the "men of substance" in Providence refused to invest in the new scheme.

Outside Rhode Island, the Canal Company fared no better: the Second Bank of the United States offered only short-term loans, and John Jacob Astor of New York flatly turned down the Canal Company's request for funds. By 1831, the Canal Company was resorting to financial machinations of impressive complexity. Brown & Ives, the Providence Bank, and the Providence Institute for Savings all invested another $55,000. They chartered the "Blackstone Canal Bank" which purchased $150,000 of new canal company stock. Brown & Ives bought $35,000 in Blackstone Canal Bank shares and loaned it $30,000 at 6 percent. The entire project now rested on a house of cards; under different guises, Nick and Tom were subscribed many times over.

The canal's woes plagued Tom Ives's final years. In 1831, he wrote of the "embarrassed situation" of the Blackstone Canal Company. The final blow came in 1835 when the Boston and Worcester Railroad was inaugurated; canal revenues immediately dropped by 20 percent. In all, the canal served less than twenty years and lost $700,000. Had Uncle John's original proposal been accepted by Massachusetts, the canal's useful life would have been more than twice as long—and perhaps could have allowed the investors to recoup their money.

Contrary to his lifelong negative attitude towards manufacturing, Nick wholeheartedly supported turnpikes and canals. Like Robert
Fulton, a pioneer of the steam engine, he believed that they tied people
together to "create a sense of mutual interests arising from mutual in-
tercourse and mingled commerce." It is not difficult to imagine his dis-
may that the Blackstone Canal was the worst investment ever made by
Brown & Ives-and that its failure may have hastened Tom's early death
in 1835. A further interesting point of speculation is whether Nick would
have embraced railroads as a new way to "bind men together" had he
been born several decades later or lived longer. Might he have become a
James Hill, a Jay Gould, a Cornelius Vanderbilt, an Edward Harriman,
or a Collis Huntington, his locomotives crossing the continent the way
his ships had plied the seas? Certainly, his successors at Brown & Ives
seized upon the opportunity with alacrity, undaunted by the debacle of
the Blackstone Canal. Nick lived long enough to see the first step taken.
When the *Boston & Providence Railroad* arrived at India Point[52] in 1835,
at the urging of Nick's son, nephews, and Edward Carrington, Brown &
Ives was a major investor in this first railroad. That such a project could
be financed despite the recent loss of $700,000 in the Canal is, in itself,
eloquent testimony to Nick's prudent lifelong stewardship of the firm.
Brown & Ives was to be involved in virtually every one of the major railroads built over the ensuing thirty years.

Nick could do little to halt either the inexorable dominance of manufacturing in Rhode Island or the demise of his beloved maritime commerce. He continued, however, to fume against the tariff and other im-
pediments to free trade. But by 1821, he admitted defeat and resigned
from the Legislature. Three years later, his mood did not improve when
John Quincy Adams was elected with overwhelming support from
industrialists. Like many former Federalists, Nick had never forgiven
Adams for defecting to the Republican camp to support the Louisiana
Purchase and the 1807 Embargo. Now Adams sought to keep potential

---

[52] The distance was covered at a speed of fifteen to twenty miles an hour, in two hours
and twenty-five minutes. Passengers were thrilled by the experience despite the deaf-
ening noise and the showers of ash and soot.

factory workers on the Eastern Seaboard by supporting protectionism and restricting Western land sales. As the 1828 election approached, the President's opponents hatched a plan to gain voter support in the West, Mid-Atlantic and North East manufacturing states. The elaborate ploy, designed to upstage Adams at his own game, involved proposing an exorbitant tariff (30 percent to 50 percent duties) that was never supposed to make it past Congress. Not for the first time in Congressional history, the plan that was too clever by half backfired and Congress did in fact approve the "Tariff of Abominations." The net result was to precipitate six years of agitation that culminated in the "Nullification Crisis" when South Carolina threatened to secede from the Union.

The agricultural South deeply resented high import duties charged on goods it could not produce locally. Furthermore, the tariffs of 1816 and 1824 had limited Britain's ability to pay for Southern cotton. Now, Southern discontent turned South Carolina's John Calhoun into a strong advocate of states' rights. When in 1829, the newly elected Andrew Jackson failed to lower the Tariff of Abominations, tensions escalated between Jackson and his Vice President Calhoun; meanwhile a radical faction was gaining popularity in South Carolina. In January 1830, one of the most celebrated congressional debates in history took place on the Senate floor between Senator Robert Hayne of South Carolina and Senator Daniel Webster of Massachusetts on the subject of states' rights and tariffs. Two years later, when John Quincy Adams in the House and Henry Clay in the Senate pushed to make the protection of domestic industry a permanent policy, South Carolina held a state convention to declare any tariff unconstitutional and unenforceable within its sovereign boundaries. The following February 1833, the state adopted an "Ordinance of Nullification" and launched military preparations. Ultimately Clay and Calhoun worked out a compromise agreement that brought the tariff down to 20 percent. Bloodshed was averted, but not before Rhode Islanders had witnessed the rather extraordinary spectacle of Tom Ives's public declaration of support for Calhoun and the Nullifiers.

One can easily imagine the effect of these torrid political developments on a man of Nick's convictions. He must have felt vindicated in his dire predictions about the tariff, but distraught as his country was torn apart. He fought his battles with tenacity and to the best of his ability. There was, however, no disguising the fact that he—and those who shared his outlook—were ultimately defeated on all fronts. It was a bitter denouement to all the hopes that had marked his coming of age and the birth of the new Republic.

CHAPTER 9

JACKSON'S AMERICA

*"There are many men of principle in both
parties in America, but there is no party
of principle." —Alexis de Tocqueville*

W hen Nick ended his formal political career in 1821, America
was still only halfway through its "Era of Good Feelings."[53] In
colonial times, society had been ordered through systems of paternalism
and dependence: most people were bound by personal ties of one kind or
another. The limited scope of the colonial economy blunted the differences between the gentry and ordinary folk. Jefferson's faith in the virtue
of the yeoman farmer seemed plausible at a time when two-thirds of the
white population owned land. The Republicans who came to power in
1801 trusted in the "people's opinion [because] no one controlled it and
everyone contributed to it."

In 1815, Americans—renewed in the belief that "the natural sociability of people was the best social adhesive"—united in a great post-war
burst of patriotic fervor. During his eight-year administration (1817-25),
President James Monroe managed to produce an appearance of political

---

[53] The term was coined in July 1817 by Benjamin Russell in the Federalist *Columbian
Centinel*, following President Monroe's visit to Boston as part of his good will tour of
America.

consensus. The collapse of the Federalist Party and Monroe's nearly unanimous 1820 re-election victory seemed to confirm this common sense of national purpose. Looking back on "The Era of Good Feelings," John Quincy Adams would say with veneration:

> . . . the production of our soil, the exchanges of our commerce, the vivifying labors of human industry, have combined to mingle in our cup a portion of enjoyment as large and liberal as the indulgence of Heaven has perhaps ever granted to the imperfect State of man upon earth.

In Rhode Island too, the rival factions within the only party, the "Democratic-Republican" (which by 1828 would be known simply as "Democratic"), generally found cooperation more beneficial than partisanship.

But even during these seemingly benign years, the underlying political reality was quite different. Behind an illusion of harmony, the atmosphere inside the White House itself was strained and divisive. The disastrous Panic of 1819, the first major peacetime crisis of the nineteenth century, and the landmark Supreme Court case *McCulloch v. Maryland* that same year, reanimated disputes over the supremacy of state sovereignty and federal power. The Missouri Compromise in 1820 reopened the explosive political debate between slave and free soil territories. As the years passed, these divisions and the passions they aroused only became more rancorous. In no respect did the tide of events move in a direction sympathetic to Nick's own principles and world outlook: an orderly, hierarchical society founded on trade and benevolence. The political history of the remaining two decades of Nick's life thus provides an essential backdrop to understanding the philanthropic journey on which he was to embark from the mid-1820's.

Throughout this whole period, America's industrialization, migration, and rapid urban growth were relentlessly disrupting traditional relationships and eroding consensual values. America was turning into a scrambling commercial society, dominated by pecuniary interests. As the population reached the ten million mark in 1810, the demographic map was undergoing dramatic change. People were moving from countryside to town, from East to West. Meanwhile, ethnically and religiously distinct European immigrants were beginning to arrive in ever larger numbers. The participation of common people in government was becoming the essence of American democracy, but each new faction was clamoring for representation: interest group politics were born. Partisanship (exactly what the Founding Fathers had tried so diligently to avoid) thus became a hallmark of American political life.

All across the nation, contradictions between the egalitarian aspirations of the American Revolution and the social realities of the Industrial Revolution were causing tensions to rise. The acrimonious presidential election of 1824 brought any remaining "good feelings" to an abrupt end. Five candidates were pitted in a contest based on regional interests: John Quincy Adams from the Northeast (not the choice of Nick or Tom); Speaker of the House Henry Clay who was popular in the West; Treasury Secretary William Crawford, from Georgia, an "Old Republican" and President's Monroe's choice; South Carolina's John Calhoun, the future champion of states' rights; and the former Senator and Tennessee Governor, General Andrew Jackson who was widely viewed as a defender of the "Common Man." Although Jackson won both the popular vote and the largest number of Electoral College votes, John Quincy Adams was elected President on the single vote cast in the House of Representatives by Henry Clay (whom the new president promptly appointed as secretary of state). What was inevitably perceived as a shabby piece of political chicanery set the scene for the forthcoming presidential term.

New battle lines were swiftly drawn. The last Federalist congressional caucus dissolved in 1825 and its remaining members, including Daniel Webster, joined with Henry Clay to launch a new "National-Republican Party." On the "Democratic-Republican" side, it became imperative to instill a new political consensus by reviving Jeffersonian principles. Southern "exceptionalism" and agrarian interests would now guide the modern Democratic Party at the national level. So began the "Two Party

System" of modern American politics. For the next quarter century, it would be characterized by high levels of voter interest and boisterous, often bitter campaigns supported by huge numbers of partisan newspapers.

John Quincy Adams did little to counter this divisiveness. Beyond authorizing a few roads and canals, no significant legislative achievement took place during his administration. Despite his great intelligence, experience, integrity, and devotion to his country, he was unable to maintain strong public support. In 1828, he failed to secure a second term. This time, Andrew Jackson was ushered into office with a decisive majority.

Ironically, "Jacksonianism infused into American democracy more elements of a monarchy than even the Federalists had dared to try."[54] Loyalty to the party was the sole criterion for political worth. Jackson used federal patronage—the "Spoils System"—to reward supporters, but he did rotate positions to stem corruption. He initially played on the traditional Jeffersonian notion that the people should be left unhindered to improve their lot. But over the course of eight years, he gradually consolidated and expanded presidential power at the expense of Congress, using the veto twelve times. Invoking "Manifest Destiny," he expanded the United States to the South and West, harshly removing the native peoples "to extend the area of freedom." For the first time in America, resentment was specifically targeted against the rich: local banks were being allowed to behave increasingly irresponsibly, while disparities between rich and poor were growing to unprecedented levels.

Opposition to Jackson reinvigorated the National-Republican Party which advocated a strong economy based on three mutually reinforcing tenets: a high tariff to protect and promote American industry, subsidies for internal infrastructure improvements generated from both the tariff and federal land sales, and a national bank to encourage productive enterprise. Its leader Henry Clay believed that national unity and harmony would result from economic interdependence among the regions. Urban

---

[54] As Gordon Wood further wrote, "Jacksonian office holders lacked the polished conversation, the graceful manner and high tone of a real gentleman; they did not look like gentlemen." Alexis de Tocqueville noted that American public officials did not possess the aristocratic distinction that Europeans expected in their government officers.

factory workers in the Northeast would consume Western foods, and the South would sell its cotton to Northern mills. Clay preached a truly "American System" and opposed party politicians who pandered to local interests. Nick would have supported Clay, had the Senator not been such firm advocate of the tariff.

Rhode Island too was swept up in these national passions, but here the debate coalesced around the question of state constitutional reform. That touchstone issue dominated the state's political agenda for the last two decades of Nick's life, and came to an explosive culmination just after his death.

Rhode Island's Royal Charter, which had seemed so progressive in 1663, was now completely outdated. It fixed legislative representation to the original seventeenth century demographics, giving Newport six seats; Providence, Portsmouth, Warwick four seats; and all other towns only two. In 1750 when Providence had 3,500 inhabitants, four seats in the Legislature seemed fair. But when the state's population rose to 23,000 in the late 1830s, the capital city was severely underrepresented. Providence—which had $1/6^{th}$ of the state's inhabitants, $1/7^{th}$ of its voters, and $1/4^{th}$ of its wealth—had only $1/18^{th}$ of Rhode Island's legislative representation. Why? Largely because the 1663 Charter restricted suffrage to landowners. During its first two centuries when Rhode Island was principally agricultural, 75 percent of white males owned sufficient property to vote. But by 1830, 60 percent of the state's free white men—including thousands of mill workers—were ineligible for the franchise. Rural town meetings—the basis of political power—were still controlled by a handful of farmers who, in turn, controlled the General Assembly and refused to reform the outmoded system.

In the immediate post-Revolutionary period, surplus Yankee farm labor had streamed into the first textile mills and brought prosperity to a countryside badly lacking in opportunity. But rural Rhode Island soon looked with growing antipathy at the new industrial workforce and resisted any improvements (even refusing to create fire districts) that might raise in taxes. When immigrants of different ethnic and religious origins began arriving in the 1830s, the farmers' antipathy became palpable.

They viewed efforts to replace the anachronistic Charter with a more representative Constitution as a threat to their very survival.

Textile entrepreneurs also wanted to keep the *status quo* to ensure a supply of docile and disciplined labor. Poor urban workers were thought to have "had no will of their own"; thus they might fall under the spell of "rich and unprincipled men" if allowed to vote, the mill owners argued. An unlikely alliance thus developed between rural and manufacturing interests.

Calls for a state constitutional convention began in 1818 and continued with mounting urgency over the next twenty-three years. Initially, the reformers believed that political re-equalization would ameliorate social distress. *The Manufacturer's and Farmers' Journal* wrote, "The free people of Rhode Island have for more than forty years submitted to a species of government, in theory, if not always in practice, as despotic as that of the autocrat of the Russias."

In 1821, the General Assembly turned the matter over to town meetings, but farmers in the state's rural South and West voted against holding a convention. Three years later, the legislature agreed to hold a convention; delegates were elected and met at Newport in June 1824. Nick, one of the four delegates representing Providence, pushed hard for the reapportionment of seats, but not for free suffrage. Although the convention's proposals were hardly revolutionary, agrarian South County prevailed and once again succeeded in preventing any greater voice for the northern, industrial part of the state.

The 1824 election of John Quincy Adams accentuated such discord on the national level: his followers refused to share power. They ignored landholders in favor of urban and manufacturing interests who strongly advocated for protective tariffs. So Adams's opponents created a new "Country Party" that attracted a hodge-podge of individuals, even former foes, united in the conviction that at least a disciplined party was the better route to political power. The Country Party leader Elisha Potter was particularly displeased with President Adams's mismanagement of American trading privileges in the British West Indies. He moved firmly into Andrew Jackson's camp, taking along his close friends Nick, Tom, and John Brown Francis. In this most convoluted fashion—and in direct contradiction of his most fundamental beliefs and principles—Nick Brown, the former ardent Federalist, thus became for a time a Jacksonian Democrat.

Nick did so just as James DeWolf withdrew from politics. His nephew George DeWolf's Cuban sugar crop failed in 1825, so he could not reimburse his London banker who, in turn, collapsed to the tune of $700,000. When DeWolf's creditors swooped in, George and his family managed to escape Bristol in the dead of night, leaving a trail of spectacular insolvencies—and ultimately the port's demise. James DeWolf resigned his seat in the General Assembly but—having diversified into manufacturing, banking, insurance, and transportation—survived handsomely. Most men of Bristol, however, were forced to seek work on whaling ships in the Pacific, or to move their families out West.

As the 1828 Presidential election soon loomed, many Rhode Island voters "trimmed their sails to catch the Jackson breeze," turning the state's Jacksonian Democratic Party into a "curious amalgam of local machinations by obscure politicians." But the Adams incumbents, supported by many of Rhode Island's new industrialists who believed that Adams would zealously enforce protection,[55] demonstrated considerable ability in defending their interests. The election took place in an atmosphere of deep sectionalism and animosity. Adams easily carried Rhode Island; only one electoral vote went to Jackson in all of New England. But Jackson won everywhere else, repeating Thomas Jefferson's landslide twenty-eight years earlier against a previous Adams. For the first time since the Presidential election of 1800, Nick found he had voted for the winning candidate.

Locally, the realignment of political parties caused by the election of 1828 brought voter suffrage agitation once again to the fore. If the "aristocrats" would not grant a new, reformed Constitution, then the people

---

[55] When President Adams visited Rhode Island on a Sunday in October 1828, he was received with "as much attention and pomp as could be expected on the Lord's Day" and given a vote of confidence by the General Assembly. But, contrary to Harvard, Brown University did not confer upon him an honorary degree.

of Rhode Island would write their own. Between March 14th and 28th of 1829, demonstrators marched in Pawtucket and Providence. Their leaders were Seth Luther, a Providence carpenter, and William Tillinghast, a Providence barber. Luther would go on to found in 1832 the "New England Association of Farmers, Mechanics and Other Workingmen," America's first workingman's organization and Tillinghast would declare, "The Jackson Party which is truly Democratic in other states does not know what a set of landed aristocrats their brethren in Rhode Island are . . . but I am determined to expose them." At first, the two men avoided radical action, undertaking instead a letter writing campaign to national and local political figures—most did not even bother to reply.

Predictably, the honeymoon between Jackson and his new-found Rhode Island supporters was brief. The new President soon recognized the support of Elisha Potter's Country Party and rewarded it accordingly. But the constant jockeying for power made federal patronage difficult to implement. Rhode Island's political leaders being ambitious men who used local issues to increase their influence. Jackson's autocratic distribution of the state's political spoils soon alienated Democrats who had so recently supported him. By the 1829 Congressional elections, Rhode Island's Democrats began disassociating themselves from the person of the President and sent National Republican representatives to Washington. Rhode Island politics needed a fresh new champion; both parties turned to Nick's son-in-law, John Brown Francis.

The only surviving child of Uncle John's eldest daughter Abby and Philadelphian John Francis, John Brown Francis had been raised in his grandfather's mansion, then entered Brown University in 1804 at age 13. After graduation he had worked for a few months at Brown & Ives, but concluded that the mercantile business was not his strength. He then enrolled in the Tappan Reeves Law School, but never took the bar. It was only at his mother's death in 1821, when he inherited Uncle John's lovely seven hundred acre waterfront property in Warwick *Spring Green*, that he discovered his true vocation as a gentleman farmer. So, in 1822 when he proposed to his second cousin, Nick's daughter Ann Carter Brown, he was the New England version of a landed aristocrat.[56] That same year he became Secretary of the Rhode Island Society for the Encouragement of Domestic Industry, which provided a platform to advance his public life. Soon after, he won a seat in the Rhode Island General Assembly.

A man with the potential to exert strong, conciliatory leadership in a time of high partisan emotion, John Brown Francis came close to the modern notion of a "dream candidate." He sympathised openly with landowners but was also a member of the state's leading merchant family. Might he thus bridge the longstanding divide between country and town interests? A man of genuinely liberal principals, John Brown Francis disdained attacks on the private character of others and—remarkably for the times—had managed to avoid such attacks himself. Though only thirty-seven years old in 1829, his prematurely white hair (which gave his piercing blue eyes an even greater intensity) lent him an appearance of gravitas considerably beyond his years.

Francis advocated creating a truly liberal party: "Why should we be chained down neck and foot to the prospects of Clay or Jackson? For one, I must protest against these party fetters." Thus, when Governor James Fenner threatened to retire as Governor in 1829 (he subsequently had a change of heart and was re-elected to a further two years), both National Republicans and Democrats courted Francis enthusiastically to run for Governor. Demurring then, he finally ran as a Democrat in 1833.

While John Brown Francis hesitated, Rhode Island politics were rocked by an anti-elitist wave that was sweeping the nation: the Anti-Masons. For nearly a century, the Freemasons had provided many Americans with social advancement and learning (Andrew Jackson was a Freemason, as had been virtually every one of the Founding Fathers). But now the middle classes felt that membership in any exclusive fraternity—particularly one as secretive as the Freemasons—conflicted with good citizenship. Opposition to Freemasonry was taken up by churches as a sort of religious crusade. Soon, shrewd political leaders capitalized on strong anti-Masonic feelings by creating vigorous new parties to

---

[56] Nick's daughter was marrying "true gentry"—well after those considerations had ceased to matter!

oppose Jackson. By 1829, the Anti-Masons had broadened their issue base to include championing internal improvements and protective tariffs, but remained staunchly independent of the National Republicans.[57] Instead, they fielded their own presidential candidates.

The Anti-Mason movement resonated in Rhode Island where anti-elitism was on the rise. Since so many legislators were Freemasons, Rhode Island politics were thrown into two years of chaos. When John Brown Francis finally did run for Governor in 1833, he did not escape the usual dose of acrimony. The Brown family was accused of belonging to a "silk stocking aristocracy that felt nothing but disgust for democracy." Elisha Potter countered by proclaiming that the Browns had "done more to promote the interests of the state, and the town of Providence, then any 10 families in it." True to form, Nick and Tom proffered advice and staunch support from behind the scenes. On March 20, 1833, Tom wrote to his nephew: "As for the report that the Rich men of Providence will all go against you—if true, it will aid you in the country, as you must be considered the head of the farming country interest. . . . I cannot judge myself having been so long estranged from Political parties in the State."

Although the son and grandson of Freemasons, John Brown Francis won handsomely and brought a Democrat majority to the General Assembly on his coat tails. Francis's election vividly illustrated how individual personalities could supersede political parties in Rhode Island. The Democrats were successful in spite of the President's policies rather than because of them. Francis went on to be re-elected annually until 1838.

Francis immediately set to work healing rifts. A symbolic reconciliation took place in June 1833 when Andrew Jackson visited Providence and Newport as part of a New England tour. The President was greeted by ninety-five-year old Moses Brown who "thee and thou'd him in Quaker manner and insisted he visit the Friends' School. . . . [Jackson]

---

[57] Henry Clay was also a Freemason.

complimented the aged philanthropist upon retaining his physical and mental faculties to so great an age."[58]

John Brown Francis's greatest challenge was to keep a lid on the growing suffrage movement. Eager to maintain its rural supporters, Rhode Island's Jacksonian Democrat leadership encouraged the *status quo*. John Brown Francis wrote to Democratic Party political leader Elisha Potter that his "warm and powerful friends in Providence" (the Browns and the Ives) would expect rural South County's political leader to suppress attempts in the Legislature to extend the suffrage. As a major property owner, he was convinced that landholders would be annihilated if the vote were granted to all men. The freehold qualification guaranteed that "those who possessed the right [of property ownership] should possess the power to protect it." It also ensured that those who had a permanent interest in the prosperity of the state should control its affairs, as opposed to the "unstable population of factory towns."

In December 1831, popular agitation resurfaced when Thomas Doyle launched the Rhode Island branch of the New England Association of Farmers, Mechanics, and Other Workingmen to push for a 10-hour workday. Then, in 1834, it was a member of the elite who came forward to lead the campaign for a Rhode Island constitution: Thomas Wilson Dorr.

Articulate and energetic, the son of China-trader Sullivan Dorr, Harvard-educated Thomas Dorr was also interested in education reform and abolition. Following his election to the General Assembly, Dorr managed to organize a new convention in September 1834 under the guise of assembling to protest Jackson's financial policies. Nick's old nemesis James DeWolf was elected president. Claiming to be non-partisan, he said he was motivated purely by his disapproval of Jackson.

The 1834 Constitutional Convention proved an even greater fiasco than the one in 1824. Almost all participants conceded that it was unfair for Providence to pay two-thirds of all taxes yet have only four representatives in the Assembly. But no one could agree on extending the franchise. Unable even to reach a quorum, the delegates departed without

---

[58] Jackson was presented with a degree from Harvard (to the fury of John Quincy Adams) but, once again, Brown University did not extend the same honor.

submitting anything to voters. Governor John Brown Francis had promised to introduce "improvements" only if sanctioned by public opinion;
now he did not "deem it a misfortune that the mass the yeomanry were so
averse to all change." Francis admitted that "The old party lines are now
entirely demolished. . . . Who is to rule the roost?" Rhode Island's elites
recognized that society was facing unpredictable and painful change. But
they sought to avoid "precipitate acts" that would disrupt the "stability
of our institutions."

Nick derived great satisfaction from his son-in-law's efforts to infuse
Rhode Island politics with much-needed calm and conciliation. But
as John Brown Francis was settling into office, yet another anti-elitist
campaign was gaining strength on the national scene, one which was to
have profound consequences for Rhode Island interests and for Nick in
particular: President Jackson's crusade against the National Bank.

Among Andrew Jackson's many iconoclastic views, two stood out:
his deep anti-clericalism, and his opposition to almost any form of borrowing. Frustrated that churches and banks lay outside his reach, he set
out to destroy the institution which embodied his prejudice against the
American financial system: the Second Bank of the United States. Under
its third president Nicholas Biddle (clearly resented by Jackson not merely
as a banker but as a rival fount of power), it had evolved into a powerful
institution that produced sound national credit and currency. Rhode
Island's mill-owners supported the Bank as the guarantor of a healthy
national economy, none more so than Nick. But as banks throughout the
nation prospered and proliferated, a vocal undercurrent of anti-banking
sentiment grew commensurately. In direct opposition to a pro-Bank
Congress, Jackson claimed the Bank was corrupt and dangerous to
American liberties. He vetoed the Bank's charter in 1832 and withdrew
all federal deposits in 1833, placing them in twenty-three private banks
controlled by Jacksonian Democrats (known as "Jackson's Pet Banks").

With no effective National Bank in control, government funds rapidly ended up in the hands of Western land speculators, launching an
inflationary spiral. Fearing for the safety of government funds, Jackson's

advisors pushed in 1836 for a "Specie Circular" that would require land to be purchased only with silver or gold. A run on hard currency resulted. Still, Biddle purposefully aggravated the financial crisis by calling in loans and refusing to grant new credit. The Senate censured Jackson. For a moment, it seemed that his downfall was imminent.

An extraordinary and wholly unrelated event then tipped the scales of popular opinion back in Jackson's favor. On January 30th, 1835, Richard Lawrence, a deranged English immigrant, tried to shoot President Jackson at point blank range on the Capitol steps. His two pistols both misfired, Jackson was unscathed, and Americans rallied behind the President. Within a year, the economy recovered its equilibrium, and Biddle simply ran out of ammunition. By the end of his second term, Jackson had won the Bank War. In reality, the victory was pyrrhic at best as the economic dislocation it caused would endure for almost a decade—well past the end of Nick's life.

The Bank War was particularly traumatic for Rhode Island's textile industry; it depended heavily on bank credit. As noted by Senator Asher Robbins, times were tough "not by the action of fortune or the perils of business with a miscalculation of folly or imprudence, but by the gratuitous and unnecessary act of [our] own Executive Government." Popular suspicion of the banking sector was rife in Rhode Island. In tough times, the public needed a scapegoat and bankers were an obvious target. The number of banks in Rhode Island had doubled over the past two decades, while capital loans and circulation had increased threefold. Many banks engaged in highly speculative activities and discounted paper of dubious origins. An 1826 review of Rhode Island's banking system revealed it to be fragile, with insufficient real capital. A commission finally was appointed in 1836 by the General Assembly to investigate complaints of excessive interest charges (some banks exacted payments of eighteen percent). Thomas Dorr was among the commission members who recommended the reforms enacted in the Bank Act of June 1836—the first such comprehensive reform in the United States. The legal interest rate would be fixed at 6 percent; the minimum capital required to charter a bank would be $50,000 (half from actual shareholders); directors could serve on only one board at a time; and every director must now swear fidelity to this new law or pay a $1,000 fine.

As major shareholders in the Providence Bank, Brown & Ives were incensed. They had already contested the relatively mild Bank Act of 1822, claiming (unsuccessfully) that the government could not tax both capital and shares. In 1836, Moses Brown Ives (who had replaced his father as the Providence Bank's President) lost no time in seeking legal counsel and confirmed that the Bank Act violated the Bill of Rights. Nick was tempted to carry the suit all the way to the Supreme Court. He even sought the advice of the great Daniel Webster who agreed that the oath was unconstitutional. But the people of Rhode Island seemed arrayed against all bankers and were "displaying a powerful excitement which pervades the community." One by one, other Rhode Island banks agreed to administer the oath to their directors. The Providence Bank stood alone. Nick realized that the public had misunderstood his motives and believed he was arrogating to himself "peculiar privileges" beyond the control of the law. Resorting to litigation over the Bank Act would merely invite legislative action adverse to the Providence Bank. Reluctantly, Brown & Ives decided to comply with the oath and to bide their time. Nick did not live to see the Act repealed.

With tariffs no longer a major topic of debate and the Bank War lost, the National-Republicans were out of arguments on the national stage. Their only recourse was to build a new party organization, using newspapers and inventive campaign techniques to increase voter turnout. So Henry Clay announced the formation of the Whig Party. Initially ridiculed as a reconstitution of the old Federalist Party, its supporters could agree only on opposing Jackson, that dangerous maverick on horseback who purged his opponents, vetoed internal improvements, and prevented modernization. But soon, Southerners who hated Jackson's power grabs and even some Anti-Masons joined the Whig ranks in supporting Clay's "American System."

Economic issues came to play a central role in party politics. Increasingly, those who felt threatened by the prospect of economic change supported the Democrats, and those committed to promoting economic development supported the Whigs. The Democrats wanted America to remain predominantly agricultural, but the Whigs envisioned a nation where agriculture's importance was equalled by that of commerce and industry. The Whigs gradually evolved a coherent belief in growth-oriented money policy, internal improvements funded by public land sales, and a social system built on public schools, private colleges, charities, cultural institutions—all wrapped in the moral overtones of a Protestant religious revival.

Andrew Jackson left office in 1836 wildly popular thanks to his backwoods past and appeal to the "everyman." He was succeeded by his Vice President, Martin Van Buren, who won with a meagre 50.9 percent of the popular vote. Indeed, by the time Van Buren finally achieved his life-long dream of the Presidency, Democrat majorities had disappeared in the South and West. Meanwhile, the Whigs began to do well in state elections.

Van Buren defined his public life in terms of party loyalty and limited government. He understood about seizing important new trends, particularly broadening the franchise, and a communications revolution[59] that now made political information widely available. He continued along the trajectory set by Jackson: endorsing popular sovereignty, opposing both a national bank and national economic planning, promoting continental expansion, and protecting slavery. But "The Little Magician," so adept at gaining power, soon demonstrated that he was ineffectual at wielding it.

Within a year of his taking office, the "Panic of 1837" was caused by a combination of factors: America's chronic capital shortage and dependence on the foreign purchase of treasury bills, a huge trade imbalance (imports had risen 250 percent under Jackson to $180 million, while exports and carrying trade totalled only $134.3 million), and a poor English harvest (Britain called in its loans to pay for imported grain). If the Bank of the United States had still been in existence, it could have

---

[59] Samuel Morse was busy working on the telegraph in the 1830s and 1840s, while new roads, canals and soon railroads greatly improved the dissemination of mail and newspapers.

intervened to assure a favorable balance of trade for the country. Instead, the country was inundated by a flood of foreign goods. The U.S. balance of payment deficit more than tripled in size, and $15 million in specie was drained to Europe. The weak American financial system could not withstand the pressure.

Another contributing factor to the crisis was Henry Clay's January 1837 "Surplus Revenue Bill" that distributed $37 million of surplus federal revenue from tariffs and land sales to state governments for infrastructure projects (Rhode Island received $386,611). Suddenly, the private banks which held federal government funds were required to come up with huge sums of cash; many lost their entire reserves. Then, in 1838, the world price of cotton collapsed due to a glut in Liverpool, England. This time the economy went into free fall.

America fell into a deep depression that would last seven long years (and so outlive Nick), a depression second in severity only to the Great Depression of 1929. Ironically, Rhode Island's banks were saved by the very anti-banking spirit that had started the financial sector's woes. The stringent 1836 Bank Law, which had forced many institutions to restructure and recapitalize, allowed the state to survive the financial crisis. Still, many Rhode Islanders blamed it on speculators, those who sought wealth without having to labor for it—"destroying men's souls" in the process.

The depression gave the Whigs a new lease on life and two clear goals: to rescue the country from executive tyranny and to restore prosperity. *The Providence Journal* noted in 1838 that "Rhode Island was the first state in the Union to acquire the memorable distinction of breaking loose from the company of Van Buren." Many people placed their hopes instead in William Henry Harrison, an erudite and distinguished Virginia gentleman who had been the hero of several battles against the Native Americans (Fallen Timbers in 1794, Tippecanoe, and Thames in 1813); he also represented the Northwest Territory in Congress and served as Governor of the Indiana Territory for twelve years before moving to the larger Ohio political stage. Harrison "claimed for the Whigs the toga of Roman virtue" by promising to exercise executive restraint, to serve only one term, and to use the veto sparingly.

Back at home in Rhode Island, Nick changed camps and became a Whig, as did James DeWolf. The Jackson administration had provided only one important benefit to Brown & Ives: compensation for ships lost almost thirty years earlier. In March 1830, the United States and Denmark agreed to a mixed commission to adjudicate the claims of American merchants who had suffered seizures of ships and cargoes during the Napoleonic wars; in July 1831, the United States and France signed a similar treaty. Both processes took several years but in 1836 Brown & Ives received a windfall $203,869 for the losses of *Hope, Robert Hale, Isis,* and *Argus* as well as for their shares in other captured ships (all long since written off their books).

Since the farmers and landholders who controlled the General Assembly opposed the increase in public spending required by the "American System," Rhode Island's Whigs remained in the opposition. But when John Brown Francis refused to do more than criticize Jackson's campaign against the Bank, the Whigs accused him of being a "pitiful, office hunting Anti-Mason" who "delight[ed] in cultivating [his] patrimonial acres and in sitting under the shade of their patrimonial trees." In response, he publicly revealed his financial condition; indeed, his assets were small in comparison to those of his Brown relatives, yet sufficient to place him beyond the influence of banking magnates in Providence.

Even though the Rhode Island Whigs soon began advocating for reapportioning the Legislature and widening the franchise, Thomas Dorr decided to form a separate "Constitution Party" in 1836 to push for reform. The new party attracted a diverse following that included labor leader Seth Luther, but never gained more than 10 percent of the vote. Frustrated by Dorr's third party activities, the Whigs expelled him. He was snapped up by the Democrats who saw an opportunity to expand their reach. But none of the would-be reformers could agree on what changes to make: Democrats wanted to include immigrants but not African-Americans[60]; Whigs were prepared to expand the vote to African-Americans but not new immigrants. No one wanted the "property-less

[60] Elisha Potter, the Democrat leader, controlled all the votes of his debtors and borrowers from his banks.

rabble." These factory workers, in turn, realized that Rhode Island's elite needed their services but were not prepared to treat them as equals.

At seventy-one years old in 1840, Nick felt the situation sufficiently grave to participate formally one last time in the political process. On December 3rd, he was driven to Bristol by his son John Carter "in his Stanhope" to cast his vote as a Presidential elector for William Henry Harrison. His candidate won the election by a landslide, with 80 percent voter turnout. Tragically, the promise was dashed almost instantly: Harrison died within a month of his inauguration from pneumonia caught while delivering his inaugural speech without an overcoat.

By a quirk of fate, the first Vice President to thus reach the Presidency through death of the incumbent was far from suited for the job. The far better qualified Henry Clay had lost the Whig presidential nomination to Harrison because of a February 1839 Senate speech advocating toleration for the evils of slavery (lest its disappearance devastate the American economy); he had then refused the Vice Presidency in a fit of pique and with the fateful words, "I'd rather be right than President." So it was that John Tyler, also a Virginian "Tidewater aristocrat" (and at fifty-one, the youngest President to date), succeeded to the White House. A dedicated Old Republican and faithful disciple of Thomas Jefferson, Tyler had joined the Whig Party only to protest Jackson's policies on Nullification and the Bank. He lost no time showing his true colors. Eager to be elected President in his own right in 1844, Tyler needed first to dislodge Clay from the leadership of the Whig Party. He therefore vetoed any measure proposed by the Whigs to save the US economy. By September 1841, just as Nick made his exit from this world, the entire cabinet resigned in protest and Tyler was expelled from the Whig Party (the only time in history when a sitting President has been ousted from his own party). He responded by purging Whig appointees and replacing them with "States' Rights" Democrats.

In Rhode Island, the franchise debate was now ready to explode in violent confrontation. It did so in October of 1841.[61]

---

[61] The timing, in fact, caused a significant delay in settling Nick's estate.

Having given up all hope of changing the state's constitution through legislative measures in the General Assembly, Thomas Dorr and his supporters embarked upon the chain of events that would become known to history as the "Dorr Rebellion" or "Dorr War." A remarkably bloodless episode, it nonetheless culminated in precisely the sort of mob behavior, demagoguery, defiance of the forces of law and order, and even armed confrontation that Nick had so feared. A so-called "People's Charter" was carried by a state-wide referendum (of questionable legality). Rival parallel elections were convened and Dorr was actually "elected" for a brief moment as a parallel Governor. In the end, the "Charterite" forces of law and order (who supported maintaining the 1663 Charter) carried the day under the leadership of their Governor, Stephen King. Dorr's resolve faltered at the critical moment and his supporters lacked the stomach for armed confrontation. The rebellion thus fizzled out before the Federal forces requested by Governor King were needed and, from Boston, Roman Catholic leaders played a role in restraining the Irish immigrants who might have added fuel to the flames.

The final outcome was a new Constitution, enacted early in 1843, framed by an alliance of Whigs and rural Democrats—John Brown Francis prominent among them—calling themselves the "Law and Order Party." It was a compromise measure which Nick would have approved of heartily. The franchise was extended to all free men, black as well as white, but not to naturalized citizens for whom the old property qualification was retained. Most of the urban immigrant population was still effectively excluded. In the General Assembly, the House (but not the Senate) was re-organized to afford greater representation to urban areas. Thus, behind an appearance of change, the status quo was preserved. It would be another forty-five years before immigrants finally received the vote in Rhode Island.

As a result of the "Dorr War," abolition was driven off the political agenda. The abolitionists' early support for Dorr evaporated after his white immigrant supporters insisted on the exclusion of free blacks from the expanded franchise proposed by the "People's Charter." The "Law and Order" Party lost no time exploiting that opportunity and gave free blacks the right to vote in the new Constitution.

But the underlying issues did not disappear. Many people were left with a profound sense of pessimism about the possibility of a free and just society; social divisions based on class, religion and ethnicity seemed unalterable. Despite the extension of the franchise, the turnout of qualified voters in Rhode Island remained the lowest of any northern state. Yet the pace of immigration continued to increase; by the 1850s, one-fifth of Rhode Island's population was foreign, and two-thirds of those immigrants were Irish (in Providence, the ratio was one in four). From the 1860's, the Irish were joined each decade by a new group of immigrants: first French Canadians, then Southern Italians, and then Portuguese—first from the mainland and then from the Azores. In response and for a brief period before the Civil War, a new anti-Irish and anti-Catholic movement took hold of state politics: the "Know-Nothing Party." Eventually, the issue of slavery would dominate public affairs and the Know-Nothings would be integrated into the new Republican party of Abraham Lincoln.

Thus, at the twilight of Nick's life, American politics were yet again in an uproar and partisanship was rife. The economy was stagnant. For all Jackson's populist rhetoric and claims to represent the common man, disparities in wealth were greater and the lot of the industrial worker worse than ever before. Economic hardship was spawning xenophobia and anti-Catholicism. Shortly before his death in 1836, Uncle Moses wrote to his son and son-in-law, "America is a young country grown old in Party Divisions and Annimosities." As he approached the end of his life, Nick doubtless shared this doleful opinion. He had done his part to fight partisanship and to uphold the Federalist cause, but that task proved impossible in the face of American society's vast transformation. Around him, society seemed much less harmonious than in the days of his youth; then, socio-economic relations were still based on precisely those mutual rights and obligations between superiors and subordinates in which he so fervently believed.

Narragansett Bay

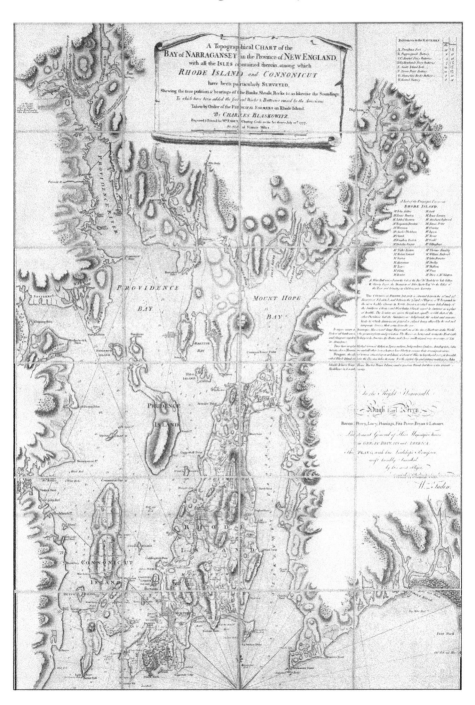

The Colonial Years

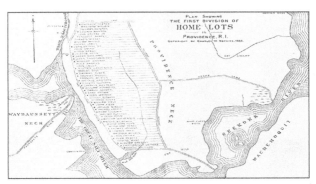

The first home lots in Providence

John Brown (1736–1803)

Moses Brown (1738–1836)

America's first product label

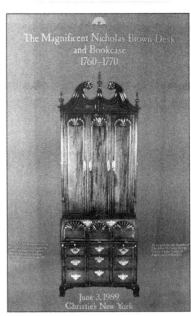

*The poster for the Christie's sale
of the Nicholas Brown desk*

The Colonial Years

The First Baptist Meeting House (1775)

University Hall (1791)

Uncle Joseph's house on Main Street (1774)

Uncle John's mansion on the hill (1788)

Slater Mill (1791)

The New Republic

Nicholas II by Chester Harding (1836)

Thomas Poynton Ives (1769–1835)

Nicholas II by Thomas Sully (1847)

The Nightingale-Brown House (1792)

Brown & Ives's ship Eliza

The New Republic

Nicholas Brown III (1792–1859)

John Carter Brown (1797–1874)

Ann Brown's daughters,
Abby and Anne in 1832

Sophia Augusta Brown (1825–1909)

Industrial Providence (1850's)

The Gilded Age

Sophia Augusta Brown holding
her grandson, John Nicholas
Brown II in 1900

John Nicholas Brown (1861–1900)

Natalie Dresser Brown and
son, John Nicholas II

The Providence Public Library (1900)

Harbour Court (1906)

The John Carter Brown Library (1904)

The XXth Century

John Nicholas Brown II (1900–1979)

Richard Neutra's Windshield
House (1938)

Nicholas VI and Diane Vernes Brown

John and Anne Brown with
their three children, Nicholas,
John Carter and Angela

J Carter Brown III (1934-2002)

Family Tree

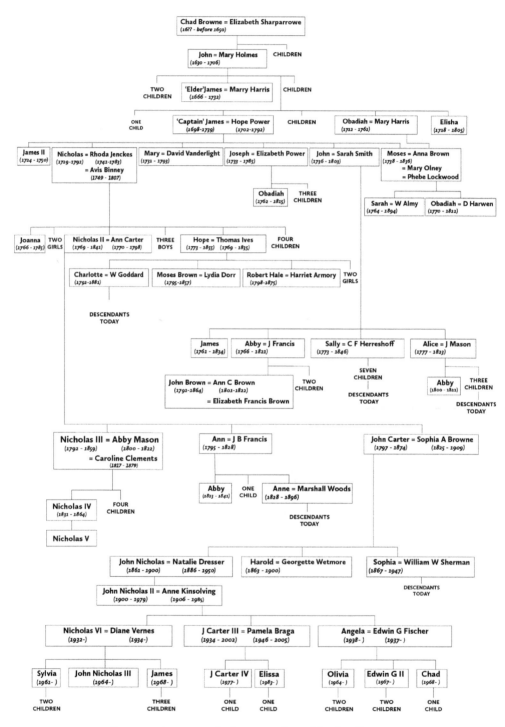

For more images and a large version of the family tree,
go to www.grapplingwithlegacy.com/gallery

CHAPTER 10

THE HAVE AND THE HAVE-NOTS

*"A man who tells you that the great Author of our
existence designed that the many should be poor
and miserable, in order that the few may roll and
riot in splendid luxury, would pick your pocket
if he had a good opportunity." —Seth Luther*

Despite his reputation as a champion of the "have-nots," Andrew Jackson paid scant attention to the dispossessed. To be fair, almost no one at the time regarded the state as an engine of social intervention or "welfare." It is nonetheless ironic that the Jacksonian Era witnessed a marked increase in the numbers of urban poor, especially African-Americans, factory workers, and immigrants. Through the 1820s and 1830s, when America achieved greater material abundance and a higher standard of living, the numbers of property-less workers and artisans with no hope of financial independence rose at an even greater rate. The white middle classes reacted with a mix of sympathy and fear. Some led reform movements to solve social ills; some felt threatened and reacted with violence. This matter was to increasingly preoccupy Nick in the later part of his life.

When the American Revolution did away with monarchy, many ordinary Americans believed it heralded a golden age of egalitarianism where "no one was really better than anyone else." In the early nineteenth century, growing commercial opportunities converted social mobility into a scramble. In one generation, paternalistic relationships were replaced by the contractual-voluntary, explicit, and often impersonal. When the continental and state revolutionary governments issued five hundred million dollars in paper money, people who had hitherto dealt only in barter were able to participate in the economy. Paper money liberated plain and "middling" men from patronage dependencies. As a result, America's entrepreneurial activity shifted from the hundreds of well-to-do creditor merchants of the colonial era who had dominated the overseas trade on the Atlantic seaboard, to thousands upon thousands of ordinary small traders and market farmers who transacted with each other all over America. The way people connected to one another changed forever. New opportunities in industry, banking, infrastructure, and Western lands now were open to anyone.

Yet America's new egalitarianism was full of contradictions. People promoted republican values of productivity and frugality, but still aspired to gentility and leisure. While most Americans exulted in forsaking European snobbery, they also copied European forms of gracious living. Etiquette books became hugely popular, but said nothing about working harder and better. Americans yearned for social and cultural homogeneity, yet unwittingly perpetuated a heterogeneous and stratified society. In Rhode Island the feudal concept of primogeniture (all inheritance to the eldest son) was maintained; only firstborn sons of freemen could vote upon coming of age.

Of the myriad forces that transformed society in the early Republic, urbanization and industrialization most marked the growing gap between the "have" and the "have-not." In the years between 1820 and 1850, the country's urban population multiplied fivefold. Urban life was far tougher than in the cities of Europe; New York's death rate was twice that of London. Sanitation was abysmal, epidemics were rife. Many large cities lacked running water; people still dug wells in their back yards despite contamination from outhouses. Authorities allowed hogs and geese to eat garbage in back alleys. Stray dogs, rats, and vultures abounded. It was not unusual to see a sign warning, "Unattended infants are in danger of being eaten." In Philadelphia or New York, the life expectancy of a new-born was only twenty-four years. Urban factories spewed their coal soot into the air. Although fire was a constant threat, fire companies were often operated by rival gangs who fought each other for the right to loot a burning building rather than to put out its flames. From his lodgings in New York, Crawford Carter wrote to his brother-in-law Nick:

> There has been one large fire; a number of smaller ones, and five hundred alarms of fire since I have been here. All we do in case of an alarm after we are in bed is just to reach the hand out of bed & feel the Wall; if it should be hot we get up, but if we should find it cool we turn over and go to sleep again; this is an established rule here.

When the Great Fire of December 16, 1825 broke out in New York, the fire brigades competed in showing off their prowess by pulling engines themselves rather than using horse or steam power. As a result, 674 structures were destroyed, including every remnant of early Dutch New Amsterdam.

Along with these environmental dangers, cities spawned a plethora of social ills. A New York diarist wrote in 1829, "The City is infested by gangs of hardened wretches . . . brought up in Taverns." Commercialized vice was big business in New York: over 10,000 prostitutes plied their trade in 1844. And yet the cities beckoned ever greater numbers. To foreign visitors such as Harriet Martineau who visited in 1837, America was full of "raw egotism, boastful men, demanding women and loud children."

As the birthplace of American industry, Providence was a microcosm of all these evils. Its population almost doubled in the thirty years following the Revolutionary War, from 6,400 inhabitants in 1790 to 11,800 in 1820, and then jumped to 17,000 in the following decade. During this period, two major calamities transformed the urban landscape: a fire and then a hurricane.

On January 21, 1801, a fire started at John Corliss's brick warehouse on
Towne Street and spread down the thoroughfare. Although sixty-three-
year old, Uncle Moses came galloping into Providence accompanied by
the fire-fighting apparatus he had perfected on his Elmgrove estate. He
arrived just in time to watch his own warehouses go up in flames. Every
able bodied man and boy turned out to fight the blaze. Several were even
posted on the roof of Uncle John's mansion to stamp out sparks as the
inferno crept up the hill. Meanwhile, Uncle Moses rode back and forth,
shouting orders through a megaphone. To stop the fire's advance, the
Clark & Nightingale warehouse was blown up, along with several older
houses. When the blaze finally was halted, thirty-seven buildings along
Towne Street lay in ruins: damages amounted to $300,000—10 percent
of the town's taxable property.

The warehouses and shops were soon rebuilt, and Towne Street was
renamed Main Street in 1807. Trade resumed, interspersed among the
dwellings and industrial plants: Zachariah Allen's distillery and sugar
house, the Dodge's silver shops (Seril made shoe buckles, Nehemiah
made gold rings and other fine jewelry), Clark & Nightingale's cooper
and blockmaker shops. A new highway, South Water Street, connected
the traditional town center at Market Square to points south. Cotton
mills sprang up just outside town in the Moshassuck, Woonasquatucket
and Pawtuxet river valleys.

The greatest amount of development took place on the "Weybosset
side" of town, directly across the Great Salt Cove from Main Street.
In the eighteenth century, the marshes and swamps of Weybosset had
been drained, the Cove partly filled in, and the reclaimed land settled
by new immigrants who were mostly laborers and artisans. Now, this
section of town was filled with dwellings, distilleries, rope houses, paper
mills, shipyards, slaughterhouses, and tan yards. The fine new Beneficent
Congregational Church was erected in 1809, the first to have a dome over
an octagonal base instead of a steeple.

The second great disaster to hit Providence started on the night of
September 22, 1815. The people of Rhode Island went to bed, little concerned about the typical seasonal storm that was looming. But during

the night, the wind increased and by dawn it was blowing from the East with hurricane force, lashing the waterfront and destroying much in its path. By noon, when the wind shifted to the southwest, the sun shone upon a scene of unprecedented destruction: water had risen to twelve feet above the high tide level. Two bridges were washed away and all the warehouses on both sides of the Great Salt Cove were severely damaged. At least twenty-seven ships lay scattered on its shores. Brown & Ives's great 520-ton ship *Ganges* had torn loose from her anchors, crashed into the bridge at Market Square, then hurtled through the Cove, her bowsprit piercing the upper story of the Washington Insurance Company building. Valuable cargo was lost, homes were carried off their foundations, tall steeples were dashed to ground, and the Second Baptist Meeting House was destroyed. Fortunately there was little loss of life.

Once again, much as they had after King Philip's War and the Fire of 1801, the people of Providence went to work rebuilding and starting afresh: "Nothing was ever the same after the Great Gale, but most everything was better." Decrepit structures on Main Street were pulled down and replaced with fifty brick buildings. The architect John Holden Greene designed many with granite facing bolted onto frames of heavy timbers, giving the center of town a more metropolitan look. Greene already had introduced the "Gothic Revival" style in 1811; his belfry to St. John's Episcopal Church was built out of local Smithfield stone. But over time, as Providence became enamored with the "Greek Revival" style, façades resembling Greek temples and Doric porticos sprung up all over town. Tom Ives's children chose a "Greek Revival" style when they married and moved into new homes.

The Weybosset Bridge was expanded for the sixth time in 1816, and connected to a new waterfront street built on filled land. Important new businesses were established on the Weybosset side of town, especially the Exchange Bank, the Providence Washington Insurance Company, and the monumental Arcade. Inaugurated in 1828, its 216-foot-long granite walls, 74-foot-wide porticos, and 21-foot-high columns—the largest in America, designed by Russell Warren and James Bucklin to imitate Napoleon's Greek Revival church of the Madeleine in Paris—were built by Cyrus Butler for $145,000. Butler struggled at first to attract shoppers away from the east side of Providence; indeed, the 78 shops of the Arcade stood empty. But when the fashionable milliner "Three Sisters" agreed to relocate to the Arcade, other tenants soon followed.

The *Providence Gazette* noted in September 1820, "There were 107 wagons of fruit and vegetables at the market, while six years before, 40 would have caused surprise." By 1825, the waterfront was dredged and fitted to allow deep-draft ships to berth in close to the shore against a sea wall of cut granite blocks. Industry moved northwest of the (much reduced) Great Salt Cove to the banks of the Moshassuck River. There, tan yards, slaughterhouses, and distilleries as well as paper, chocolate, and fulling mills (to wash wool cloth) dumped their waste into the water. Construction of the Blackstone Canal also led to public improvements: new streets, a boat basin and tidal lock, and two bridges (many funded in 1829 by the Providence Washington Insurance Company which Brown & Ives controlled). By 1837, all tidal land was filled in and stone walls were erected along the Providence River.

By 1832, Providence was the leading metropolis of southern New England. India Point, Uncle John's former dockyard, was chosen in 1835 for the new Boston and Providence Railroad terminal. There, passengers were met by steamboats on regular runs to Newport and New York. John Brown Francis bought a large house in the neighborhood that originally had been built by James Mason in 1810 (he had married Uncle John's youngest daughter Alice). Francis converted it into a three-story hotel known as Tockwotton Hall, Providence's seventh hotel. The public flocked to the hotel simply to gawk at the comings and goings of the first railway travelers.

But as India Point evolved from dockyard to rail yard, overcrowded tenements sprung up around Uncle John's former warehouses. Slums also appeared north of the Cove at "Snowtown" where a cluster of shacks built on posts in the sand became home to many free blacks. Congestion was apparent all over town. People lived two or three families to a house, and many families included eight or ten members. Homes were modest: only one white family in ten lived in a house worth more than $700, only one in a hundred lived in a house worth more than $3,000.

By 1812, the wealthier residents had moved up the hill on the east side of town, away from the crowds and incessant din of iron wheels on the paving stones of Main Street. Uncle John had led the way in 1788, soon followed by the Clark and the Nightingale families; their matching mansions, designed by John Holden Greene in 1789 and 1792, each occupied their own blocks on Benefit Street. The newfound prosperity of the early Republic was reflected everywhere in grand houses. Although the purer lines of the "Federal" style were already fashionable in many cities, the Providence elite still preferred the balanced and classically inspired "Georgian" style with its three-part symmetry and central doorways flanked by identically placed windows. But after living in Uncle Joseph's Georgian house on Town Street for a decade, Thomas and Hope Ives built their own brick house in 1806 in the delicate Federal style, adding a Corinthian porch and a classical balustrade. Inside, there was an oval-shaped back parlor and a *"tour de force"* (freestanding) staircase. They filled their new home with stylish furniture, including pieces inlaid with African ivory.

The 1810 Sullivan Dorr Mansion, also by John Holden Greene, included fashionable Gothic revival elements. Its drawing room walls were painted with Italian scenes. Black butlers wore a special livery of striped britches and black velvet jackets with brass buttons, white stockings, and slippers with large brass buckles. Born in Boston, Dorr had spent four years in Canton representing his family firm and other New England mercantile houses, including Brown & Ives, before settling in Providence in 1804.

On the next street over from the Ives House, Edward Carrington bought and enlarged the Corliss House in 1812. The delicate two-tier porch (reminiscent of galleried houses in the South) and helical main staircase were both unusual for Providence. After ten years of service as the U.S. consul in Canton, Carrington had married a China trade heiress, Loriana Hoppin, and decided to settle in Providence. With twenty-six ships on the seas, he could afford to fill his home with teakwood furniture and gold lacquer, and his large garden with exotic plants. The painted silk wallpaper in the back parlor was a present from a Hong merchant.

The captains and supercargoes reporting to his counting room were impressed by the Chinese lounging chair that stood inside the door.

In Thomas Halsey's 1801 home on Prospect Street, live terrapins were kept in the basement to prepare turtle soup. The Clark House—considered the most lavishly decorated in Providence—had wall-to-wall carpeting woven to look like a Highland plaid and covered in leopard skins, "looking glasses" (mirrors) from New York, a sofa and two "sophetts" covered in silk, and fashionable orange damask striped silk window curtains. Artificial flowers, orange trees, fringes, tassels, and a "tambour writing table" completed the look.

Mrs. Nightingale's house across the street was not deemed half so fashionably furnished and needed repairs. Yet it was precisely this house that Nick finally bought on August 18th, 1814. Years earlier, he could have built himself an imposing house on the hill in the new Federal style, one like Tom's mansion. Yet he had preferred to remain near his beloved wharves and warehouses. Elizabeth Nightingale fell on hard times after her husband's death in 1791, so in the depths of the 1814 wartime recession, Nick was able to buy the house, barns, stable, woodshed, and orchard for $16,000 (still a considerable sum when a fine federalist dwelling with elegant furnishings cost $3,000). Art historian Demian Hess described the Nightingale-Brown in an application to the National Register of Historical Places:

> Nicholas Brown II's conservatism, often disguised by Thomas Poynton Ives's business audacity, comes out in his choosing an old-fashioned house design and how long he took to move there—five years after Thomas Ives built his own much more fashionable brick house.

The Nightingale-Brown house had an entry parlor, dining room, kitchen, bedroom, and back dining room on the ground floor, with the same pattern of rooms repeated above. Its carved wood moldings represent the lingering Georgian taste. Mary Stelle Brown set about preparing their new home, although Nick would have been happy to continue using his old-fashioned colonial furniture from the old family house on Main Street. The Townsend-Goddard desk no longer reigned in a front parlor, but was placed in the "breakfast room."

As was the case with all wealthy homeowners in Providence, most of the live-in servants were people of color. In the years between 1790 and 1825, the free African-American population of Providence more than tripled to reach 1,414 in 1825. It formed a fairly homogenous group, one quite distinct from the poor and illiterate fugitives from the South who generally ended up in Boston (Providence was traditionally hostile to any stranger who risked becoming indigent and would require town charity). In the 1820s, half of black men lived in white homes where they were employed as servants. The remainder rotated through seafaring and land-based jobs. But by the 1830s, a property-owning skilled African-American artisan class slowly began to emerge. Within a decade, more than half of the people of color in Providence would own their homes and find work as grocers, bakers, draymen, shoemakers, and saloon keepers, or as servants living out.

Many worthy Providence townspeople viewed the growing autonomy of African-Americans almost as a form of deviance which must be brought into line. After all, did middle class ladies not need servants if they were to pursue charitable activities outside the home? In October 1830, a group of prominent men decided to solve the problem with a novel approach: financial incentives to overcome "habits of idleness and dissipation" among servants. The "Society for the Encouragement of Faithful Domestic Servants" launched with ninety-eight subscribers who each paid three dollars annually for access to servants it had vetted. Servants nominated for good conduct and continued service would receive "a handsome octavo Bible" or two dollars at the end of their first year of employment, with bonuses increasing up to ten dollars after five years (the equivalent of one month's wages for a cook, or six weeks for a housemaid). Fifty-five servants initially registered with the Society. Not surprisingly, the scheme did not endure.

Access to education or places of worship was of great concern to the African-American community. When Sarah Latham opened a "School for Blacks" in 1815, she was criticized for "making servants proud and less faithful." She had to explain that the school existed to inculcate correct morals as an essential service to the wider community, especially at a time when, in the words of William J. Brown,[62] "to drive a carriage, carry a market basket after the boss, and brush his boots, or saw wood and run errands, was as high as a colored man could rise." When better opportunities appeared in the 1830s, an African-American barber with his own shop was "considered the upper crust of the colored population," according to Brown. Even when racism was not openly manifested, paternalism was rife. As noted by Brown, "The white people seemed to be combined against giving us anything to do which would elevate us to a free and independent position. The kindest feelings were manifested towards us in conversation and that was all."

William J. Brown started work at age eight, but managed to piece together an education by attending Sabbath school before the start of the church service, as well as other schools "for colored youth" whenever teachers could be found. He apprenticed to a shoemaker and made enough to rent two rooms for forty dollars a year—a large dwelling for a family of six African-Americans. While he was growing up, the black community in Providence began establishing its own organizations for mutual support and defense: the African Union Meeting House and School in 1821, the Young Men's Union Friendly Society in 1828, a second black Masonic lodge in 1826 (the first had been founded in 1799), and the Black Temperance Society in 1832.

Rhode Island's woeful lack of public education was not just an issue for the African-American community; until 1828, no town other than Providence would fund public schools. In February 1799, the Providence

---

[62] Born in 1814, William Brown was the grandson of Cudge, one of the slaves owned jointly by Nicholas Brown and his three brothers. Two of Cudge's siblings, Thomas and Sharp, worked for Moses as teamsters on his farms. Following his manumission, Cudge purchased a lot on Olney street with funds from Moses, then worked for Thomas Ives. Born in 1781, his third child Noah had numerous extraordinary adventurers as a seaman before finally settling down with Alice Prophet from the Narragansett tribe (whose mother Chloe had purchased a black husband because "the treatment the Indian women received from the husbands they had purchased was so satisfactory that others were encouraged to follow their example"). William was Noah and Alice Brown's fourth child.

Association of Mechanics & Manufacturers and the city's shopkeepers joined prominent merchants in petitioning the Legislature for a state-funded system of public schools. They pointed out that, "Under a Republican form of government, liberty and security . . . depend on a general diffusion of Knowledge among the people." An ignorant people could only too easily be swayed by the "charms of an ambitious despot." After much debate, an "Act to Establish Free Schools" was passed in 1800. But the General Assembly refused to administer the school system directly and placed this responsibility on Rhode Island's towns (allowing them to keep 20 percent of their yearly tax quotas).

Farmers, who had little reason to favor schools that took away their children's labor and increased their taxes, simply refused to comply. Within three years, the Act to Establish Free Schools was repealed. Sunday schools in the mill towns became the only source of formal education outside of Providence (where the Town Meeting voted to take over Whipple Hall, the Brick Schoolhouse, and two other small schools). Even after a new free school act was voted in 1828, less than 45 percent of school age children attended school regularly. When a superintendent of schools finally was appointed in 1839, he reported that all the school buildings were "unfit for use in their present condition . . . either too small, too dilapidated, or too badly constructed to be worth rebuilding."

Rhode Island thus lagged behind the rest of the nation whose educational standards actually surpassed those of most Western European countries. Americans were motivated to be literate in order to conduct business; as a result, three-quarters of men could read and a slightly smaller percentage could write (female literacy, however, was much lower). The desire for learning was fueled by America's first "communications revolution." Even in Rhode Island, newspapers flourished, often subsidized by political parties. In 1814, Nick's father-in-law, John Carter, sold his printing business and the *Providence Gazette* to Hugh Brown (Nick's distant cousin) and William Wilson. Among the many newspapers published in Providence in the 1830s was the ancestor of today's *Providence Journal*, which started as the semi-weekly *Manufacturers' & Farmers' Advertiser* in 1820. Printed by Miller & Hutchens whose shop was in the "Old Coffee House" at Market Square where political and business affairs were conducted, it became a daily in 1829 as the *Providence Daily Journal and General Advertiser*. Support from the business elite allowed it to become "more enterprising in getting the news."

By 1820 (when the term *businessman* was first used), few if any in the North dared publicly to claim that they did not work for a living. But nowhere was the relationship to work more fundamentally transformed than in the textile mills of Rhode Island. In one generation, the quiet of nature and the rhythm of the seasons was replaced by "a world of precisely structured hours, close confinement and the noise of machinery." Hours were no shorter (5:00 a.m. to 7:00 p.m.) nor easier than on the farm. In fact, tasks needed to be performed more rapidly. Work became largely less physically exhausting but instead was unrelenting, intense, and much more numbing.

Initially, factory work had been welcomed as a means of providing employment to women and children. By 1832, 1,731 men, 3,297 women, and 3,472 children worked in Rhode Island's mills. Samuel Slater's first operatives were all children between the ages of seven and twelve. Since children had always contributed to family support, factory work seemed perfectly natural and even benign when compared to a farmer's life. Hard work made children virtuous: "Better to be overworked than to pine in sloth, rags and wretchedness." By 1831, three quarters of all American children under the age of twelve working in cotton mills were employed in Rhode Island.

A typical newspaper advertisement might read "Wanted. Families with not less than four children each to work in the mill." In 1812, an average mill worker's salary was seventy-five cents a week for six days of work; youths received forty-two cents. Wages began increasing in the 1820s when a family of six could earn a combined weekly income of eight dollars. Wages often were paid as vouchers in the company store or as rent in company tenements. Housing was marginally adequate at best. A typical four-family tenement accommodated thirty to thirty-five people, including twenty children. Once children were grown, parents were forced out to make room for new families. But mill families often stayed no more than a year, moving restlessly from one village to another, always on the lookout for a better situation.

Child labor would continue in Rhode Island long after it had ceased elsewhere in America. Rather than upgrade their equipment, mill owners would keep using obsolete machinery that could be tended by children. In contrast, the "Lowell method" pioneered by the Lowell brothers at by Waltham, Massachusetts, sought specifically to avoid creating a permanent factory class by recruiting thousands of single women to work before marriage. Despite its noble intentions, the Lowell method proved no more enlightened than the Slater approach. An 1839 *Boston Daily Times* editorial described "girls compelled to work in unhealthy confinement for too many hours every day. . . . [T]heir food both unhealthy and scanty, . . . they are crowded together in ill-ventilated apartments, and in consequence they become pale, feeble and finally broken in constitution." Yet for young women used to long hours on the family farm at no pay, the promise of $3.60 a week (with $1.50 deducted for room and board) compared very favorably to the dollar a week they could earn for live-in domestic work.

Indeed, factory salaries exceeded the pay of unskilled laborers such as canal workers, stevedores, and seamstresses. In 1835, workers received about $2.50 a week, still too little for a minimal standard of living when beef cost eight cents a pound, flour cost $4.50 a barrel, and a glass of beer in a tavern was three cents. However, a skilled artisan could earn 75 percent to 100 percent more, enough to purchase a modest dwelling.

The first textile mills owners found it difficult to recruit workers; popular fears about the industrial process were deep-rooted, as was a widespread distaste for the rigorous discipline required in a factory setting. Cottage spinners and weavers, who had always set their own hours and often held several jobs, were particularly resistant to the regimentation of the factory system. To avoid replicating the industrial slums of England, Almy & Brown created the first mill village in 1806 at Slatersville as a model community to house workers in rows of neat, sturdy cottages. Taking a paternalistic role, they provided a wide array of services: company stores, churches, and recreation halls were intended to promote a "wholesome" mill village life. Almy & Brown insisted on "sobriety," "faithfulness," "steady habits," and "correctness." But despite their owners' best efforts, mill villages often were viewed as hotbeds of immoral behavior (with some justification). Pawtucket, the first manufacturing community in America, developed the reputation of being a rowdy, riotous town.

Ironically, while the American middle classes advocated "making something of one's life," factory workers were fast losing control over their destinies. Everyone was gaining access to a host of new, cheap consumer products (inexpensive shoes finally differentiated between the left and right foot), but mass production was dehumanizing the workplace. Before industrialization, journeymen had worked independently or with others in small shops, directed by a master craftsman who supervised production for a local, custom-made market. At the beginning of the nineteenth century, every artisan's ambition was to become a master someday. Thirty-five years later, that dream was almost dead.

In the eighteenth century, there were almost no large employers in America—the 100 workers of the Hope Furnace were a rare exception. Now, many Rhode Island mills employed at least that number under one roof; in Massachusetts, some factories had eight hundred workers. The mechanization of work would fundamentally transform the United States: as tasks were broken into piecework and goods increasingly mass produced in factories, the means of production moved to the hands of capitalists. Substantial wealth and easy access to credit enabled them to contract for massive orders, while the size of their operations allowed them to cut prices below those fixed by masters and journeymen.

Faced with so many marketplace variables beyond their control, mill owners considered work hours and wages to be the only factors they could regulate to their advantage. Employees became factors of production, so working conditions reflected a general indifference to health, safety, and comfort. As a Fall River, Massachusetts mill foreman declared, "I regard my work people just as I regard my machinery. . . . When my machines get old and useless, I reject them and get new, and these people are part of my machinery." Little was done for the workers' safety or comfort. When the Rhode Island General Assembly finally voted in 1840 to require three months of schooling for all child factory workers, the law was roundly ignored.

Smaller "manufactories" (unmechanized factories that could be started up on a shoestring) also played havoc with the artisan system of production. To increase their profits, manufactories introduced the "sweating system," either demanding greater productivity from skilled workers or resorting to cheap labor: women, children or unskilled immigrants. Technological innovation only intensified the downward spiral. As the division of tasks grew more complex, artisans became piece workers. The boom-bust swings of immature corporate capitalism—coupled with long hours, low wages, unpredictable layoffs, and uncompensated industrial accidents—created a climate of economic uncertainty for all. Once steam engines and factory mechanization was introduced in the 1830s, unskilled workers could be employed in large numbers. Fear of unemployment kept them in line.

When skilled artisans complained, the courts accused them of "artificial interference with the natural operations of the free market . . . Pregnant with public mischief and private injury." In contrast, factory workers made few attempts at protest. Only in 1824, when Pawtucket mill owners announced an additional hour to the work day and a twenty percent reduction in wages to compete with smaller rural mills, did a hundred female weavers respond angrily that they would "abandon their looms unless allowed the old prices." A riot occurred the following day, so the mill owners resorted to a lockout. Two years later, the Providence Association of Workingmen was organized to secure a ten-hour day—with little success. The first trade union, a merger of separate journeymen societies, was launched in 1833 to push for a ten-hour workday (the law finally was implemented in Philadelphia in 1835 and became a federal statute in 1840). In Rhode Island, social forces were arrayed against organized labor. Immigrant workers squabbled incessantly among themselves: The French Canadian looked down on the Irish who, in turn, brought to America their ancestral family feuds. When workers did attempt to organize, the response was harsh: Andrew Jackson became the first presidential strike breaker, sending troops against canal workers in 1834. It was easier for a disgruntled factory worker simply to move out West (although the 1837 depression limited that option, too).

The first manufacturers wanted only highly trained artisans from England or Scotland, or else Protestant Irish weavers from Ulster. Almy & Brown initially avoided hiring immigrants, claiming they were "unsteady, not faithful and some of them very intemperate." But by the 1820s, they had no option but to employ the Irish laborers who had first arrived to work on the Erie, and later the Blackstone, Canals. More followed to build the Providence Railroad from 1831 to 1835, then stayed to work in the mills. Waves of Poles and Italians would come after the Civil War. All down the Eastern Seaboard, numbers of immigrants swelled from a trickle of 8,385 a year in 1820, to over one thousand a week by 1840.

Within Providence, the Fox Point neighborhood attracted large numbers of immigrants eager to work in its burgeoning factories and bustling harbor. A small group of Irish established Rhode Island's first Roman Catholic church in 1813. By 1827, there were two hundred Irish immigrants in Providence and four hundred Roman Catholics within a four-mile radius of Pawtucket, enough for Mass to be celebrated in the Old Town House. The Bishop in Boston was asked to send a resident priest. A year earlier, the Bishop had acquired land for a church in Newport for the many Irish laborers who built Fort Adams or worked in the coal pits at the northern end of Aquidneck Island; Christ Church on Temple Street finally was erected in 1834.

Most of the Irish immigrants could not afford to move out West, so they accepted jobs for very low pay. Since they owned no land, they could not vote in Rhode Island, so their rise to power was slow. There were too few Roman Catholics in Rhode Island in 1830 to elicit the nativism that would later characterize the state's politics. But from 1842, anti-Irish sentiment began to mount; immigrants were accused of producing "5/8th of the criminal business before our Municipal Courts, and the majority of the inmates of our Jail and Asylum and almost the entire rank and file of our street beggars."

Racial tensions ran high as the Irish competed for employment with trained black freemen. Though most factories refused to employ African-Americans, white artisans and laborers nevertheless feared that trained black freemen would take away their jobs for lower wages. Local newspapers were filled with reports about gangs of rowdy boys who set upon black pedestrians, loitered at street corners, disrupted evening Sabbath services. Sometimes daily harassment escalated into deadly violence. On the night of October 18, 1824, a mob decided to "punish" a group of African-Americans for not stepping off the sidewalk to allow whites to pass. It set fire to black homes on Addison's Row, off North Main Street in a neighborhood known as "Hardscrabble." The town watch did not intervene. By dawn, twenty houses had been destroyed or damaged—including property owned by Nick. During the ensuing trial, a defense attorney representing the ten indicted men claimed his clients had simply struck a blow for "the morals of the community" by demolishing a notorious nuisance that had long been "the resort of the most corrupt part of the black population." The case was dismissed.

Frightened, the citizens of Providence called for a central police agency. The town watch was increased by two hours each day and doubled from twelve to twenty-four men. But public disorder remained a problem. In September 1826, a memorial to the town council deplored "the alarming increase of the vice of Intemperance . . . the multiplication of common dram shops . . . and the introduction of new places of resort [and] amusement of different grades furnished with every variety of refreshments including strong liquors." The city's elite favored municipal incorporation as had happened in Boston. But the proposal failed to obtain the required 3/5ᵗʰ majority when it appeared on ballot in 1830; people once again feared increased taxes.

Then on the night of September 21, 1831, a brawl erupted between white sailors "on frolic to some house of ill fame" and black residents of "Snowtown" by Olney Lane (which had become filled with bars and brothels). This time, a white sailor was shot dead and the remainder driven off. The next night, a mob of white vigilantes returned to Olney Lane to strike at the source of "midnight revels, the succession of severe and bloody affrays and the frequent, bold and open riots." Four days of chaos ended only when the governor called in the state militia. Pelted with stones, the soldiers fired into the crowd, killing five. In the end, it took the Governor, the Sheriff, and four companies of state militia, complete with field artillery, to drive out the rioters. Eighteen houses lay in ruins and the "good people" of Providence were thoroughly frightened. Municipal incorporation, with an elected mayor who would be a "vigorous and efficient Executive Magistrate," empowered to detain "any dissolute person" was now unquestionably needed to replace the old town meeting system. Samuel Willard Bridgham, who had served as a Federalist in the General Assembly alongside Nick, was elected in June 1832 as the first mayor of Providence and served until his death in 1840. In his inaugural speech, he remarked that Providence had grown "too heterogeneous and unmanageable."

Indeed, all of America was struggling to keep its unruly growth in check. Urban rioting was spreading, incited by ethnic, religious, and racial animosities. Mobs and gangs were composed of mostly unconnected and anonymous people, full of class resentment, and were thus all the more frightening. Over a three-year period from 1834 to 1847, the entire United States was in the grip of "the present supremacy of mobocracy," according to the *Richmond Whig*. In January 1834, several factions of Irish canal workers brawled, followed in February by two volunteer fire companies in New York. In April, a Democrat mob looted a branch of the Bank of the United States in Portsmouth, New Hampshire. In the New York mayoral race of April 1834, the new Whig party challenged the Democrat "bullies" who kept the city in the control of Tammany Hall. Thousands poured into the streets; the mayor himself was clubbed to the ground (there was no professional police force in New York City until 1844). Philadelphia experienced race riots in August and election unrest in October. In November, there was an uprising of Irish railway workers in Baltimore. The most shocking incident was the burning of an Ursuline convent in Charlestown, Massachusetts in August 1834, an act of impromptu violence that reflected the growing discontent of the working classes and the extent of extreme anti-Catholic sentiment in New England.

The number of riots only increased the following year, 1835, in reaction to abolitionist campaigns in the South. New Yorkers (who depended on the cotton trade) generally opposed abolition. Out West, vigilantes took law enforcement into their own hands. In 1838, the young Illinois lawyer Abraham Lincoln commented that "accounts of outrages committed by mobs form the everyday news of the times." Many Americans, including Nick, felt that mob rule was a greater threat to liberty than any foreign tyrant. The quest for law and order became the concern not just of the factory owner who wanted a disciplined workforce, but of the ordinary man who feared simply walking in the street. Anxiety compelled people to find ways to tame the anarchic exuberance of the new nation. It was a far cry from the Founding Fathers' vision, instilled into Nick at a tender age and cherished by him ever after, of a close-knit society living in Christian harmony under the benign oversight of a patrician elite.

CHAPTER 11

THE BENEVOLENT EMPIRE

*"The new reformers wanted to imbue people not
with deference and dependency but with 'correct
moral principles'; they aimed to change the
actual behaviour of people." -Gordon Wood*

Nick was greatly upset by the economic, political, and social forces
that were turning the new nation away from his own treasured
vision and beliefs. But the response of many Americans to the upheaval
of the New Republic's early years caused him even further distress. A new
middle class was emerging which, with its craving for respectability, its
emphasis upon equality of opportunity, and its belief in moral redemp-
tion, was to define the modern American ideal. Although its values were
by no means inimical to Nick, its obsession with systemic reform clashed
with his essentially paternalist eighteenth century outlook.

In the midst of turbulence and uncertainty, Americans of the 1820s
and 1830s grasped at any means to create an appearance of stability and
control, starting with illusions of decorum and genteel restraint in their
own homes. Cast iron, fuel efficient cook-stoves, oil lamps, mass produced
furniture, textiles, and carpets gave families of even modest means access
to new levels of domestic comfort. Those who could afford to do so set aside
a room in the house for formal occasions where the best and newest of their

possessions could be displayed. Cultivating a taste for refined adornment, such as matching upholstered seating and the pianoforte,[63] had little productive purpose but provided a reassuring sense of well-being.

Now that houses were warmer, a new concern for privacy moved the parental bed into a separate bedchamber where a French "low post" bed was exchanged for the traditional unventilated high post bed. Previously in the eighteenth century, sexual relations had been part of serious courtship, but the nineteenth century values changed: passions should be controlled and sexual behaviour limited. In 1790, one third of New England brides had been pregnant at marriage but now that number fell with the new emphasis on chastity and easier birth control.[64] These new standards of behavior had a direct impact on a woman's freedom of movement. Gone were the days when Mother Hope ran her own shop; women were now expected to be pure, pious, domestic, and submissive to their husbands and fathers. By the late 1820s, wealthy women made social calls in the morning (unless the weather was too cold or wet for young ladies to leave the house), left cards (according to an increasingly complicated protocol), and participated in sewing circles or female benevolent societies. Countless books on child-rearing extoled the virtues of motherhood and of the "mother-citizen" who was responsible for instilling strength of character and self-control in her children.

Leisure time was supposed to be filled with rational, family centered activities. Dancing—once taught by French or Italian dancing masters—was condemned as licentious by almost everyone outside the elite. Theater, so popular at the turn of the century,[65] was now considered "a

---

[63] The ultimate badge of gentility was a pianoforte, which cost from $200 (six months' wages for a carpenter) to $600 (the price of a small house or the annual salary of a country minister), and could be afforded by only one in 100 families. Pianofortes became part of the ritual of courtship in affluent households where young people gathered to sing sentimental British parlor songs.

[64] However, venereal disease ravaged all ranks of society and became a major source of infertility in the nineteenth century.

[65] In 1792, after the repeal of the theater ban, a building at the rear of the coffee house on the corner of Westminster and Mathewson Streets was fitted out (with substantial contributions from Uncle John) as *The Providence Theater*. During intermission, "liveried servants entered the circles, bearing trays laden with wines and sherbets, and served them to their masters and mistresses."

nursery for vice on par with brothels, grog shops, and gambling dens."
The quest for proper behavior extended to all walks of life, and was codified and encouraged by a vast number of etiquette books. "Sophisticated"
people began using a fork rather than eating only with a knife. Snuff
replaced pipes. Landscaped "rural cemeteries" replaced graveyards, and
grief was expressed through "mourning fashions."

Dress too evolved considerably over America's first thirty years as
colonial fullness gave way to Republican trimness. Men began wearing
pantaloons and by 1815 dressed in knee britches only for the most formal occasions. Longer "frock coats" appeared in 1816 and became the
mainstay of a man's wardrobe throughout the rest of the century. By
the late 1820s, wigs had completely disappeared: men wore their hair
"Roman emperor style" and virtually all Americans were clean-shaven.
The high-waisted, diaphanous dresses of the 1800s that exposed arms
and the upper body became far more modest by the 1820s; once again the
female figure was disguised under voluminous layers of fabric. Women's
hair was piled high at the back of the head, with masses of bows and sau-
sage curls. Machine-made and machine-printed textiles allowed women
to own more than two dresses. Men too could afford more than a single
jacket and two pairs of pantaloons. Cheaper shirts also meant better
personal hygiene, since most Americans wore a "chemise" day and night.
Ladies' shoes evolved from sandals and slippers with ribbon straps to soft
ankle boots. By 1835, Yankee shoemakers were producing over fifteen
million pairs of inexpensive, ready-made shoes a year.

But domestic and personal hygiene improved only marginally.
Chewing tobacco was widespread and led to incessant spitting. American
women were internationally famous for their bad teeth. By 1820, almost
all families used English-made ceramic chamber pots, but soap served
only to wash clothes; it was quite unthinkable to wash anything more
than the face and hands once a day. Over the course of 150 years, a more
abundant and varied diet had allowed Americans to tower over their
European counterparts. By the Revolution men had an average height of
5-feet 8-inches, with many over six feet tall. A white New Englander who
survived until the age of twenty-one could expect to live past age sixty,

but one in four did not reach adulthood (one white baby in six died in infancy, another 10 percent died before age two). As women continued to have close to seven babies on average (fertility rates did not fall to an average of six children until 1840), the nation was youthful; the median age was only sixteen in the first quarter of the nineteenth century.

Medical health did not improve at all. Although the prosperous had access to better nutrition and better resistance, they could not buy real protection from infectious disease. Many ordinary people understood contagion, yet little was done to alleviate overcrowding. Doctors—most of who simply learned the trade as apprentices—still practiced the Galenic Theory of the four humors which relied on removing "humoral fluids" through bleeding, purging, blistering and puking.[66] The remarkably low mortality rates of the eighteenth century were overtaken in the nineteenth century by yellow fever, cholera, and tuberculosis (a quarter of all deaths) as population densities increased and new diseases were imported from the four corners of the globe. Wealth could not guarantee of longer life.

Indeed, disease and death were the great equalizers in a society that now placed a premium on egalitarianism. People were encouraged not to ape their social superiors, but rather to develop an innate sense of duty. The handshake (instituted by Thomas Jefferson) replaced the colonial era's doffed caps, deep bows, and lowered heads. Visitors found Americans more affable than their European contemporaries, pointing to greater mobility, a wider franchise, and more frequent elections as an explanation. On his 1831 visit to the United States (ostensibly to report on the prison system), the twenty-five-year old Frenchman Alexis de Tocqueville noted, "Nothing struck me more forcibly than the general equality of conditions among the people." Flattered by these comments, Americans took pride in promoting social homogeneity and egalitarian rhetoric.[67]

This desire for social equality was largely propelled by the Second

---

[66] The one exception was smallpox. Inoculations had become a commonplace family health measure by the 1820s, thanks to the introduction in 1796 of Edward Jenner's cowpox vaccine, milder than the one used by Moses Brown.

[67] Europeans also considered American servants strikingly forward and rather inefficient by the standards of their well-run aristocratic households.

Great Awakening, a huge religious revival that swept the country through the first decades of the nineteenth century. Back in the 1740s, the First Great Awakening had preached an intensely personal experience of spiritual rebirth. Now, people yearned for something to help cope with their anxieties other than the cool scepticism, deism or rational Christianity practiced by the Founding Fathers. Preachers such as Presbyterian lawyer Charles Finney began holding revival meetings, declaring that Christian teachings could solve social problems. The 1801 Cane Ridge Camp meeting in Kentucky attracted a crowd of 20,000 and spawned numerous non-denominational churches based on fundamental Christian tenets. A decade later, over three million Americans—a quarter of the population—had attended a camp meeting. By 1820, one observer noted, "Everything which goes forward seems to be preaching, praying, exhorting and singing without any time or disposition for reflection."

Evangelical denominations enrolled thousands of new members attracted to the concept of man's spiritual equality before God. The Methodist Church converted numerous frontier families through an efficient network of "circuit riders" drawn from the common people. Other revivalist churches challenged the traditional assumptions that human worth depended on race, gender, and class. The first African-American Methodist bishop Richard Allen was consecrated in 1816. Among the Baptists, the new "Freewill" denomination offered a religion of practical and simple beliefs which became popular in Rhode Island's agrarian areas as well as in emerging industrial centers. Some of the more established denominations in Providence also began to abandon theological purity in favor of moral reform and improving society. They moved away from the Calvinist concept of predestination (that God has preordained who is to be saved or damned) in order to rehabilitate the importance of human volition. The Brown family adhered to this "New School Calvinism" that reconciled human responsibility with divine omnipotence.

Another major theological movement was Unitarianism, launched in Boston in 1782. Rejecting such concepts as the trinity of God, the divinity of Christ, original sin and predestination, it spread to Providence where it particularly appealed to small merchants and grocers.[68] Indeed, the Second Great Awakening was the crucible in which the "middling sorts"—laborers, artisans, and small shopkeepers—formed a culture of their own making. As religion became more personal and voluntary, it empowered individuals to participate in an increasingly impersonal marketplace. Since many converts believed that the Awakening heralded a new millennium, they initiated a variety of reform movements to transform society at all levels. The more formal denominations also embraced the trend by launching missionary, tract, and educational societies. Their "organized evangelism" prepared the ground for organized charity.

By the 1820s, hundreds of thousands of shopkeepers, mechanics, and artisans were thinking of themselves as a national moral community whose values represented the broad public interest. They would be the guardians of a work ethic that provided the moral underpinning of an open, meritocratic society. Convinced of their superiority, these middling sorts condemned the vices of both the poor and the very rich. In the Colonial era, those aspiring to the rank of "gentleman" had yearned not to work. A half century later, labor had been rehabilitated as a means to attain opportunity, progress, and self-improvement. The new "manly type" was sober, dignified, self-possessed, and viewed the growing number of "degraded factory operatives" as blighting the social order. The poor and the deviant were the products of a faulty environment and must thus be removed to asylums, away from harmful influences.

This emerging "redeemer nation" in the Northern half of the United States also believed that great wealth caused idleness, extravagance, and dissipation. Self-discipline was encouraged, replacing traditional deference to authority. The rich must be turned away from the corrosive effects of greed, which "manufactures drunkards, chains and lashes the slave, and crowds down and oppresses the poor, the friendless, and the destitute: it is the father of all crime from the days of Adam until the present time."

---

[68] Unitarianism even took over the Congregationalist stronghold of Harvard. When the Providence's Congregational Church on Benevolent Street was rebuilt in 1816, it became the First Unitarian Church.

The new middle class believed it could transform society by instilling correct moral principles to achieve the social and cultural stability
for which it so yearned. It sought to harness human progress to "elevate
universally the intellectual and moral character of our people." It was
obvious that the individual, paternalistic acts of charity of the colonial
era could not solve the deep, systemic problems resulting from industrialization and urbanization. The new benevolent institutions were not
simply handing out alms, they were agents of compassion. These new
reformist associations attempted to impose self-restraint in the face
of urban violence and mass anonymity by fusing volunteerism with a
Christian message. At its peak in 1820, the frenzy for organized charity
produced two thousand mutual benefit societies, fraternal, and reform
organizations, as well as Bible and missionary societies.

Given Rhode Islanders' reluctance to pay taxes, there never was any
public money available to remedy the fundamental causes of poverty.
That burden fell on the elite who continued the longstanding tradition
of Christian stewardship and paternalistic compassion. For two hundred
years, Rhode Island's leading citizens had believed that pious, moral
leadership and individual acts of charity could bring society's conflicting interests into harmony. Now times had changed. Benjamin Franklin
had been among the first to recommend shifting from pious works and
personal charity to promoting the general welfare. At the turn of the
century, the Providence elite gingerly began adopting this new institutional approach. In 1772, there were just three charitable organizations
in Rhode Island; by 1817 the number had grown to 49. A typical early
initiative was the "Providence Female Charitable Society for the Relief
of Indigent Women and Children," founded in 1801 and funded by the
town's wealthiest men. Its ambitious agenda included binding out impoverished children to learn a trade, purchasing cloth and materials
to give "idle" women employment, and establishing a home to teach
young girls a domestic craft. But twenty years later, a new generation of
reformists was moving beyond simply solving the problems of the poor
to improving the quality of all human life. As a writer in the *Christian
Spectator* noted in 1822, "The peculiar characteristics of the benevolent

efforts of our age . . . entirely different from those of any former age . . . [are] marked by UNITED, VIGOROUS, SYSTEMATIC efforts."

Since this new approach to reform had originated with the Second Great Awakening, many of the new initiatives focused on spiritual health. As mill villages crept closer to Providence, concerned townspeople noticed that the workers spent their only day off "in slothful inactivity or sports and recreation." Some believed that "if this nation falls, Sabbath breaking will be one cause of the awful catastrophe" and sought to prohibit business, travel, recreation and even the mail on Sundays. Missionary activity was revitalized as a plethora of new organizations sprang up to send preachers, Bibles and other books of piety to "heathens" at home and abroad. Poor boys with a talent for preaching were sponsored to become missionaries or to run Bible societies and evangelical publications.

Sunday school was another focus of reformist activities. Samuel Slater had started a Sunday school in 1796 for the children working in his mills, whom he initially taught himself, but only in secular subjects. A decade later, the Reverend David Benedict was put in charge of Slater's Sunday schools to provide religious instruction. In 1815, the "Providence Female Tract Society" was formed to bring "Christianity to the industrial masses" in the 140 mills surrounding Providence. It merged with the "Rhode Island Sunday School Union" in 1825 to establish a "Sunday school in every village, factory establishments and neighbourhood." By 1838, the "Sunday School Union" was running 160 non-denominational schools for 12,000 pupils. It was one of the few activities outside the home considered sufficiently "respectful" for upper-class women.

In 1831, Alexis de Tocqueville noted that "Americans of all ages, all conditions, and all dispositions constantly form associations." Since associations were seen to be the answer to problems of immorality, more and more benevolent organizations were launched-sometimes they impeded one another. Such faith in the power of reason and persuasion would have seemed preposterous to colonial New Englanders. But now people felt they lived "in an age replete with remarkable occurrences of divine Providence." Technology would provide the tools to overcome social ills, just as it was enabling an era of unprecedented economic achievement.

While in colonial times it had been thought that moral education could only be inculcated in children, now many believed that adult "wrongdoers" could be "reclaimed." Lyman Beecher referred to "the practicability of suppressing vice by means of societies instituted for that purpose." The popularity of such societies stemmed also from the kinship bonds they offered in an increasingly anonymous and hostile world. They ranged from small, local initiatives to huge, nationwide movements, with a few misguided attempts in between. Providence had its fair share of each.

"The Providence Shelter for Colored Orphans," founded in March 1838 by Uncle Moses's only granddaughter Anna Jenkins, was a typical small venture that combined an asylum and a benevolent society. Its medical officer was Dr. Samuel Tobey, who also treated the Brown family. Located on North Main Street in a building owned by Anna, the shelter's aim was to rescue children who were "subjected to the blighting influence of evil example, surrounded by the effects of intemperance and vice, taught and encouraged in the practice of wickedness by those whose duty it is to train them to habits of useful industry." By removing African-American children from an unwholesome environment to one "more conducive to virtue and socially acceptable habits," the shelter aspired to influence an entire generation. The founders soon realized they should also welcome children who needed to be separated from their "vicious" parents, as well as children whose parents were in domestic service. A boarding program was offered for fifty cents a week.

At the other end of the scale, the nationwide temperance movement was the most ambitious of all the early nineteenth century reform initiatives. In 1800, liquor consumption was four times greater than it is today. Drink figured prominently in the work and leisure of all social classes and was considered healthy (at least it did not kill like water). "Good morning Mr. A, won't you walk in and take a glass of brandy?" was a common greeting; alcoholic beverages lubricated every social occasion, whether a state visit by French General Lafayette, a cotillion party, or a large supper after a funeral. Liquor was the largest inventory item in any country store. Artisans took two breaks daily for a drink, at 11:00 am and 2:00 pm. There could be no more impossible challenge for a reformer than promoting temperance—yet it succeeded.

In April 1827, several hundred townspeople assembled in Providence to frame a set of temperance resolves. They were inspired by the Reverend Daniel Pickering, Pastor of the First Universalist Church, who preached that "intemperance had converted many useful and industrious members of the community . . . into contemptible drones." Pickering in turn was influenced by the *Six Sermons on Intemperance* of Lyman Beecher, founder of the "American Society for the Promotion of Temperance," which sought not "to impose the slightest restraint or dictation upon any individual," by placing its faith in "the concentration of public opinion."

Grocers condemned prohibition as "an infringement of individual liberty not consistent with a free government." Nevertheless, the consumption of alcohol fell by two-thirds within little more than a decade. Thousands of Rhode Islanders took the temperance pledge, including all 275 members of the Mechanics Association who felt their workshops had become "scenes of disorder and ruin." Breaking with precedent, the organization's president John Howland offered cash rather than the customary liquor to the carpenters who were building his new house. A "Providence Association for the Promotion of Temperance" was founded in 1830, with branches for women, African-Americans, sailors, and youths.

When the first cholera epidemic ravaged the Eastern Seaboard in 1832, people became convinced that "intemperance is a powerful predisposition to cholera." Public pressure shifted from moral suasion to legal compulsion, including the strict regulation of liquor licenses and/ or banning the sale of liquor on Sundays. On an election day in Newport, Governor Fenner gave a hundred dollars to the public school fund rather than treat his voters to a drink. Taverns ceased to be centers of community life; attendance fell at racing and blood sport events. One by one, the Congregational and Baptist churches in Rhode Island insisted on abstinence from "ardent spirits" as a condition of membership. In 1832, the First Baptist Church adopted a temperance pledge that all members must accept; it then expelled twenty-six members for intemperance. The

General Assembly passed state-wide prohibition laws in 1838 and 1852. By the 1840s, alcohol consumption across America had decreased by two-thirds. Sobriety was now equated with respectability.

The rich, however, continued to consume liquor in their homes and clubs. As a result, the temperance movement became anti-elitist: "Not a year went by in which temperance spokesmen did not denounce the reluctance of the upper classes to abide by the cold water convention of an abstemious majority." The "bibulous wealthy" were attacked as agents of society's decline since they were role models for their "social inferiors, who are always emulous to ape their examples." Nick, who believed above all in moderation, saw the impractical side of the temperance movement. In a late nineteenth century *Providence Journal* article, an anonymous observer recounted:

> In him the temperance reform found an ardent but tem-
> perate friend. Meeting one time at the home of one of the
> sea captains in his employ, whose habits were verging
> to an extreme, he observed to him: "Captain, do you
> know that some people find fault with you and me?"
> "What now?" asked the captain. "Well, well," Mr. Brown
> replied, "They say I drink too much wine, and you drink
> too much rum."

> After the eloquent Dr. Hewitt had addressed a large as-
> sembly of the citizens of Providence in the First Baptist
> Meeting House, urging the fullest measures of total ab-
> stinence, Mr. Brown came up to him and said, "Very
> well, Mr Hewitt, very well: but how can I get along load-
> ing and unloading my ships without the 11 o'clock and
> the 4 o'clock grog rations?[69]

---

[69] Most of the anecdotes in this chapter come from an anonymous, undated biographical newspaper article— probably from the late nineteenth century, that was found in
a family scrapbook.

The same shopkeepers, artisans, and skilled laborers who were attracted to temperance responded enthusiastically when a new abolition movement was launched in the early 1830s. This was the reform movement, beyond all others, that would most agitate Nick and pose for him a near-insoluble conundrum. The new version of abolition of the 1830s brought into direct conflict two of his most fervent ideals: utter detestation of the institution of slavery on the one hand, and an impermeable belief in law, order and the sacred rights of property on the other.

Forty years earlier, Nick had been bitterly disappointed when the Providence Abolition Society, the first cause he ever had taken to heart, had faded into irrelevance. After the unsuccessful 1791 Gardner trial, Uncle Moses had realized the futility of enforcing a state law that all seemed bent on subverting. He had hoped that the opportunities in manufacturing would eventually convince slave traders to invest in other enterprises. William Ellery, the Customs Collector at Newport, had noted woefully that slave traders would not change their trade "for the slow profits of the manufactory," any more than "an Ethiopian could as soon change his skin." Uncle John had been far more biting in pointing out the fallacy in his brother's quest:

> I hope the abolition society will promote our own manufactories, especially the cotton manufactory, for which great experience has accrued and is accruing. This is most certainly a laudable undertaking, and ought to be encouraged by all; but pause a moment—will it do to import the cotton? It is all raised from the labour of our own blood; the slaves do the work. I can recollect no one place at present from whence the cotton can come, but from the labour of slaves.

So Uncle Moses had transferred his crusade to the federal level. After the Fugitive Slave Law was adopted in 1793, he had opened his Elmgrove home to runaway slaves. He had lobbied George Washington personally and on March 22, 1794, Congress had passed a federal law prohibiting Americans from fitting out vessels "for the purpose of carrying on any trade or traffic in slaves, to any foreign country." Over the next six years, slave traders were restricted by an unbroken line of Federalist prohibitions.

But in Rhode Island, the *Providence Abolition Society* had never managed to win a landmark case. In 1796, it had sued Cyprian Sterry, the premier slave trader in Providence and a trustee of the College, who had sponsored twenty voyages in the past two years; he had settled out of court. Also in 1796, the Society had attempted to prosecute John Brown for a slaving venture the previous year. A distraught Moses had urged his brother to settle out of court, but Uncle John had refused, "puffed up by the slave trading interests of Newport." America's first prosecution for illegal slave trading had ended disastrously for the anti-slavery forces. Uncle John was acquitted (although his ship was impounded) and a judgment for costs was awarded against the Providence Abolition Society. Uncle Moses had attributed the verdict to "The Peculiar Turn" of the Newport jury, as well as to other kinds of favoritism "which I forbear to describe." From that point, the Providence Abolition Society had gone into rapid decline. The handful of subsequent cases it had brought to trial invariably had ended in acquittal as slave traders hired the best attorneys in New England who prolonged cases indefinitely or hid behind legal technicalities.

In the meantime, Brown & Ives had sought to develop "legitimate" commerce with Africa in wood, gold and ivory. Its captains received strict orders not to engage with any trader who might be associated with slaving.

In the first forty years of the New Republic, the notion of resettling freed slaves in Africa had surfaced periodically. It had been actively promoted in 1816 by Paul Cuffee of Westport, Massachusetts, who had transported thirty-eight settlers to Sierra Leone on his own vessel. Cuffee, of Aquinnah Wampanoag and West African Ashanti descent, had been a successful merchant and the wealthiest African-American of his day. He had believed that "Negroes" could more easily "rise to be a people" in Africa than in the United States. Although Cuffee died prematurely in 1817 before realizing his dream of a mass emigration to Sierra Leone, he had convinced a number of influential Americans to endorse the concept.

Encouraged by Thomas Jefferson, the "The Society for the Colonization of Free People of Color of America," known as the American Colonization Society, had been founded in December 1816 by the Reverend Robert Finley of New Jersey. James Monroe, Andrew Jackson, Francis Scott Key, and Daniel Webster all had attended its inaugural ceremonies. Others had endorsed the Society for more overtly racist reasons, as a way of ridding the South of potentially "troublesome" agitators who might threaten the plantation system of slavery: "We must save the Negroes or the Negroes will ruin us." To its supporters, colonization was an ideological middle ground between nationwide abolition and perpetual black bondage.

The American Colonization Society funded the establishment of a colony on the African "Pepper Coast," which became known as Liberia. Despite difficult beginnings (twenty-two of the first eighty-eight emigrants died within the first three weeks), 2,638 African-Americans emigrated to Liberia through the 1820s, supplemented by freed slaves from the West Indies and captives from slave ships intercepted by the British and American navies. Congress, however, never agreed to subsidize the Society.

But most African-Americans in Philadelphia, New York, and Boston were united against colonization, equating it with expulsion. They were determined to fight against slavery and for full citizen rights in America. Uncle Moses, who continually encouraged and supported African-Americans to improve their welfare, strongly disapproved of colonization. Responding to a solicitation from the Society in March 1828, he had condemned its plan as "wholly impracticable & inefficient to the extinguishing of Slavery. . . . [T]he money so bestowed [is] worse than thrown away." Written in his 90th year, Moses's critique of the Society's President Gerrit Smith's proposal is remarkable for its lucidity and prescience. Not surprisingly, the Society had little success convincing Rhode Island African-Americans to leave for Africa. Only one group of thirty-two had departed in January 1826 for Liberia, led by Newport Gardner who declared upon departure, "I go to set an example for the youth of my race. I go to encourage the young. They can never be elevated here. I have tried it for sixty years. . . . It is in vain."

But contrary to his Uncle Moses, Nick felt that colonization provided an orderly solution to the emancipation conundrum and would promote Christianity in Africa. Comforted in the knowledge that the concept of colonization had originated with an African-American, he became a life member of the Colonization Society in 1832, donating $1,000, and later served as Vice President for the New England chapter. More fundamentally, perhaps, the idea of colonization seemed to offer a way for Nick to reconcile the principal dilemma which confounded his stance on abolition. In common with many Americans of means at the time, he despised the institution of slavery. But he was concerned that abolition, in particular immediate emancipation, was so inimical to the principles of property and respect for the rule of law that it might fatally undermine the established order he regarded as sacrosanct. He would have no truck with slavery or the slave trade himself. He would advocate in the strongest terms that the institution was an evil that should be eradicated. But he would not countenance coercion. It was a conflict of principles which was a sure recipe for yet more frustration and disappointment.

When the new abolition movement sprung up in the early 1830s, the issue had been dormant for thirty years. Rhode Island Senator James Burril had strongly opposed the 1820 Missouri Compromise, but free blacks had lost the franchise in 1822. The state had come to depend increasingly on Southern cotton for its textile mills and Southern markets to sell its products. Over those years, many Rhode Island mills (although not Brown & Ives) had begun specializing in "kersey cloth" (a coarse cotton wool blend for slave clothing), slave blankets, and "bagging" (sacks for harvesting cotton).[70] Rhode Island now was the nation's leader in what Massachusetts Senator Charles Sumner called a union of "the Lords of the Lash and the Lords of the Loom."

Then in 1833, the North American press reported at length about the British "Immediate Emancipation Act," the culmination of a long

---

[70] By 1850, "Negro goods"—kerseys, jeans and linseys—would comprise 79 percent of the total cloth produced in Rhode Island mills, for Newport was attracting more and more Southern visitors in the summer months.

abolitionist campaign. From August 1st, 1834, slavery was abolished in al-most the entire British Empire. The British campaign had followed a sim-ilar timeline to that of its American counterpart, beginning when a group of Quakers and Evangelical Protestants had formed "The Committee for the Abolition of the Slave Trade" in 1787. Like Uncle Moses, its most prominent leader William Wilberforce had viewed his personal battle against slavery as a divinely ordained crusade. On February 10th, 1807, the British Parliament prohibited the slave trade. Thereafter, the mighty Royal Navy patrolled the seas and established a West Africa Squadron that ultimately seized over 1,600 slave ships and freed 150,000 Africans. A "British Anti-Slavery Society" was founded in 1823 to push for eman-cipation, a decade before its American equivalent. But it was only when a peaceful strike by Jamaican slaves was brutally repressed on Christmas Day 1831 that Parliament took decisive action. The British government agreed to pay £20 million in forty thousand separate awards to compen-sate slave owners for the loss of their "business assets"—40 percent of the crown's total expenditures for the year 1834.

British emancipation put great pressure on the United States and struck a chord with members of the growing American middle class al-ready active in "moral improvement." Among the crusaders demanding immediate emancipation were Theodore Weld, the brothers Arthur and Lewis Tappan, and William Lloyd Garrison. Born in 1805, Garrison had been deeply affected by the publication of an incendiary pamphlet by African-American David Walker calling for active resistance on the part of slaves. In 1831, at age twenty-five, Garrison received funding from the Tappan brothers to set up his own anti-slavery newspaper, *The Liberator*. For the next thirty-five years, the publication would be the most prominent voice of a distinctive anti-slavery position that preached immediate eman-cipation, no compensation for masters, and no deportation of freed slaves.

The South, whose enslaved population of two million had tripled since the Revolution, still felt extremely bitter about the North's rejection of slavery. It blamed the "Northern criticism of slavery which incited blood-shed" for the bloody Nat Turner uprising of August 1831. Garrison, how-ever, seized the opportunity to organize the "New England Anti-Slavery

Society" in January 1832, with dozens of affiliates and several thousand members (particularly women whom he encouraged to take action). In October 1832, Garrison came to Rhode Island to speak before the new "Black Temperance Society" at the Beneficent Congregational Church. In the audience sat Nick's former partner George Benson with some of his nine children, including his second-youngest daughter Helen (born in 1811) who was enthralled by Garrison's oratory. Benson invited the speaker to his home in Brooklyn, Connecticut. Soon, Garrison became a regular caller and, in September 1834, he and Helen Benson were married.

The "Providence Anti-Slavery Society" was formed in 1833, in parallel with an "American Anti-Slavery Society" that grew to 1,350 delegates representing 250,000 members in 1838. In contrast with Uncle Moses's Abolition Society of forty years earlier, there were few wealthy men in its ranks. In 1834, two agents from the New England Society settled permanently in Rhode Island but the movement only truly expanded past the confines of Providence and Pawtucket when Henry B. Stanton was appointed its agent in mid-1835. Membership in the Society increased steadily to three thousand, and its capital to $2,000 (Uncle Moses added a codicil to his will, gifting the organization $500). The organization opened a permanent office in the Arcade building. Initially, Rhode Island abolitionists strove to maintain a reputation for non-violence by relying on "uncompromising moral suasion." Asked how they would achieve their aims, the reply was "by means precisely like those which have been employed with so much effect towards the subversion of Intemperance."

But when nothing came of Virginia's 1835 "Great Debate" following the 1831 Turner Rebellion, Garrison and his New York counterpart Elizur Wright decided to launch a major propaganda offensive. Their objective was to reach twenty thousand influential Southern whites, especially those known to espouse moderate views on slavery. Relying on the Federal Post Office's legal obligation to deliver mail, they printed and posted 175,000 tracts (the number would grow to a million by year's end). Incensed, the Southern authorities took the law into their own hands and broke into local post offices to destroy the tracts. In a dramatic intervention, President Jackson allowed local postmasters to leave the tracts undelivered, and branded the abolitionists "monsters." From the Senate, John Calhoun tried to introduce a bill requiring the Federal Post Office to enforce state censorship laws. With mass mailings no longer an option, the abolitionists turned to circulating anti-slavery petitions in Congress. In response, Southern congressmen introduced the "Gag Rule" of May 1836: petitions could be received by Congress but would be immediately tabled.

As Americans watched Congress tamper with the Post Office and free speech, they began to fear that their constitutional rights might be jeopardized. Abolitionists exploited these fears, and antislavery sentiment spread rapidly in the Northeast. Incidents of mob violence led many to wonder if abolitionists, "whose mistaken enthusiasm bred a mania that jeopardized the safety of church and state," might not be making the situation worse. Even if they did not preach violence, the fact that they *caused* mob violence was disquieting.

Nick was extremely upset by this threat to law and order. It was undeniable that he deplored slavery. But, like many Americans, he felt that immediate emancipation would produce even greater evils. National unity was still fragile and property rights were still being redefined in this early stage of industrialization. The 1832 Mill Acts[71] had dethroned landed property from its supreme position; now emancipation would mean the forceful seizure of personal property. "Predisposed to reform but resistant to radicalism," Nick was particularly opposed to this new incarnation of the abolition movement because it set one portion of the community against the other. On one occasion, when the Friends of Temperance asked for his consent to hold a meeting in the First Baptist Meeting House, he replied that he would "rely upon the well-known wisdom and integrity of Dr. Mark Tucker (the pastor of the Beneficent Congregational Church, who planned to attend) so that the subject of slavery should not be introduced. The peace of the church is very dear to me."

But as the "exaggerated Statements and inflammatory appeals" of abolitionists began sparking mob violence, Nick and others of his

---

[71] In 1832 the Supreme Court ruled that eminent domain could be used to allow a mill owner to expand his dam and operations by flooding an upstream neighbor.

background and outlook decided further action was required to avert a "Crisis . . . big with peril to the Union of the States and to the supremacy of the laws." He was not alone in his concern. Rhode Island wanted to reassure its southern trading partners that the "large majority of Northern communities, including their most prominent citizens, discountenanced abolitionist activities."

One of the great ironies of the struggle between the manufacturing interests and the abolitionists in Rhode Island was the extent of anti-slavery sentiment among the mill owners. Rowland Hazard, the state's largest kersey cloth manufacturer, authored several anti-slavery tracts and prided himself on having helped to free dozens of kidnapped freemen in New Orleans. But he also viewed the young, fiercely committed abolitionists as menaces. Indeed, by the 1830s, Rhode Island's paternalistic industrial leaders were controlling public opinion and setting the tone for the rest of society—much like the merchant princes of the Colonia Era. The mill owners felt that the abolitionists were threatening this traditional order by claiming a higher authority from God to sanction their stand on slavery and civil obedience.

In the late spring of 1835, three dozen men of means gathered to discuss the situation. Mostly Episcopalian or Unitarian (considered the more "restrained" and affluent churches), they represented the top 10 percent of the town's property owners. At their head was Samuel Bridgham, the first mayor of Providence, whose specific mandate had been to restore law and order after the Olney riots. Nick was the group's most prominent member. Moses Brown Ives, Professor William Goddard (married to Tom Ives's daughter Charlotte), Edward Carrington, and many industrialists were also present, as well as former governor James Fenner and future Senator John Clarke. On November 2nd, 1835, they unanimously adopted ten resolutions (although "several gentlemen spoke in a very spirited manner").

The constitution of the "Anti-Abolition Society" began with a ringing condemnation of slavery:

> It having pleased the Creator of mankind to make of one
> blood all nations of men, and having, by the diffusion of his

light, manifested, that however diversified by colour, situation, religion, or different States of society, it becomes them
to consult and promote each other's happiness, as members
of one great family: It is therefore the duty of those who
profess to maintain their own rights, and especially those
who acknowledge the obligations of Christianity, to extend,
by the use of such means as are or may be in their power,
the blessings of freedom to the whole human race; and in
a more particular manner to such of their fellow-creatures
as by the laws and constitution of the United States are
entitled to their freedom, and who by fraud or violence are
or may be detained in bondage.

It is important to understand that the goal of the Providence Anti-
Abolition Society was to calm public sentiment and meet the "dire threat
to community stability." The Reverend Francis Wayland, president of
Brown University, best summarized the Anti-Abolitionists' perspective:

Slavery in this country will yet cease, for it is wrong. But
it will never be made to cease by the present efforts. . . .
They may destroy the union, plunge this country into a
civil war, break us up into a half dozen different confed-
eracies, but abolish slavery as they are now attempting
to do it—they never will. You may note my words, they
never will.

Within a month, four more Rhode Island communities held anti-
abolitionist town meetings. The Anti-Abolitionists were very careful to
aim their criticism only at the anti-slavery agents (they called Garrison
a "fanatic" whose mistaken enthusiasm bred a mania that jeopardized
church and state) but not at the rank and file of the movement who
"did not suspect the criminal designs of those leaders." Soon similar
groups sprang up all over the Northeast, careful to promote the same
anti-slavery, anti-violence message. As Calvin Cotton of Massachusetts

wrote, "We do not yield to the abolitionists one whit in our opposition to slavery; we differ from them only as to the mode of getting rid of the evil."

For a while, the Anti-Abolitionists appeared to succeed. It would not be until the mid-1850s, over a decade after Nick's death, that Rhode Island public opinion would move firmly into the abolitionist camp, following the South's aggressive attempts at expansion into the Western territories and political tampering with their new state constitutions. The 1850 Fugitive Slave Act would cause outrage among even the most die-hard anti-abolitionists. As textile magnate Amos Lawrence would write in 1854, "We went to bed one night, old fashioned, conservative Union Whigs, and waked up stark made Abolitionists." Many manufacturers would follow Lawrence's lead and join the "Conscience Whigs," which evolved into a new "Republican" Party. In Rhode Island, the Hazard family would abandon the "Negro cloth" business in 1848 and Rowland Hazard would lead the 1856 presidential campaign for John Fremont (who was defeated by the pro-slavery Democrat, James Buchanan).

It is interesting to speculate as to how Nick might have aligned himself in the 1850s, had he been alive to express a view. The Anti-Abolitionist campaign was a rare instance of Nick's taking such an intransigent and public stance in the two decades following his retirement from government service. Like the reformers of the 1830s, he sought to transform "the intellectual & moral standard of the community." His objective was to teach men "that while they are labouring for the good of the whole, they are labouring for the good of themselves."[72] He was not, however, willing to contemplate the upending of the established forces of law and order as the price of achieving that end.

---

[72] These are the words of William Gammell who married Tom Ives's granddaughter Elizabeth.

CHAPTER 12

FATHERS AND SONS

"The <u>poor</u> <u>lunatic</u> talks of doing good &c. &c. why not do some good now to his grand- children since he will not to his children?"
—*Nicholas Brown III to Moses Brown Ives*

O f all the frustrations and disappointments experienced by Nick in the 1820s and 1830s, none was more painful to bear than his dissat- isfaction with his own sons. When Nick was a child, the family unit was the foundation of society. The Fifth Commandment ("Honor thy father and thy mother") provided the benchmark for the "order which God hath placed among Mankind." In his 1765 *Letters on Education*, John Witherspoon (who founded of the College of New Jersey, the future Princeton University), noted that parents had "to establish as soon as possible, an entire and ab- solute authority" over their children. They must be caring and affectionate, but not too much so; they were not to indulge their children. This had been exactly Nick's own upbringing. His own father and Captain James before him had rarely demonstrated much tenderness. And there was never any question that sons would not follow in their fathers' footsteps.

After the Revolution, the forces of industrialization, urbanization, western expansion and emigration overwhelmed paternal authority; families exerted less influence in the lives of young people. They in turn looked more to their peers rather than to their fathers for models of behavior. Grown children increasingly considered themselves the independent equals of their parents. As the historian Harriet Cooke noted, "Probably in no enlightened country on the globe are children more anxious to be esteemed, or earlier permitted to become men and women than our own." When fathers did not accede to this desire for autonomy, clashes inevitably ensued.

The first of the Brown family to rebel was James, Uncle John's son, born in 1761, eight years before Nick. While James was still at school, his father had written to him:

> I do very much Fear that from Your Backwardsness in writing or in other words that from Your being so very Loth to write at this period of Life, You will not hereafter Give that Attention to Bussiness which I so Ardently have Ever Indeverd to Inculcate in Your mind & Disposition.

Since the College of Rhode Island was shut down during the Revolution, Cousin James was sent to Harvard where he graduated in 1780, then to live with the Tench Francis family of Philadelphia (agents for the Browns before the Revolution). Mrs. Francis was the former Anne Willing, whose brother Thomas had been in partnership with Robert Morris and who was now president of the National Bank. Anne Willing Francis felt great affection for the charming young James: "He is now become Absolutely necessary here having My Sons all from me, he has assumed their rank and fills his Station with great Address. . . . And I assure you he has entered with Sport into all the Amusements of the City Gallants."

Cousin James became adept at selecting the best tea and sugar, the finest cloth and the most handsome horses, but he did not inherit his father's ability to drive a bargain. When Uncle John asked him to purchase a "chariot," James plunged into the project with gusto and ordered a carriage "tall and impressive [as a] fairy coach, painted in robin's egg blue with gold leaf edging the doors and window frames, . . . a chariot of such fragile beauty that, after its purchase, it had been driven all the way from Philadelphia, to avoid possible injury in transporting it by sea." He also greatly overspent his father's budget, paying $800 for horses when Uncle John wanted to spend no more than $500.

Some of the time, Uncle John appeared indulgent of James:

> You Know I am not a Favorite to Extrevigence merely for Extrevigence Sake, but Anhtuing that is Really Convenient & Elegent can be Expected with out Extree Expense. Theirfore I Leave it wholly to you to do as you may think best.

But at other times his frustration showed through:

> Every man is born for some purpose or other I have an anxious desire that you should be a usefull member of Society in some sphere or other, as you do not incline to that of a Merchant so much as to spend your time in that Branch, the Law nor Phisics Does not Ingrosse your attention, The Statesman therefore is what I wish you to be and the sooner you begin your attention to it the better you'l please me and all your relations.

Upon his return to Providence, Cousin James steadfastly refused to engage in his father's enterprises. Did he simply lack ambition? Uncle John had once said, "before I was 7 years old I knew what property was and consequently what a Despicable figgur in Life I mySelf and my children after me would Cut without a shear theirof." Did James wish to avoid clashing with his father over business decisions? One of Uncle John's former associates said of him, "Mr B. will always hang on you a heavy load if you are willing to submit and I am of opinion that his speculations are hazardous and imprudent and must occasion his pressing hard on his Conncetions for support in them." Or did he simply not have the stomach to emulate his father's attitude towards risk?

Uncle John finally gave up on his son James and took as partner Tench Francis's son, John. The relationship strengthened a number of valuable contacts in Philadelphia—notably the Willing family and its access to Robert Morris. Fortunately, Cousin James and John Francis got along extremely well and shared an interest in architecture and design, which was deployed to good effect in the building of Uncle John's grand new brick house on Benefit Street.

Following his father's death in 1803, Cousin James remained for thirty years in the house he had done so much to design, surrounded by his widowed sisters and their children. He never married but, endowed with the "great gift of being well, wherever he went," devoted his life to developing this gift. He filled his days with visits to his Federalist "Cold Beef Club" (they rejected the refined French food introduced to America by Jefferson), hunting expeditions to Prudence Island, and riding his old-fashioned phaeton to Uncle John's country estate *Spring Green* in Warwick.

Having been disappointed by his son, Uncle John turned all his formidable energies to his grandson, John Brown Francis, born in May 1791:

> When six weeks old John Brown Francis left Philadelphia for Providence where he was Received on the wharf & taken into the arms of his Grandfather Brown who from that moment to the hour of his death in September 1803 thirteen years uniformly & unceasingly regarded him with the tenderest care & solicitude.

The bond grew even stronger when John Francis died in 1796—his little son was only five years old. John Brown Francis accompanied his grandfather everywhere; aboard the great "Indiamen" up the Bay on their return from the Orient or crouched at the great man's feet in a sulky (there was room on the seat only for Uncle John's enormous hulk). "He is certainly prodigiously attached to that child," noted Anne Willing Francis, the child's paternal grandmother. Following a carriage accident in 1802, John Brown would ask his grandson to rub his legs every evening. On his deathbed, his last words were "Good night my dear, dear Boy."

Little did Nick realize at the time that his own sons too would resist following in his footsteps. His eldest, Nicholas III, was only a year
younger than John Brown Francis, but as moody and rancorous as
Francis was amiable and conciliatory. Even the most complimentary
biographies of Nicholas III note his short fuse and belligerent nature. In
The Chad Browne Memorial, the 1888 Brown family genealogy, an entry
penned by Rush Hawkins (Nicholas III's son-in-law) noted euphemisti-
cally, "One of his fine traits of character was his openness of speech and
manly frankness; as his opinions were founded on honest convictions,
he was not ashamed to express them."

Born October 2nd, 1792, Nicholas III initially had distinguished himself among his Brown University class of 1811 contemporaries for his
breadth of knowledge and prodigious memory. Nick envisaged a future
in politics for his son, and sent him to the prestigious Tappan Reeve Law
School at Litchfield. In his reminiscences of his own time at Litchfield,
Roger Baldwin commented on his classmate: "smart, but lazy, drinks."
Nicholas III refused to sit the bar (unlike his cousin Moses Brown Ives,
three years his junior, who also attended the Tappan Reeve Law School),
so Nick sent him to a man he much admired, his brother-in-law Dr.
Benjamin Carter, who was living in London. Thus, in the spring of 1816,
Nicholas III became the first Brown to visit England, 178 years after Chad
Browne had crossed the Atlantic.

Benjamin Carter was a remarkable man. He had entered the College
of Rhode Island in 1782, the same year as Nick, although he was only
eleven at the time. Benjamin had written his senior exhibition on
"The Four Elements" in flowery blank verse at age 15. He stayed on
for a Master's degree in 1789, then enrolled in the Medical College of
Philadelphia (at the University of Pennsylvania) where he studied under
Benjamin Rush and other notable physicians. After a very dull summer
practicing medicine in Connecticut, Benjamin moved to Charleston,
then to Savannah, returning to Providence in 1798, just when Brown &
Ives needed a ship's doctor for the *Ann & Hope*.

For seventeen dollars per month and a one ton "privilege" (the right to carry a ton of cargo in his own name), Benjamin Carter set sail for Botany Bay (the future Sydney, Australia), and then to Canton. His journal vividly describes such varied events as a spear-throwing battle between aborigines, rescuing a marooned Indian, Cantonese life, diseases of the Orient, and a skirmish with a French privateer. Nick asked the *Ann & Hope*'s captain to be "helpful to our brother-in-law and friend," and over the next three trips Benjamin's privilege increased to the point where he had built a "handsome competency." On one voyage, the ship discovered some of the Fiji islands. On another, *Ann & Hope*—now sheathed in copper—returned so fast from loading sugar in Batavia that she reached England before her documents had arrived from America. Since she could not sell her cargo in England, she sailed for Amsterdam where Benjamin visited mathematicians and scientists at the Universities of Leyden and Utrecht (the conversations took place in Latin). He also was able to purchase medicines in Amsterdam, which he later sold in New York for a large profit. While in St. Petersburg, he met Czar Alexander I and visited Russian hospitals, conversing in classical Greek with Russian priests. As a member of the Mount Vernon Lodge in Providence, he attended several Masonic meetings in Europe.

On a voyage to Canton aboard Brown & Ives's *Asia* in 1804, Benjamin decided to remain in China, lodging with Edward Carrington who had succeeded Samuel Snow as the second U.S. consul from Providence. After just one year, he was able to send home over $16,000 gained from a lucrative medical practice in the European concession and from trading in Chinese goods (he asked Brown & Ives to manage his money). He learned Mandarin from a Chinese Jesuit with whom, in 1805, he translated the first letter from the U.S. government to a Chinese official of the highest rank. Benjamin also lobbied the U.S. State Department for a native speaker on the consular staff in Canton to assist American merchants who were being cheated of large sums by the Chinese. However, the post was not created; he suspected that his strong Federalist leanings were being held against him by the Republican administration.

Benjamin Carter returned to Providence in the spring of 1806. Within twelve months, he moved to England where he remained for the next eleven years, attending lectures in mathematics and medicine in Cambridge and London, studying Hebrew and Syriac, and making numerous famous acquaintances. Following the Battle of Waterloo in 1815, he spent a year in Paris but much preferred England over France, and wrote as follows to his brother John Carter, Jr.:

> There is a better country than America where your abilities would be more likely to meet with encouragement among men of learning and religion than among the brutal, ignorant, impious and atheistical Americans. The country I mean is England. I sometimes entertain the hope that I may be permitted to spend the remainder of my life on the classic ground of England.

It is understandable that Nick felt the extraordinary Benjamin Carter might be a steadying influence on his wayward son.

Uncle Benjamin first took his nephew to Scotland in the summer months to visit several cotton factories.[73] Uncle and nephew greatly enjoyed the impressive public works around Edinburgh, the "romantic and sublime" Western Highlands, and the "many peculiarities" that the Scots exhibited in "speaking." They were disturbed by the "wretched hovels" of the "Highlands [which] appear to have gone backward in civilization," but intrigued by the differences between American firs and pines as compared to Scottish native woods. On their way back to London in October, they visited the ironworks at Newcastle, a glass factory, and a woolen manufactory in Leeds where they witnessed the process of spinning and weaving fine wool.

As the son of Providence's leading printer and bookseller, Benjamin Carter had inherited his father's passion for books, particularly those on historical topics. So he took his nephew to numerous booksellers and libraries. In one, they saw an Egyptian mummy and Kennet's *Bibliotheca American*. They were awed by the 50,000 volumes of the University of

---

[73] He noted that the Scots were sufficiently enlightened not to employ boys under the age of ten, as was the practice in Rhode Island.

Edinburgh library, including "a beautiful Manuscript of Virgil [and] a copy of St. Jerome's Latin Bible." Whenever possible, they called on collectors of books pertaining to American history.

In London, the two were frequent guests of a widow, Anne Grant of Laggan, an author who had spent her early married life in the Mohawk country of the New York state and had written *Memoires of An American Lady, 1808*. Uncle Benjamin agreed with her observation that America was a land of promise but not of performance. They met a Baptist preacher, Doctor Charles Stewart, who showed them copies of several books by Roger Williams, a very old map of New England engraved on wood, and "an account of Mrs. [Anne] Hutchinson" (who had led the colonists on Aquidneck Island in the 1630s). Under his uncle's guidance, Nicholas III purchased enough books to fill two trunks, which he shipped home.[74]

In their time spent together, Uncle Benjamin transmitted to his nephew a keen interest in American history but did not manage to quell his discontent. Nicholas III returned to Providence just as angry and unsettled. Perhaps unfairly, Tom Ives blamed Benjamin Carter who wrote angrily to Nick about the "perfidious counsels of Ives—[he] has proved himself a most destructive enemy." The unfortunate consequence was to destroy the close relationship between the brothers-in-law. Benjamin lamented:

> My heart was wrung with the keenest sensations to see the destruction that was preparing for my unfortunate relations, who seemed insensible of their approaching fate & laughed at my warnings. I stretched out my hand to help them but some of them tried to bite off my hand & came near destroying me. My want of success does not indispose me from doing any good action but it suggests the necessity of prudence & discrimination.

---

[74] One small volume, bought on November 11, 1817, from "The Widow Tweedy" had margins filled with indecipherable symbols; these finally were interpreted in 2014 by a Brown University undergraduate and two professors who determined they were an essay on adult baptism by the strapped-for-paper Roger Williams.

Benjamin Carter finally returned to the United States in 1819, settling in New York. He remained active in literary clubs and private libraries, but aged into a crusty, irascible, elderly bachelor. Much of his ire was directed at the pro-slavery Republicans and their "falsely" egalitarian preaching. However, he remained devoted to his Brown nephews and they to him.[75]

Following his return to Providence in 1819, Nicholas III spent the next four years floundering about. He courted his second cousin, Abby Mason (daughter of Uncle John's youngest child, Alice who had married James Mason) who charmed him with her inquisitive mind and brilliant intellect. They married on July 5th, 1820 and appeared happy, filling their home with the finest China trade furnishings. But soon Abby began coughing blood. Desperate to prolong her life, Nicholas III took her to New Providence in the Bahamas in October 1822. She died a week after her arrival.

Nicholas III did not tarry long in Rhode Island after Abby's burial. He moved to New York in early 1823, lodging in a series of boarding houses and leading a pleasant enough life, attending the races on Long Island and occasionally travelling to Washington and Philadelphia for Brown & Ives. He also tried his hand at various ventures but none flourished; "his mind changes so often I know not what he will finally conclude," declared his younger brother in exasperation. His uncle, Crawford Carter (a much younger brother of Ann Carter Brown, Nicholas III's mother, and Benjamin Carter), also seeking his fortune in the city, wrote home: "I see little or no chance for anything like permanent business in New York" (but would eventually run a successful print shop). Fortunately for Nicholas III, Brown & Ives's New York agent provided cash and the income from the $15,820 in bank stocks that Nick had given his son. At a time when the average unskilled laborer earned seventy-five cents a day, he could have lived comfortably.

In later years, Nicholas III would claim that he had been compelled to

---

[75] At Benjamin's death in 1831, the bill for the funeral was sent to Nicholas III. But Brown & Ives attempted to claim eighty-eight cents from Benjamin's estate for a "freight expense" for the trunks of "historical books on America" shipped thirteen years earlier. This petty gesture shocked Benjamin's sister, Huldah Carter.

live "in a cellar or garret" because his father had refused to provide him with adequate financial support. That the story was so utterly lacking in truth is less important than the mindset it reveals; one that would reassert itself with tremendous venom in Nick's last years and after his death.

Fortunately, Nick's second son, John Carter or JCB (as he was known to all) had a far more amiable personality but, as would become apparent, no greater proclivity for the family trade. Named for his distinguished grandfather, the printer John Carter, JCB was born August 28, 1797, five years after Nicholas III. "Modest and always tolerant of dissent," he appeared to have little in common with his fiery and tempestuous older brother. After learning the "Three Rs" and oratory at the Providence Academy on George Street, and boarding at George Jeffrey Patten's co-educational School in Hartford, JCB entered Brown University in 1812. His prep school had been notable for its relaxed and benevolent atmosphere, so the fifteen-year old JCB found university rather stifling. The curriculum had hardly changed since his father's day. His theological texts were the works by Anglican prelates, written to prove the rationality of religious beliefs in general and the irrationality of Enlightenment skeptics. He was particularly affected by William Paley's *Principles of Moral and Political Philosophy* (a required text at Cambridge University, which advocated "complete toleration of all dissenters from the established church").

To counter the college's overemphasis on writing and public speaking, JCB joined the "United Brothers Society," a student discussion club whose members kept their own library and educated themselves in modern history, modern literature, and current events. Founded in 1806 in reaction to the Federalist and elitist "Philermenian Society," the United Brothers espoused a more Republican political view. JCB enthusiastically took part in their debates on the downfall of Napoleon, on relations between the New and Old Worlds, and on the territorial expansion of the American Republic. He enjoyed discussing such thorny issues as "Should Congress encourage manufacturing?" or "Should the Republicans welcome immigrants?" The United Brothers did not hesitate to question the relevance of the Brown University curriculum by sponsoring a debate en-titled, "Are the advantages derived from knowledge of the dead languages sufficient to compensate for the time and expense necessary to gain that knowledge?" JCB and the others members voted "NO."

Graduating "Phi Beta Kappa" (an honor society for the liberal arts and sciences) in 1816, JCB pronounced one of the twenty-eight com-mencement orations. He chose the only historical topic, "The Revolution of Empires," which examined both Napoleon and the revolts in South America—a far cry from his father's oration on commerce thirty years earlier. Then, like his grandfather, father, brother, and cousins before him, JCB began his apprenticeship in the family business.

He joined his older cousin, Moses Brown Ives, who had started his apprenticeship three years earlier (Nicholas III was traveling in England at the time). A serious, diligent young man, Moses Ives gave full sat-isfaction to his father. In his first year at Brown & Ives, he was sent to investigate real estate in Ohio and the tobacco trade in Kentucky. In 1818, he was allowed to sign in the firm's name and crossed the Atlantic to spend a year with the Scotsman Daniel Crommelin, Brown & Ives's agent in Amsterdam. Moses Ives called on mercantile houses in Antwerp, Le Havre, Paris and London before returning to Providence in 1819. It was later said that "while abroad, his object seems to have been not so much to see sights, and walk through galleries, as to observe men, and acquaint himself with the habits and manners of merchants of distinction."

Tom and Hope Ives's second son, Robert Hale, born in 1798, arrived in the counting house a year later. While Moses was being groomed for a career in maritime commerce, Robert showed great interest in industry and would push to expand his family's investments in manufacturing.

Since Moses Ives had greatly benefited from his travels, JCB and Robert were sent on similar trips to gain firsthand experience, starting with a "tour of observation" to the Ohio Valley in 1819. The cousins were charged with finding ways to improve trade and new opportunities for investments in Ohio land, Kentucky tobacco, and Georgia cotton. On November 2nd, they boarded a steamboat from New London to New York, then the mail coach to Philadelphia. They crossed through Pennsylvania, to Ohio, Kentucky, Tennessee, and Northern Georgia until they reached Augusta, a total journey of a thousand miles. They were allowed to transact only one deal—purchasing bulk tobacco and arranging for its shipment by riverboat to New Orleans—and that only under the supervision of John Corlis, Brown & Ives's commissioning agent in Lexington. Little was left to their discretion: they were told how much to buy (200-250 hogshead barrels), how much to pay (three to five dollars a hogshead), and what bank would clear their payments. Nick and Tom even asked their friend Sullivan Dorr, who was in Ohio at the time, to keep an eye on the young men (Moses Brown Ives would marry Dorr's daughter fourteen years later in 1833). In his diary, JCB noted that things in Kentucky were "pretty much the same as in Providence—the inn at Paris, KY was better than the one back home, but that the holiday parties in Lexington were equally boring."

Two summers later, in 1822, twenty-four-year old JCB was deemed ready to sign on as supercargo aboard *General Hamilton*, bound for Gibraltar, with instructions to sell a cargo of tobacco in exchange for 30,000 Spanish milled silver dollars which then would be used to purchase naval stores in St. Petersburg. Once that transaction would be completed, it was decided that JCB would follow in Moses Ives's footsteps across Northern Europe, calling on merchant houses in Hamburg, Bremen, Copenhagen, and Amsterdam, before catching passage home from London.

But nothing worked out as planned. After a swift 35-day crossing, tobacco sales were very poor due to the Spanish Revolution. Then, ten days out of Gibraltar, on July 22, 1822, the *General Hamilton* ran aground on the coast of Normandy. No cargo was lost but the French arrested the entire crew for attempting to smuggle silver into France and JCB was held for twenty days under armed guard in a fisherman's shack. Brown & Ives got their silver coins back but *General Hamilton* was sold for salvage (it was a bad summer for Brown & Ives: they lost not only *General Hamilton* but also *Hector* carrying a shipment of iron from Sweden). Thoroughly disheartened by his first experience with European bureaucracy, JCB was nonetheless delighted to be allowed to remain in Europe until the following spring. In fact, he would spend the next two years footloose and fancy free, his "business trip" transformed into a Grand Tour (with perhaps all too predictable consequences).

First, he spent five months in Paris as the guest of a baronial banking family whose matriarch was the former Martha Redwood of Newport. There he attended the theatre, opera, and toured cathedrals. In March 1823, he crossed the Channel to Britain, first to London where he scorned the foppery and affectations of London "bucks" at the opera in Covent Garden,[76] then on an extensive tour which took him from Shakespeare's Stratford-on-Avon to the top of Ben Nevis in Scotland, where he almost froze to death in a freak blizzard. At Glamis Castle, the setting of Macbeth's murder, he noted, "In the long hall are to be seen a great number of family portraits. I don't know how it is but whenever I am in one of these famous old establishments, I take more pleasure and satisfaction in viewing the portraits of a long line of illustrious ancestors than in any other paintings." Given his respect for history and historical facts, he was offended by the Duke of Atholl's proposed "theme park" dedicated to the mythical Gaelic bard Ossian. He was also appalled by the rural poverty in Ireland and in the Scottish Highlands.

With no Uncle Benjamin to accompany him, JCB flatly refused all entreaties from Brown & Ives to visit the great textile mills of the British Midlands, telling his father that all factories were "alike." In fact, he agreed with Thomas Jefferson that the best course for the United States was to avoid building factories and to let England continue to be the workshop of the world (at least, he had the humility to add "but what do I know about it?"). He nevertheless went to Amsterdam for four months with Brown & Ives's agent Daniel Crommelin.

When Robert Ives joined him, the two young men set off from London on a leisurely tour of the South of England that pointedly, once again, did not include factory visits. They returned to London at the end

---

[76] Everywhere he travelled, JCB carried his treasured copy of Benjamin Silliman's *Journal of Travels in England, Scotland and Holland,* which he initially had borrowed from the United Brother's Society Library while at Brown University, then bought for himself in 1820. Silliman emphasized the commonalities between America and Britain.

of September to find a letter of rebuke waiting from Nick, chiding his son for allowing himself to be distracted from business matters. JCB was again urged to observe the new machinery and processes which gave English industry its dynamism—and took away business from Rhode Island mills. Contrite, JCB responded at length, enclosing a list of numbers and market quotes to show that he had mastered current trade figures. However, he also took the liberty of noting:

> In all your letters to me you have mentioned the subject
> of trades, manufactures, etc. without stating anything
> specific on either of these points. I could have wished
> that you had been more full in these particulars so that I
> might have reflected at my leisure on any plans you may
> have in view. . . . In Europe it is customary for young
> men to purchase (or their parents purchase for them) a
> share in an established house and to partake in propor-
> tion of the loss or gain. . . . I don't know that this thing
> is yet understood with us.

Returning to the Continent to spend Christmas 1823 in the South of France, he then explored Italy before returning to Paris in May 1824, where Brown & Ives asked him to enquire about "indemnities to un-justified searches and seizures [that had taken place] under the reign of Bonaparte." Voyaging north in June and July 1824 to Northern Germany, he again met up with Robert Ives, then humored his father by visiting the Brown & Ives correspondents in Hamburg and in Amsterdam where he inspected his family's ships. Finally, he returned to England and, after a last excursion to the West Country (under the guise of visiting factories in the Midlands), set sail for Providence from Liverpool in November 1824. Robert stayed on in Europe, travelling to Italy in the Spring of 1825, from where he sent home samples of marble and alabaster, as well as an engraving.

While in Europe, JCB missed his sister-in-law Abby Mason Brown's tragic death in December 1822 and his brother Nicholas III's abrupt departure from Providence. When he came home, Nick fervently hoped that he would show some enthusiasm for Brown & Ives. But after such exhilarating years abroad, Providence seemed very dull to the twenty-four-year old. New York offered so much more: "Indeed I have often thought that if a person was not satisfied in that City, he would be obliged to search very far upon this Continent at least, to find a better place." Only the intervention of his Uncle Tom Ives dissuaded him from making the move. He thanked his uncle for the advice, saying:

> I have for a long time thought, that the City of New York was much the most eligible situation of a young man & presented prospects infinitely superior to any provincial town. . . What you are pleased to call my "situation" & "prospects" & those other circumstances which you say are such "very strong inducements" for me to locate myself in R'd I'd are deserving, I confess, of great consideration & are such as should have full weight with every one before he decides upon changing his residence. . . . I agree it is not every one that betters his condition by emigrating.

Though he continued to serve Brown & Ives, JCB never let business concerns overshadow his interests in history, the arts, and literature. Beyond his Uncle Benjamin Carter, JCB's influential mentor was none other than James Brown, John Brown's bachelor son, the refined, somewhat eccentric man who had once dared stand up to his own father. When Cousin James died in 1834, JCB wrote in his diary, "Perhaps with no person in Providence have I been upon such terms of familiar intimacy as with Mr. Brown—especially since my return from Europe now ten years since. Accustomed to visit him <u>at all hours</u>, I always received a cheerful smile & the welcome hand of friendship."

Nick did his best to accommodate his younger son's interests, evidently anxious not to strain their relationship. He sent JCB to lobby on behalf of the firm in Washington, D.C. and to New York to check on investments that included the Shakespeare Hotel (named after Grandfather Carter's shop, *The Sign of Shakespeare's Head*). But politics did not excite JCB any more than commerce. He was even bored by the speeches of the great orators John Calhoun and Daniel Webster, whom he heard in Washington : "Only let me have a cool million & others may have the [political] offices" he wrote. As a biographer would note many years later, "his tastes for active business were never very strong or controlling. He did not like the daily restraints it imposes, and had little relish for the excitement it involves."

At least Nick could console himself that JCB upheld a sense of family. A rather slight figure (he noted in his diary that he only weighed 113 pounds at the age of thirty-six in 1833), JCB made the effort to get along with everyone. Family members would rely on him for advice and support until the end of his days (his aunt, Huldah Carter, made him her executor in 1840). From time to time, he escaped from his father's roof to more cosmopolitan centers, especially Saratoga in "the season," from whence he sent amusing letters to his cousins (in 1835, he complained the resort was full of politicians and "not as fashionable as formerly"). He made every effort to maintain cordial relations with his brother Nicholas III, visiting him whenever business or a spa holiday took him to New York state. He also followed in his father's footsteps, becoming a trustee of Brown University in 1828, "in place of my brother who resigned." Toward the end of Nick's life, the relationship between father and son softened noticeably. In his diaries, JCB began referring to "my father" rather than only to "Mr. Brown," and treated the old man with gentle consideration—"I ride out with him every day which refreshes him, or at least releaves the tedium of confinement."

Uncle Tom Ives was also an important influence on JCB. When Tom died in 1835, JCB noted in his diary: "a most excellent man & estimable citizen & who always was a warm friend to me & every individual of my father's family, one in whose sound judgment I placed all confidence & whose advice I sought on all occasions." The Ives family was warm and caring. Tom felt strongly that "the children must be near & taught to love each other." In addition to Charlotte, Moses, and Robert, there were two more girls, followed by baby Thomas who lived only five months in 1804. Sadly, the fate of the two younger daughters cast a pall on this otherwise cheerful family.

Born in 1796, Elizabeth (known as Eliza) was charming and vivacious like her Aunt Joanna; she also died at age seventeen in 1813. While she was alive, Eliza kept the family much amused. A note appended by Tom to a letter from Eliza to her older sister Charlotte at school in Philadelphia reveals much about his relationship with his children:

> After Eliza's amusing description of Dances & dresses, it may not be amiss to add, that there are many imployments much more useful & important than those—altho' I am very far from supposing that young people should be deprived of these innocent pleasures.... Your Ma & myself have been laughing at Eliza's descriptive talent & seeing what she has written induced me to make these remarks.... You are, my dear child, continually in our thoughts—this separation—has repeatedly been the means of calling our attention to past scenes & we love to dwell on the many amiable traits that your character has unfolded to us. It is impossible for a child to have parents more affectionately attached, than yours, my dear, are to you--we love you tenderly--& this regard, is the true cause of our being now separated—it became very necessary that you should have soon, more advantages of Education, than our town affords if longer delayed you might think yourself rather too old to suffer the confinement & assiduity necessary.

Hope, born in 1802, was afflicted with epilepsy. Gentle and much loved by all, she bore her illness with great fortitude although she could not attend boarding school like her sisters. Several times, the family took her to the spa at Saratoga, but to little effect.

Tom's demonstrations of fatherly affection were a considerable contrast with Nick's household while his children were growing up. Mary

Stelle Brown did her best to raise her step-children with care and affection, which they returned in equal measure. But Nick, whose own father had never demonstrated much warmth, seemed uncomfortable with any public display of emotion and could not bring himself to express such easy feeling. In a letter to her "beloved mother" (her stepmother, Mary Stelle) from Mrs. Bereton's school in New York, Ann noted that she preferred writing to her father over speaking directly with him. In his diaries, Nicholas III was more blunt, calling his father "that gray-haired Jughernaut." Indeed, both boys preferred dealing with their Uncle Tom. Reminiscing about his father many years later, Nicholas III would tell his cousin Moses Brown Ives:

> My father & his children always lived upon terms of nothing more than common civility—that he never in conversation, or writing, would reply or take notice of what was advanced by either of the children. Of course, no confidence could exist where there was no interchange of views—or where what was advanced by one party was treated with contempt by the other. And the principal reason why your father [Tom Ives] and myself always lived on terms of cordial friendship was that he heard & replied to whatever I advanced—sometimes he adopted my views . . . [and sometimes] I adopted his views.

This reliance on uncles for advice and guidance was nothing new in the Brown family; after all, Nick had owed an enormous debt to both his uncles Moses and John. The pattern was simply repeated from one generation to the next. Nick's correspondence with his much younger brother-in-law, Crawford Carter, contains more marks of affection and concern than do letters to his own sons. While he wanted his sons to remain under his supervision in Providence, he urged young Crawford to travel the world. In 1803, he suggested that the boy to apply for "the place of a clerk on the Ship Patterson to Canton. . . if they can't pay you, go for the privilege of bringing an adventure home." Three years later, he suggested that Crawford go to China aboard *John Jay* rather than risk the "sickly climate" of Indonesia, but he was careful to add "May you be directed to do what may be for the best . . . what may Eventually turn out for your future good." When the *John Jay* was wrecked, Crawford sailed instead as supercargo to Batavia for another firm. He was taken ill, the captain died on the voyage, and her owners went bankrupt. Nick tried to cheer Crawford up: "You have many friends, & I will serve you—therefore keep in your spirits . . ." and recommended that the young man read the Bible daily, "Solomon will tell you the importance of a good character to a Young Man & point out the dangers & snares of life. . . . I am affectionately solicitous that you preserve such a steady line of conduct as will tend to your own peace, while it will be joyful to your family."

The apple of Nick's eye was his charming and gracious daughter Ann who, albeit all too briefly, provided him with as much pleasure as her brothers did worry. She was much loved by her little brother JCB who wrote "whilst young I passed some of the happiest days of my life rambling about the fields with my dear departed sister." Nick was delighted when on June 18, 1822, Ann married her second cousin, Uncle John's adored grandson, John Brown Francis.

From the outset, the young couple seemed blissfully happy at *Spring Green*, while Francis's political career was blooming. Nick's first grandchild was born in September 1823, a little girl named Abby after her paternal grandmother. A boy, John, was born in 1825 but lived less than a year. Anne was born April 23, 1828. Then, tragedy struck again. Less than a week later, Ann died from the complications of childbirth. Her death had seemed senseless: "perhaps no woman was ever more happily situated than Ann was," noted her obituary. The widowed John Brown Francis was stricken with grief, so Abby and her baby sister went to live with Nick and Mary (who became their legal guardians), ably assisted by the trusted Amey-Ann Stelle (Mary's spinster sister) who had raised Nick's own children.

Much as Uncle John had doted on his grandson John Brown Francis, Nick's great solace in his last years were his grand-daughters, Abby and Anne. The two girls spent much of their childhood in Providence and allowed Nick to demonstrate the affection he had been unable to give his own children. He remained on amicable terms with his son-in-law John Brown Francis, who in 1831 remarried a Philadelphia cousin on the Francis side, the widow Elizabeth Willing Francis Harrison (who already had a daughter, Mary). The new marriage produced four children: Elizabeth (1833), Sally (1834), Sophia (1836) and John Brown Francis II (1838). As step-sisters, Mary and Abby were close in age, attended Miss Searle's School together outside Boston, and became the closest of friends. Abby was heartbroken when Mary died suddenly in January 1841 (Abby would die that October).

There were, however, moments of friction between Nick and his son-in-law John Brown Francis over the girls' upbringing. Once, feeling particularly frustrated, Nick wrote:

> Your notes my dear sir are wearing down to the grave, my best Earthly friend. . . . I am desirous of dividing any unpleasant feelings & pray to you, to think more favorable of us all under this Roof, where we have all endeavored to make you so welcome and comfortable, & it is your own fault, that things are as at present.

Nick was nevertheless always mindful to give John Brown Francis final word on any important decision, even when it upset his own plans. In 1836, Nick made arrangements for Abby to travel back to school on the new railroad, accompanied by both his clerk and his personal physician. At the last minute, John Francis detained Abby at *Spring Green*. With the train leaving at 8:00 the next morning, Nick waited until sunset to send a message to his son-in-law. His exasperation was palpable. John Brown Francis later noted in his diary that Abby made a trip to Boston "against my wishes—but I yielded to the pressing invitation of her Grandfather."

Abby was a charming but very sickly child. By her 15th year, in August 1838, she was bedridden at *Spring Green*, "subsisting on liquids & refusing every kind of food." Two years later, she still had not recovered and languished, "totally prostrate, reduced to a mere skeleton & unable to eat anything or sit up twenty minutes at a time." Yet she bore her many sufferings with patience and cheerfulness: "no grieving, no repining at her hard fate but in the midst of all her afflictions a cheerful smile at all times greeted her friends." The family placed their trust in Doctor Tobey and did their best to make Abby comfortable.

When she seemed to revive in July 1839, JCB arranged for a cruise to Long Island Sound thinking that sea air would do her good. The first day was pleasant, followed by "a cool Ev'g & beautiful moonlight." But upon retiring to their cabins, the passengers were attacked by bed bugs "who had mustered in great force." The following night was spent in an "indifferent" hotel and Abby cheered up with ice cream. For a few weeks, the excursion had a beneficial effect, but soon she began to languish again. She was moved to Nick's house in Providence. After four years as an invalid, Abby died, just three weeks after her grandfather. She was only 18.

Anne, meanwhile, attended the new "Young Ladies' High School" which Brown alumnus John Kingsbury had opened in 1828. It was extremely progressive as the students learned "not the usual feminine accomplishments, but Latin, Mathematics and Science (Kingsbury's detractors ridiculed him as "the man who teaches girls Latin.") Just a few doors down from the Nightingale-Brown house on Benefit Street, the school boasted of astonishing luxuries such as carpeted floors and broadcloth covered desks.

Affection for the two little girls was not Nick's exclusive preserve; they drew together the whole Brown family. In December 1830, they received sugar plums from their cousins, Tom Ives's oldest grandchildren, Charlotte Hope Goddard, born in 1823, and William Goddard II, born in 1825, with a note: "My dear Cousins. William and myself send you some sugar plums because it is William's birthday. We wish you all a happy Christmas. Your affectionate Coussins [sic], William & Hope." Another cousin, Anna Herreshoff (born in 1802 to Uncle John's daughter, Sarah Brown Herreshoff), sent a charming note from the family estate at Point Pleasant in Bristol:

My dear little Anne. There is a little girl that I want to see
very much. I long to feel her soft arm around my neck,
to receive a dozen of her sweet kisses and to hear her say,
"I love you cousin Anna." This little girl is now reading
these lines and she is the darling of my heart. How I do
miss you my dear one!

JCB too doted on his nieces, just as he had adored his big sister Ann, and
got along well with John Brown Francis. In May 1828, just a month after
Ann's death, JCB took the distraught widower on a tour of the countryside
around Boston, hoping to distract him from his grief. The two men visited
agricultural facilities and many of the great manufacturing centers including
Lowell and Woonsocket, as well as the theological seminary and academy
at Andover, Massachusetts. JCB was impressed by the landscape around
the seminary which "presents a very different appearance from the grounds
around Brown University. I always feel mortified at the dirty, filthy, slovenly
appearance of everything around my own Alma Mater. . . ." Once back in
Providence, JCB showered his little nieces with affection. He relished visiting
them at *Spring Green* or sharing the same roof in Providence. He rejoiced
when their health was good and agonized over their childhood illnesses:

Even now in my waking dreams I sometimes fancy, Ann
is not dead, but sleepeth and that ere long I shall again
enjoy her society and receive her counsel and advice –
how elusive are these expectations. . . . Her dear little
daughters are with us—for their mother's sake I should
love them, but now that she is no longer with us, they
will be ever doubly dear to me. The Infant has taken a
Strong hold of my affections.

To her uncle, Abby seemed "like gold seven times purified." In 1835, JCB
commissioned the famous portraitist Chester Harding to paint his nieces—a full three years before Nick acquiesced to sit for his own portrait
by Harding (commissioned by Brown University).

Predictably enough, Nicholas III refused to participate in this
happy display of family closeness. He rarely visited Providence.[77] In
November 1831, aged almost 40, he finally remarried twenty-four-year
old Caroline Matilda Clements of Portsmouth, New Hampshire. A
son, Alfred Nicholas Brown (later known as Nicholas Brown IV), was
born the following September 1832.[78] The arrival of a child accentuated
Nicholas III's financial anxieties, for which he blamed his father. Nick's
charitable and philanthropic giving, the subject of forthcoming chapters, provided the catalyst for much of his ire. While Nick was pouring
money into the Baptist Church and Brown University, he, the eldest son
of an immensely wealthy man, was struggling to make ends meet. In
desperation, he hatched a plan: his father's attitude was so extreme that
he must be declared insane. On February 9th, 1833, Nicholas III wrote
to Moses Ives:

> I feel it my duty to submit to you my views on the subject
> of my father's conduct toward the public, & toward his
> own family, & to say that the opinion which John [JCB]
> & myself entertain of the unsoundness, of his mind is, by
> daily acts of his, most abundantly confirmed. . . To state
> the matter more logically—one of two things is true viz.
> 1. He is either a malignant fiend—a devil—determined
>   to injure his children
>   or
> 2. He is a Lunatic, laboring under that species of
>   Lunacy called idiocy.
> Now for his own sake, & for the honor of human nature
> I will draw the most favourable conclusion viz. that he is
> An Idiot"

[77] He made an appearance for his sister Ann's funeral in May 1828; his father noted that
he made an effort to "appear quite sympathetic."
[78] Nicholas III asked JCB to be the godfather and the first Episcopalian Brown was
baptized at St. Clement's Church, New York.

The letter goes on to suggest that Nick should be put under the care of guardians through a competent tribunal, or at the very least prevented from:

> . . . ruining his family, & intercepting my GdFather's property from going where he intended it should go, viz. to benefit his posterity. And further, it is the duty of us children to stand forth in our own defense: it is the duty of those who care one fig for my GdFather's descendants to be up & doing on this subject.

In paragraph after paragraph of pure vitriol, Nicholas III listed examples of his father's latest benevolence: $2,000 for a new Baptist seminary, a $3,000 organ for the Baptist Church, a chapel for Brown University, "a subscription of ten thousd dolls for some purpose or other," declaring "Here then is proof, proof, proof that this hurry of ideas has become confirmed Lunacy of the species called idiocy. . . ." Nicholas III also pointed to the fact that his father never had bought his own daughter Ann a piano, nor built his son JCB a house. "If he must subscribe for the benefit of those who send their sons to College in RI why not subscribe something for the future benefit of his Gd Son here. The poor lunatic talks of doing good &c &c why not do some good now to his grand-children since he will not to his children." Nick's decision to make large donations in his lifetime rather than merely leaving posthumous bequests was admittedly unusual for the times. His son worried that "if the poor lunatic does these things now, he will not make his will & leave those sums for the same purposes." He ended by asking Moses Ives, "If you have an influence over my poor shatterbrain'd father let me request you to lessen (if it is impossible to prevent) the amount of his donations: this I know you can do."

When Nicholas III and Caroline moved to Rockland County (near Tappan, New York) in May 1833, Nick agreed to purchase a 7 ¾ acre property for them but, true to form, placed the deed in JCB's name. Nicholas III pressed Brown & Ives for funds to repair the house, claiming his father had promised $1,000 to purchase a horse and chaise, as well as a piano for Caroline, "musick being an agreeable recreation in a country as well as town, & there being neither rhyme nor reason why we should not be gratified, in this respect, as well as the Baptist Congregation" (an allusion to the fine organ Nick had purchased recently for the First Baptist Meeting House). When no money arrived, Nicholas III's tone became harsh: "our little boy, has for his middle name that accursed name Nicholas . . . & for no other purpose than to gratify the foolish family pride in names. . . . The lunatic has not presented his g'd child with even a rattle to play with. Any other man on earth would have put a few thousand into some Bank to accumulate until he reached 21 yrs."

A daughter was born to Nicholas III and Caroline in February 1835, named AnnMary after her grandmother (Ann Carter) and step-grandmother (Mary Stelle). To support his growing family, Nicholas III again tried borrowing from Brown & Ives's New York correspondents, using his various investments as collateral. But the partners held firm and sent him no more than his regular allowance. In 1837, Nicholas III attempted a different tactic: he returned to Providence for an extended stay, while Caroline gave birth to a second daughter on March 9. Two weeks later, little AnnMary died of scarlet fever so the new baby was given the name of her dead older sister. Perhaps thanks to this tragedy, a brief rapprochement of sorts was effected between father and son; Nicholas III was able to borrow $3,000 directly from Brown & Ives. Later he would claim that in this period of "amiable feelings," his father had invested in the "Insurance company at Providence" and in "the bank at Newport" on behalf of his son and talked of purchasing an estate for him in Rhode Island. The warm feelings did not last long and Nicholas III returned to Rockland. A fourth child, John Carter Brown II, was born in March 1840, but Caroline recovered with difficulty. So, in November 1840, Nicholas III took his wife to St. Croix in the West Indies, leaving young Alfred Nicholas in his grandfather's care. As Nick's health was fast fading, the boy spent time at *Spring Green* with the Francis family. Upon their return to the United States in April 1841, Nicholas III and Caroline stayed almost two months in Providence and frequently visited *Spring Green*. With Nick's death fast approaching, everyone tried to be on their best behavior.

For a man of traditional outlook like Nick, imbued with such a strong sense of family and of family obligation, the unsatisfactory situation concerning his sons must have been a bitter pill to swallow. The fact that he at least enjoyed cordial relations with the younger one, while no doubt some consolation, hardly compensated for the failure of either son to embrace the family's prodigious merchant heritage. Admittedly, Nick's inability to surrender control made it difficult as a general proposition to foster relationships of trust and confidence with the next generation and prompted something of a crisis within the partnership when Tom Ives died in 1835.

Nicholas Senior had been made a partner at the age of eighteen by his uncle Obadiah, and Nick was awarded the same status at the age of twenty-one, but his son and nephews were only made junior partners in 1832 when Moses Ives was thirty-eight, JCB was thirty-five, and Robert Ives was thirty-four. However, while this obsession with control may provide a partial explanation of the exceptionally fractious relationship between Nick and Nicholas III, it is clearly not the whole story. The harsh fact seems to be that through whatever quirk of genetic disposition Nicholas III was, by common consent, an unusually angry, embittered, and ungrateful man. It is interesting to speculate about the extent to which this unhappy experience of fatherhood drove what was to become Nick's obsession with the higher education of young men.

CHAPTER 13

FROM CHARITY TO PHILANTHROPY

"The true use of riches" —*Francis Wayland*

It is fortunate for posterity that Nick finally agreed in 1836 to have his portrait painted by Chester Harding. That this picture hangs today in Brown University's Sayles Hall is no small feat. Other than Uncle John who sat in 1794 for a miniature by Newport artist Edward Malbone,[79] no Brown had ever commissioned a portrait—it evidently offended their Baptist sensibilities. The University had initially requested the portrait (along with a monumental statue) in 1822 to commemorate Nick's donation of Hope Hall, its second building. Nick flatly refused the statue and made the university wait fourteen years to sit for the portrait, after Harding had painted his little grand-daughters.

This is an instance where a picture really is worth a thousand words. The setting evokes the stately portraits of an earlier era: a marble column, great swags of crimson velvet framing a view of Narragansett Bay. Nick is seated at a table laden with maps and ledgers. Behind him, a tall

---

[79] There also exists a sketch of Uncle Moses, but it was secretly drawn in 1823 by a nephew hiding behind a bush (and turned into a painting the following year by John Wesley Jarvis).

bookshelf is filled with volumes, many worn in appearance and leaning to the side, the artist's way to indicate frequent use. Most striking, however, is Nick's clothing. By 1836, all men wore "pantaloons" (trousers) and short boots; he wears black silk britches and buckled shoes. The fashion was for frock coats with cinched waists; he wears a loose dress coat. His frilly white shirt with a soft, turned-down collar was also out of date in an era when men wore pleated fronts, black ties and upturned collars. Indeed, the only "modern" items in the portrait are the chair and table cloth which most probably came from the artist's studio.

It is hard to imagine a more eloquent depiction of the sixty-five-year old. Consciously and unabashedly old-fashioned in his appearance, he harks back unashamedly to the long dead Federal era and the simple certainties for which he never ceased to yearn. In Harding's portrayal, Nick is the quintessence of the successful, wealthy merchant prince in the faded glory of his declining years. Above all, he appears utterly self-assured and certain of his place in posterity.

However accurate the rest of the depiction, the self-assurance and certainty are but a bold façade. We know from Nick's obituary that "the structure and habits of Mr. Brown's mind were somewhat peculiar. He had no relish for general reading or for prolonged conversation, or for mixed society." His inability to express emotion publicly was therefore well known. Instead, "on paper, he expressed himself always with freedom and clearness, sometimes with force. His power of observation was singularly quick and searching, without the aid of intermediate processes, or without being able to communicate such intermediate processes to others."

This explains why his daughter Ann, whom he adored, nevertheless felt more at ease writing to her father than addressing him in person.

So confident in other ways, Nick also was never at ease about his riches. His preoccupation with the "burden and complexity" of managing vast wealth is noted in several posthumous accounts. Once, when Judge Robert Crandall of Exeter asked Nick his opinion on the passage in Matthew 19:24 about the rich man entering the Kingdom of Heaven, Nick apparently replied: "Well, Judge, I have often thought of it, and the matter has given me some trouble. I sometimes fear my property will keep me out of heaven; but I don't mean it shall." Another time, he supposedly confided in Mr. Bowler, the cashier at the Providence Bank: "I think more and more of the old prayer that we find in the Bible. Were I to begin life again, I would pray: Give me neither poverty nor riches."

This fundamental shyness and emotional restraint reappeared three generations later in my grandfather, John Nicholas Brown II (1900-1979). Both Nick and he were known for their "remarkably even and kindly temper." The statement made in the 1841 *Providence Journal* obituary could just as easily have applied to his great-grandson:

> He was in the best and only true sense, a man of the People and for the People. He had a deep stake in general welfare; he wanted no official emoluments, he sought no political power; he was tempted to promote no interest hostile to the interest of the masses around him.

The modern notion of social responsibility had been introduced at the turn of the nineteenth century by College of Rhode Island President Jonathan Maxcy who admonished, "the condition of men and their connexions and dependence in civil society entailed obligations that impinged upon the conduct of all." But as a rule, "few capitalists are willing to part with a portion of their treasures for the luxury of doing good," as noted by the Rhode Island Sunday School Union. Nor did other famous benefactors show much interest in "exerting the power which God has given us upon the spirit of man . . . for the purpose of promoting happiness & confirming his virtue."

French-born Stephen Girard of Philadelphia (1750-1831), one of the richest Americans of all times who personally had saved the U.S. government from financial collapse during the War of 1812, had felt no obligation to cure social disorder. However, he did leave $7 million in his will for civic improvements, canals, a loan fund for the Freemasons, the Pennsylvania Hospital, and a boarding school for white orphan boys. Conversely, Edward Delavan (1793-1871), the principal funder of the temperance movement, felt that "I have given in my lifetime what I felt it was my duty to give. I think my family is entitled to what is left of my estate." Brown University graduate and great educator Horace Mann (1796-1859) disagreed: "A fortune left to children is a misfortune since it takes away the stimulus to effort, the restraints from indulgence, the muscles out of the limbs, the brain out of the head, and virtue out of the heart." Others, such as the textile magnate Amos Lawrence gave liberally (but made no charitable bequests), hoping "that I may at last be received among the faithful stewards, with the "Well Done" promised; and thus secure what is beyond price compared with anything Earthly."

Growing up in a family of maritime traders during times of war and economic crisis had taught Nick that wealth can disappear in an instant; it therefore should thus be used wisely while the opportunity permits. Money had bought his father power but not the health of his children. Nor could money buy family harmony. But money could be used to improve society. William Gammell, a Brown University professor who married Tom Ives's granddaughter Elizabeth, offered a valuable insight into Nick's outlook:

> [It] was not commerce alone that engaged his attention and tasked the energies of his mind. He had large interests at stake in the country and he could not be indifferent to its government or its political progress. To achieve success as a merchant and to amass wealth was not with him the greatest result to be accomplished. From the outset of his career he was accustomed to recognize other interests, and other claims upon his attention than those of his profession alone, & he always cherished a comprehensive sympathy with the future of the country and his race.

The most profound influence on Nick's social conscience was his Uncle Moses. He in turn had been inspired by the Reverend Samuel Hopkins of Newport, his partner in many abolition campaigns, who preached that beyond saving souls, "benevolence should be practiced towards all beings, particularly the poor, the illiterate, the slaves, the downtrodden, and even the untold millions of heathens in Asian and Africa." As a Quaker, Uncle Moses saw no conflict between living well and endeavoring to improve the world. The Quaker leader William Penn, who believed that class distinctions were an essential part of the divine order, had said, "men are indebted to God not only for their wealth but for their very being, and accountable to Him for the way they spend their lives as well as their fortunes."

Uncle Moses's faith as a Quaker was based on social action. In addition to his anti-slavery efforts, he was a founder of the Rhode Island Bible Society and, in 1816, Vice President of the American Bible Society. Two years later, with the assistance of Thomas Arnold and George Benson, Nick's former partner, he established the Rhode Island Peace Society and financed the distribution of thousands of pamphlets. He also supported the Connecticut Asylum for the Deaf and Dumb at Hartford, established in 1817. His fascination with the state's early history and his love of books led to his involvement with the American Antiquarian Society in 1812 in Worcester, Massachusetts, the Rhode Island Historical Society in 1822, and the Providence Atheneum in 1838. He opened his Elmgrove estate as a waystation on the Underground Railroad. But the greatest source of satisfaction in his old age and his most enduring legacy was his third and finally successful attempt to establish a New England Yearly Meeting Boarding School.

Ten years after the Brown brothers' failed 1767 attempt to introduce free public education in Providence, Uncle Moses had tried to provide Quaker children with a "guarded education" that included subjects with an immediate practical value. But the attempt failed after just two years for lack of teachers. Like the Baptists, most Quakers were indifferent towards education, relying instead on the "Inner Light" as their guide. The wealthy sent their children to private schools; the poorer Friends put them out as apprentices to learn a trade. In 1782, Uncle Moses made a second attempt at opening a school at Portsmouth, Rhode Island, just as America fell into a post-war economic recession. By 1788, the school closed. He bided his time, carefully investing the few hundred dollars saved from the second failed attempt; by 1813 it had grown to $9,000. Though already seventy-six years old that year, he convinced other New England Friends to pledge $10,000 for a third attempt. Ground was broken in Providence in 1816, with Almy & Brown in charge of construction (Uncle Moses sometimes advanced money when cash was running low). The school finally opened in January 1819; Moses was 81. Three years later, his son Obadiah died, leaving a $100,000 gift to the school—the largest single financial contribution to an American educational institution to date.

In the first few decades of Nick's adult life, when maritime commerce was in its golden age, when the Federalists still wielded influence, and when the wealthy, educated elite still held sway, Nick was content to undertake innumerable, ad-hoc gestures of personal charity, similar in type—if greater in quantity—to those of many other affluent men. An anonymous writer observed:

> I think I do not at all overstate the fact, when I assent, that for the last 25 years, whenever any person among us, in almost any rank of society, was in pecuniary distress, the first person to whom he would spontaneously apply for relief was Nicholas Brown. Nor was his reputation for charity confined to his native place. Almost every mail brought him applications for assistance from every part of New England, and even from the remoter States; & rarely, it is believed, were such appeals unavailing.

Nick was particularly known for providing funerals for the indigent and attending the ceremonies in person: "almost invariably he might be seen in his chaise following the little funeral trains, however small they were, to the burying grounds." He was also famous for delivering care packages himself to poor families. Stephen Mason, a clerk in a grocery store at the foot of College Street, recounted that:

Mr. Brown would often come in and say: "Stephen put me up a half a peck of meal, half a gallon of molasses and half a pound of tea." Stowing these into his chaise, he would drive off. Perhaps in an hour he would return and say: "Stephen, put me up a peck of potatoes, a peck of meal and half a dollar's worth of sugar." These would be packed into the old chaise and carried to another needy family. This ministry went on for years. He rarely carried much money in his pocket, but he was always distributing little checks. At his office he distributed silver pieces as some citizens scatter crumbs of bread to the hungry sparrows. Indeed his door was thronged by applicants for charity.

At Thanksgiving, he left orders with the butchers on Market Square to supply fowl, meat, and vegetables to destitute families. But Nick did not mean to encourage dependence. On one occasion, when a butcher gave a large piece of beef to one man and a smaller one to another, the recipient of the lesser pieces complained to Nick that the other man actually owned three fat hogs. Nick apparently replied "He has? Well, well, he is an industrious man; a fine, industrious man. Go back and tell the butcher to give him another piece."

A donation here, a Thanksgiving turkey there—this assortment of individual actions would provide temporary relief but do little to improve society. Perhaps, as William Gammell later suggested, it was his experience of the China Trade that inspired Nick to form "large views and liberal principles." Since he was far too inhibited to play a major public role like his Uncle Moses, Nick embarked upon his own philanthropic journey by channeling his influence through institutions that promoted social stability and "which tended to affect the course of human action and human thought." Inevitably, he was influenced by the reformist spirit of the era that believed "when an individual has once formed a habit of doing good, we of course consider it probable that he will continue to do good." Benevolent organizations were providing, he felt, both individual

regeneration and social reconstruction. But Nick carried the concept
to a much greater degree than any of his contemporaries, certainly in
Providence where his initiatives were "suggested by no conspicuous
models in the community in which he lived." He was also among the
first to seek lasting change, rather than short-term, palliative measures,
by promoting "agencies of perceived good [and] opening fountains of
beneficence whose streams should flow thro' successive generations."

The church was an obvious port-of-call on this philanthropic journey. Like his father, Nick never was baptized (thus avoiding a public
profession of faith) and preferred studying the Bible in private, "leaning
back on one chair with his feet on another and his book in hand before
him." But he firmly believed that church attendance promoted social
order. And one way to encourage church attendance was to subsidize
the cost of pews. The first churches in Providence had been funded by
lottery and private subscriptions. By the 1830s, public pew auctioning
and an ongoing pew tax became the new means to finance construction
for all denominations. In 1832, when the old square pews were torn out
of the First Baptist Meeting House, Nick bought nineteen new long pews
for $2,000, many more than he could fill with family, and often not in
"prime locations." His willingness to buy relatively undesirable seats and
to pay taxes on them was an important contribution to the welfare of the
church. It also illustrated the way "bourgeois Protestants" could combine
displays of financial success with great generosity.

Nick continued in his father's efforts to increase church decorum
and formality. He was the Moderator of the Charitable Baptist Society
for thirty years. His first major gift was a fine house on Angell Street
to serve as a parsonage. From 1817, he pushed the church to accept an
organ; it finally was installed seventeen years later at a cost of $3,000.[80]
Church concerts and recitals now became standard fare. When the balcony for African-Americans was removed in the 1832 renovation, the
church showed it unequivocally favored a more fashionable, wealthy,

---

[80] The installation of an organ completed the transformation that had begun in 1771
when Elder Winsor and forty-eight members had resigned because "singing in public
worship was very disgustful to him."

and white congregation. Nick pointedly sought to remedy this imbalance by contributing generously to "poorer" churches, and attended the services of many other denominations. In a letter to his grand-daughter Abby, Nick noted, "This morning Yr Uncle John [JCB] took me to hear a Roman Catholic Priest who surpassed my Preacher. I would [agree] in most respects certainly."

The Brown family was particularly associated with the pioneering African Union Meeting House and School. Nick approved that it was "open and free for all Christian professors and not confined to any one profession of the Christian religion."

Until the 1820s, African-Americans attended Providence's main churches; ten percent of the First Baptist Meeting House's members were black. They sat high up in the second balcony, which felt like "a pigeon hole" to William Brown. In May 1805, a delegate from Boston visited Nick in order to raise funds for a black church. Nick sent him on to Uncle Moses with a note "Boston abounds in free Blacks & as many of us have aided in promoting the Abolition of Slavery, I think we Can't do better than to assist in forming their morals & instructing them in religious Dutys." Nick hoped that Uncle Moses would contact former members of the Abolition Society, "to join in contributing to the plan proposed. . . . I myself will subscribe handsomely."

Nothing came of this 1805 initiative, but by 1819 it was obvious that the growing African-American community in Providence needed its own non-denominational church and especially a Sunday school. Some African-American leaders—notably Frederick Douglass—denounced separate black churches as "Negro pews on a higher and larger scale." But others felt that they "sought to achieve dignity for Black people" and allowed the community to better assert itself.

The first few planning meetings took place in the First Baptist Meeting House's vestry, led by the African-American George Williams, with major encouragement from Stephen Gano, the First Baptist's pastor (widowed from Uncle Joseph's daughter, Mary) and Henry Jackson, the Sunday School superintendent. Uncle Moses donated the land and Nick covered some of the construction costs. He was concerned that the building should be "on a lot easy of access," so that attendance would not decline after the novelty of a new meeting house wore off.

Henry Jackson preached the first sermon when the African Union Church and its adjoining parish house (with a capacity of five hundred) were inaugurated in August 1821. A school house also opened in the African Union Meeting House vestry for two hundred children who paid $1.50 a quarter. It offered the "Lancastrian" plan of instruction whereby the older students helped teach the younger ones. But teachers were hard to find (they received only fifty dollars a quarter), and often resigned after just a few months. Due to the lack of decent education, opportunities for black children, any parents of color simply indentured their children to white households (20 percent of all children of color in 1820), where they were supposed to be provided instruction.

Nick also assisted the Colored Freewill Baptist Church on Pond Street. In 1822, he told his Uncle Moses about a "Mr. George Dods," a former cooper employed by the Brown family, who was "engaged in the laudable undertaking" of establishing a meeting house, also to be used as a day school on Tockwotten Hill, near India Point. Since Uncle Moses had "generously aided the uptown Meeting House [The African Union Church]," Nick hoped he "may feel a freedom to Encourage the one now raised on Tockwotten Hill," as "it has proved a lasting benefit to that extreme End of our Town." Nick was concerned "to have the Blacks instructed in Religious Duty & every thing tending to improve their morals and to make them Industrious, honest & prudent."

This tone of paternalism marked all of Nick's dealings with the African-American community in Providence, as indeed it marked his charitable assistance to the poor and needy in general. As with Uncle Moses, many in Providence came to him for assistance. In 1809, Nick told his uncle about helping a man build a house in the Olney Lane neighborhood. A typical instruction to a supplier might read:

> Sir, I told the Bearer Noah, who I believe an honest
> well behaved Black man, that I would give him Twenty
> Dollars to assist him in Building his new house. He

says he wants to pay it to you, towards bricks & lime. I
thereby engage to pay you twenty Dollars in course of
September and presume this will answer Noah's purpose & be as good as money.

The tone of paternalist superiority, amounting almost to arrogance, cannot but shock modern susceptibilities, however benign and well-meaning
the intention. Still, as many historians concede, such attitudes were "an
inevitable sequel to slavery, a necessary prologue to the establishment
of a free Negro community in the state." It was, in short, very much the
conventional attitude of the day on the part of the well-to-do toward
those less fortunate—when they bothered to notice them at all.

Nick was also enthusiastic about missionary work, whether at home
or abroad. He suggested to Ebenezer Thresher, Secretary of the Northern
Baptist Education Society, a "Sinking Fund" (endowment) so that "no
young man of suitable talents & Peity, should be put off." From 1823 until his death in 1841, he chaired the non-denominational "Rhode Island
Bible Society,"[81] organized in 1813 to supply local Sunday schools with
Bibles and books. He also donated large sums to the "Northern Baptist
Education Society," the "American Tract Society," and the "American
& Foreign Bible Society," and paid for the publication of sermons by
eminent preachers such as Yale's president Jonathan Edwards. In 1832,
a young woman named Harriet Ware started a Sunday school for children, an evening school for adults, a Sunday morning service, and a
Sabbath School for the inhabitants of India Point. She was surrounded
by "drunken revels, endless profanity and even murder." Slowly she won
the people's confidence and Brown University students came to help on
Sundays. Impressed by Ware's tenacity, Nick bought her a new building
in a more salubrious part of town.

---

[81] With a Quaker moderator (Uncle Moses) and a Congregational minister and an
Episcopalian bishop among its senior officers, the Rhode Island Bible Society sought to
unite many disparate denominates to serve the needs of the community – an approach
that greatly pleased Nick.

When subscription papers were presented to Nick, he usually would say: "Well, well, you raise what you can, and then bring the paper to me and I will double the figures." When the American Baptist Missionary Board faced a deficit of $40,000, a collection was proposed in the First Baptist Meeting House. Nick declared "raise all you can, and I will double it"—six hundred dollars were subscribed. He directed that some of his bank stock dividends go to poor Baptist ministers. As Brown University President Asa Messer wrote "There is no Baptist here, if anywhere, whose liberality is comparable to his and there are not many whose property is greater. It is certainly a pleasing consideration that his liberality is always directed to religious or charitable or literary objects."

Another means to promote social order was to build libraries to improve "intellectual standards." Since 1753, when Nicholas Brown had participated in the formation of Providence's first library, the Browns had supported many "literary objects." Nick had been a member of the American Antiquarian Society since 1813. In the melioristic climate of the 1830s, a new library, "larger, better arranged, more useful and more attractive than that within the means of any individual share-holder," would "open to men a new path to social distinction" so that wealth "becomes in a less degree an object of envy." The library would "render knowledge, valuable knowledge, accessible to the whole com-munity." And so a library was started in rooms 42 and 44 on the second story of the Arcade in 1831. Five years later, Nick and his Ives nephews, Moses and Robert, acquired a plot of land on Benefit Street and offered $6,000 to erect an "Atheneum," so long as a further $10,000 would be raised by others (three hundred members purchased shares worth fif-teen dollars each). They also contributed $4,000 for books, requiring an equivalent match by the town's other "learned societies." Ground was broken in 1837. At the 1838 inauguration of the neoclassical stone building, President Wayland of Brown University hailed the Atheneum as a bonding force in the community, proclaiming: "Without access to useful knowledge, Americans would fall prey to sensual indulgence or the opportunities that the country's wealth multiplied for the gratification of passions."[82]

There were moments when even Nick's resources were not enough to cover all his donations. In 1831, he wrote "I have a great many heavy money plans to carry into effect in the ensuing year...." He applied his entire share of the French spoliation claims to his charitable giving. From his correspondence, it is clear he studied each request carefully in order to "master the subject well." In his last decade, philanthropy became his passion; "His charities became with advancing years, greater; and they followed each other in more & rapid succession... He not only sowed the seed, but was himself permitted to reap the harvest."

All these various initiatives, if only by virtue of their scope, scale, and potential for long term impact, lifted traditional charitable giving to a status more closely akin to modern notions of philanthropy. They were, however, but the precursors to Nick's one true, great, and single-minded philanthropic cause—and the one which was destined to define his posterity— namely that of the university which to this day continues to bear his name.

That cause will be discussed in detail in the next chapter. Beforehand, it is appropriate to speak of Nick's final, posthumous philanthropic act. In many ways his most daring donation, it was certainly his most remarkable, not least because it had almost nothing to do with moral reform. This gift was aimed, purely and simply, at alleviating the plight of the most vulnerable, forgotten members of society. As such, it may also be the most eloquent testimony to Nick's sense of unease with the good fortune he had the lifelong privilege to enjoy.

In March 1840, when Nick's health was failing and he knew his end was near, he drafted a remarkable codicil to his will: he now wished to sponsor an asylum for the insane in Providence. Funding a "lunatic asylum" was a complete departure from his usual support for educational institutions, churches, tract and missionary societies, and libraries. His will gave little explanation for the decision:

---

[82] The Atheneum boasted that it was the cheapest institution of its kind in the country; nevertheless, the five dollar annual membership fee and only rare evening hours placed it out of reach for the working classes.

> And whereas it has long been deeply impressed on my
> mind that an Insane or Lunatic Hospital or Retreat for
> the Insane should be established upon a firm and per-
> manent basis, under an act of the Legislature, where the
> unhappy portion of our fellow beings who are by the
> visitation of Providence deprived of their reason may
> find a safe retreat and be provided with whatever may
> be conducive to their comfort and to their restoration to
> a sound mind, where any person regardless of class or
> religion could better themselves.

It is possible that Nick may have been influenced by the new breed
of philanthropist that had appeared in the late 1830s. They not only
funded but actively assisted segments of society that were previously neglected or deemed beyond help. Thomas Hopkins Gallaudet (1787-1851)
was working with deaf-mutes; Dr. Samuel Gridley Howe (1801-1876)
was advocating for the blind; and Horace Mann (1796-1859), a Brown
University graduate, was crusading for free education and good schools.
But Dorothea Dix (1802-1887) only published her fiery report on the
care of the indigent insane in Massachusetts in 1841, after Nick's death.

New Englanders generally (just as their cousins back in England) and
Rhode Islanders in particular had always shown a pronounced distaste
towards caring for the poor, the needy, the infirm and the weak-minded -
between whom they made little distinction. The first law empowering towns
to build a "house of correction for vagrants" and "to keep mad persons in"
dated from 1725. In 1742, the General Assembly had given the care of the
"insane and imbecile" to the town councils, with the power to appoint
guardians to their estates. Most of the time, Rhode Island towns equated
public charity with increased taxes. They instituted strict vagrancy laws
and insisted that elderly manumitted slaves be the responsibility of their
owners. Care of the poor was auctioned off to those who accepted the least
money. A recommendation to build an almshouse for the poor and another
for "the idle, intemperate and disorderly" was never implemented. It was
only in 1830 that the Dexter Asylum was erected through the generosity

of Ebenezer Knight Dexter, who left $60,000 and forty acres of land, the majority of his estate, to support the poor. Of the sixty-four inmates who first occupied the Dexter Asylum, over a quarter were deemed mentally ill.

The general consensus was that the poor and the deviant were the products of a faulty environment and should be removed from the harmful effects of society. In New York, Thomas Eddy founded the New York House of Refuge for juvenile delinquents in 1825. The reformers John Tuckerman (1778-1840) and John Griscom (1774-1840) launched the New York Society for the Prevention of Pauperism, a critic of most charitable endeavors for poor relief, which "relieved the sentiments of the 'comfortable classes' but did more harm than good to the poor." The Society advocated instead for savings banks and life insurance rather than simply dispensing pious advice.

Jacksonian America discovered asylums as a way to control both vice and dependency. But these almshouses and other institutions for the confinement of mentally ill were in reality human warehouses, designed more to segregate the allegedly insane than to provide for compassionate treatment. Insanity was classified with criminality and violent behavior as a threat to the community, so many people believed that physical punishment was the only way to correct or at least nullify "moral anomalies." Massachusetts physician R. C. Waterston (1812-1893) expressed the opinion of only a tiny minority when he asserted, "disease should be met with pity not with punishment; and of all diseases, surely there is none more worthy of compassion than that under which the lunatic suffers." Only Dorothea Dix begged legislature after legislature to "have pity on them; for their plight is hid in darkness, and trouble is their portion." Though conditions for the insane in Rhode Island's poor houses were equally horrific,[83] there were few voices pushing for enlightened care.

---

[83] In his 1851 "Report on the Poor and Insane in Rhode Island," Thomas Hazard described in graphic detail inmates of the Newport Asylum such as Rebecca Gibbs, "who had lost her reason through disappointed affection, and thereafter had been for thirty years a charge of the town. She seemed to be in a sense folded together... caused by her having for several winters been shut up in a cell without fire and without clothes."

Nick's method of funding the new asylum was well in character: his gift would launch the fundraising effort and his (posthumous) notoriety would influence others. In order to pay for this major new gift, Nick decreased some of his charitable bequests, particularly the cash he planned to leave to his granddaughters and to Brown University.[84] The will stipulated a grant of $30,000, "hoping that my sons and other friends will cooperate in the humane and benevolent design that the benefit of the Institute may soon be realized."

In fact, the opposite happened. Only a few weeks after Nick's death, the start of the "Dorr Rebellion" put all public life on hold for the next two years. Then, Nicholas III did all in his power to contest his father's wishes, even suing his brother and cousins to prevent the insane asylum. One can only imagine his indignant reaction to hearing of this bequest in light of his earlier accusations of "lunacy" toward his father; the thought must surely have crossed his mind that Nick had seen that infamous letter to Moses Ives and resolved to pay his eldest son back in kind for the insult. The family firm finally settled, paying Nicholas III $10,000 to withdraw his suit.

When Nick's bequest was released in 1844, the General Assembly issued a charter for a "Rhode Island asylum for the Insane." A committee was appointed to discuss raising the additional funds necessary to erect and furnish a building. Among its members was Alexander Duncan, a nephew by marriage and close confidant of the wealthy industrialist Cyrus Butler. Duncan wrote to his uncle:

> The undersigned have reason to know that you have often directed your attention towards the object which they now commend to your favorable regard, and they rejoice in the persuasion that you are not less anxious than they are that the proposed Institution should be established upon broad foundations, and be made in all

---

[84] By then the President's House, library fund and "building for minerals" (Rhode Island Hall) all had been completed.

its arrangements at least equal to kindred Institutions in other states. They ask you, Sir, to impart to this philanthropic enterprise, an impulse which will render certain its success.

It took Butler only five days to respond favorably:

> As soon as I was informed of the very liberal bequest he [Nick] had made, in contemplation of some future action as to this matter, and the very judicious condition on which he had authorized his Executors to pay the same, I determined to come forward in the establishment of such an institution, provided it could be carried out according to the enlarged and correct views of my late friend, and on a plan suited to the wants of this State, and equal in all events to any in the country.

He offered to fund $40,000 if an additional $50,000 endowment could be raised. The project captured popular imagination and $128,000 was raised from 1,039 subscriptions (414 for less than ten dollars each). In 1845, a large tract on the shore of the Seekonk River, known as the "brick house farm," was purchased. The building—a Victorian gothic structure in a park designed by Frederic Law Olmsted—was laid out by Dr. Luther V Bell, superintendent of the McLean Asylum near Boston, "in accordance with the most modern practices of the time in caring for the mentally ill." Dr. Isaac Ray, who had opened the first hospital for the insane in Maine, was engaged as the Superintendent and went on to become a leader in the field. Bell and Ray travelled together to Europe to visit leading institutions. They believed in a homelike atmosphere, walks in the park, music, and "innocent pleasures rather than ascetic constraint." In May 1844, a few months after the asylum had been approved, Dorothea Dix heard of the project while on a visit to Newport. She wrote to Brown & Ives "the plan is excellent and a few modifications would it seems to me add to the comfort and convenience of those who may become occupants." Thus, "the asylum was not the dream of an architect but the result of the thinking of two outstanding psychiatrists of the time."[85]

In 1847, six years after Nick's death, the Butler Hospital commissioned Thomas Sully, one of America's finest portraitists, to produce two "founders' portraits." The one representing Cyrus Butler shows a man in a setting and dress typical of his era. However, the portrait of Nick is once again revealing for the message it conveys. Unable to paint from life, Sully simply copied the head and hands painted by Chester Harding in 1836, but placed them on a figure standing by the water's edge, holding a telescope in one hand (signifying vision) and a letter (symbolic of steadfastness) in the other. A sloop under sail is clearly visible in the background. The old-fashioned shoes have acquired shiny buckles. Most curious is a Quaker-style hat, balanced on its brim, like a horn-of-plenty spilling the wisdom of its bearer onto the world. While Harding had emphasized Nick's love of books and business, Sully chose to focus on his passion for maritime commerce. The Quaker hat is probably in homage to Uncle Moses. The factor common to both artists is the ineluctable sense of a better age already long past. This, surely, is how Nick would have wanted to be remembered.

---

[85] In 1850, an act was passed which forbid keeping insane persons in jail; by the following year, there were five institutions in Rhode Island to "care of the unfortunate."

CHAPTER 14

BROWN UNIVERSITY

*"American citizens have the duty to promote the
means for elevating universally the intellectual and
moral character of our people." —Francis Wayland*

Nick's philanthropic journey reached its apogee in the late 1820s
when he decided to devote his energies to Brown University.

In the first two decades that followed his landmark gift of 1804,
Nick's attitude toward the University followed his general pattern of
giving: reactive to need, but not particularly strategic. In 1805, he gave
$500 to purchase books; in 1811, Brown & Ives subsidized the costly
textbooks of the new medical school. In 1815, at his son JCB's urging,
he funded a "Philendean Society" to lend books to poor students. A
dedicated librarian was hired in 1824 and, by the mid-1820s, the Brown
University Library catalogue listed 5,818 volumes. Nick also underwrote
the university's expansion. In 1821, when it was obvious that the College
Edifice was too small for 152 students, he spent $5,189 to purchase land
and $20,000 to build a three-story "elegant brick building-containing
forty-eight rooms."[86] Completed in January 1823, the new building was

---

[86] He enlisted Uncle Moses to negotiate with Mr. Waterman to obtain the land on reasonable terms ["reasonable" underlined twice], "as it will fall on me, the College being
poor &c . . ."

named "Hope College" (the College Edifice was renamed "University Hall"). For the first time, trees were planted and the two buildings were surrounded by a fence: a real campus was born. Nick explained his gift in a letter to the Corporation:

> ... believing that the dissemination of letters and knowledge is the great means of social happiness . . . I avail myself of this occasion to express a hope, that Heaven will bless and make it useful in the promotion of Virtue, Science, and Literature, to those of the present and future generations, who may resort to this University for education.

While he was engrossed in his business affairs and legislative duties, Nick limited his involvement with the University's administration to his role as Treasurer of the Corporation. But the mid-1820s heralded a new chapter in his life, shaped by the confluence of the various distressing developments already described: his eldest son had stormed out of Providence and his younger boy showed little proclivity for commerce; maritime trade was in rapid decline; his dream of cohesive, decorous, and well-ordered society lay in tatters. America seemed to have lost its moral compass.

Nick could have shut himself off from the world and spent the remainder of his days railing against the perpetrators of this turmoil, as had his Uncle Benjamin Carter. But Uncle Moses's teachings about the perfectibility of human nature had made a lasting impact. If the dissemination of letters and knowledge was indeed the great means of social happiness, then Nick would train the young men in *his* university to navigate America's stormy seas. He could not provide a quality education for all, but he could at least train some of the country's future leaders.

His was an ambitious objective but, as was said in his eulogy, "He was endowed in an unusual degree with that quality, . . . largeness of mind. A plan or an enterprise was attractive to him, other things being equal, in proportion to its extensiveness. . . ." Nick may have mulled over his strategy for several years. Finally, in 1825, when the university faced a crisis that threatened its very existence, Nick saw his opportunity arise and sprang to action.

Under the twenty-year presidency of Asa Messer, the University had made steady progress in broadening its curriculum. The faculty was expanded to include distinguished professors such as Tristam Burges, the "Webster of Rhode Island" (a former Chief Justice and now a Congressman at the zenith of his career), who taught rhetoric and oratory (the chair Nick had endowed). In 1825, there were sixty seniors in the graduating class.[87] Messer had an abiding aspiration to bring the benefits of college life within the reach of as many young men as possible. He maintained tuition at the remarkably low rate of sixteen dollars per annum and even instituted a long winter holiday so that the poorer students might earn money teaching in rural schools. However, his "common touch" was interpreted as a sign of weakness. Over the years, unruliness increased markedly, ranging from pranks (filling the bell tower's door lock with lead) to acts of vandalism. Messer, fearing that "rusticated" (suspended) boys might fall behind in class, did not tighten discipline. Student disorder became such a problem that a committee, that included Nick, was formed in 1824 to investigate the situation.

To compound the problem, Messer did not demonstrate a zealous adherence to traditional Baptist doctrine—a matter of no small consequence in the years following Unitarianism's arrival in Providence. Although a committed Baptist, Messer found certain aspects of the Unitarian doctrine highly compatible with his personal beliefs (particularly the Unitarian view that Christ was not God, but the Son of God): "All men have full liberty of opinion," he maintained, "and ought to enjoy it without subjecting themselves to the imputation of heresy." In 1815, he preached at the now Unitarian First Congregational Church, and in 1820 accepted an honorary degree from "heretic" Unitarian Harvard. Stephen Gano, Pastor of the First Baptist Meeting House, railed that Messer used "a language,

---

[87] This would be the largest graduating class until 1870.

which is so far from being calculated to promote the morals of young men [that it] is fit for the brothel, and not for refined or virtuous society."

Initially, Messer's detractors were a minority since the University was run by a large, bicameral corporation representing several denominations, with an Episcopal bishop as Chancellor. But as Baptists began feeling increasingly threatened by Unitarianism's popularity, they clamored increasingly loudly for Messer's removal. Fortunately, two University fellows died in 1825; one had been an intransigent Baptist cleric. Nick lost no time in resigning as treasurer (the position was taken over by Moses Brown Ives) to become a fellow. His new position would make it easier to manage the clerical zealots while remaining civil in his dealings with old family friends. It was said that he managed to steer "a cautious, responsible course which helped the University to survive," not as an ally of the Baptist sectarians but independently, for what he believed were the best interests of the University.

The easy solution would have been to let Messer go and move swiftly to appoint a successor better suited to conciliate dissenting opinions. Nick, however, did not favour expediency; he had very definite and cogent ideas as to how a seat of learning should be run. Messer was far from ideal, but Nick was not about to exchange one imperfect character for another. So he set himself to the delicate and dangerous task of keeping Messer in place while waiting for the right man to become available.

Nick paid the price incurred by anyone who seeks to reconcile the irreconcilable—he made himself deeply unpopular with almost everyone. Messer's supporters claimed:

> [he] ought not to be swayed by the influence of those whose patronage has been bestowed with a liberal hand, and who from long established reputation, for the immensity of their wealth, may be by him looked upon as a Species of Demi-God, whose frowns can blast and whose smile can save.

In contrast, Messer's detractors felt that Nick was too lenient:

> It would be nothing more or less that supererogation, to allude again to the undue influence had over the affairs of Brown University by a wealthy and liberal donor, who, in giving alms, expects an equivalent, in the loud and lasting blasts of fame, which may be blown in his behalf. Nor shall we do so, any further than to suggest to him, the propriety of exerting that influence to obtain another President.

Vitriolic articles in the *Literary Cadet and Saturday Evening Bulletin* in the summer of 1826 blamed Nick for the University's woes:

> The influence had on this institution by the individual to whom we allude, has been productive of the most baleful consequences and the angry feelings, which are now in full tide of successful operation in that seminary [and] may be traced to that fruitful source of discord.

In September 1826, when five of the twenty-eight seniors refused to participate in Commencement exercises, Messer had no choice but to resign. Invoking his long service, he expressed the hope that on leaving the world, "I may be enabled to think that I have served my GOD as faithfully as I have served Brown University." In December 1826, the Corporation voted to appoint as President a young man considered by many to be the most promising Baptist minister in America: Francis Wayland.

So began a partnership, characterised in equal measure by profound mutual respect and by the clash of two iron wills that would shape the character of Brown University for the rest of Nick's life and for decades beyond.

Born in 1796, just three years after his parents emigrated from England, Wayland was just a year older than JCB. After indifferent preparatory schooling, he was admitted as a sophomore to Union College at the age of only fifteen, where he came to the attention of Dr. Eliphalet Nott, a famed Presbyterian minister and educational innovator. Following his graduation in 1813, Wayland studied medicine in Troy and New York City. Then, changing to theology, he entered Andover seminary in 1816 as a charity student. Too poor, however, to continue with theological studies, he became a tutor at Union College for the next four years and "learned from [its President] Dr. Nott the unique methods of teaching and novel rules of college administration."

But his ambitions were far greater.

In 1821 he was appointed pastor of the First Baptist Meeting House in Boston where his reputation grew considerably. Despite the success of his widely distributed 1823 "Sermon on The Moral Dignity of the Missionary Enterprise," he realized he had little future as a preacher. When he married Lucy Lincoln in 1825, he knew that his pastor's salary would not support a family.

The same year, Wayland was also named a trustee of the Brown University Corporation. It is unclear whether the appointment was at Nick's behest, although his suitability soon became apparent. Nick wrote to Wayland: "The cause there absolutely and imperiously demands a man like you. . . . Besides, Providence College [Brown] must have such trustees or be ruined forever. Radical changes must be made in order to save it." Wayland seemed to be a willing collaborator in a discreet campaign to push his candidacy for the Presidency. However, when he grasped that the process of replacing Messer would not be swift, Wayland accepted the Chair of Natural Philosophy and Mathematics at Union College in the spring of 1826.

It was not until the October following Messer's resignation that Wayland finally received a much-anticipated letter from Nick, offering the presidency and expressing this heartfelt sentiment:

> The prosperity of the College here, should lay [sic] near the heart of all dear friends, as the period has arrived which has been so much desired by many with its late President. I have been on intimate habits with him

for a long while & hope to be in the confidence of his
Successor.

Nick explained that Wayland's confirmation would have to wait until
the Corporation met in December 1826, but that "there will be not one
dissenting voice." A subsequent letter gives an insight into Nick's vision
for the University and his ecumenical perspective:

> I hope they [our Baptist friends] will be prudent, & not
> desirous that we should become altogether a Sectarian
> institution, if so, it will hurt us and lessen our numbers.
> As much of a Baptist as I am, the best policy should be to
> hold out a liberal view, and make the College a nursery
> of Science &c, instead of Sectarian Interests."

Evidently Wayland did not quite believe the assurance. He had heard
rumors to the contrary and asked Dr. Nott for advice. Nott warned "if
there is not a clear deck and a cordial crew, it will be very difficult to give
an old ship a new direction. . . . If things are go[ing] on in the old way
you don't want the place."

Those doubts, however, proved to be misplaced. Nick's careful handling of the situation paid off and he was able to write to Wayland in
December 1826: "Every Extertion will be made by us in meeting Your
views as to salary on Your taking the Presidency of the college here." Nick
also asked Wayland to stay on another two months at Union College so
that he could "acquire many good ideas in the government and also in
the course of study to be pursued [at Brown University]."

So it was accomplished. Without question, Nick was satisfied that
he had secured the best man to steer a new course at *his* university. Like
so many successful partnerships, that between Nick Brown and Francis
Wayland was marked equally by what divided as by what united them.
Each was possessed of an iron will and a resolute determination that
he must have the final word. It is testament to both men's fundamental

strength of character that their mutual respect and esteem survived intact to the day of Nick's death.

The common ground between the two men was so extensive that it is tempting to see Wayland's teachings as a mouthpiece for many of Nick's convictions. Both professed to be ecumenical in the catholic spirit of the Brown charter which excluded all sectarian tests and teachings. They sought for the University the same end: to produce educated men imbued with Christian belief and a high sense of social responsibility, capable of making a positive contribution to society. Both applauded the divinely sanctioned "fruits of individual acquisitiveness," but feared that unbridled greed would tear America apart. Both believed that members of society owed each other obligations and duties, particularly the wealthy and well educated. Education allowed men to discover, apply and obey the laws of the Creator, particularly "the necessity of benevolence" that was being increasingly neglected in times of prosperity. With the disappearance of traditional forms of patronage, with the fluctuating redistribution of wealth, and with widening commercial opportunities for middling men everywhere, the gentry's position in Northern society was becoming more and more anachronistic. But now it was possible to *learn* virtue and talent in order to think and act like a gentleman. If kinship, patriarchy and patronage no longer worked to bind society, then love and benevolence could underpin a new order based on "real worth and personal merit."

The republican values extolled by the Enlightenment and so admired by Nick in his youth had been based on the writings of classical antiquity. Yet no one in the United States, however educated, seemed able to resist the lure of the marketplace or to achieve the level of self-sacrifice required for true "disinterestedness." The American people seemed incapable of achieving the degree of virtue needed for true republicanism. Nick finally admitted that it was utopic to expect people to give up their private interests for the sake of public good. Rather, they needed a moral compass, a set of values that would guide them through the era's stormy seas. If he could provide those destined to be leaders—the students at *his* university—with the correct moral and aesthetic sensibilities, then he could achieve a positive effect on national life.

The culmination of this endeavor was Wayland's senior year course in moral philosophy, meant to synthesize all a student's higher learning and to reconcile religious doctrines with secular studies. In 1835, Wayland compiled his lectures into the book *Elements of Moral Science*; it sold over 200,000 copies. His teachings were steeped in the "Scottish approach," a reaction against the rational philosophies of the eighteenth century that had turned so many away from religion. Better suited to the optimistic American character of the New Republic, the Scottish philosophies valued man's innate knowledge and natural judgment. They were based on common sense, the existence of God, and high standards of morality. John Witherspoon had made the College of New Jersey (the future Princeton University) a Scottish stronghold, and Scottish texts had been introduced at Harvard in 1792. At Brown, Wayland sought to instruct students on choosing the morally correct course of action in life by placing History, Theology, Science, Law, Government, Economics and social relations within a single ethical framework. Moral law codified life's problems and provided answers to theological questions.

Like Nick, Wayland had little faith in the continued progress of man unless strengthened by the practice of Christianity. The natural theology that both men admired sought to reconcile science and the scriptures: "God's creation and his word must agree," said Wayland. It was a recipe for harmony which greatly pleased Nick. In both men's opinion, the foundation of moral obligation was the will of God, and man's ultimate aim should be to spread the Gospel. But duty to his fellow man followed close behind. Wayland labeled this principle the "Law of Reciprocity," followed by its important corollary, the "Law of Benevolence"—the obligation to help those who have no claim on you.

Wayland did not believe that capitalism was intrinsically sinful, but he criticized those obsessed with the accumulation of riches. Wealth should be a recompense for doing something useful and could be used as one pleased, so long as it did not infringe on the rights of one's neighbors.

But it should be tempered by the "true use of riches" for the public good. Both Nick and Wayland felt that the 1837 depression was a moral crisis resulting from speculative practices which violated the laws of morals and economics.

Wayland thus sought to harmonize classical economic thought with traditional moral principles. Like many of his age, he believed in the perfectibility of man; he thus supported efforts to expand public education (actively participating in the report that led to reinstatement of the Public School Law in 1828), to reform prisons, and to improve hospitals. Wayland deplored, however, the more radical reformers who advocated women's rights, extending the suffrage, or immediate emancipation.

While almost unanimous about their goals, the two men differed with respect to the way in which these goals would be achieved. Wayland was wedded to Adam Smith's principle that vocational skills, allied to a virtuous lifestyle, formed the best education, one which "united practice with theory so the mind acquires the habit of acting in obedience to law and thus is brought into harmony with a universe which is governed by law." He firmly believed that universities should offer classes relevant to the new professions of the industrial age in order to remain competitive in recruiting students. The University's function was not just to train ministers or lawyers, nor should it "entice young men into the learned professions who would be more useful in other departments of life." Education must be practical. Yet the traditional "classical course" offered at Brown University was not practical; it produced a "superficial habit of mind in those who yielded themselves to its influence," according to Wayland.

The debate about higher education had been ongoing for a long time: seventy-five years earlier, Benjamin Franklin had recommended supplementing the traditional diet of Latin and Greek with courses suited to the requirements of particular careers. But when the College of Philadelphia (the future University of Pennsylvania) was founded in 1751, Franklin's ideas were watered down and the classical curriculum prevailed. However, more recent attempts at reform had met with greater success. In 1824, The Rensselaer School had awarded the first degree in civil engineering in the English-speaking world. A year later, Thomas Jefferson had convinced the University of Virginia to allow students to enroll in one of eight separate schools depending on their aspirations and abilities—a far cry from the traditional imposition of Classics, *Belles Lettres* and Rhetoric. While at Union College, Wayland had observed Dr. Nott planning a "parallel course" that substituted modern languages for the classics. Universities now realized that funding could be obtained from a new elite of entrepreneurs, financiers and industrialists prepared to pay for technological and commercial instruction. Even some of the more venerable institutions introduced a more student-centered approached. George Ticknor, Harvard's first professor of modern languages, convinced President Kirkland to permit some students to progress according to their abilities, as was being done at the University of Göttingen in Germany.

Brown University was undeniably in sore need of reform. Over a decade earlier, an anonymous pamphlet had appeared setting forth a plan for improving the curriculum and making it more useful to society by establishing a law school, adding a new building, and raising funds through a lottery to increase the faculty. But given the University's precarious financial base, Asa Messer had not dared change the required course for fear of losing students. At the height of the Messer controversy in August 1826, Medical School Professor John DeWolf wrote to the Corporation that Brown was "no more than a tolerable academy, compared with Yale or Amherst." He urged that the college offer an education closely related to the needs of the community it served: "Let those who wish to be classical scholars have all facilities, but let those who mean to come out merchants or manufacturers, have something useful."

It was therefore no great surprise when Wayland announced that he wished to develop a "popular course," emphasizing modern languages, English literature, and science. Nick disagreed. While acutely conscious of Brown University's need for reform, he felt deeply that intellectual values should not be dictated by the vocational needs of a materialistic society. A university should be a center of learning:

> The introduction of studies on the ground of their practical utility is subversive of the college. It is not the office of the college to make planters, mechanics, lawyers, physicians, or divines. Its business is with minds and it employs science only as an instrument for the improvement and perfection of minds.

Nick concurred with Yale President Jeremiah Day, a staunch defender of the "Old Order" whose influential 1828 report reiterated that the purpose of college education was to train the faculties of the human mind, rather than teach all the branches of knowledge.

Not a complete reactionary, however, Nick concurred with Harvard professor George Ticknor's concept that higher education should respond to the needs of American society with an "enriched program of liberal studies." But he did not believe that a university should *solely* prepare students for commercial or industrial pursuits. The purpose of a higher education was to "train and invigorate intellectual powers"—practical education for making a living should come *after* college. An undergraduate classical education was essential because it was the only way to make "ancient manners familiar" and to "produce a reconciliation between disinterestedness and commerce." Thus a liberal education from Brown University would reconcile the spirit of capitalism with the ethics of Christianity; the love of profit with the love of God.

Nick possessed an overwhelming advantage in this debate: he held the purse strings. The Corporation took an entire year to consider Wayland's "grandiose plans" before announcing that they were beyond the limited means at its disposal. Nick did not clash openly with Wayland. Instead, he simply told the President to raise the monies himself for curriculum reform, but knowing full well that Wayland hated fundraising. Benjamin Hallett, a Brown graduate and journalist in Boston, sympathized with Wayland's frustrations: "With the materials the President of Brown

University has, it is in vain to attempt to model a Harvard or Yale or even a Union. Here we rely almost wholly upon popular favor."

Prevented from making drastic changes in the curriculum, Wayland concentrated on improving the discipline and quality of teaching of an institution which now was referred to by some as "the disgrace of the city." He even contemplated moving the university away from the temptations of Providence. His first order of business was to make "study not a sham, but a reality, and discipline not a form, but a fact." Vacations were shortened and "frivolous pastimes"—such as singing in one's room—were banned. At Commencement, the edifice no longer would be illuminated nor alumni awards given for declamation: "all gaiety at exercise in the meeting house" ended. Hard liquor was replaced by cider, now available only at set times. "Officers of instruction" once again visited students' rooms; "[Wayland] had a heavy foot for a student's door when it was not promptly opened after his official knock." Though absences and violations were reported to him daily, a few pranks still occurred.[88] He reinstated an exclusive power to dismiss students, dealing directly with parents and sending home report cards at the end of every term. He made no exceptions for attenuating circumstances and refused to shield students from the law "by making every young man feel that he must be accountable for his own actions, prepare him for becoming a member of society"(in later years, he would refer to the "great mental stress" that some severe cases had caused him).

Contemporaries described Wayland's "vast amount of primitive power, . . . made more effective by passion, wit, and a gift of trenchant speech." Tall, with strongly chiseled features, he impressed by his imperial spirit and his "lordly and penetrating glances." As one alumnus later recounted, "At the top of College Hill, Dr. Wayland was ruling with a rod of iron." But in later years, many alumni wrote of their admiration for Wayland, notably James Angell, Class of 1849, who became President of the University of Michigan: "The discipline of the college was wholly in

---

[88] In a letter to President Everett of Harvard, Wayland mentioned that a pony had been carried up two flights of stairs and put in his recitation room.

his hands. In administering it he was stern, at times imperious. *But no graduate of his time ever failed to gain from him higher ideals of duty or lasting impulses to a noble and strenuous life.*" This was precisely Nick's objective.

The new president set about improving academic standards by tightening entrance requirements and providing an "intellectual tonic" to the university. The number of recitations was increased; textbooks were no longer allowed in recitations, except in the Learned Languages. He added courses in Chemistry, Physiology, Political Economy, Algebra, Calculus and a term of Astronomy.[89] The strong measures paid off. Justice Joseph Story of the Supreme Court wrote in his memoirs that "he could distinguish a graduate from Brown University [during Wayland's presidency] by his power of seizing upon the essential points of a case and freeing it from all extraneous matters."

Wayland also increased salaries to $1,000 for resident professors, $400 for tutors, and paid himself $1,500. Tuition rose by 80 percent in order to fund these raises and to attract "energetic and conscientious instructors." Although he believed that education should be a commodity available to all—"[If] it is good for one class in the community it is good for all classes"—Wayland opposed financial aid. But the Corporation felt that higher education was to a great extent eleemosynary and that funds should be devoted to the payment of professors and to student aid. In the fall of 1828, the Corporation announced that the University would provide free tuition for thirty-five indigent students, twenty of whom must be Baptist ministerial candidates. Wayland confided to a friend, "I'm strongly opposed to the policy, but I yield to the present emergency, and I hope only for the present."

There was one change to the curriculum that Nick not only supported but positively demanded. In selecting Wayland to preside over *his* university, Nick had not forgotten his principles of *laissez-faire* economics and free trade. Political economy became a required course for seniors at Brown, and included study of the Frenchman Jean-Baptiste Say who

---

[89] He also managed to introduce French—although it was dropped in the period between 1831 and 1842.

proclaimed that universal exchange was as necessary to human welfare as universal production. Again, Nick's perspective was at odds with current trends. In a state that so strongly backed protectionism, the press lashed out against Nick. In an editorial in the *Rhode Island Statesman,* a "True Friend of the College" fumed:

> The College is becoming a *nursery of anti-American doctrines,* a mill for the manufacture of young theorists ready to meet the world in arms, and fight for the principles of *free trade*! Yes! A course of instruction in political economy, founded on the theories of Say, is now going on in a College situated in Rhode Island, the heart and soul of the manufacturing interest, and is annually sending forth young men to combat the doctrines upon which, nine-tenths of the people of New England say, depends the prosperity of the Country!

Insofar as Nick was concerned, it was water off a duck's back.

Wayland's most controversial reform was approved by the Corporation on March 15th, 1827. It required that all tutors, professors and other officers must live on campus for the whole of each term—Wayland himself set the example by living in Hope College. By instituting the "family model" of college community which had existed at Harvard since 1821, he strove to establish close personal relations between officers and students, and to increase supervision. All the medical school professors were fired (they lived and maintained practices off campus in order to teach *pro-bono*), with the exception of George Bowen who became the College Librarian and John DeWolf who founded the Department of Chemistry. Most famously, Wayland dismissed Tristam Burges, despite his holding the Nicholas Brown Chair in Oratory and *Belles Lettres.* Burges countered that he held his "professorship as a matter of honor, and [that he] was not concerned with salary." Known as "Old Bald Eagle," he in fact shared many educational principles with Wayland's, notably that moral philosophy was the most important field of knowledge. The *Providence*

Journal of September 30, 1830 accused Wayland of having deprived the University of one of its best and ablest professors. Undeterred, Wayland held firm. The 1831 Commencement marked the final battle between the two great orators, and became known as "The War of the Greeks." Burges, president of the "Society of the Federal Adelphi," and Wayland, who had opened a chapter of Phi Beta Kappa at Brown, each pronounced speeches. Opinion differed as to the winner, but Wayland prevailed.

Nick did not endorse this treatment of Tristam Burges. In 1826, Nick had specifically requested that the funds accumulated since his 1804 donation should support Burges's chair. He had worked with Burges for several years to establish a prize for the graduating class's best speeches and essays—the medals were donated by Moses Ives. The two men were close friends, despite political differences (Burges was resolutely anti-Jackson). But Nick held his tongue, sensing that at this critical juncture Wayland needed his full support.

At first, Wayland's reforms met with a storm of protest. Enrollment declined drastically and student rebellion threatened. The Providence community too was up in arms over this outsider who had increased fees, introduced "foreign academic practices," suspended oratorical and medical instruction, and fostered sectarianism. Other critics disliked the increased Baptist influence at Brown; it was still important to many that the college be governed by the liberal principles of Manning and Maxcy who welcomed students of all religious persuasions. They were alarmed that tuition had risen and that the new collegiate course was designed for an "intellectual aristocracy." A series of articles in the *Rhode Island American* were particularly scathing and claimed that Brown University had become "wholly inefficient and worthless as a *general* school. That institution belongs to a particular sect; is patronized by a single family, and must, in the nature of things, be directed by sectarian views and family influence."

Only a few applauded the "new regime." A New York paper wrote "*In fine*, under the administration of President Wayland and his able assistants, it is believed that the reformation has been such that the university will assume a proud rank among those of greater age and more richly endowed."

Nick and Tom advised Wayland to persevere and so he did, even threatening to dismiss the entire senior class for insubordination. In his memoirs, Wayland described:

> The leading members of the corporation, however, co-incided with me in opinion, and, assuring me of their cordial sympathy, advised me to continue fearlessly in the course which I had commenced. I cannot omit to mention the name of one gentleman connected with the corporation to whom I was especially indebted for wise counsel and generous encouragement—the late Thomas P. Ives, a man whose quiet opinion carried more weight than that of any ten men in Providence.

Wayland remain steadfast. In an era where Harvard's chapel was bombed and the Chairman of the Faculty of the University of Virginia murdered, Brown University never experienced an outright revolt. As one alumnus Charles Thurber acknowledged, "I think Dr. Wayland entered upon the presidency of the college at a time when to discharge its duties faithfully and efficiently required more nerve and courage and greater capacity than had been required at any previous period in its history."

Eventually, the students fell into line and reconciled with the new order; their enthusiasm for study reappeared. By the 1830s, increased tuition revenue made possible an expansion of the faculty and a balanced budget, including new professorships in the Natural Sciences, Rhetoric, Literature and the Classics. Most of the appointments were offered to recent outstanding graduates. In 1829, Brown & Ives funded the purchase of European scientific instruments "adequate for any purpose of scientific illustration." In 1831, the Corporation authorized $25,000 for a perma-nent library fund (the most ambitious sum ever raised by subscription for an educational project in Rhode Island). The first $10,000 came from Nick—Wayland himself was one of the largest subscribers at $200. Nick also gave $18,500 in 1834 to build Manning Hall which would house the 10,000-volume library downstairs and a chapel upstairs. Designed by Russell Warren and James C. Bucklin (who had built the Arcade), it is an exact model, although twice the size, of the graceful temple of Diana Propylea at Eleusis. At its dedication on February 4th, 1835, Wayland delivered a speech on the "Dependence of Science on Revealed Religion."

In 1838, when the need arose to "erect another hall for Natural Sciences and Philosophy," Nick was again the principal donor. Inaugurated in 1839, Rhode Island Hall had two lectures rooms on the first floor, a "cabinet of mineralogy and geology" on the second floor, and a "chemical laboratory" in the basement. Nick also paid to landscape the college grounds.

Although Nick and the Corporation prevented Wayland from enlarging the student body to provide "a liberal education for many persons in all classes of the community," he was grateful for his benefactor's active interest in "every discussion that involved the welfare of the university, . . . appear[ing] at all times ready to cooperate in every plan for the enlargement of the [University's] resources and the improvement of its situation."

The cost of "intellectual life" rose again to $128 in 1833. Since Wayland continued to disdain fundraising as he believed that seeking funds for "eleemosynary distribution" detracted from his more important intellectual pursuits, so the endowment remained at $32,300—still too small to yield significant income. Wayland considered that faculty members should be responsible for their own revenue by ensuring that sufficient numbers of students attended their courses; an element of insecurity would stimulate instructors and students to improve education. To this end, Wayland obtained permission in 1830 for students to register for partial courses, and in 1833 began selling public tickets to lectures.

Brown University was not the only college to have financial problems. In 1839, only eleven American institutions enrolled more than 150 students. Yale in 1830 received less than $3,000 a year from its endowments, while Columbia in 1850 still had debts of $68,000. The faculty of Amherst averted a crisis by teaching for several weeks with no pay at all. Gifts and bequests occasionally provided aid, but they were infrequent and remarkably small. In contrast, William Gammell termed Nick' generosity:

> A series of benefactions, so large in amount, bestowed on a single institution of learning, [that it] forms a brilliant example of private philanthropy and unostentatious munificence, which at that time had seldom, if ever, been paralleled in the history of American colleges. His example shone almost alone in the generation to which he belonged....

It is interesting to note, however, that Nick does not appear to have taken personal interest in the students at Brown—an echo of his relationship with his own sons. Uncle John's commencement dinners for undergraduates had been famous in their day. Uncle Moses's door was always open to young men seeking advice. But Nick seems to have preferred keeping an arm's length relationship with the students at Brown, directing Wayland to implement his vision.

Both men were subjected to frequent accusations of elitism. Wayland was criticized for his intimacy with wealthy patrons who sought to transform the University into a Harvard or a Yale to serve exclusively the needs of an American aristocracy, "a learned institution of high repute patronized by the rich and serving to prepare their sons for a life of culture and comfort as well as usefulness." Both became conservative Whigs in 1835. Both valued a disciplined society. Both sought every mean to deflect social conflict; indeed, historian Martin Burke described Wayland as "one of the most prominent antebellum proponents of class harmony." Both deplored the institution of slavery, while abhorring in almost equal measure the prospect of violence inherent in the radical abolition movement.[90]

Nick's death in 1841 marked only the halfway point in Wayland's tenure as President. On his arrival in 1827, he had found three professors and two buildings; at his departure in 1855, the University would have twenty departments, eight professors, four buildings, and a library of 30,000 volumes, and was established beyond question as one of the leading liberal arts institutions in America. It may well have been Wayland who implemented their joint vision, but without Nick's lifetime contribution of over $160,000 (close to the entire amount he had inherited from his father), their grand dream never could have been realized.

Wayland was not in Providence when Nick died. In 1840, the Corporation of Brown University had persuaded him to take a leave of absence. Travelling to the European continent, he did not much like France or Germany, and then found English universities to be old-fashioned institutions that cultivated narrowness.[91] He also formed an unfavorable impression of British society, especially the privileged aristocracy, the established churches, and the vast gulf between the classes. He came home more committed than ever to democracy and evangelical Protestantism. In his view, American education must serve the needs of the masses; the college curriculum must thus be popularized.

[90] Wayland also maintained a close relationship with Professor William Giles Goddard (1794-). Married to Tom Ives's eldest daughter Charlotte Rhoda, Goddard had graduated from Brown University, studied law and edited a newspaper in Massachusetts, then purchased the *Rhode Island American* and lectured at Brown University from 1832. Unashamedly aristocratic in his tastes and reactionary in his political views, Goddard was convinced of the inherent value of liberal studies, especially literature and the arts, as a refining and civilizing influence in a society predominantly concerned with material acquisition.

[91] However, he was impressed by how readily prizes, scholarships, fellowships, and other rewards for high attainment seemed to stimulate students. On his return to Providence late in 1841, he founded the "President's Premiums," a special examination in Latin and Greek. He used Nick's bequest for scholarships to underwrite these prizes, explaining: "Reward rather than subsidize." However, few students signed on. In 1846, the Corporation called for a re-examination of the premium system, fearing that Nick's last legacy was being misused. In the end, the funds were restricted to tuition grants and scholarships.

Upon his return, Wayland's first order of business was to preach the eulogy at Nick's memorial service:

> He . . . deserves a most honorable & conspicuous place among those who have stood forth as leaders and pioneers of their age, in the true appreciation of seminaries of learning, and in liberal benefactions for their foundation and support. These benefactions like the others which proceeded from his hand were bestowed by him with singular judgment and care, and their fruits will remain until the end of time, for the culture of the human mind, for the elevation of character, and the improvement and adornment of society.

Then Wayland proceeded to draft "Thoughts on the Present Collegiate System in the United States," proposing once again that colleges should adapt their courses to the different capacities and wants of students. But the Dorr Rebellion—during which the University's buildings were used as barracks—distracted everyone in Rhode Island. When college life returned to normal, there seemed little reason to take action on Wayland's proposals; the institution appeared in good health.

Then enrolment began a gradual but steady decline (attendance fell by 20 percent between 1835 and 1849), while financial pressures increased commensurately. Wayland knew that something was fundamentally wrong. Frustrated, he suddenly resigned in 1849. Stunned, the Corporation pleaded for his return and named him head of a "Committee on Advice" to reshape Brown's future.

That Committee's report, delivered in March 1850, was one of the most radical set of proposals ever made for restructuring an American university. It began by noting that "with the present century, a new era dawned upon the world. A host of new sciences arose all holding important relations to the progress of civilization." It accounted for the pressures of industrialization and westward expansion. It stated bluntly that the outdated curriculum was impeding the nation's intellectual and material progress. The proposed remedy was the practical, vocationally-based education that Wayland had wanted since the beginning of his tenure. A new program of fewer requirements and more electives should be tailored to the "wants of the community," with new courses, a Ph.D. program, and easier admission requirements. The "New Plan" did not abolish the classics but placed them on "their own merits," equal to any other group of subjects. It did not abolish morality or religion; instead it hoped to lay the basis for a better relationship between science and religion so that "truth could be incorporated in all knowledge."

Not surprisingly, the concept was received with delight among the manufacturers but was condemned by Bishop John Lancaster Spalding who claimed it brought "education to a point where its worth is measured by the power it gives to amass wealth." Wayland dared to openly denigrate the "aristocratic college of his former associates" which produced "cultivated gentlemen" rather than useful and industrious workers. Despite this thinly veiled criticism of Nick, JCB and Moses Brown Ives joined their fellow trustees in supporting Wayland's plan by contributing $65,000 of the $125,000 it required.

Although large, the sum was woefully inadequate to cover such an expansion in the number of subjects and professors. The only solution was to increase the number of pupils, which meant greatly lowering academic standards. Other schools had done well by offering a "practical education": The Dartmouth School of Engineering, Rensselaer Polytechnic Institute, the Wharton, Tuck and Harvard Business Schools; but all these received philanthropic support. Soon it became obvious that the university could not serve the moral aims of a classical college while also contributing to the advancement of knowledge. "The value of religion was emotional and moral, not intellectual"; attempting "a scientific study of religion" was doomed to failure. The Brown degree became debased as the quality of students suffered. Barnabas Sears, who succeeded Wayland, would complain a few years later: "We are flooded by a class of young men of little solidity or earnestness of character, who resort to this college not so much for the sake of sound learning as for the sake of cheap honors. We are now literally receiving the refuse of other colleges."

Wayland must have been acutely conscious of this loss of prestige. Deeply disappointed, he pleaded extreme fatigue when he stepped down in 1855, although he remained as a fellow until 1858. For the next decade, he devoted himself to reform movements including temperance, antislavery, peace organizing, as well as prison and hospital reform. He died of a stroke on September 30, 1865, age 69.

In the end, much that Nick had striven for and funded so handsomely was dissipated in little more than a decade after his death. The lesson for future generations of donors was clear: without substantial endowment to continue the good work into the future, lifetime contributions are not by themselves enough to ensure enduring change. Yet, by investing in "results long distant" rather than seeking the instant gratification of an act of direct charity, Nick clearly made his mark as a forerunner of modern-day strategic philanthropy.

CHAPTER 15

LEGACIES

"I have always served the public to the best of my ability. Why? Because, like every other man, it is to my interest to do so." —*Cornelius Vanderbilt*

A t the end of March, 1841, JCB returned from a "Washington tour" to find "to my sorrow & astonishment . . . my hon'd father very much altered since I left him some weeks ago, Some cruel disease seems to have reduced him to a very feeble state. From having been comparatively hale & active when I last saw him, his appearance now is that of an infirm old man—& yet his age is short of 72." Nick was suffering from heart disease (then known as "dropsy") and fading fast. Over the next few months, Abby's poor health and the disheartening news of President Harrison's untimely death only added to his afflictions. JCB did what he could to distract his father, taking him out daily on carriage rides. His July 5ᵗʰ, 1841 diary entry reads: "Delightful weather. I took father out to ride this forenoon & to avoid the noise of the Town. We went over into Seekonk—he enjoyed the fine air & the green fields very much. Alas, poor man, his engagements in this world are fast diminishing in number."

On a more positive note, everyone was cheered that Abby was well enough to spend three months at *Spring Green* that summer, the first time she had returned home in two years. But by the end of August, Nick's conditioned had worsened and Abby was determined to be with her grandfather in Providence. The two would spend the last weeks of their respective lives together and die just three weeks apart.

On September 27th, 1841, Nicholas Brown II died at twenty minutes to four in the morning. "Thus has my venerable parent gone down to the grave full of years. I shall see his face no more," wrote JCB in his diary. Francis Wayland, then in England on a sabbatical, would write "His manly and venerable form will no more meet us at his hospitable fireside, in the mart of business, or in the house of God." On September 30th, following a funeral service in the First Baptist Meeting House by the Reverend Robert Patterson, a lengthy carriage procession made its way up North Main Street to the North Burial Ground. Nick was laid to rest next to his two wives. Nicholas III and his family, who had rushed up to Providence, led the mourners in the first carriage, with JCB in the second. In the third carriage were John Brown Francis and his family; Hope Ives followed, accompanied by her son Moses and his family; Robert Hale Ives and his family were next in the procession, with other members of the Ives family in succeeding carriages. In the 22nd carriage were the "President, Fellows, Trustees, Faculty and Students of Brown University," followed by members of the Charitable Baptist Society, various other relatives, "friends in Carriages and others on foot." Thirty days of mourning were declared at Brown University during which all students and faculty wore black mourning bands.

The good citizens of Providence read Francis Wayland's eulogy and William Goddard's lengthy obituary, but what really interested them— just as it had fifty years earlier at Nicholas, Sr's death—was Nick's will.

The most recent version had been drafted in August 1838. In the preamble, Nick referred to himself as a merchant and mentioned the three people whose loss he felt most acutely: his "honored and affectionate wife," his "kind and beloved daughter," and his "highly esteemed friend, partner and brother," Tom Ives. His executors would be JCB, Moses Brown Ives, Robert Hale Ives, and Thomas Burgess. The will was comprised of two parts: the first dealt with the distribution of Nick's estate to his heirs, the second provided for numerous charitable bequests.

Other than his house, carriages, and furnishings (all left to JCB), the entire estate would remain under the control of Brown & Ives. Each son would receive $1,500 in cash, but any further revenues would be distributed solely at Brown & Ives's discretion. Thus, while Nicholas III and JCB would share their father's holding in the family partnership, only JCB would have any say in its management. Even in death, Nick still controlled the purse strings.

These instructions were shockingly severe; Nicholas III was outraged. John Brown Francis wrote in his diary on October 2nd, "N Brown (Nicholas III) 49 years old this day exceedingly dissatisfied with his father's will & not without cause." His daughters, Abby and Anne Francis, were left a considerable fortune in prime Providence real estate including the "Jenckes estate" in central Providence, and $20,000 in cash. Since Abby died on October 19th, thirteen-year old Anne inherited the entire amount. Since his daughters had been raised by Nick, John Brown Francis petitioned the Court to be appointed his Anne's guardian.

Alfred Nicholas, Nicholas III's son, received half the rent on the old family house on South Main Street, occupied at the time by the Blackstone Bank. Otherwise, there were only three other individuals who inherited directly from Nick. His sister-in-law, the devoted Amey-Ann Stelle, who had raised his children and grandchildren, was given lifetime use of Avis Binney Brown's house on Thomas Street, as well as revenue from a farm and from pews in the First Baptist Meeting House. Nick's distant cousin, the printer and ardent abolitionist Hugh H. Brown, inherited a house and lot on the Weybosset side. Sarah Noyes Bolles,[92] who was living under his roof with her son Nicholas Brown Bolles, was given shares in the Providence Bank, the "Corey estate," revenue from pews in St. John's Episcopal church, and $600 for her son's education.

The remainder of Nick's 1838 will contained an extensive list of

---

[92] She was the widow of the Reverend Lucius Stillman Bolles, Jr., a Brown University graduate and son of the eminent Reverend Bolles, Sr., a protégé of the Reverend Doctor Samuel Stillman, a Fellow of Brown University, and the founder of both a Bible Society and a Foreign Mission Society based at his church in Salem, Massachusetts. When the younger Lucius Bolles died in 1837, Nick had not hesitated to take in the young widow and her two infant boys.

gifts to the charities and causes he had supported all his life: Brown University received rental income to fund scholarships, as well as real estate and cash for a new President's house and a library fund; three Baptist churches in Providence, as well as eight education societies, tract societies and missionary organizations would receive annual sums for ten years, ranging from $60 to $500; Hope Ives was left $500 to distribute to charity as she pleased.[93] And of course, there was the remarkable gift to found an insane asylum.

Nicholas III was furious to learn that he would be tethered for life in a lesser position in the family business. At first, he tried to rally his brother JCB and his former brother-in-law John Brown Francis to his cause—but the three men soon quarreled. In January 1842, Nicholas III demanded an "inventory and estimate" of his father's "Com[pan]y Property," questioning whether Brown & Ives could lock up his rightful inheritance. The executors replied dryly that Nicholas III's ownership of property did not make him a co-partner. They felt that Nick had been justified in giving his eldest son "one-third of his portion subject to the casualties of the business operations of Brown & Ives" and that he had "no right whatever to interfere in the [company's] management." The letter concluded rather unkindly that Nick had intentionally sought to exclude his eldest son.

Nicholas III's letters alternated among a variety of approaches. In some he demanded advances on his portion of the estate; in others, he pleaded on behalf of his wife and children, or questioned the methods and motives of the executors. He quibbled with the minor terms of the will and engaged the New York law firm of Tucker & Crapo to investigate a "hidden fund" that Brown & Ives might be keeping from him. Other letters directed the partners on how to invest HIS money or manage HIS property. He even admonished Brown & Ives for charging the Reverend David Benedict too little rent for a house owned by the estate: "this chap has plundered the family enough in all conscience, by means of the

---

[93] In a later codicil, drawn just three months before his death, Nick directed a little more income for Nicholas III, in the form of "half the rents from the Jenckes estate."

malign clerical influence exercised over an unfortunate & priest-ridden individual."

In contrast with the passionate tone of his arguments, Nicholas III was cold and formal when referring to his father, only ever using the word *Testator*. He did not hesitate to point out that "I am in fact the only person concerned who is in want of money—one heir had no expense at all." In May 1842, he claimed that he would have to pawn his watch for fifty dollars, noting "I did hope that on his death whether I lived here or elsewhere, I should no longer be compelled to live in the miserably straightened manner I had done for years previous to his exit."

At other times, Nicholas III assured the executors that he bore them no ill will. "I have taken that open, honest, honourable, manly independent course—so characteristic of myself." Any proposal they might make would be "listened to and replied to, in the right spirit with promptitude." Most extraordinarily, he wrote in October 1843, "I have no recollection of ever during the whole course of my life, having asked the Testator for money—house—land having always been extremely anxious to do nothing which might, by any possibility, endanger the existence of reciprocal good feeling & friendly relations."

In the first year of battle over his father's estate, Nicholas III came regularly to visit his brother JCB in Providence. Then, after a six-week visit between September and November 1842, he stayed away. JCB attempted a reconciliation in December that year, presenting his sister-in-law Caroline with a portrait miniature of himself. His diary never mentions the feud though it must have been painful.

Then, in January 1844, Nicholas III came up with a new tactic: he now considered the "insane clause[bequest]" invalid and would sue in the courts of New York (as an impartial decision could not be had in Rhode Island) to prevent the funding of a mental hospital. He argued that Nick had overestimated the actual value of his estate and that such a gift would leave his grandchildren "poor and smarting under the wretchedly injudicious conduct of their Grandfather's will." He alleged that he had consulted with several lawyers, all of whom assured him that funding a hospital was legally invalid.

Brown & Ives were understandably deeply troubled by the threat. A public airing of family matters showing disharmony among the cousins and criticism of their handling of the estate would harm the business and only enrich the lawyers: "We may consume years in protracted litigation and expend thousands after thousands of dollars and finally end where we began but with wasted means and estranged feelings." They hoped that Nicholas III would "upon further consideration of the matter acquiesce in the conclusion to which we have come after much reflection and able legal consultation that the request for an insane Asylum is valid and must be carried into effect." But Nicholas III stood firm: "My children will be poor & smarting under the wretchedly injudicious conduct of their G'dfathers will. . . . I wish to leave no legacy of law-suits to my posterity[;] whatever of this is necessary to be done, I prefer to do it myself. . . . Why there exists so much desire to pay so large a sum is mysterious to me; considering that the Testator has already done so much for the public in his life & in his will."

Finally, the executors offered to pay Nicholas III $10,000 if he would withdraw the law suit. Nicholas III accepted the settlement, but not without asserting that the executors had deliberately overestimated his father's estate and that his father had died "wholly ignorant" of how much he was really worth.

The rancor did not end with Nicholas III's settlement. He then sought a greater allowance from Brown & Ives to pay for his children's education: Alfred Nicholas must go to New York where he could board with a "cheap family," and the others needed "advantages not found in common country schools." Surely, his father "who felt 'great anxiety to educate the children of others' would consider that a knowledge of the french spoken language & also the same of Italian & Spanish is not merely a luxury but an absolute necessity." Nicholas III also negotiated a new career. Now that he had access to funds, he dreamed of a position of power and influence far from Providence and New York, which both held bad memories. A diplomatic post seemed the answer, so he secured from President Polk an appointment as American Consul in Rome.

As Nicholas III prepared to leave for Italy with his family in

September 1845, Robert Hale Ives urged him to come to Providence so that family members could meet in a "spirit of mutual confidence and amity," without lawyers present. The partners promised that he would always be entitled to his share of "the accumulated dividends of B[rown] & I[ves] Company."

Following this visit, Nicholas III and his family spent a few days in New York before embarking (and even went to P.T. Barnum's show). JCB came too, escorting his niece Anne Francis back to her boarding school. Nicholas III took his brother aside and showed him the two cases of books which he had bought in England twenty-eight years earlier. Would JCB like to purchase them for $10,000? JCB was stunned; he had never spent that much money on anything. A few months earlier, he had met Henry Stevens of Vermont who proposed to settle in London to search for books of "American interest" for a handful of clients. These two crates therefore seemed like the perfect way to kick-start a collection. JCB tossed and turned for three nights before making a decision: yes, he would buy the books.

Nicholas III's Italian adventure turned into a brief, shining moment in his restless life when he rose above his usual state of acrimony and resentment to show great courage and resolve.

When Nicholas III, Caroline and their children arrived in Rome in November 1845, they found Italy in turmoil. The land was still divided among a multitude of duchies, states and kingdoms. Nationalism was on the rise and the people yearned for a strong leader who would drive out the foreign powers present in the land, namely conservative Austria, and unify Italy into one nation. On June 16, 1846, a new Pope, Pius IX, was elected who immediately launched a number of political and economic reforms (including such basic progress as allowing railways to pass through the Papal States) that gave liberals and the poor great hope. The new Pope even appointed a secular Prime Minister but balked at leading a war of liberation against Roman Catholic Austria. Further, he refused to allow laymen in his administration; the people were severely disappointed.

It did not take long for Nicholas III to meet the men who were pushing for reform. Word got back to Washington that he was hosting radicals
in the U.S. consulate. In April 1847, Caroline's brother H.H. Clements
wrote to Crawford Carter about Nicholas III having "fallen into bad
odour with one Mr. James R. Polk [the U.S. President]," asking him to
intercede with "Governor Francis" to use his political connections on
Nicholas III's behalf.

Then, in November 1848, the Prime Minister was assassinated. Rome
rose in violent rebellion and the Pope fled to the Kingdom of Naples.
The revolutionaries, led by Giuseppe Mazzini, declared a "Rome of the
People" and promised elections, freedom of the press, land redistribution, and lay schools. From his exile in Gaeta Fortress, the Pope sent a
scathing message to the foreign diplomatic corps and they all flocked to
him—all except Nicholas III.

Throughout the upheaval, the official stance of the United Sates
government was to steer a neutral course. But Nicholas III enthusiastically sided with the revolutionaries. In December 1848, he wrote a long
dispatch to Secretary of State James Buchanan describing events in a
positive light, and arguing that greater involvement was in America's
best interest. In February 1849, he marched with the newly elected con-
stituent assembly through the streets of Rome, dressed in his grand
diplomatic uniform; he attended a solemn Mass at St Peter's Basilica; he
invited revolutionaries to the American consulate to celebrate George
Washington's birthday. Although officially not authorized to treat the
Roman Republic as a sovereign state, Nicholas III did everything in his
power to show his support.

There was a far deeper explanation for Nicholas III's behavior, beyond the thrill and excitement of participating in a historic event. The
Roman Republic was an opportunity to enshrine the principles of Roger
Williams: separation of church and state, freedom of religion (the revolutionaries opened Rome's Jewish ghetto), and of Rhode Island's 1663
Charter—representative government and free elections. He was convinced that it was the "bright example of our country shewing as a great
beacon light to the world, the sure road to wealth, to greatness, & to

happiness" that the people of Italy had risen against their sovereigns, and Americans could not but feel responsible for the outcome of revolutions they had inspired. Moreover, he felt this was a unique opportunity for the United States to sell its technology to the backwards nations of Europe:

> The United States, called by the exact extent & boundless fertility of her territory, the illimitable increase of her population, her numberless resources of every kind, & the immense facilities afforded by Fulton's great invention [the steamboat], to far higher destinies, [must] become, 'ere long, for her own sake, an actively mediating, if not controlling power, in all that regards the European continent.

It is an interesting point of speculation that, while Nick might well have balked at the flagrant challenge to established authority, he would surely have approved of his son's sentiments. Nick could possibly even have felt a touch of pride that the family heritage had not, after all, been wholly wasted on his wayward older son.

The U.S. State Department responded by sending another envoy, Lewis Cass, with specific instructions not to recognize the Roman Republic. Cass's letters to Secretary Buchanan were the antithesis of Nicholas III's reports: Rome was in chaos, the Austrians were marching south. Cass was correct; by late April, four Roman Catholic nations were sending troops to reinstate the Pope. The French landed in north of Rome on April 25th, 1849. At first, the revolutionaries, led by General Giuseppe Garibaldi, repulsed the French but soon the situation became untenable. The Revolutionaries thanked Nicholas III for his efforts, although his increasingly desperate letters to Washington had made little difference to U.S. policy. Instead, Nicholas III used his position to provide American passports to many revolutionaries. The famous American journalist Margaret Fuller, in Rome to cover the revolution, mentioned Nicholas's bravery in her dispatches to the *New York Tribune*.

On June 29th, 1849, the day French troops breached the walls of Rome,

Nicholas III submitted his resignation to the U.S. State Department. When French troops invaded the American consulate, he repelled the assault, American flag in one hand and sword in another. Afterwards he made a speech and the Italians cheered. For this brief moment, after a lifetime of discontent, he was a hero, one praised for his moral courage. Sadly, no other family members were able to witness these events. All they heard was that Nicholas III had upset the foreign policy of the United States.

On July 12, 1849, Pope Pius IX was escorted back into town by French soldiers (who would remain until 1870). Nicholas III boarded a ship for Genoa, taking with him several revolutionary fugitives dressed as his servants. He remained in Europe for another three years, visiting Nice, Barcelona, Geneva, Madrid, and Paris. Caroline Clements Brown kept up a correspondence with a number of European luminaries (she had been introduced to the French author Georges Sand by Mazzini), and Nicholas III commissioned a marble bust and several portraits including a fanciful depiction of his grandfather, the printer John Carter. The family finally returned to Rhode Island in 1853 where Nicholas III lost no time reverting to customary form.

For several years, Nicholas III had been obsessed with finding a proper house. Even before his departure for Europe, he had insisted that Nick promised him the "Brattell Estate" back in 1837. John Brown Francis was concerned since the house had been inherited by his daughter, Anne. Nicholas III then set his sights on Uncle John's brick mansion which Sarah Brown Herreschoff had left to her youngest son James. In 1851, James Herreschoff sold the house to Robert Ives who in turn gave it as a wedding present to his daughter Elizabeth upon her marriage to Brown University Professor William Gammell. Nicholas III made certain that everyone he met during his European travels knew how "cheated" he felt by the sale of the Herreschoff house. While on a visit to Paris in 1852, Anne Francis (who by then had married Marshall Woods) was greatly upset by these accusations and wrote to her father; John Brown Francis responded that this was "the story of a Madman or a liar as everyone knows him to be. I am sorry that you are to be disgust whilest in Paris." In the end, Nicholas III decided to purchase a 200-acre waterfront property in Warwick and to build a large Italianate house, *Choppaquonsett*—right next door to John Brown Francis at *Spring Green*.

Completed in 1855, the mansion featured large, high ceilinged rooms and great halls with opulent furnishings, English hand-printed wallpaper, imported plants in the garden, and a long avenue of fir trees. Nicholas and Caroline's hospitality became famous since Pawtuxet was a popular summer escape for the wealthy residents of Providence.[94] John Brown Francis was understandably displeased about his new neighbor whose dogs caused havoc among the *Spring Green* sheep. In turn, Nicholas III suspected Francis of influencing the authorities to raise the property tax on *Choppaquonssett*. He also continued badgering Brown & Ives for more money and did not hesitate to meddle in the firm's affairs, despite the assurances made before his departure for Italy. Once, in 1854, when he heard that Brown & Ives planned to donate to a school a parcel of land which Nick long ago had lent to an African-American man, he wrote to Robert Ives: "I always understood that the lot on which Negro George's house stands was undivided property of the late Testator [e.g., Nicholas, jr]. If I am correct, I beg to object to anyone erecting a school—or other house there without payment of rent."

Fortunately for Brown & Ives, Nicholas III had political aspirations and so hired a sensible attorney, Stephen H. Smith, to handle his relationship with the firm. In 1854, Nicholas III became a member of the "Know-Nothing" political party and two years later, successfully sought the Republican nomination as Lieutenant Governor under the "Know Nothing" Governor, William Hoppin.[95] But before starting his year in high office, Nicholas III managed to fit in one last family quarrel.

Thirteen years after Nick's death, Brown & Ives announced that an obelisk would be erected to his memory at the Providence North Burial Ground. All family remains would be moved to a new location near the

---

[94] One notable visitor in 1855 was Paul, Duke of Brunswick, Queen Victoria's cousin.
[95] After Nicholas III's adventures in Italy, the anti-Catholic "Know-Nothing" party seemed most appealing. . . .

monument; JCB would pay for the entire project. Nicholas III objected, insisting that he should be involved in such decisions. He resented the "profound secrecy that JC Brown Esq. [JCB] had observed towards me . . . he did not wish me to know what were his plans, views, ideas, and intentions." Nicholas III wanted the monument erected in Swan Point Cemetery. He also wanted to take a cast of his father's skull so that a bust might be commissioned in Rome. Brown & Ives demurred. Once again Nicholas threatened legal action because the executors were taking on a role which should have been left exclusively to Nick's heirs. Fortunately, Nicholas III then became engrossed in his government responsibilities and Stephen Smith settled the matter. Then, less than two years after his excursion into Rhode Island politics, Nicholas III died suddenly at age sixty-six on March 2nd, 1859, while visiting a friend in Troy, New York.

Although Nicholas III produced five children (two more children arrived after Nick's death: Caroline Matilda, known as Carrie, in 1841, and Robert Grenville in 1846), there are no descendants alive today. Alfred Nicholas, who married Anna Mauran, died at the age of thirty-two in 1864, leaving behind a two-year old son, also named Nicholas V, who died in 1891 unmarried. All the others died childless; the sons, John Carter II and Robert Grenville, in 1907 and 1896, respectively. Nicholas III's daughters both married devoted husbands who built several memorials to their wives. In 1860, AnnMary married the colorful Rush Hawkins who raised a regiment ("Hawkin's Zouaves") and finished the Civil War as Brigadier General. An amateur historian (who compiled many of the Brown family papers), art collector and bibliophile, Hawkins commissioned the tomb-like "Annmary Brown Memorial" on the Brown University's campus after her death in 1903 to serve as a library, art gallery, and mausoleum. At age 35, in 1875, Carrie met in Providence an equally colorful member of the Italian diplomatic corps, Count Paul Bajnotti. Too old for children, they traveled the world from a base in Turin. After her death in 1896, Bajnotti commissioned two memorials in Providence: a large bronze sculptural fountain (designed by a woman) in 1898 for the city's new Burnside Park, representing a female angel of life trying to break free from three male tormentors representing the woes of the world, and, in 1904, a 95-foot brick clock tower on the Brown University campus, whose bells rang the start and end of lessons. The base is inscribed "Love is Strong as Death."

Just as Nicholas III continued true to form after his father's death, so too did JCB. He never wavered from his "equable temperament" and lack of ostentation; he did not overtly display his great wealth. Like his father, he may have appeared formal and reserved to strangers, although in times of crisis he showed "firmness and nerve." But contrary to his father, he was "unusually fond of society" and liked to entertain, whether at home on Benefit Street or on his frequent trips away from Providence. He easily could have maintained the pleasant life of a wealthy bachelor, much like Uncle John's son James Brown, with a minimal presence at the counting house, interspersed with business trips to Washington, New York or Philadelphia, and holidays in Saratoga.

But in 1845, JCB discovered a passion that changed his life. The fortuitous coincidence of meeting Henry Stevens and of purchasing Nicholas III's two crates of books ignited in him a new sense of purpose. Thanks to his Carter genes, he had always cared for books. The pleasure he experienced turning the pages of the "Mazarin Bible" in Paris in 1822 remained with him for life (he would buy that volume in 1873 for £3,400). He enjoyed collecting Latin and Greek classics printed by the Aldine Press in Venice between 1490 and 1597, along with beautifully illuminated "Polyglot Bibles." But once he dove into his brother's books, JCB became captivated by the voyages of discovery, the development, and "civilization" of the American continents. Soon he was able to say "My Bibles stand quietly on their shelves, as they have done for ages past & gone; nobody troubles them." Rather, he became fascinated by the complexities of religion, business, and politics in a brand-new environment: how the "Old World" and the "New World" inspired and shaped each other. This fascinating question he called "The Great Subject."

Until the Spanish American wars of the early nineteenth century, few people were interested in the history of the Americas. In 1829 Obadiah

Rich opened a bookshop in London specializing in early works he had amassed during his years as U.S. consul to Spain. In 1832, 1835, and 1844, he issued the first catalogues of "Americana," books *about* America. A French collector, Henri Ternaux-Compans, also published a bibliography on the topic in 1837 (JCB would instruct Henry Stevens to purchase for him every volume listed in that bibliography that had been printed before 1700). Soon, he had a network of correspondents on the look-out in London, Amsterdam and Paris. For close to thirty years, JCB had little competition and managed to obtain extraordinary items such as the Second Latin edition of the 1493 letter in which Columbus announced his discovery of America. When he decided to include works on indigenous peoples, the "collection became a powerful instrument of scientific study, no longer restricted by romantic notion of common destiny, or by the casuistic idea of Manifest Destiny but organized by genuine and complete dedication to learning and knowledge." Ecumenical like his father before him, JCB bought books irrespective of the author's religious persuasion, if they advanced the study of the Americas. His library became a world-class standard that continues even today when book dealers note "not in the JCB Library" to signify a true rarity.

From the start, JCB was adamant that his collection should always be accessible to scholars and enlightened amateurs. He was even willing to send valuable books on loan across the Atlantic. Eminent men flocked to Providence and were treated with "unexampled courtesy." But such liberality took much effort. By 1855, JCB realized he needed a full time assistant. He was fortunate to find the dynamic John Russell Bartlett, born in Providence but educated in French Canada. Bartlett had helped Albert Gallatin create the American Ethnological Society's survey of archeological finds in 1847, and had worked as a surveyor of the Mexican border from 1850 to 1855. It took him seven years to compile the catalogue of JCB's *Bibliotheca Americana*.

Beyond giving JCB a passion that would advance scholarship in countless ways, books also found him a soulmate. In 1859, at age sixty-one, he met a vivacious thirty-four-year old bibliophile, Sophia Augusta Browne. She was the youngest daughter of the Anglo-Irishman Patrick Browne (a senior member of Her Majesty's Council of the Bahamas, Registrar of the Court of Admiralty and Assistant Justice of the Court). Her mother was Harriet Thayer of Providence, a direct descendant of Roger Williams. To everyone's amazement, the two were married on June 23, 1859. Three children were born to this unusual couple: John Nicholas, on December 17, 1861, Harold in 1863, and Sophia in 1867. Sharing her husband's passion for collecting (although preferring the late nineteenth century fashion for illuminated manuscripts, examples of fine printing, and Shakespeare folios), Sophia Augusta's "lively pen" is found in much of the correspondence relating to her husband's library. In 1862, she helped oversee the addition to the Nightingale-Brown house of a fireproof library wing designed by Richard Upjohn (a decade earlier, JCB had added a carriage house by Thomas Tefft). She redecorated her Georgian home in the latest Victorian taste: flocked velvet wallpaper, potted palms, and hanging brass gas lamps. The Townsend-Goddard desk was relegated to the second-floor hallway. In summertime, the family rented a house on Bellevue Avenue in Newport.

JCB lived for seven years after the birth of little Sophia, dying on June 10, 1874 at the age of 77. Just as his father, he died in a period of economic turmoil. One year earlier, the "Panic of 1873" had hit Rhode Island hard. Like its predecessors, this financial crisis had several origins: post-war inflation, rampant speculation in railroads, property losses in the 1871 Chicago and 1872 Boston fires, a large trade deficit, and ripples from economic dislocation in Europe following the Franco-Prussian War. Due to profound structural flaws in Rhode Island's economy, the recession would last until 1879; there were too few types of manufactures, and too many communities dependent on a single industry. Increasingly larger mills meant that capital could not easily be shifted to new products or different types of enterprises. But with over $66 million invested in manufacturing and 50,000 workers employed in the sector, strong vested interests opposed any change. If an investor wanted diversification, plenty of opportunities were available in real estate, railways, and mining elsewhere.

JCB was never motivated by financial success. With ambitious, hard-working cousins looking out for his business interests, he did not feel much pressure to remain involved in Brown & Ives's day-to-day affairs after his father's passing. Nor did he feel the need to undertake new charitable endeavors to bolster his place in society. Rather, he recognized that in America, "It is cash and cash alone that gives a man credit & substantial consequence in this country[;] the more I mix with mankind, the more I am confirmed in this opinion[,] & mankind & womankind too, I have long since found, rate an individual according to his rent-roll." He was full of admiration for his father's generosity,[96] and continued supporting his father's favorite causes, but he could hardly be called a philanthropist.[97] JCB sat on the board of the Butler Hospital from 1844 to 1867, and was its president from 1867 to his death in 1874. He served on the Corporation of Brown University for forty-six years, and regularly made major donations[98] (which equaled the $160,000 given by Nick) both during his lifetime and in his will. He was an early supporter of Rhode Island Hospital, taking a great interest in the first building that was erected in 1863 when he donated $84,000. Like his father, he often gave to educational institutions, especially schools in the new Western states. But, engrossed in collecting as well as in his new wife and young family, JCB acted out of filial duty rather than actively seeking to make his mark on the community.

By the time of JCB's death in 1874, sea changes were taking place. The "Age of Benevolence" of his father Nick's lifetime—when it was believed that improving the character and morals of the poor would solve most of society's evils—was giving way to a more pragmatic tone as the first "reformer philanthropists" adopted a scientific approach to researching abuses and challenging inertia. Americans began relying on formal organizations to diffuse knowledge, self-respect, self-control, morality, and

[96] One his longest diary entries is a list of his father's gifts to Brown University; but he makes no comment other than noting that they represented "a very large sum of money."
[97] Charity engages individuals in concrete, direct acts of compassion. Philanthropy seeks not so much to aid individuals as to reform society by applying reason to the solution of social ills and needs, often in an institutional framework. The ultimate goal of philanthropy is to make charity unnecessary. . . .
[98] He donated $70,000 for books and new philosophical apparatus" (scientific equipment), scholarship funds, and $70,000 for a new library building.

religion. They became conscious of critics such as Ralph Waldo Emerson who condemned the "miscellaneous popular charities and thousand-fold relief societies" which simply offered advice to the poor. For example, prison reform now centered on preventing crime and on finding work for discharged prisoners, rather than simply giving them Bibles. Charles Loring Brace (1826-1890), who founded the New York Children's Aid Society, believed that the best charity was an opportunity to work. Brown University alumnus Horace Mann (1796-1859) promoted education as the way to overcome poverty through free, public, entirely tax supported education for all children "without any stigma of charity."

By the 1850s, the decade after Nick's death, slavery had emerged as the single most central issue in American politics, and was taken up by national organizations that commanded national audiences. Although apparently not moved by other social issues, JCB did feel strongly about slavery. His Uncle Benjamin Carter had been a strong influence, just as Nick's thinking had been informed by Uncle Moses. And like his father, JCB preferred intervening behind the scenes, as his obituary noted:

> Long before the great crisis in our history was reached, he was accustomed to encourage and aid all judicious efforts for organizing public opinion to resist its encroachments. He did not approve of violent or boisterous demonstrations against it, but, in his own quiet way, he did not fail to give to the anti-slavery cause his sympathy and pecuniary support.

Before the Civil War, JCB continued his father's financial support of the American Colonization Society but also contributed to contemporary initiatives in the fight against slavery. When Charles Sumner delivered his famous speech in the Senate on the "Crime Against Kansas" (which was being flooded with settlers from the South to force its admission as a slave state), he specifically mentioned JCB's support for Kansas as a free state. Throughout his life, JCB collected books and pamphlets relating to the slavery question, and paid to have several reprinted and distributed.

As an early member of the New England Emigrant Aid Society (that promoted and subsidized the settlement of frontier lands by northerners), JCB bristled when he was accused of a cynical real estate ploy. In 1859, when he was about to retire from its board and John Brown's raid on Harper's Ferry took place, JCB immediately wrote the Society to withdraw his resignation: "This is not the time for a man with the name of John Brown to hold back."

The anti-slavery movement paved the way for other causes to command national platforms, notably Dorothea Dix's campaign for the insane. Her initiative was ground-breaking in its approach to research and inquiry, its efforts to arouse public opinion through the press and memorials to legislatures, and its cultivation of powerful figures. In 1854, after six years of lobbying by Dix, Congress passed a law granting twelve million acres of public lands for insane asylums and institutions for the blind, deaf and dumb. But the act was vetoed by President Franklin Pierce who declared, "I cannot find any authority in the Constitution for making the Federal Government the great almoner of public charity throughout the United States." The "Pierce Veto" would characterize federal involvement with public welfare for the next eighty years until the Great Depression.

Thus, it was private charities, free-lance "reliefers" such as Clara Barton, and volunteers (especially women) who provided critical social services during the Civil War. The privately funded U.S. Sanitary Commission united thousands of local relief societies (15,000 Soldiers' Aid Societies in the North alone) into a national organization responsible for health and relief in military encampments, one that also gave thousands of civilians a sense of purpose and participation. Rigorously professional and relentlessly bureaucratic, the Sanitary Commission replaced politics and sentimentality with disinterest and science.

After the Civil War, the South's economy and infrastructure lay in ruins. Millions of emancipated slaves—jobless, landless, and uneducated—had to be integrated into a new political and economic system based on free labor and universal civil rights. For the first time, the Federal Government undertook an ambitious, multi-state program. Reconstruction was entrusted to the Freedmen's Bureau under General Oliver Otis Howard, an evangelical with years of experience in Protestant voluntary associations. JCB was a major funder of this initiative, along with George Peabody who poured $3 million into the 1867 Peabody Education Fund, and later Samuel Slater's nephew who launched the John F. Slater Fund in 1882. But these philanthropists were no match for the brutal economic and political repression of African-Americans all over America. Reconstruction ended in failure.

JCB could afford his pace of collecting despite his modest day-to-day involvement in business because Brown & Ives was going from strength to strength. Nine months before Nick's death in 1841, his son and nephews, still only junior partners, had obtained his approval to transform the Blackstone Manufacturing Company from a partnership (shared with the Butler, Wheaton, and Carrington families) to a "body corporate and politic" by act of the General Assembly. Immediately after Nick's death, the firm was further reorganized into an effective three-way partnership which lasted until the death of Moses Brown Ives in 1857. Robert Hale Ives became the dominant day-to-day partner due to his expertise in the textile industry. Moses Brown Ives, president of the Providence Bank, took a special interest in the civic, philanthropic, and legal aspects of the partnership. Their sister Charlotte Ives Goddard also became actively involved after her husband's sudden death in 1846 (from choking on a piece of meat). Three years after Nick's death, a twist of fate allowed Brown & Ives to purchase a burned-out mill on the site of the original Hope Furnace. The mill was rebuilt and the Hope Company incorporated in 1847. With this addition to its Blackstone and Lonsdale operations, Brown & Ives fast became one of the largest textile manufacturers in New England. The partners never hesitated to adopt the latest technology, such as George Corliss's revolutionary rotary steam engine.

In 1851, the two eldest of Charlotte Ives Goddard's five sons— William, Thomas, Moses, Francis, and Robert—formed a separate agency, Goddard Brothers, to handle procurement and marketing for Brown &

Ives under a salary arrangement. This allocation of tasks allowed for better product differentiation (one of its specialties was "umbrella cloth"). Goddard Brothers also performed the duties of a selling house, backed by the exceptional liquidity of Brown & Ives. Since the firm no longer had to account for maritime trade risk, it could underwrite all the credit needs of the Blackstone, Lonsdale, and Hope companies. Brown & Ives could even discount commercial paper for its subsidiaries and thus benefit from their interest payments.

New business adversaries appeared. Much as the DeWolfs of Bristol had been Brown & Ives's foes in the first decades of the nineteenth century, the Sprague family became their great rival in the second half. Its investments in factories, Maine timber, and South Carolina waterpower, "street railways," ironworks and five banks made it the most powerful conglomerate in Rhode Island. The Spragues employed 12,000 workers and did not hesitate to tell them how to vote. The family also produced two governors, William Sprague who defeated John Brown Francis in 1838, and his nephew, also named William who was elected in 1860 (William Goddard Jr. thought him "half crazy"). In 1843, the Spragues were involved in a controversy still debated in Rhode Island today. On New Year's Eve, Amasa Sprague, William's brother was beaten to death. Six months earlier, he had orchestrated having a liquor license withdrawn from Nicholas Gordon, an Irish immigrant who ran a pub near Sprague's Cranston factory where workers drank during their lunch breaks. Gordon and his brothers were blamed for the alleged revenge killing. John Gordon was hanged. The jurors were "told ... to give greater weight to Yankee witnesses than Irish witnesses."[99] But the $19 million Sprague "empire" was built on credit and was thus vulnerable to economic downturns; it collapsed spectacularly in the panic of 1873, with bankruptcy proceedings dragged into the 1920s.

By the 1860s, Rhode Island had become the most highly industrialized state in America thanks to the development of metal and machine industries in addition to textiles. That year, the state's population was

---

[99] Seven years after Gordon's death, Rhode Island abolished the death penalty and more recently, in 2010, the Rhode Island Legislature confirmed Gordon's innocence.

174,000: a 154 percent increase since 1820. With 50,666 inhabitants, Providence had grown in that period 1,000 percent. A good harbor for heavy goods such as coal and raw cotton, a railroad hub for inland distribution, and a surrounding market of 75,000 people made it the economic pivot of southern New England. Of course, the boom hid many ugly realities. Only 45 percent of school-age children regularly attended class. The illiteracy rate was unusually high for a northern state (growing at 367 percent while the population was increasing only by 50 percent). With tacit approval, Rhode Island mill owners continued to operate simple, obsolete machinery which could be tended by children. Manufacturers regularly ignored the 1840 law prohibiting the hiring of children unless they attended school three months a year as well as the 1853 law excluding their employment on night shifts and for more than eleven hours a day. Only considerations of economy (the cost of light and heat), not humanity, reduced the working week from seventy-eight hours in the 1840s to sixty-nine hours in the 1850s. Economic and social divisions were magnified by religious and political antipathies. The Irish immigrants made no secret of their disdain for the anti-slavery cause. Rhode Island opposed the Fugitive Slave Act of 1850 and voted for Lincoln in 1860, but was often swayed by its close economic relationship with the South.

As the Civil War began, Brown & Ives was in pole position to supply cloth for tents and army uniforms. The firm opened a new mill in Cumberland, Rhode Island in 1861, a second mill village at Ashton (1867), a steam powered mill at Berkeley (1872), and the huge *Ann & Hope* steam mill (1886)[100]. As Nick had envisioned, Brown & Ives stock remained in a "United Fund" (similar to a modern mutual fund) whose assets were over $2 million. Profits were reinvested or used to pay large dividends to the partners: in the twelve months between 1871 and 1872, their Lonsdale investment yielded 65 percent. Other investments provided consistently

---

[100] Bought by Martin Chase in 1946, the mill was rented out to several tenants. In 1953, Chase and his son Irwin transformed a recently vacated space into a discount retail factory outlet. By 1969, the *Ann&Hope* chain was generating $40 million in revenues; known for innovations such as large parking lots, shopping carts, central check-out counters at the front, and a liberal return policy, *Ann&Hope* stores still exist.

high returns, ranging from ten to 32.5 percent. During these years, Rhode Island's economy was experiencing a "golden" age; the combination of Yankee ingenuity and the sweat of thousands of immigrants made the state a world leader in silverware and jewelry, machine tools and rubber.

In time, a new generation took its place in the counting house. Thomas Poynton Ives, Jr. joined Brown & Ives shortly before his father Moses Brown Ives's death in 1857. An avid amateur scientist, he pursued medical studies after his graduation from Brown University in 1855. Then in 1860, Robert Hale Ives welcomed his son, Robert III, to the counting house. A graduate of Brown University Class of 1857, Robert III, traveled and studied in Europe before joining Goddard Brothers as junior partner in 1860. On the eve of the Civil War, it appeared that the second generation of the Ives family could look forward to a secure and seemingly limitless future. This was not to be.

At the Civil War's outbreak in 1861, Brown & Ives possessed large amounts of ready capital to speculate heavily in commodities. The textile mills enjoyed increased profits as the North geared up for the wartime economy. Although the family shipped gold to London for safekeeping, it seemed that the Civil War would provide an economic windfall for the partnership—more wealth than could possibly be spent in a lifetime. With almost no tax burden, this capital would provide for trust funds and investments for several generations to come. Then tragedy struck. All the Ives and Goddard men of suitable military age enlisted in the Civil War. Less than a month after his departure from Providence in September 1862, Robert Hale Ives III died from wounds received at Antietam. His father never recovered from the grief. At the same time, Thomas Poynton Ives II contacted tuberculosis. Increasingly ill throughout the Civil War years, he travelled to Europe in 1865, hoping to restore his health. There he met and married Elizabeth Cabot Motley, daughter of the American minister to Austria. But his health continued to deteriorate rapidly and within months he was dead. By November 1866, sixty-eight-year old Robert Hale Ives was now the only living male representative of the Ives line. The future of the firm lay in the hands of the Goddards.

At JCB's death in 1874, all financial interests of the Brown family were removed from Brown & Ives, and his estate moved into a separate space at 50 South Main Street called the "Trustee Room." From this location, senior trustee George W. R. Matteson managed JCB's vast holdings for the next thirty-four years, representing Sophia Augusta and her children at board and stockholder meetings, initiating investment purchases, and managing all aspects of the fortune in consultation with the other trustees. JCB's investments kept Sophia August and her children in fine style.

When her husband died, Sophia Augusta immediately had the children (aged thirteen, eleven and seven) baptized Episcopalian, then whisked them off to Europe. The family and their entourage of staff, nannies and tutors spent two years abroad: winters in Cannes on the Riviera, and the rest of the year touring museums, churches, and private libraries. John Nicholas and Harold often accompanied their mother to booksellers and private collectors. At an early age, they were shown priceless works: a Columbus letter, the papers of Leonardo daVinci, a note by Galileo. Sophia Augusta also gave them beautiful English and American silver, porcelain and artworks.

She was an indomitable force in an era when women were discovering a role for themselves in the charitable sector. Many of the middle-class women who had tasted activism during the Civil War were finding outlets for their energies in promoting political equality and moral reform causes. Their organizational and advocacy efforts resulted in the Eighteenth Amendment (prohibition) and Nineteenth Amendment (women's suffrage) to the Constitution. Women now sat on the governing boards of non-profit organizations, while nursing, social work, teaching, and other careers in the "helping professions" offered them new professional options. For Sophia Augusta, perpetuating her husband's mission through the sound management and enhancement of his collection was her way of contributing to the advancement of knowledge and understanding among peoples.

In 1881, John Nicholas entered Brown University but left after only two years due to poor health. He continued to educate himself in history, architecture, languages, and classics, and traveled extensively.[101] He joined Brown & Ives, under the tutelage of his cousin William Goddard II, and was made President of the Lonsdale Company. In 1888, he formed a partnership with his brother Harold, JN & H Brown, to offer mortgages and to invest in real estate in Providence and out West—much as the Estate of John Carter Brown was doing under the eagle eye of George Matteson. But John Nicholas's business activities left him plenty of time for other interests: The Episcopal Church, the Domestic and Foreign Missionary Society, the YMCA, the Providence Charitable Fuel Society, the Southern Negro Orphan Asylum, and a variety of more esoteric causes including a project to repopulate Alaska with reindeer (and to teach animal husbandry to the indigenous populations). Like his grandfather, John Nicholas was interested in politics, particularly issues such as free trade and the Puerto Rican Tariff. He did not seek elected office but was proud to serve as President of the Rhode Island Republican League and as a presidential elector for Benjamin Harrison in 1888. Thus John Nicholas followed squarely in the footsteps of the father he had lost so young.

From her sons' earliest age, Sophia Augusta ensured they would develop an appreciation for the care, condition and housing of books.[102] They were tutored first by John Russell Bartlett, then from 1895 by his successor George Parker Winship. On his trips to Europe, John Nicholas was expected to report back to Bartlett with his assessment of the books he encountered. He sought to "perfect" his father's collection, searching for better copies of books bought in haste or for missing works of importance, often adding beautiful bindings. When he turned 22 in 1883, Sophia Augusta entrusted him with the care of the library.

John Nicholas also seems to have been the first Brown to show interest in art: "I think that old books and new pictures are weaknesses of mine. The former I do know something about, the latter nothing."

---

[101] In 1895, Brown University voted to confer him a degree as a member of the class of 1885.

[102] But Harold preferred forming his own collection on the history of religious bodies in Colonial America.

Nevertheless, he admired the Impressionists and bought several important paintings while in Paris. In 1889, his portrait was painted by the notable French portraitist, Léon Bonnat.

Harold emulated his older brother in many ways. He spent only a year at Brown University in 1885 but asked George Matteson to guide him in acquiring business skills (in one letter concerning a mortgage he wrote "need I say it is like Hebrew to me"). Deeply spiritual, he gave $100,000 to the Domestic and Foreign Missionary Society of the Protestant Episcopal Church, as well as numerous donations to other churches, but he also owned a box at the Metropolitan Opera House in New York City. On October 4th, 1892 Harold married Georgette Wetmore Sherman (1872-1960) from Newport, with whom he shared a keen interest in French Empire furniture and objects with Napoleonic associations. The couple's grand house in Newport was decorated to form a suitable backdrop for their collection.

On September 8th, 1897, thirty-six-year old John Nicholas Brown married twenty-eight-year old Natalie Bayard Dresser. A descendent of Peter Stuyvesant and George Washington's aide-de-camp Colonel Nicholas Fish, Natalie and her siblings had been orphaned at an early age and taken in by their maternal grandmother Susan Elizabeth Fish Leroy of Newport. In 1892, Natalie and her three sisters had used their small inheritance to move to Paris where Natalie had studied painting. Soon after her return to America in late 1896, she had met the courtly and reserved John Nicholas.

Following their marriage, the couple spent an extended honeymoon in Europe. They returned to the United States the following year to set up a winter household in Providence on Brown Street and a residence on Fifth Avenue in New York City, summering in Newport. Although Natalie did not share John Nicholas's love for all things nautical (she was so seasick on his steam yacht *Ballymena* that he sold it soon after their marriage), the couple was very happy. A son, also named John Nicholas, arrived on February 21st, 1900, born in New York under a Rhode Island flag.

Upon his return to Providence in 1898, John Nicholas finally gained formal ownership of his father's collection which was referred to as "*La Grande Bibliothèque*." Only at that moment did he begin to think as a philanthropist. Scholarly inquiries (the first photo request came in 1864) and loan requests (including the 1893 Chicago World's Fair) continued to be encouraged, as in the days of JCB. However, John Nicholas felt that *La Grande Bibliothèque* would better serve humanity if it were housed in a purpose-built building under the auspices of an institution with strong curatorial capacity. He began to plan this extraordinary gift by outlining in a new will his thoughts which reflected the trends taking place around him.

Since the 1870s, metropolitan centers such as Boston, New York, and Philadelphia boasted constellations of cultural, educational, and charitable institutions, tightly linked by interlocking boards of directors. In states with charity-friendly laws, such as Massachusetts, institutional endowments were among the largest capital pools available, a source of funding for industry and western railroads. The rough-hewn, self-made men of the early industrial decades were being replaced by young men with a university education who belonged to a tight web of professional, political and social networks. Harvard's president Charles Eliot spoke in 1869 of a new "functional elite" whose authority was based on "public-serving scientific expertise."

This new generation believed that private charity should be purged of its sentimentality and organized into an effective force. The first duty of the community was not to feed the hungry or to clothe the naked, but to prevent people from becoming hungry and naked. They sought to replace the "kindly but mistaken charities" that continued to spring up "profuse and chaotic" in times of economic downturn, with efficient organizations where the head triumphed over the heart. Consolidation and cooperation were the order of the day, as exemplified by the United Hebrew Charities (Philadelphia in 1870 and New York in 1874) and the Charity Organization Society which promoted national collaboration and higher standards of efficiency among the older relief-dispensing agencies. By 1900, people of all classes were embracing the progressive

ideal—the belief that defects of their economic, social, and political institutions could be remedied by the application of scientific principles,
compassion, and expertise.

Most importantly, an unprecedented number of Americans had
become rich and powerful enough to shape community and national
affairs. "The Gilded Age" was characterized in equal measure by acquisitiveness and excesses, as well as by enormous generosity and altruism.
Indeed, its philanthropists were the very titans of industry who caused
many of the afflictions that reformers sought to undo. . . . In 1870, there
were only a hundred American millionaires. Over the next twenty years,
this number grew to 4,047. By 1916, it would reach 40,000, with John D.
Rockefeller and Henry Ford counted as billionaires. The fortunes of the
wealthiest among them have still not been equaled to this day. When
wealth is measured as a percentage of the economy, only two of the thirty
richest Americans of all times are alive today: Bill Gates and Warren
Buffet. Using this approach, John D. Rockefeller (1839-1937) would have
been worth $192 billion at his death, Cornelius Vanderbilt (1794-1877)
$143 billion, and John Jacob Astor IV (1864-1912) $116 billion—in comparison with Bill Gates's current $79 billion.

In June 1889, there appeared in *The North American Review* an article entitled "Wealth"—it would become the most famous document
in the history of American philanthropy. Penned by Andrew Carnegie,
it sought to reconcile the inequality caused by industrial development
with the equality needed for continuing social and economic progress.
Breaking with traditional American views, Carnegie believed that millionaires were not servants of God but forces of civilization who had
achieved success through competitive "survival of the fittest." He urged
his fellow millionaires to use their proven business acumen and judgment to create "the ladders on which the aspiring can rise"—in effect,
replacing traditional equality of condition with equality of opportunity.
The challenge was not to gain wealth but to dispose of it effectively
in one's lifetime ("it is a disgrace to die rich") so as to bestow lasting
benefit on weaker and poorer members of the community. Carnegie's
philanthropy included public libraries, parks, concert halls, museums,

swimming pools, institutions of higher learning and other agencies providing the means by which people could pull themselves up by their own bootstraps.

Contrary to Carnegie, the oil magnate John D. Rockefeller, a devout Baptist, still adhered to the old-fashioned doctrine of stewardship: "The good Lord gave me the money." But he cautioned, "We must always remember that there is not enough money for the work of human uplift and that there never can be. . . . How vitally important it is, therefore, that the expenditure should go as far as possible and be used with the greatest intelligence."

To this end, in 1891 Carnegie hired a professional staff to manage his "business of benevolence properly and effectively." Soon, other wealthy individuals decided to structure their philanthropy along a corporate model, one more flexible than the traditional English "charitable trust." These new "foundations" were to be scientific instruments of reform and problem solving, and would address the root causes of social ills. Most importantly, they would have a very broad mission: the advancement of knowledge and human welfare. In this spirit, Margaret Olivia Sage (1828–1918), the widow of financier Russell Sage, launched one of the earliest modern foundations in 1907:

> [it] should preferably not undertake to do that which is now being done or is likely to be effectively done by other individuals or by other agencies. It should be its aim to take up the larger and more difficult problems, and to take them up so far as possible in such a manner as to secure co-operation and aid in their solution.

Over an eleven-year period, Sage donated virtually all of the $75 million-dollar fortune bequeathed by her husband, thereby anticipating both think tanks and policy research institutions as well as the grant-making foundations we know today. Her lofty ends were to be achieved not by direct political action but by studying conditions, making findings available to influential citizens, and by mobilizing public opinion to bring about change. Such a relationship between academic experts, professional bodies, business, and government would become the paradigm of a new kind of process—one based on policy rather than partisan politics.

In addition to the foundation, another significant product of this era was the private research university. Intentionally crafted to serve the needs of a people engaged in a rapidly growing industrial economy, this new brand of university was distinctively secular in orientation and systematically cultivated relationships with the nation's wealthiest men. Business wealth poured into a host of new institutions—Cornell (1865), Johns Hopkins (1876), Stanford (1891), and the University of Chicago (1891)—allowing them to hire faculty internationally and make huge investments in the libraries, museums, and laboratories essential to carrying out path-breaking research.

John Nicholas Brown pondered these realities as he decided the future of the family's most important treasure. His father had cared little for politics and politicians (and considered public officials "more self-servants than servants of the people"), so giving his father's collection to the City of Providence was not an option. In an 1870 letter to John Russell Bartlett, JCB had clearly rejected "build[ing] up an Institution mainly at my own expense and then to have it controlled and managed by a set of political jugglers." It was imperative that the collection remain independent, although intellectual attachment to an academic institution was acceptable.

There were several libraries in Providence from which to choose. John Nicholas had followed his father and grandfather in supporting the Providence Atheneum and the library at Brown University, but he was attracted particularly to the innovative mission of the Providence Library. Founded in 1871 by representatives from Rhode Island's leading scientific and industrial societies, this library was privately supported to serve the people in the best "public" sense of the word. The librarian William E. Foster developed innovative methods and practices "that were observed with interest by the entire library world," including establishing "contacts" such as schools, museums, foreign groups, local industries, hospitals, the blind, and individual readers interested in self-education. It was the first library to stage lectures, to purchase books requested by readers, to notify city officials and businessmen about new books in their fields, and to loan small collections of books to organizations. With such an ambitious program, the library soon outgrew its first space. John Nicholas stepped forward with the remarkable sum of $268,500. A classic Renaissance building, with 93,000 volumes and thirty-nine employees, was thus inaugurated on March 15th, 1900 with John Nicholas in attendance.

This would be his last public act. Less than a month later, he contracted typhoid fever and died in New York on May 1st, 1900. His brother Harold Brown who was in London received the news by telegram and rushed back to America on the first available ship. But while at sea, he became gravely ill from "pleurisy, pneumonia and erysipelas" and died on May 10th, 1900, the day after his arrival in New York. Within the space of ten days, Sophia Augusta had lost both her sons. Their heir was the two-month-old baby, John Nicholas Brown II.

CHAPTER 16

Transforming The
Human Experience

*"Scholar, sailor, humanist
who brought art into life
and made of life an art"*
Epitaph on the gravestone of John Nicholas Brown II

John Nicholas Brown was only thirteen when his father died. His son John Nicholas Brown II was orphaned at two months old and never knew his father. Thus two successive generations of Brown children grew up under the influence of remarkable mothers – Sophia Augusta Browne Brown, and Natalie Dresser Brown - with a keen aesthetic sense, but with little input from the male-dominated world of business. They did both experience, however, the "golden age" of American philanthropy—that period between 1890 and 1930 marked by the combination of extraordinary wealth, no income taxes, and radically new attitudes towards giving (which, we have seen, had been percolating for the past half-century). John Nicholas I's philanthropic potential was cut short by his premature death at 39; however, his son considered himself a "professional philanthropist."[103]

---

[103] He tried to use these words on his passport application, but was rejected and told to write "real estate."

When John Nicholas II inherited both his father's and his uncle's great wealth in May 1900,[104] the press wrote that he was "The Richest Baby in America . . . Maybe the World." His mother Natalie Dresser Brown did her best to shield him from prying eyes and to protect his fragile health. She chose to raise him in Newport, but far away from Gilded-Age Bellevue Avenue; they lived in the French château-style house that she built in 1906 on a steep hill overlooking the harbor, *Harbour Court*. In 1913, she bought *Camp Yawgoo* in South County for his recreation. Noting that he had inherited his ancestors' love of the sea, she provided sailing lessons and boats. Mother, son, and a retinue of servants often traveled throughout Europe by automobile and train (they were present at the 1911 coronation of George V and Queen Mary), and throughout the American West when Europe was inaccessible during the Great War. In 1919 they spent the summer in Japan and, in 1923, chartered a specially outfitted (due to the physical height of the Brown family) paddle wheel boat on the Nile. John Nicholas II was thrilled to witness the excavation of Tutankhamun's tomb by Howard Carter before touring the Holy Land.

With no father to guide him, John Nicholas II drew his own lessons from the events he witnessed. At age four, the little boy in his cream sailor suit presented Brown University president Faunce with the keys to a magnificent *beaux-arts* building on the campus green. Three years earlier, in 1901, his father's executors had decided to offer the collection of books under an agreement of shared authority that "preserves its individual identity as a whole," with a separate endowment always to have "its own separate and special housing, . . . and to be kept separate and distinct from any other Library." To this day, the John Carter Brown Library is owned by the University Corporation but is operated as a semi-autonomous institution with its own administration and funding, under its own committee of management. The executors also directed that $150,000 be spent to erect an appropriate building. In 1904, 12,000 books were moved out of the Nightingale-Brown house on Benefit Street,

---

[104] Estimates vary from $30 million to $100 million ($25 billion to $83 billion in modern economic power—an amount of wealth relative to the then total output of the U.S. economy).

and another $500,000 was placed in the Library's endowment. This final chapter in JCB's collection was overseen by two women: Sophia Augusta (until her death in 1909) and Natalie (who remained deeply involved until her son took over on the management committee in 1923).[105]

John Nicholas II's inheritance was organized into two trusts; Natalie was a beneficiary and received a dower on the provision that she not re-marry (she would remain a widow for fifty years). George Matteson (who by 1900 had been handling the family's affairs for over three decades) and, after 1908, his son Frank managed the investment portfolios for the various trusts. Cautious by nature, the Mattesons invested in municipal bonds, blue chip stocks, real estate, and mortgages. In her position as guardian, Natalie was apprised of all transactions and often included in the decision-making. She took particular interest in the real estate investments out West (now known as the Brown Land Company), and construction projects such as the Turks Head Building in Providence.

All around her, the philanthropists of the Gilded Age were funding open-ended programs for the "improvement of mankind." The 1913 Federal Income Tax Act exempted institutions "organized and operated exclusively for religious, charitable, scientific or educational purposes," and in 1921 tax relief was granted for personal giving. As a result, the number of American foundations climbed steadily, from twenty-seven in 1913 to two hundred in 1930, with an aggregate endowment of $1 billion. In 1928, there were twenty professional fundraisers offering their services in New York City alone.

Although this scale of benevolence did much to make wealth accept-able, public opinion reacted strongly in 1913 when John D. Rockefeller sought a Congressional charter for his $100 million foundation—just at the time when his Standard Oil Company was being prosecuted for violating the Sherman Antitrust Act. Progressive presidential candi-date Theodore Roosevelt strongly opposed Congressional endorse-ment, proclaiming "no amount of charity in spending such fortunes [as

---

[105] Of the four Brown family members who have sat on the JCB Library's board to date, half have been women.

Rockefeller's] can compensate in any way for the misconduct in acquiring them."

Meanwhile, the "machinery of benevolence" looked for ways to democratize philanthropy so that middle and working-class Americans would become more civically engaged. In 1900, a "Community Chest" was launched in Cleveland to collect donations from corporations, employees, and individuals on behalf of nonprofit organizations, so as to minimize the duplication of fund-raising appeals while aligning charitable and business agendas (the United Way is a descendant of the Community Chest). In 1913, the first "Community Foundation" was also started in Cleveland to encourage small donors to establish charitable trusts, placed under common management. Thus, at the beginning of the twentieth century, Americans came to think of philanthropy not only as acts of personal charity, but also as a form of community citizenship.

During World War I the federal government promoted "mass philanthropy" for humanitarian purposes, reinforcing the perception that giving was part of being American. After the War, a notable increase in the standard of living (the average annual salary rose 30 percent from $696 in 1914 to $898 in 1929) further bolstered giving by all levels of society. In 1928, Americans collectively gave $2 billion; including five hundred lump-sum gifts of $1 million or more. Many of the organizations we know today were founded at this time: the Girl Scouts, the American Cancer Society, Goodwill Industries, the NAACP, and the National Urban League.

Though he probably did not set out to do so, John Nicholas II grew up to become a model for early twentieth century philanthropy, described by Robert Bremmer, a historian of American philanthropy, as "the direct conversion of massive capitalist wealth into public assets under the guidance of the wealthy themselves." Like John Simon Guggenheim who included "the appreciation of beauty" among his broad goals, John Nicholas II felt that art and culture were a vital component of the human experience. He was convinced of the positive impact of great architecture, whether the structure was centuries old or cutting edge modern.

The breadth of his interests would run from historic preservation to promoting leading contemporary architects. Although the primary beneficiary of his munificence would be Providence, he would also fund major projects far from home in Istanbul, Athens, and Rome.

Raised in an era when philanthropy prized scientific research, John Nicholas II realized early that he needed the right education to develop his personal paradigm. After being home-schooled by tutors in his early years, he attended Episcopalian St. George's School in Newport as a day boy (where his favorite subject was Sacred Studies). When the time came for university, President Faunce assured him of an "easy experience" if he would attend Brown University. Instead, John Nicholas II chose Harvard where he designed an independent concentration in "The History and Literature of Classical Cultures" that required fluency in Latin and Greek. There, he formed life-long friendships and met important scholarly mentors. After graduating *magna cum laude* with a John Harvard Fellowship in 1922, he embarked with his mother on a year-long tour "taking moving pictures of still objects" of Europe's medieval cathedrals and other religious sites (with a Rolls Royce and attentive professor at his command). Upon his return to Providence in 1923, he later recalled:

> I was duly installed in the chair my father vacated 23 years before from which I was supposed to "run the estate." In the adjoining room sat Mr. Matteson, a large and impressive figure, who had indeed run the estate since my infancy. All day long delegations waited upon Mr. Matteson, were admitted, smoked long cigars, and took a noisy departure. Meanwhile, since no one ever bothered me, I sat alone reading a pocket edition of Dante. I don't know how long this might have continued had I not been liberated by a sudden attack of appendicitis.

After his recovery, John Nicholas II decided to return to Harvard for a Master's degree in "historic architecture, Christian iconography and the history of painting." Natalie bought a Boston apartment nearby for which her son designed a "modern" bedroom—the "first modern room in New England," he would claim. This time, John Nicholas II studied under the legendary Paul Sachs, the father of professional museum curatorship. While still at Harvard, he established the Medieval Academy of America and its magazine *Speculum*. He began collecting Old Master drawings. He purchased furniture for *Harbour Court* from a monastery in Burgos, Spain, and had his bedroom redecorated to resemble a Spanish monk's cell (he briefly considered becoming a Roman Catholic monk). But his crowning project in those years was to commission the architect Ralph Adam Cram (who had designed *Harbour Court* and Natalie's 1901 memorial to her husband, Emmanuel Church in Newport) to build a neo-English Perpendicular Gothic chapel for St. George's School, so that the students would no longer have a long walk to church. After four years of close collaboration during which John Nicholas II was involved in every detail, the chapel was consecrated in 1928.

As A. Lawrence Lowell once observed, "When I first knew John he was a classicist, then he became a mediaevalist, and now I hear he's a modernist. What may we expect next?" In fact, John Nicholas II also discovered a passion for colonial architecture and preservation in 1928 when he became involved with the rehabilitation of the Old Brick Market house in Newport. As a result of all these initiatives, the American Institute of Architects elected him a lay member in 1931 (in an interview given shortly before his 70th birthday, he remarked that, could he live his life over again, he would have been an architect). His life-long interest in historic preservation would continue with saving the Arcade building in Providence (1945) and Slater Mill in Pawtucket, as well as helping to found the Providence Preservation Society in 1956. Another obvious project was to restore to its former colonial glory Nick's home on Benefit Street (which he had to purchase from the descendants of JCB's daughter, Sophia Augusta Brown Sherman). In 1936, he would also buy John Brown's brick mansion from the estate of Marsden Perry, the industrialist who had purchased it from the Gammell family in 1901. After extensive renovation, the house was sold for $10 to the Rhode Island Historical Society in 1942.

All these new endeavors were in fact a way to postpone returning to the counting house—in the spring of 1929, John Nicholas II and his mother even chartered the world's largest yacht *Iolantha* to cruise throughout Greece and Turkey. Then, two events changed his life forever.

While on the Mediterranean cruise, John Nicholas II met Europeans and read newspapers that made him aware of looming financial disaster. He cabled the counting house that all his shares should be sold; his financial managers did not listen. Then, as the Great Depression took hold in 1930, Frank Matteson created a consortium of twenty-five investors (mostly leading Providence families) to corner the Chicago rye market. It was a disaster; John Nicholas II insisted on reimbursing each investor from his personal funds. Although he would recover from that debacle, this and two subsequent episodes of egregious mismanagement in later years severely depleted his assets.

The second event was decidedly more positive. A prolific correspondent—who, like his ancestors, revealed little about himself—John Nicholas II was one of the first Americans to be psychoanalyzed (he recognized a "mother fixation"). He was determined to lead a useful life, but realized that he needed the encouragement and support of an energetic partner. On his way to an Episcopalian convention with his mother in early 1930, the shy, lanky young man (he was almost six foot seven) stopped for tea in Baltimore where he was introduced to Anne Kinsolving. Born in 1906, she was the fourth of the seven children of the Reverend Arthur B. Kinsolving and Sally Bruce, both of Virginia. The Kinsolving family has contributed innumerable famous bishops and priests to the Episcopal Church; the Bruces are a distinguished Virginia dynasty (Sally became Poet Laureate of Maryland). Anne always seemed to attract attention: a parishioner paid for her to attend private school, another lent her a horse, yet another wanted to adopt her. But bored by school and left to her own devices in the rectory of Old St. Paul's Church in Baltimore, she started smoking at age 11, learned Russian and the violin, and discovered that she had a biting wit and a winning way with words.[106] Anne dreamed of becoming America's leading female journal-

---

[106] She once described a celebrated lady cellist as "an enormous crab embracing an indifferent oyster."

ist, so went to work as a reporter for Hearst's *Baltimore New American* where she covered Rudolf Valentino's funeral, flew upside down in a plane over the Washington monument with a military air ace, and struck up a friendship with the opera singer Enrico Caruso. In 1926, she left Baltimore for a year to tour of America as "personal press agent" to legendary French tennis star Suzanne Lenglen. By 1930, she had become the newspaper's music critic and was earning far more money than her brothers. When John Nicholas II met her, she had the independence, high spirits, and powerfully assertive sense of self that complimented him perfectly.

He was enthralled. Their third date was in New York for the premier of Stravinsky's *The Rites of Spring*. On the train back to Baltimore, Anne collapsed with appendicitis. When she awoke in hospital after surgery, John Nicholas II was standing by her bed with an engagement ring. He warned her however that he might have lost all his money in the rye pool. Anne did not care. They were married on October 18th, 1930. Anne wore a Russian wedding head-dress and the headlines read "Millionaire baby marries Cinderella girl." The couple then set off on a year-long honeymoon[107] during which Anne indulged in her childhood fascination with tin soldiers (which eventually would develop into her legendary knowledge of military minutiae and America's finest collection of books and prints on military uniforms, now at Brown University).

Anne complimented John Nicholas II admirably. "Anne has often tried me," he once said, "but she's never bored me." She understood that his immense wealth precluded him from the professional career he would have enjoyed as an architect or curator (his son, John Carter III would fulfil that dream). Instead, she encouraged him to undertake large, complex projects that would stimulate and stretch his abilities. But, she insisted, he must take control over his financial affairs and become master of his own fate. In the interim, Frank Matteson had died and his lieutenants resigned. As John Nicholas II described the situation:

---

[107] Natalie insisted that John Nicholas II's nanny accompany them.

With no business training of any kind, I suddenly found myself an officer of several land companies, a large textile concern, and a director of a few banks. Fortunately for me they were all too sick at the time to distinguish between the ministrations of the doctor and the first-year student, and in the years before their recovery I had plenty of time to learn the hard way. I became quite coy towards my various patients as each wooed me in turn with her own special set of complexities. In the end, after a valiant struggle, it was the land that won.

John Nicholas II also continued to sponsor initiatives well beyond the borders of Rhode Island. He had been a founding member of the Byzantine Institute of America (now housed at Dumbarton Oaks in Washington, DC), and had underwritten the restoration of the mosaics of Haghia Sophia in Istanbul (1931). Now he funded the restoration of Karyie Camii in Istanbul, the treasury of San Marco in Venice, as well as the Stoa of Attalos in Athens. When the river Arno flooded Florence in 1966, he coordinated much of the American rescue effort. He also helped found St. Dunstan's College of Sacred Music in Providence.

After his marriage, John Nicholas II deepened his interest in modern art and architecture. Historian George Goodwin has aptly described how he did so:

> [John Nicholas II] never viewed architecture as warring against itself. Indeed, he enjoyed and understood architecture on many levels: as providing bodily comfort, as expressing artistic yearning, as ennobling human behavior, and as sustaining the soul. Architecture, for Brown, represented a continuum in which the past lived within the future, the future within the past.

While at Harvard, he had joined the Society for Contemporary Art and, after graduation, the Museum of Modern Art's junior committee, chaired by Nelson Rockefeller. In the mid-1930s, he commissioned modernist architect Richard Neutra to build the first *Bauhaus*-inspired home on the East Coast: *Windshield* on Fishers Island, New York—complete with rubber floors, aluminum frame windows and two Buckminster Fuller-designed *Dymaxion* bathrooms.[108] In the late 1930s, he pressed for the appointment of Alexander Dorner as director of the Rhode Island School of Design Museum. Dorner was a radical exponent of contextual displays who had recently come from Germany and "would put the museum on the map as it had never been before." When Dorner was falsely accused of Nazi sympathies and fired, John Nicholas II stood by him and resigned from the RISD board.

Natalie once commented about her son's marriage, "Anne was the stirrer-up, John was the smoother-over." Natalie had instilled in her son an interest in civic affairs. A strong proponent of woman's suffrage, she had also presided over the Newport Civic League, campaigned for Democratic candidates (from 1929, she was President of the Newport Democratic Club), and served as the first woman ever on a jury in Newport County, as well as on a task force to study the effects of prohibition. During World War II, she would be president of the Maple Leaf Club to knit for the armed services and chaired the Women's Committee for the Council of National Defense.[109] Now, Anne encouraged her husband to take a more public stance on causes that mattered. JCB had said, "Speak to the past and it shall teach thee." His grandson would put these words to action, using his considerable charm and diplomacy to honor the past but influence the future.

---

[108] He was probably influenced by both the first American exhibition about the *Bauhaus* presented in Cambridge in December 1930 and sponsored by the Harvard Society for Contemporary Art, and by The Museum of Modern Art's 1932 "Modern Architecture: International Exhibition." My cousin, Carter Brown's daughter Elyssa, produced the documentary "Windshield: A Vanished Vision" in 2016, with a score by another cousin, Chad Brown Fischer, son of Angela Brown Fischer.

[109] Natalie also continued to paint and exhibit her work at the Newport Art Association, over which she presided. She also remained an active member of the Episcopal Church, attending national conventions and overseeing "her" parish in Newport, Emmanuel. After a year-long illness, she died on March 27, 1950 at *Harbour Court*.

John Nicholas II began his career in public service by accepting President Roosevelt's 1933 appointment to head the Rhode Island division of The Public Works Administration. In 1935, he chaired the Rhode Island State Planning Board (which "struggled feverishly to dig, pave, and bridge Rhode Island out of the Great Depression"), followed by a seat on the Newport City Council (his only elected position) and its Council of Civilian Defense, the War Fund Campaign for the Rhode Island Red Cross, and the Governor's bi-partisan committee to plan for postwar problems. Then in 1945, he was appointed special cultural advisor to General Eisenhower, attached to the Monuments, Fine Arts and Archives Commission (known as the *Monuments Men,* the subject of a recent eponymous film directed by George Clooney), which worked to identify and restore public artworks looted by the Nazis. It was a frustrating assignment but he was influential in convincing the American government to return looted works to the venues from which they had been stolen, rather than keeping them as war reparations. On his return, he was tapped to chair the (ultimately unsuccessful) initiative to locate the newly formed United Nations Organization in Rhode Island. Then, having been appointed by President Truman in November 1946 as Assistant Secretary of the Navy for Air, he wrote in 1948 a memorandum outlining steps for the Navy to desegregate and embrace "non-discrimination" on a broad scale; he held the post for two and a half years before resigning in March 1949 and returning home to Providence. In his home state, he served on for forty-two years and chaired the board of the Rhode Island Foundation (a community foundation), as well as the Rhode Island Turnpike and Bridge Authority, and the Rhode Island Council on the Arts. Throughout his life, he attended numerous conventions of both the Episcopal Church and the Democratic Party.

John Nicholas II also chaired or served on committees that "brought art into life": for example, the Harvard University Committee for the Visual Arts which examined the role of fine arts in the university curriculum (1954), the President's Committee on an American Armed Forces Museum (1957), the Smithsonian's Board of Regents (1957 to 1979) and the Smithsonian's National Portrait Gallery Commission (1963). But in Rhode Island, he faced an interesting challenge.

Henry Wriston, the first Brown University President who was not a Baptist clergyman, steered the university through the critical events of 1937 through 1955, including the Depression, World War II, and the GI Bill. He is credited with changing Brown from "an essentially regional institution" into "a major American university." This endeavor required vast new facilities and major funding. In a relationship that evoked the one a century earlier between Nick and Francis Wayland, Wriston depended on the generosity of John D. Rockefeller, Jr. (Class of 1897) But as the university began acquiring land and tearing down houses to build its new campus, Rockefeller insisted the new structures be in neo-Georgian style (at the time, he was engrossed in the restoration of Colonial Williamsburg)—"In a strange sense, the university demolished old buildings to erect new buildings that looked old."

The University's neighbors were in an uproar. At the same time, the City of Providence was loosing much of its manufacturing base and a substantial portion of its population; many neighborhoods were blighted and renewal plans were based on massive slum clearance. Unless heroic efforts were taken to restore its tax base, Providence faced further decline and squalor.

Back in 1936, John Nicholas II had been invited to serve as vice chairman of the state's advisory board of the "American Historic Buildings Survey," a national initiative to catalogue America's architectural patrimony. There he had met Antoinette Downing, an architectural historian and activist. On February 20, 1956, the two called a meeting at John Nicholas II's office in the Joseph Brown House on South Main Street to launch the Providence Preservation Society. Although its initial purpose was to safeguard against Brown University's further incursions on College Hill, the society quickly evolved to protect the character and beauty of the entire East Side of the city. By August it had gathered nearly three hundred members (annual dues were five dollars per year). A few weeks later, as the City Plan Commission prepared to demolish thirty-two acres of run-down homes on Lippitt Hill, the Preservation Society undertook to "demonstrate methods and techniques of developing a feasible program of preservation, restoration, and renewal." John

Nicholas II did not believe in "preservation for sentimental reasons . . . but to assure a richer and more varied whole. . . . The inestimable value of the old is honored as a vital part of the present."[110] Rather than recreate a museum village exemplified by Colonial Williamsburg, East Siders sought to reinvigorate a living neighborhood.

Then, in 1962, John Nicholas II was asked to chair the Building & Planning Committee at Brown University (he had started on a sub-committee in 1957). Now "inside the lions' den," he finally had a chance to introduce modernism to campus. The experience was only moderately successful: he brought Philip Johnson to build the laboratory to house a new IBM 7070 computer (1961) and the List Art Center (1971), but both projects required years of bureaucratic wrangling and painful negotiations (Johnson resigned in 1968). During his ten-year chairmanship (in the same period, he was appointed Secretary of the Corporation), the university continued to expand at a furious pace. As John Nicholas II noted with typical understatement, the building program was "my most absorbing interest."

Fortunately, he always had a multitude of other interests to provide respite from endless planning meetings, including deriving genuine pleasure from his real estate investments out West: "This is a challenge I cannot resist in a world of ephemeral values and atomic fission, where only the land and the spirit are left to remind us of our origin and our destination."

Early in his marriage, Anne had convinced him to take up the cello so that the family could play chamber music; the couple hosted several concert series at home in JCB's former library and on Fisher's Island. But

---

[110] A report published in 1967 demonstrated that Providence and its Preservation Society had made enormous progress: none of the East Side's "priority" buildings had been destroyed, more than 140 structures had been restored, and a rich array of educational programs had been launched, including a Benefit Street tourist "trail," a festival of historic houses, and 150 plaques placed on restored buildings. However, the gentrification of the East Side largely benefited middle-income and upper-income families. Longtime property owners and tenants—many of them African-Americans—were forced out of the neighborhood. Rhode Island did not pass a fair-housing law until 1965.

his true passion was sailing. Throughout his life, he built a number of boats; the most famous, *Bolero*, was designed in 1949 with revolutionary features and broke numerous records. He was on his yacht *Malagueña* on October 9th, 1979, when he collapsed from a massive heart attack and died.

Anne stayed on at *Harbour Court*. Over the years she was an instrumental force in a number of civic organizations, notably the Newport Music Festival and the Preservation Society of Newport County, in addition to publishing several major works of military history. A fervent Republican, she never hesitated to voice her opinions and appeared as a character witness for Claus Von Bulow at his infamous trial. She died of lung cancer on November 21, 1985.

John Nicholas II and Anne had three children: Nicholas VI born in 1932, John Carter III (known as Carter) born in 1934, and Angela Bayard born in 1938. Both boys were sent to the Arizona Desert School (there were fears of U-boats in Narragansett Bay), followed by the Groton School, and then Harvard. Nicholas was to become a diplomat and so majored in Russian language and literature. But midway through his freshman year, he realized that his life lacked purpose; the best diplomatic posts were now going to political appointees. He had no desire to end up in Providence, playing second fiddle to his illustrious father—what could he do on his own merit, not based on his name?

While John Nicholas II was posted in Washington as Assistant Secretary of the Navy, Nicholas had met several heroes of World War II who sparked his enthusiasm for the Navy. So, in the spring of 1952, his junior year at Harvard, he dropped out to start all over again as a plebe at the U.S. Naval Academy in Annapolis. He would remain in the Navy for twenty-seven years, notably serving as Executive Officer to the Navy's first African-American Admiral Samuel Gravely. A year after graduation, Nicholas met Diane Vernes, a sparkling young French woman who was visiting Fishers Island with her family. The Vernes were prominent Huguenot bankers; Diane's maternal ancestors were shippers and silk merchants. They married in Paris on June 27, 1957. Diane then followed Nicholas around the world, moving house twenty-seven times.

Following his retirement from active service, Nicholas became Director of the National Aquarium in Baltimore, an unusual choice given his lack of academic credentials ("All he really knew about fish was how to cook them," said one observer). But the Aquarium was the centerpiece of Baltimore's Inner Harbor redevelopment and played an essential role in the city's rebirth. After twelve years at the National Aquarium, Nicholas returned to Providence in 1995 to take over Preserve Rhode Island, the statewide preservation advocacy organization founded by his father. Today, he continues to serve on numerous non-profit boards, contributing strategic and management advice.

Angela, the youngest, also attended Harvard and married a Boston neurosurgeon, Edwin Fischer. Her life has been dedicated to service in the non-profit sector. With her two brothers out of state, she single-handedly maintained the family's legacy in Rhode Island for decades, including the Corporation of Brown University and the John Carter Brown Library.

Meanwhile Carter, the second son, perpetuated his father's belief in "the redemptive powers of art." Deciding at a young age that he wanted to be a "cultural engineer," Carter also spent considerable time educating himself: Harvard, Harvard Business School (long before "arts management" existed as a common course of study), and another Master's degree at New York University's Institute of Fine Arts, interspersed with a year with Bernard Berenson in Florence, and *l'Ecole du Louvre* in Paris. In 1961, Carter Brown was hired by the National Gallery of Art in Washington, DC as an assistant to the Director John Walker and was soon groomed to be Walker's successor. Appointed assistant director in 1964, he supervised the construction of the museum's East Building designed by I. M. Pei, (which would inspire museums around the world to commission great architectural projects). In 1969, at the age of thirty-four, he became director the National Gallery.

Carter's ambition as director was to attract larger crowds to the nation's art museum through "blockbuster" exhibitions (such as "The Treasures of Tutankhamun"), technology (such as the Audioguide), and a wide variety of topics (from African sculpture to Old Masters). During his twenty-three years as director, the National Gallery added over 20,000 works to the collection. The annual budget increased from $3 million to $52 million and the endowment from $34 million to $186 million, at a time when many museums and cultural institutions were losing public funding. Its rivalry with the Metropolitan Museum of Art in New York was widely reported in the press. One of Carter Brown's most significant achievements was to persuade Congress to indemnify art on loan from abroad, which freed American museums from the impossible burden of insuring borrowed art.

Through his high-profile leadership of the National Gallery, Brown became one of the leading public intellectuals in American and the champion of American art. His chairmanship of the U.S. Commission of Fine Arts, which oversees public art and architecture in the nation's capital, and of the Pritzker Prize for Architecture, deeply influenced architecture and design not only in Washington, D.C. but throughout the world. After his retirement, as chairman of Ovation (the arts cable network he helped found), he remained fascinated by the possibilities of film and television for the promotion of art and music. Tragically, Carter died in 2002 at the age of 68.

As noted by his biographer Neil Harris, "It was the notion of becoming a mediator, an interpreter, an intermediary between performers or artists on one side and a set of publics on the other that captured Carter's imagination and never surrendered it." Often referred to as a "populist patrician," Carter was, according to his *New York Times* obituary, an "unlikely figure to champion mass culture, with which he was eternally fascinated but sometimes charmingly unfamiliar." He defended his career choice by saying that foundation work was "getting your kicks out of vicarious funding of other people's creativity" but, an art museum was "hands on with real objects and real creativity."

That search for direct engagement defines those of my generation in the Brown family who continue to be involved the non-profit sector. The wealth is now largely depleted; John Nicholas II's fascination with technology led him to make disastrous investments in early pollution control equipment shortly before his death, and my father's lifetime of public service did not replenish his coffers. Now we can offer principally our time and energy.

Almost a century ago, Franklin Roosevelt introduced the revolutionary concept of government responsibility for what the U.S. Constitution calls "the common welfare" by funding it through taxation. For the past ninety years, government has also worked in tandem with key institutions from the non-profit sector to take responsibility for basic social needs. Steeply progressive taxes on personal income and estates, combined with high corporate tax rates, have created powerful incentives to direct private and corporate resources into cultural, educational, health, and human welfare services. In 2015, $373 billion was directed to nearly 1.5 million public charities (a number that has increased twelve fold over forty years), employing full-time staff by the tens of millions, and supported by over 100,000 private foundations and the volunteer efforts of more than 25 percent of our adult population. The next four decades will witness an extraordinary "generational wealth transfer" conservatively estimated at $48 trillion, of which $20 trillion will be earmarked for charity (Boston College report, 2014). These funds will move into non-profit organizations from donors at all income levels, not just America's wealthiest individuals.

Today the income of the top one hundredth of a percent of the American population is once again about the same as it was hundred years ago. At this end of the spectrum, the *Chronicle of Philanthropy* lists a series of bequests made in 2015 that very much resemble those made by the philanthropists of the "Gilded Age": $605 from the estate of John Santikos to the San Antonio Area Community Foundation, $400 million from John and Jenny Paulson to Harvard's School of Engineering and Applied Sciences (the largest in its history), $177 million from Chuck Feeney's Atlantic Philanthropies to the University of California at San Francisco and Trinity College Dublin to create a Global Brain Health Institute, $150 million each from David Koch and Steven Schwarzman for Memorial Sloan Kettering Hospital and Yale University, respectively. To date, 141 of the world's wealthiest individuals and families have publicly adhered to the "Giving Pledge," a commitment launched in 2010 by Bill Gates and Warren Buffet to dedicate the majority of their wealth to philanthropy. When asked, only one cites "guilt" as a reason. Others cite the responsibility to engage in serious philanthropy that is commensurate with great wealth; the opportunity to "make a difference" and to see it happen; the feeling of indebtedness to one's community; concerns about poverty and need to find solutions; worry about leaving too much to children, coupled with the desire to teach them about giving back.

In contrast with these billionaires, the fastest growing sector in philanthropy is small family foundations, many with assets under $1 million, who often target very specific causes rather than large institutions. Indeed, one of the unique characteristics of American philanthropy is not "a matter of the rich helping people in need, but of people, rich or not, providing for their own future." Philanthropy gives energy and purpose to citizens in a democracy by creating linkages and reinforcing a sense of community.

Amazingly, only a third of Americans do any research before making a charitable donation. Philanthropic decisions must not be taken lightly; misguided giving, or choices led only from the heart and not also from the head, can cause unintended consequences or even irreparable damage. This is why donor education is so critical. The very wealthy are surrounded by advisors—lawyers, asset managers, philanthropy consultants—but there is little guidance available for those who simply want to ensure they are giving in the most effective way possible, no matter what the amount.

There have never been so many innovative ways to engage one's time, talent and treasure: from investing in a social enterprise to building a non-profit's management capacity, from local giving circles to crowd funding platforms, from social media-based advocacy campaigns to volunteering in an after-school program. Now that the Brown family has less to distribute, my mission is to help others learn how to assess root causes, identify the full spectrum of possible solutions, find potential partners, and measure the results. In this way, I can leverage several generations' worth of philanthropic experience to a greater benefit.

Throughout my student and professional years, I was deeply involved with development economics and the Global South (even starting doctoral research in India). I spent a decade in New York working with emerging markets in project finance and investment promotion; I then married a French UNHCR official who took me to the Bosnian-Croatian border during the Yugoslavia war, the Pakistan-Afghan border during the rise of the Taliban, and Slovakia when the Schengen Agreement opened Europe's internal borders. There, I ran income generating projects and launched a microfinance initiative. We then settled in London where I raised our two children, while remaining deeply involved with a number of international organizations. In 2006, following two bitter experiences in misguided charitable projects, I signed up for a course in strategic philanthropy run by The Philanthropy Workshop (started by the Rockefeller Foundation). It changed my life; impact became a priority—where could I make the most difference? The path led me straight home to Rhode Island.

I began the Prologue to this book by outlining a voyage of discovery upon which I was provoked to embark by two seminal events, separated by a distance of fifteen years, and which presented two such very different perspectives on my family's role and motivations since my forbear Chad Browne helped to found the state of Rhode Island nearly three centuries ago. It is only fitting to end by trying to summarize what I have learned along the way.

As Nicholas Brown II was the individual who gave ultimate embodiment to the family propensity for philanthropy—and is the principal character in my narrative—I feel obliged to ask what would my great-great grandfather think of his legacy today? Brown University continues to offer a rare intellectual freedom of choice while ensuring that the humanities remain at the core of the college experience. Its graduates are, to use the words of historian Ted Widmer, "intellectually more voracious about the world." But as they often choose creative or public service careers, growing the endowment continues to be challenging. However, Nick probably would be distressed by how liberal the campus has become. He would also be deeply upset to learn that Rhode Island has one of the worst unemployment rates and "climates for business" in the country, although huge efforts currently are being undertaken to turn these statistics around. He would be fascinated by the possibilities of social enterprise and impact investing, combining "doing good" with "doing well." I often think of him when I coach a budding entrepreneur, attend a board meeting of the John Carter Brown Library, or stroll down Benefit Street.

As for my own personal development, it has been a voyage of discovery more varied, complex and contradictory than ever I envisaged. The propensity to philanthropy remains baked into the Brown family character, in the process both informing and reflecting the national ethos. But I cannot accurately judge to what extent altruism, self-interest or genetic make-up has been the predominant influence. All three have played their part, in differing proportions and according to the circumstances of the moment. As an eleventh-generation descendant, there is great deal to be proud of, a considerable amount to be less than proud of, and a certain amount that simply defies attempts at rational analysis. Motivations have often simultaneously combined elements of both altruism and self-interest, and all the usual laws of unintended consequences have manifested themselves in full measure. It is for the reader to decide whether the good that has been done over nearly three centuries outweighs the errors and misjudgments along the way. Speaking for myself, what I have unearthed is a complex, sometimes burdensome legacy, but also an undeniable source of pride and inspiration.

Thanksgiving Day, 2016

LIST OF ILLUSTRATIONS

Page 203

Map of Narragansett Bay. Courtesy the Rhode Island Historical Society. RHi X42 85. Charles Blaskowitz. Chart of Narragansett Bay. Rhode Island. 1777. Ink on paper. ENGRAVING. Map #1032

Page 204

The first home lots in Providence. Courtesy the Rhode Island Historical Society. RHi X17 2762. Charles W. Hopkins. Plan Showing the First Division of Home Lots in Providence, RI. 1886. Lithograph. PRINT. Graphics – Maps – Map #14337.

John Brown (1736–1803). Courtesy of New York Historical Society. Malbone, Edward Greene, "John (1736–1803) Brown." Watercolor on ivory. The Louis Durr and Aurthur Jones Funds. 1794.

Moses Brown (1738–1836). Courtesy the Rhode Island Historical Society. RHi X5 9. Kinney, Henry E., Attributed to. Portrait of Moses Brown. ca. 1898. Oil on canvas. PAINTING. Museum Collection: 1907.6.1

America's first product label. Courtesy the John Carter Brown Library, Brown University.

The poster for the Christie's sale of the Nicholas Brown desk. Brown Family Private Archive.

Page 205

The First Baptist Meeting House (1775). Courtesy the Rhode Island Historical Society. RHi X5 362. Joseph Partridge. President Street, The First Baptist Meeting House and Adjoining Buildings. Providence, RI. 1822 ink and watercolour on paper. PAINTING. Graphics. 1971.8.1

University Hall (1791). Meriden Gravure Co. A S.W. view of the college in Providence, together with the President's house & gardens. Silk screen on paper. After David Leonard's drawing for Samuel Hill's engraving of ca. 1795. Brown University Archives.

Uncle Joseph's house on Main Street (1774). Smolski, Chester. "Historic Joseph Brown House." Mar 1974. Chester Smolski Collection, James P. Adams Library, Rhode Island College, http://digitalcommons.ric.edu/smolski_image/269/. Accessed 11 January, 2017.

Uncle John's mansion on the hill (1788). Courtesy the Rhode Island Historical Society. RHi X17 376. David Shultz. View of the John Brown House Museum from the Southeast Corner. Providence, RI. 2009. Graphics.

Slater Mill (1791). Slater Mill Historic Site – Pawtucket, Rhode Island by Doug Kerry used under CC BY-SA 2.0.

Page 206

Nicholas II by Chester Harding (1836). Harding, Chester, "Nicholas Brown (1769–1841)," Oil on canvas. Brown University Portrait Collection.

Thomas Poynton Ives (1769–1835). Lincoln, James Sullivan, 1835, after an original by Chester Harding, "Thomas Poynton Ives." Oil on canvas. Brown University Portrait Collection.

Nicholas II by Thomas Sully (1847). Sully, Thomas "Mr. Brown, Deceased." Oil on canvas. Hirschl & Adler Galleries, New York. 1847.

The Nightingale-Brown House (1792). Brown Family Private Archive.

Brown & Ives's ship Eliza. Brown Family Private Archive.

Page 207

Nicholas Brown III (1792–1859). Ingham, Charles Cromwell, "Nicholas Brown III (1792 – 1859)." Brown University Portrait Collection.

John Carter Brown (1797–1874). Courtesy the John Carer Brown Library, Brown University.

Sophia Augusta Brown (1825–1909). Courtesy the John Carter Brown Library, Brown University.

Ann Brown's daughters, Abby and Anne in 1832. Courtesy the Rhode Island Historical Society. Chester Harding. Abby and Anne Francis. Providence, RI. c. 1832. Oil on canvas. PAINTING. Museum – Painting.

Industrial Providence (1850's). Courtesy the Rhode Island Historical Society. RHi X32 30. J.P. Newell. Providence R.I. – View From the West Bank of the River. Providence, RI. 1858. Ink on paper. PRINT. Graphics - Prints.

Page 208

Sophia Augusta Brown holding her grandson, John Nicholas Brown II in 1900. Brown Family Private Archive.

John Nicholas Brown (1861–1900). Brown Family Private Archive.

Natalie Dresser Brown and son, John Nicholas II. Brown Family Private Archive.

The Providence Public Library (1900). Courtesy of the Providence Public Library. Vanderwarker, Peter (2013). *Providence Public Library Outer Washington Street.*

The John Carter Brown Library (1904). Courtesy the John Carter Brown Library, Brown University.

Harbour Court (1906). Photograph by Cram, Ralph Adams. 1906. Brown Family Private Archive.

Page 209

John Nicholas Brown II (1900–1979). Brown Family Private Archive.

Richard Neutra's Windshield House (1938). Brown Family Private Archive, copy presented to the family of the photo taken by Costain, H. Horald (1939), "Windshield, view from southeast." UCLA Special Collections, Young Research Library, Neutra Papers.

John and Anne Brown with their three children, Nicholas, John Carter and Angela. Brown Family Private Archive.

Nicholas VI and Diane Vernes Brown. Brown Family Private Archive.

J Carter Brown III (1934-2002). Brown Family Private Archive.

BIBLIOGRAPHICAL NOTES

It is fortunate for writers and scholars that primary sources concerning the history of the small but mighty state of Rhode Island, as well as that of the Brown family, are housed almost entirely within a square mile on the east side of Providence, primarily in three institutions: The Rhode Island Historical Society Library (RIHSL), the John Carter Brown Library (JCBL), and the John Hay Library (JHL)–the latter two on the Brown University campus. In addition to these three sources, I was privileged to inherit my grandfather's collection of books, pamphlets and manuscripts on Rhode Island, many of which were privately printed and presented to him by their authors. I also had access to manuscripts still in private hands, notably the diaries of John Carter Brown and John Brown Francis.

The Brown family papers form the largest collection of family business papers in America. In 1952 Brown University Professor James B. Hedges published the first volume of *The Browns of Rhode Island and Providence Plantations: The Colonial Years* (Harvard University Press, Cambridge, MA) following a herculean effort to compile and analyze these documents, some of which were still on metal spikes. Volume 2, Hedges's posthumous *The Nineteenth Century* completed this magisterial study in 1968 (Brown University Press, Providence, RI). But neither book delves much into private lives or personalities. The only other overviews of the family are Abby Isabelle Brown Bulkley's 1888, *The Chad Browne Memorial: Consisting of Genealogical Memoirs of a Portion of the Descendants of Chad and Elizabeth Browne; with an Appendix, containing Sketches of Other Early Rhode Island Settlers, 1638-1888,* privately printed but available at https://archive.org/stream/chadbrownememor-i00bulkrich#page/n7/mode/2up; along with R.A. Guild's 1880 *Ancestors* and Descendants of the Hon. Nicholas Brown after whom Brown University was Named; and H.M. Chapin's 1919 *The Browns of Rhode Island and their Connections*, both available at the RIHSL. Two further genealogical studies were completed in the twentieth century: Kathleen Goddard's 1987 initiative for the Rhode Island Historical Society *The Chad Brown workbook: A continuing family genealogy of the descendants of Chad Brown;* and Christine Lamar's 1998 *Ancestry of the Tenth Generation Browns with Allied Maternal Lines*, privately printed but available at the RIHS and the JCBL. Much family lore can be found in Francis W. Goddard's 1870, three-volume *The Political and Miscellaneous Writing of William G. Goddard* (Sidney S. Rider and Brother, Providence, RI).

The few biographies written about specific family members focus exclusively on the eighteenth century Browns and are mentioned below under the chapters to which they pertain. The one exception is Neil Harris's 2013 *Capital Culture: J. Carter Brown, the National Gallery of Art, and the Reinvention of the Museum Experience* (University of Chicago Press, Chicago, IL).

In 1993 The John Nicholas Brown Center for the Study of American Civilization at Brown University, in partnership with the John Carter Brown Library and the Rhode Island Historical Society, received a grant from the National Endowment for the Humanities to arrange, describe and catalog records relating to the Brown family. A finding aid compiled by Catherine Osborne DeCesare and Carole Foster was published in 1996 and is now housed at the JCBL. Finding aids for other Brown papers at the Rhode Island Historical Society (notably the Moses Brown's papers compiled in 1996 by Rick Stattler, based on notes by Pam Narbeth) are available on line at http://www.rihs.org/library/master-list-of-finding-aids/. Finding aids to the Brown family papers that are housed at the John Hay Library, notably those of the late nineteenth century and twentieth century Browns, can also be found on line through the Rhode Island Archival and Manuscript Collections Online website, http://www.ri-amco.org/.

As these notes will show, most of my sources on the history of Rhode Island were printed before 1970. The last history of the entire state was

William G. McCoughlin's 1986 *Rhode Island: A History* (WW Norton & Co., New York, NY). More recently, however, Rockwell Stensrud's beautifully illustrated N*ewport: A Lively Experiment* (The Redwood Library and Atheneum, Newport, RI, 2006) covers much of the state's history too.

Older but useful sources include Thomas W. Bicknell's 1920 five-volume *The History of Rhode Island and Providence Plantations* (The American Historical Society, New York, NY); Edward Field's 1902 three-volume *State of Rhode Island and Providence Plantations at the End of the Century* (The Mason Publishing Company, Boston, MA); Welcome A. Greene's 1886 *The Providence Plantations for 250 Years: The People and Their Neighbors, Their Pursuit of Progress* (J.A. & R.A. Reid, Providence, RI), available in a digital reproduction; George W. Greene's 1877 *A Short History of Rhode Island* (J.A. & R.A. Reid, Providence, RI); Samuel G. Arnold's 1859 *History of Rhode Island and Providence Plantations;* and Edward Peterson's 1852 *History of Rhode Island* (John S. Taylor, New York, NY).

Sources that give a good overview of Rhode Island's particular spirit and idiosyncrasies are George H. Kellner and J. Stanley Lemons's 1982 *Rhode Island the Independent State* (Windsor Publishers, Woodland Hills, CA); Peter J. Coleman's 1963 *The Transformation of Rhode Island-1790-1860* (Brown University Press, Providence, RI); Charles Caroll's 1933 four-volume *Rhode Island, Three Centuries of Democracy* (Lewis Historical Publishing Company, New York, NY); and Irving B. Richman's 1905 *Rhode Island: A Study in Separatism* (Houghton Mifflin, New York, NY). Three articles that address this general topic well are William G. McLoughlin's 1986 "Ten Turning Points in Rhode Island History," *Rhode Island History*, 45:2, 41-45; J. Stanley Lemons's 1986 "Rhode Island's Ten Turning Points: A Second Appraisal," *Rhode Island History*, 45:2, 57-64; and Peter J. Coleman's 1963 "The Entrepreneurial Spirit in Rhode Island History," *Business History Review*, 37:4, 319-344. Many other more specific sources are noted under the chapters to which they pertain.

When historians shifted their attention to the central roles of class, race and gender, the stories of Rhode Island's elite fell from grace. Tales of old Providence that now seem quaint and dated nevertheless have provided me with invaluable anecdotes about my ancestors. These include John W. Hayley's 1939 three-volume *The Old Stone Bank History of Rhode Island* (The Providence Institute for Savings, JC Hall Co., Providence, RI); George Laswell's 1924 *Corners and Characters of Rhode Island* (The Oxford Press, Providence, RI); and Katherine Pyle's 1914 *Once Upon a Time in Rhode Island* (The Colonial Dames of Rhode Island, The Country Life Press, Garden City, NY), all available at the RIHSL. Other similar sources are noted under the chapters to which they pertain.

Finally, I must draw attention to a few of my sources of general information on the history of the United States in the nineteenth century and on the history of philanthropy, which provided me with invaluable background and context: Gordon Wood's 2009 *Empire of Liberty: A History of the Early Republic, 1789-1815* (Oxford University Press, New York, NY), and Daniel W. Howe's 2007 *What Hath God Wrought: The Transformation of America, 1815-1849* (Oxford University Press, New York, NY), both in The Oxford History of the United States Series; as well as Olivier Zunz's 2014 *Philanthropy in America: A History* (Princeton University Press, Princeton, NJ) in the Politics and Society in Modern America Series, and Robert H. Brenner's 1988 *American Philanthropy* (The University of Chicago Press, Chicago, IL) in The Chicago History of American Civilization series. But the book that most influenced and helped me understand my ancestor Nicholas Brown II was Professor Woods's 1992 *The Radicalism of the American Revolution* (Alfred A. Knopf, New York, NY).

PROLOGUE

Christie, Manson & Wood International, Inc. produced a special publication accompanying the auction catalogue: *The Magnificent Nicholas Brown Desk and Bookcase*, Christie's, New York, NY, 1989. The desk had been mentioned in a *Rhode Island History 1959* editorial, *The Secretary Desk*, 8:4, 127.

The 2006 *Report of the Brown University Steering Committee* can be found on http://www.brown.edu/Research/Slavery_Justice/report/. Brown University's Center for Slavery and Justice holds a video of the March 18, 2004 symposium entitled "Unearthing the past: Brown University, the Brown Family, and the Rhode Island Slave Trade: A symposium on the forgotten history of slavery and slave trading in Rhode Island, featuring historians Joanne Pope Melish, J. Stanley Lemons, Rhett Jones, and Joaquina Bela Teixeira." *The New York Times* article by Pam Belluck, "Brown U. to Examine Debt to Slave Trade," appeared March 13, 2004. *The New Yorker* article by Frances FitzGerald, "Peculiar Institutions," appeared in the September 23, 2005 edition. *The Providence Journal* five-part series entitled "The Unrighteous Traffic, Rhode Island and the Slave Trade" by Paul Davis appeared March 13-17, 2006 and includes a very complete bibliography. Most recently, Craig S. Wilder's *Ebony and Ivy - Race, Slavery, and the Troubled History of America's Universities* (Bloomsbury Press, New York, NY) was published in 2013.

CHAPTER 1–SEIZING OPPORTUNITY

Sarah Vowell is quoted from her 2008 *The Wordy Shipmates* (Riverhead Books, New York, NY) and Ted Widmer is quoted in his 2015 *Brown, The History of an Idea* (Thames and Hudson, New York, NY). In addition to *The Chad Brown Memorial* cited above, further information on the first Brown in America can be found in William B. Browne's 1926 "Chad Browne of Providence, RI, and Four Generations of his Descendants," *New England Historic Genealogical Society Register*, 73-86 and 170-179. Of the many biographies of the founders of Rhode Island, the most up-to-date are John M. Barry's 2012 *Roger Williams and The Creation of the American Soul: Church, State and the Birth of Liberty* (Viking (Penguin), New York, NY) and Eve La Plante's 2005 *American Jezebel: The Uncommon Life of Anne Hutchinson, the woman who defied the Puritans* (Harper Collins, New York, NY). J. Stanley Lemons's 2001 *First: The First Baptist Church in America* (The Charitable Baptist Society, Providence, RI) presents a very clear and complete history of the denomination in Rhode Island.

The story of the founding of Rhode Island is told in Patrick T. Conley's 2012 *Peoples, Places, Laws and Lore of the Ocean State: A Rhode Island Historical Sampler* (Rhode Island Publications Society, Providence, RI), and in his 2010 *The Makers of Modern Rhode Island* and *Rhode Island's Founders: From Settlement to Statehood* (both published by The History Press, Charleston, SC); in Carl Bridenbaugh's 2005 *Cities in the Wilderness, The First Century of Urban Life in America 1625-1742* (Alfred A. Knopf, New York, NY); in Sydney V. James's 2000 *The Colonial Metamorphosis of Rhode Island: A Study of Institutions in Change* (University Press of New England, Hanover, NH), as well as in his 1984 "Rhode Island: From Classical Democracy to British Province," *Rhode Island History*, 43: 4, 119-135; in Richard L. Bowen's 1943 *The Providence Oath of Allegiance and Its Signers 1651-52* (General Court of the Society of Colonial Wars in the State of Rhode Island and Providence Plantations, Providence RI available at the RIHSL); in Gertrude S. Kimball's *Providence in Colonial Times* (Houghton Mifflin, New York, NY); in William B. Weeden's 1910 *Early Rhode Island, A Social History of the People* (The Grafton Press, New York, NY); in John Russell Bartlett's magisterial ten-volume *Records of the Colony of Rhode Island and Providence Plantations in New England* (printed between 1856 and 1865 by A.Crawford Greene & Bros, State Printers, Providence, RI); and in William R. Staples's 1843 *Annals of the Town of Providence from its First Settlement to the Organization of City Government in June 1832* (Knowles & Vose, Providence, RI).

Sources that specifically cover the early years of Providence include John H. Cady's 1957 *The Civic and Architectural Development of Providence* (privately printed by Ackerman Standard Press, Providence, RI but available at the RIHSL); Alice Gleeson's 1926 *Colonial Rhode Island* (privately printed, Pawtucket, RI); Henry R. Chace's *Maps of Providence, Rhode Island, 1650, 1765, 1770* (privately printed in 1914 but available at the RIHSL); his *Owners and Occupants of the Lots, Houses and Shops in the Town of Providence in 1798 Located on Maps of the Highways of that Date*, and his *Owners or Occupant of Houses in the Compact Part of Providence in 1759*; Charles W. Hopkins's 1886 *The Home Lots of the Early Settlers of the Providence Plantations* (privately printed by the Providence

Press Company, Providence, RI but available at the RIHSL); Richard M. Bayles's 1891 *History of Providence County, Rhode Island* (New York); and *The Charter and Ordinance of the City of Providence, Together with the Acts of the General Assembly Relating to the City,* 1854 (Knowles, Anthony & Co, Providence, RI).

The story and meaning of the 1663 Charter are explained in the excellent pamphlet *A Lively Experiment: Reflections on the Charter of 1663: One Document, A world of Change,* produced in 2013 for the 350th anniversary of the Charter by the Rhode Island Council for the Humanities.

An interesting perspective on King Philip's War appears in Zachariah's Allen's 1876 *Defense of the Rhode Island System of Treatment of the Indians and of Civil and Religious Liberty: An address delivered before the Rhode Island Historical Society April 10, 1876, the Bicentenary of the Burning of Providence in 1676* (Pamphlet, The Rhode Island Historical Society). More recently, Fred Zilian penned "Despite Roger Williams, Providence Burns Down" in the May 29, 2016 *Providence Journal* "My turn" column.

Further details on Pardon Tillinghast can be found in William R. Tillinghast's 2001 *Tillinghast Genealogy* (Pamphlet, RIHSL) and in Rose C. Tillinghast's 1972 *The Tillinghast Family, 1560-1971* (privately printed, available at the RIHSL).

Elder James Brown's sermon "Truth and Error" is discussed in the 1872-74 edition of *Rhode Island History,* 28-33; and in Mac Thompson's 1962 *Moses Brown, Reluctant Reformer* (University of North Carolina Press, Chapel Hill, NC). His writings also are found in Daniel B. Updike's 1917 *James Brown: His Writings in Prose and Verse* (Merrymount Press, Boston, MA). Captain James Brown's ledgers are analyzed in John Carter Brown Woods's 1929 *The Letter Book of James Brown of Providence, Merchant* 1735-1738 (privately printed).

Rum distilling is described in Ann Pinson's 1980 *The New England Rum Era: Drinking Styles and Social Change in Newport, RI, 1720-1770,* Department of Anthropology, Brown University, and in William D. Houlette's 1954 "Rum Trading in the American Colonies before 1763," *Journal of American History,* 28: 129-152.

Background on colonial education practices can be found in Arthur W. Calhoun's 2004 *The American Family in the Colonial Period* (first published in 1917 by Arthur H. Clarke as *A Social History of the American Family, Vol 1* (Dover Publications, Mineola, NY); in Alice M. Earl's 1899 *Child Life in Colonial Days* (Berkshire House Publishers, Stockbridge, MA, reprinted 1993); and in The Providence Institute for Savings' 1944 *Vignettes,* "Colonial schools and schooldays," available at the RIHSL.

Further information on colonial accounting practices is noted in W.T. Baxter, Ed.'s 1962 *Accounting in Colonial America* (in Studies in Accounting Theory, Richard D. Irwin, Inc., Homewood, IL).

Details on the early years of the Brown brothers can be found in the following books and articles. Concerning Joseph: see Stuart F. Crump, Jr.'s 1968 "Joseph Brown, Astronomer," *Rhode Island History,* 27:1, 1-12; and Walter J. Wilson's 1945 "Joseph Brown, Scientist and Architect," *Rhode Island History,* 4:3, 67-79 and 4:4, 121-127. Concerning John: see Charles Rappleye's 2006 *Sons of Providence: The Brown Brothers, the Slave Trade, and the American Revolution* (Simon & Schuster, New York, NY), and Henry A. Brown and R. Walton's 1988 *John Brown's Tract* (Rhode Island Historical Society and Phenix Publishing Company, Canaan, NH). Concerning Moses: see, in addition to Mac Thompson's biography cited above and Charles Rappleye's *Sons of Providence,* see Robert Hazelton's 1957 *Let Freedom Ring: A Biography of Moses Brown* (New Voices Publishing Company, New York, NY); the pamphlet *The Course of True Love in Colonial Times—Being the Confessions of William Parfrey of Boston and the Friendly Advice of Moses Brown of Providence Concerning Polly Olney* (Merrymount Press, Boston, MA, 1905 available at the RIHSL); and Augustine Jones's 1892 *Moses Brown: His Life and Services* (Rhode Island Historical Society, Providence, RI).

General background on Rhode Island's maritime commerce in the colonial era can be found in John J. McCusker and Kenneth Morgan, ed.'s 2000 *The Early Modern Atlantic Economy* (Cambridge University Press, New York, NY); in Lance Davis and Stanley Engerman's 1999 "The Economy of British North America: Miles Traveled, Miles Still to Go," *William and Mary Quarterly,* 56:1, 9-22; in David Hancock's 1995

Citizens of the New World, London Merchants and the Integration of the British Atlantic Community, 1735-1785 (Cambridge University Press, New York, NY); in Joseph A. Goldenberg's 1976 *Shipbuilding in Colonial America* (University Press of Virginia, Charlottesville, VA); in James F. Shepherd and Gary M Walton's 1972 "Trade, Distribution and Economic Growth in Colonial America," *Journal of Economic History*, 32:1, 128-145; in Stuart Bruchey's 1966 *The Colonial Merchant: Sources and Readings* (Harcourt Brace and World, New York, NY); in W.T. Baxter's 1965 *The House Of Hancock: Business in Boston 1724-1775* (Russell and Russell, New York, NY); in W.E. Minchinton's 1961"Shipbuilding in Colonial Rhode Island," *Rhode Island History*, 20:4, 119-124; in Richard Pares's 1956 *Yankees and Creoles: The Trade Between North America and the West Indies Before the American Revolution* (Harvard University Press, Cambridge, MA); in Arthur H. Cole's 1959 "The Tempo of Mercantile Life in Colonial America," *Business History Review*, 33:3, 277-299; in The Providence Institute for Savings 1944 *Vignettes* on "Shipbuilding" (available in the RIHSL); in John William McElroy's 1935 "Seafaring in Early New England," *New England Quarterly*, 8:3, 331-3; in Howard W. Preston's 1932 *Rhode Island and the Sea* (Office of the Secretary of State, Providence, RI); in Jacques M. Downs'1969 "The Merchant as Gambler: Major William Fairchild Megee (1765-1820)," *Rhode Island History*, 28:4, 99-110; in The Massachusetts Historical Society's 1914 *The Commerce of Rhode Island, 1726-1800* (Massachusetts Historical Society, Boston, MA); and in Samuel A. Drake's 1886 *The Making of New England* (Charles Scribner & Sons, New York, NY).

The 1755 painting by John Greenwood, *"Sea Captains Carousing in Surinam"* (now at the St Louis Art Museum), is analyzed in the catalogue of The Metropolitan Museum of Art's 2009 exhibit "American Stories: Paintings of Everyday Life 1765-1915" (The Metropolitan Museum of Art, New York, NY and Yale University Press, New Haven, CT); and in Robert W. Kenny's 1977 "Sea Captains Carousing in Surinam," *Rhode Island History*, 36:11,107-117.

In addition to descriptions in James B. Hedges's *The Browns of Rhode Island and Providence Plantations,* the activities of Obadiah Brown &

Co. and of Nicholas Brown & Co. are further explained in Thomas M. Doerflinger's 1984 "How to Run an Ironworks," *Pennsylvania Magazine of History and Biography*, 108: 357-366; and in Stuart Bruchey's 1958 "Success or Failure Factors: American Merchants in Foreign Trade," *The Business History Review*, 32:3, 272-292; and Eric S. Doescher's 2006 Brown University Master's Thesis "First Family of Fortune: The Rise of Nicholas Brown and Company, 1750-1770."

Background on maritime trade, privateering and later the China trade comes from Alexander B. Hawes's 1999 *Off Soundings–Aspects of the Maritime History of Rhode Island* (Posterity Press, Chevy Chase, MD) which makes frequent references to the Browns of Providence.

Manuscript Sources: As a general rule, the letters and archives of the first four generations of Browns (Chad, John, James, James) are housed at the RIHSL. But when we get to the fifth generation-the famous "four brothers," their letters and archives are split between the JCBL and the RIHSL. Business papers concerning Obadiah Brown & Co, Nicholas Brown & Co, Brown & Benson, and Brown & Ives are at the JCBL. However, Moses Brown personally bequeathed his enormous archive to the RIHSL (of which he was a founder in 1822). These exist on microfilm as part of the "Papers of the American Slave Trade," also housed at the Library of Congress. Family correspondence by the descendants of John Brown (Francis, Herreshoff, Mason) are at the RIHSL. Ancillary branches of the Nicholas Brown family (Carter, Danforth, Woods) are at the RIHSL, with some later nineteenth century manuscripts having found their way to the JHL.

CHAPTER 2—BECOMING GENTLEMEN

Of the many sources I consulted on the social taxonomies of colonial America, I found particularly useful Gloria L. Main's 2001 *Peoples of a Spacious Land – Families and Cultures in Colonial New England* (Harvard University Press, Cambridge, MA); Martin J. Burke's 1995 *The Conundrum of Class: Public Discourse on the Social Order in America*

(University of Chicago Press, Chicago, IL); James A. Henretta's 1973 *The Evolution of American Society, 1700-1815* (D.C. Heath & Co., Lexington, MA); and Christopher Clarke's 2006 *Social Change in America: From the Revolution to the Civil War* (Ivan R. Dee, Chicago, IL).

The Enlightenment, its impact on eighteenth century values and aspirations, and its manifestations in the American colonies are described in Dorinda Outram's 2006 *Panorama of the Enlightenment* (Thames and Hudson, London, UK); in Robert Ferguson's 1997 *The American Enlightenment – 1750-1820* (Harvard University Press, Cambridge, MA); in Richard L. Bushman's 1992 *The Refinement of America: Persons, Houses, Cities* (Random House, New York, NY); in Kenneth Lockridge's 1969 "Land, Population and the Evolution of New England Society 1630-1790," *Past and Present*, 39: 62-80; in Lewis B. Wright's 1957 *The Cultural Life of the American Colonies, 1607-1763*, (Dover Publications, Mineola, NY).

Background on the accumulation of merchant wealth in the American colonies can be found in T. H Breen's 2004 *The Marketplace of Revolution: How Consumer Politics Shaped American Independence* (Oxford University Press, New York, NY); as well as in his 1988 "Baubles of Britain: The American and Consumer Revolutions of the Eighteenth Century," *Past and Present*, 119:73-104 and his 1986 "An Empire of Goods: The Anglicization of Colonial America, 1690-1776," *Journal of British Studies*, 25:4, 467-499; and in Alice H. Jones's 1972 "Wealth Estimates for the New England Colonies about 1770," *Journal of Economic History*, 32:1.

Background on the life of women in colonial Providence comes from Laurel T. Ulrich's 1980 *Good Wives: Images and Reality in the Lives of Women in Northern New England 1650-1750* (Oxford University Press, New York, NY).

In addition to sources on the civic and architectural development of Providence mentioned under Chapter 1, other useful works include

Elyssa Tardiff and Peggy Chan's 2013 *Providence's Benefit Street* (Arcadia Publishing, Charleston, SC); Robert A. Geake's 2013 *A History of the Providence River with the Moshassuck, Woonasquatucket and Seekonk Tributaries* (The History Press, Charleston, SC); William M. Woodward's 2003 *Guide to Providence Architecture* (Providence Preservation Society-American Institute of Architecture, Rhode Island Chapter, Providence, RI); Patrick T. Conley's 1986 *A Pictorial History* (Donning, Norfolk, VA); William M. Woodward and Edward F. Sanderson's 1986 *Providence, A City-Wide Survey of Historic Resources* (Rhode Island Historic Preservation Commission, Providence, RI); Lynne Withey's 1984 *Urban Growth in Colonial Rhode Island: Newport and Providence in the Eighteenth Century* (State University of New York Press, Albany, NY); Arthur Wilson's 1947 *Weybosset Bridge in Providence Plantations 1700-1790* (The Pilgrim Press, Boston, MA), in Norman Isham's 1918 *Providence and its Colonial Houses–An Architectural Monograph* (privately printed but available at the RIHSL); and Henry C. Dorr's 1882 *The Planting and Growth of Providence* (privately printed but available at the RIHSL).

Charming anecdotes of early Providence can be found in the books by Gertrude S. Kimball mentioned under Chapter 1, as well as in Florence P. Simister's 1968 *Streets of the City-An anecdotal history of Providence* (The Mowbray Company, Providence, RI); in Margaret D. Uroff's 1968 *Becoming A City - From Fishing Village To Manufacturing Center* (Harcourt, Brace & World, New York, NY); in John H. Cady's 1948 *Highroads and Byroads of Providence* and his 1942 *Walks Around Providence* (privately printed by The Ackerman Standard Press, Providence, RI but available at the RIHSL); in George L. Miner's 1948 *Angell's Lane-The History of a Little Street in Providence* (privately printed by the Ackerman Standard Press, Providence, RI but available at the RIHSL); in Arthur Watson's *Angell's Apple Orchard* (privately printed by The Ackerman Standard Press, Providence, RI but available at the RIHSL); in Isaac P. Noyes's 1905 *Reminiscences of Rhode Island and Ye Providence Plantations*; in Lyman P. Powell, ed.'s 1898 *Historic Towns of New England* (G.P. Putnam & Sons, New York, NY); and in The Merchants

National Bank's 1918 *Old Providence- A Collection of Facts and Traditions Relating to Various Buildings and Sites of Historical Interest in Providence* (privately printed, at the RIHSL).

The story of the female newspaper printer can be found in Nancy F. Chudacoff's 1973 "Woman in the News 1762-1770: Sarah Updike Goddard," *Rhode Island History*, 32:10, 98-105.

Descriptions of the fine furniture and household goods purchased by the Brown brothers appear in Patricia E. Kane's 2016 *Art & Industry in Early America: Rhode Island Furniture 1650-1830* (Yale University Press, New Haven, CT) in which John Brown's desk is illustrated (Cat. 60); in Robert P. Emlen's 1984 "Wedding Silver for the Browns: A Rhode Island Family Patronizes A Boston Goldsmith," *The American Art Journal*, 16:2, 39-50; in Michael Moses's 1984 *Master Craftsmen of Newport: The Townsends and Goddards* (MMI Americana Press, Tenafly, NY); in Joseph K. Ott's 1972 "Rhode Island Housewright, Shipwrights and Related Craftsmen," *Rhode Island History*, 31:4 65-79; and in Norman Isham's 1927 "John Goddard and His Work," *Bulletin of the Rhode Island School of Design*, 15:2, 14-16.

The Brown family coat of arms is described in a 1929 *Rhode Island History* editorial "Colonial Heraldry: The Browns of Providence," 22:1, 22-24.

The anecdote about John Brown's defending a theater troupe in Providence is told in several sources, notably Constance D. Sherman's 1958 "Theater in Rhode Island Before the Revolution," *Rhode Island History*, 17:1, 10-14.

Colonial charity and the treatment of the poor are described in the general histories of American philanthropy cited above. The specific situation in Providence is analyzed in Bruce C. Daniel's 1981 "Poor Relief, Local Finance, and Town Government in Eighteenth Century Rhode Island," *Rhode Island History*, 40:8, 75-82.

The story of the first library in Providence is recounted in Horatio Rogers's 1878 *Private Libraries of Providence with a Preliminary Essay on the Love of Books* (Sidney S. Rider, Providence, RI, available at the JCBL). The building of the market house is told in John H. Cady's 1952 "The Providence Market House and its Neighborhood," *Rhode Island History*, 11:3.

The founding of Brown University is depicted in numerous sources besides Ted Widmer's 2015 *Brown: The History of an Idea,* cited above: see, for example, Janet M. Philips's 1992 *Brown University: A Short History* (Office of University Relations, Brown University, Providence, RI); Martha Mitchell's 1993 *Encyclopedia Brunonia* (Brown University Library, Providence, RI) whose digital edition is being constantly updated online; Richard Luftglass's 1985 "Nicholas Brown to Isaac Backus: On Bringing Rhode Island College to Providence," *Rhode Island History*, 44: 4, 121-125; Walter C. Bronson's 1914 *The History of Brown University 1764-1914* (Brown University Press, Providence, RI); Robert Perkins Brown and Henry Robinson Palmer's 1909 *Memories of Brown: Tradition and Recollections Gathered from Many Sources* (Brown Alumni Magazine Company, Providence, RI); and Reuben A. Guild's 1867 *A History of Brown University with Illustrative Documents* (Providence, RI).

In addition to J. Stanley Lemons's 2001 *First: The First Baptist Church in America,* cited under Chapter 1, the building of the First Baptist Meeting House is described in his 2009 "The Browns and the Baptists," *Rhode Island History*, 67:7, 74-82; as well as in his 1958 "Early Music in Rhode Island Churches," *Rhode Island History*, 17:2, 33-44; in The Providence Institute for Savings' 1931 *Vignettes*-The First Baptist Meeting House (available at the RIHSL); in Norman Isham's 1925 *The Meeting House of the First Baptist Church in Providence–A History of the Fabric* (Charitable Baptist Society, Providence, RI); and in William Hague's 1854 *An Historical Discourse Delivered at the Celebration of the Second Centennial Anniversary of the Baptist Church in Providence* (privately printed by the First Baptist Church but available at the RIHSL).

Further useful sources on Rhode Island politics in the colonial era include Daniel P. Jones's 1992 *The Economic and Social Transformation of Rural Rhode Island, 1780-1850* (Northeastern University Press, Boston, MA). Specific information relating to the Brown family and the Ward-Hopkins feud can be found in David S. Lovejoy's 1955 "Uncle Brown Grabs a Town," *Rhode Island History*, 14:2, 47-51.

Biographical information on Stephen Hopkins can be found in William E. Foster's 1884 *Stephen Hopkins, A Rhode Island Statesman: A Study in the Political History of the 18ᵗʰ Century* (S.S. Rider, Providence, RI).

CHAPTER 3—TURBULENT YEARS

Considered the American Revolution's first violent act of civil defiance, the burning of the *Gaspee* is recounted by numerous sources, notably Rory Raven's 2012 *Burning the Gaspee-Revolution in Rhode Island* (History Press, Charleston, SC); Neil L. York's 1992 "The Uses of Law and the *Gaspee* Affair," *Rhode Island History*, 50:1, 3-21; Samuel W. Bryant's 1966 "HMS *Gaspee* -The Court Martial," *Rhode Island History*, 25:3, 65-72; and John M. Ray's 1961 "Rhode Island Reactions to John Brown's Raid," *Rhode Island History* 20:10, 97-108. The excellent *Gaspee* Virtual Archive continues to be maintained at www.gaspee.org.

The capture of John Brown is told in detail in Charles Rappleye's 2006 *Sons of Providence*, with further details available in the *Rhode Island History* editorial 1951 "John Brown's Attempt at Conciliation with the British,"10:2, 62-63; and in William G. Roelker's 1949 "The Patrol of Narrangansett Bay (1774-1776) - Seizure of John Brown," *Rhode Island History*, 8:2, 45-63. The story of John Brown's devoted apprentice Elkanah Watson is told by Hugh M. Flick in his 1958 Columbia University PhD dissertation "Elkanah Watson, Gentleman Farmer," and in Watson's 1856 biography (edited by Winslow C. Watson), *Men and Times of the Revolution or Memoirs of Elkanah Watson including Journals of Travels in Europe and American From 1777 to 1842 with his Correspondence with*

Public Men and Reminiscences and Incidents of the Revolution (Dana & Co, Publishers, New York, NY).

The revolutionary period in Rhode Island is described in Leonard J. Panaggio's 2003 "The Navy in Newport," *Redwood Library and Atheneum*, 7:3, 5-6; in the catalogue to The Society of the Cincinnati's 2001 exhibit "Rhode Island in the American Revolution" (Library and Museum Collections of the Society of the Cincinnati, The Society of the Cincinnati, Washington, DC); in Joel A. Cohen's 1967 "Lexington and Concord: Rhode Island Reacts," *Rhode Island History*, 24:4, 97-102; in David S. Lovejoy's 1958 *Rhode Island Politics and the American Revolution, 1760-1776* (Brown University Press, Providence, RI); in Robert A. East's *Business Enterprise in the American Revolutionary Era* (AMS Press, New York, NY (reprinted from Columbia University Press, New York, NY, 1938); and in Frederick B. Weiner's 1930 "The Rhode Island Merchants and the Sugar Act," *New England Quarterly*, 3:2, 464-500.

The specific activities of the Brown family are noted in Jeanette D. Black and William Greene Roelker, ed.s' 1949 *A Rhode Island Chaplain in the Revolution. Letters of Ebenezer David to Nicholas Brown, 1775-1778* (Rhode Island Historical Society, Providence, RI); in Hope S. Rider's 1978 *Valour Fore and Aft: Being the Adventures of America's First Naval Vessel* (U.S. Naval Institute Press, Annapolis, MD); in William M. Fowler Jr.'s 1976 *Rebels Under Sail: The American Navy During the American Revolution* (Charles Scribner & Sons, New York, NY); in Richard K. Showman, Ed.'s 1976 *The Papers of Nathaniel Greene* (University of North Carolina, Chapel Hill, NC); in George L. Miner's 1943 "John Brown's Katy, Afterwards Continental Armored Sloop Providence," *Rhode Island History*, 11:3, 73-82. Moses's relief activities are told in all of his biographies and in Mack F. Thompson's 1956 "Moses Brown's 'Account of Journey to Distribute Donations 12th month 1775,'" *Rhode Island History*, 15:4, 97-121. The story of "soldier's blood makes good varnish" told about John Brown is in Isaac Pitman Noyes'1905 *Reminiscences of Rhode Island and Ye Providence Plantations*, op.cit.

A recent biography of Nathaniel Greene is Gerald M. Carbone's 2008 *Nathaniel Greene: A Biography of the American Revolution* (Palgrave Macmillan (St Martin's Press), New York, NY). The adventures of Esek Hopkins are recounted in Edward Field's 1898 *The Life of Esek Hopkins* and in his 1898 *Esek Hopkins, Commander in Chief of the Continental Navy During the American Revolution 1775 to 1778* (both The Preston & Rounds Co., Providence, RI).

The post-Revolutionary period in Rhode Island – the Impost Debate, the rise of the Country Party, the paper money crisis, and the ratification of the Constitution – are best told in Patrick T. Conley's 1987 *First in War, Last in Peace: Rhode Island and the Constitution 1786-1790* (Rhode Island Publications Society, Providence, RI); in both Irwin Polishook's 1969 *Rhode Island and the Union, 1774-1794* (Northwestern University Press, Evanston, IL); and in Hillman Metcalf Bishop's 1949 *Rhode Island History* series on "Why Rhode Island Opposed the Federal Constitution": "The Continental Impost," 8:1. 1-10; "The Paper Money Era," 8:4, 33-43; "Paper Money and the Constitution," 8:7, 85-94; and ""Political Reasons," 8:10, 115-125.

George Washington's visit to Providence is described by many sources, notably Howard W. Preston's 1926 *Washington's Visit To Providence* (Privately printed but available at the RIHSL),

Manuscript Sources: James Manning's comments on Rhode Islanders "must be considered as foreigners" is in a letter of May 21st, 1789 in the JCBL, Brown Family Papers, Library Correspondence 1767-1865, Folder 5.

A letter from James Brown to Thomas Willing about his brother-in-law, John Francis's alcoholism, is in the JCBL, Brown Family Archive, Library Correspondence 1767-1865, November 4th, 1795.

In addition to the sources on education in the colonial era mentioned in Chapter 1, further background information is provided in Alice M. Earl's 1899 *Child Life in Colonial Days* (Berkshire House Publishers, Stockbridge, MA—reprinted 1993), and in The Providence Institute for Savings 1944 *Vignettes*' "Colonial schools and schooldays" (available at the RIHSL). The letters of little Nick, as well as those of his sisters Joanna and Hope, are compiled in *The Letters of Three Dutiful and Affectionate RI Children to their Honored Parents* (pamphlet, privately printed but available at the JCBL). The fascinating account of Susan Lear's visit to the Brown family in 1788 appears in Jane Lancaster's 1999 "By The Pens of Females: Girls' Diaries from Rhode Island, 1788-1821," *Rhode Island History*, 57:8, 59-113.

Benson & Brown's problems with pirates in the Caribbean are recounted in Earl C. Tanner's 1962 "Piracy in the Caribbean: A Rhode Island View," *Rhode Island History*, 21:3, 90-94.

Avis Binney Brown's new house is described in Robert P. Emlen's 1995 "A House for Widow Brown: Architectural Statement and Social Position in Providence, 1791," *Old Times New England*, 77:2, 5, and in George L. Miner and W. Chelsley's 2007 *The Providence Arts Club: A Compilation* (Providence Arts Club, Providence, RI).

Manuscript Sources: George Benson's description of Moses Brown's death is in a letter dated March 7th, 1791 (JCBL, Box 371, Folder 1).

Correspondence between Nicholas Brown and his sister, Mary Vanderlight, about the illness and death of Joanna are in the JCBL, Library Correspondence 1767-1865, Folder 3 (July 26th and 31st, 1784, August 8th and 24th, 1784, September 7th, 1784).

There is an extremely interesting one-box collection of love letters between Nicholas Brown and Avis Binney at the RIHSL, quite distinct from those at the JCBL. These may be the letters referred to by Avis Binney's impoverished nieces in a series of threatening letters sent to Tom Ives in the 1820s. Letters from Avis Binney to her step-children are in the JCBL, Brown Family Archive-Library Correspondence 1767-1865, Folder 7.

Descriptions of Nicholas Brown's death are found in John Brown's letter to his son James, May 30th, 1791 (JCBL), James Brown to Abby Brown Francis, his sister, May 27th, 1791 and June 5th, 1791 (James Brown papers, RIHSL). Nicholas's inventory at his death in in Box 52 of the Brown Family Archive at the JCBL.

A description of Avis Binney Brown's funeral dated Augsut 24th, 1807 is in Box 376 at the JCBL, Brown Family Archive.

CHAPTER 5—A CHOICE OF ROLE MODELS

The quote about Uncle John driving his carriage is from Henry A. Brown's 1989 monograph "John Brown of Providence and his Chariot" (Rhode Island Historical Society, Providence, RI). He is also described in Ruel P. Tolman's 1958 "The Life and Works of Edward Malbone, 177-1807" (The New York Historical Society, New York, NY). Other vignettes of John Brown can be found in Clarkson A. Collin's 1951 and 1952 multivolume series "Pictures of Providence in the Past 1790-1820–The Reminiscences of Walter R. Danforth," *Rhode Island History* 10:1, 4, 7, 10 and 11:1, 4.

The most complete study of Rhode Island's role in the Transatlantic slave trade is Jay Coughtry's 1981 *The Notorious Triangle: Rhode Island and the African Slave Trade, 1700-1807* (Temple University Press, Philadelphia, PA). Other useful works include Lin Chernos's 2002 "The Rhode Island Slave Traders: Butchers, Bakers and Candlestick-makers," *Slavery and Abolition,* 23:3, 21-38; J. Stanley Lemons's 2002 "Rhode Island and the Slave Trade," *Rhode Island History,* 60:11, 94-104; Richard S. Newman's 2002 *The Transformation of American Abolitionism: Fighting Slavery in the Early* Republic (University of North Carolina, Chapel Hill, NC); David B. Davis's 1999 *The Problem of Slavery in the Age of*

Revolution 1770-1823 (Oxford University Press, New York, NY); Joanne Pope Melish's 1998 *Disowning Slavery: Gradual Emancipation and "Race" in New England, 1780-1860* (Cornell University Press, Ithaca, NY); Louis P. Masur's 1985 "Slavery in Eighteenth Century Rhode Island: Evidence from the Census of 1774," *Slavery and Abolition*, 6:2, 139-150; Elaine F. Crane's 1980 "The First Wheel of Commerce: Newport, Rhode Island and the Slave Trade, 1760-1776," *Slavery and Abolition*, 1:2, 178-198; Virginia B. Platt's 1975 "And Don't Forget the Guinea Voyage: The Slave Trade of Aaron Lopez of Newport," *William and Mary Quarterly*, 32:4, 601-618; Dale Porter's 1970 *The Abolition of the Slave Trade in New England, 1784-1807* (Yale University Press, New Haven, CT); Irving Bartlett's 1954 *From Slave to Citizen: The Story of the Negro in Rhode Island* (Urban League of Rhode Island, Providence, RI-reprinted in 1972); R.A. Brock's 1894 "New England and the Slave Trade," *William and Mary Quarterly*, 2:3, 176-178; Bruce M. Bigelow's 1931 "Aaron Lopez: Colonial Merchant of Newport," *New England Quarterly*, 4:4, 757-776; and William D. Johnston's 1894 *Slavery in Rhode Island* (Rhode Island Historical Society, Providence, RI).

The voyage of the *Sally* is recounted in Darold D. Wax's 1975 "The Browns of Providence and the Slaving Voyage of the Brig Sally 1764-1765," *American Neptune*, 35, 289–301.

Moses Brown's manumission of his slaves is recounted in all his biographies and in James F. Reilly's 1951 "Moses Brown and the Rhode Island Anti-Slavery Movement," Master's Thesis, Brown University. Reilly also examined the founding of "The Providence Abolition Society," in 1962 in *Rhode Island History*, 21:2, 33-48.

The challenge of building America's first spinning mill is described in Brooke Hindle and Steven Lubar's 1986 *Engines of Change: The American Industrial Revolution, 1790-1860* (Smithsonian Institute Press, Washington, DC); and in Paul E. Rivard's 1974 "Textile Experiments in Rhode Island 1788-1789," *Rhode Island History* 33:2, 35-46. A useful biography of Samuel Slater is Barbara Tucker's 1984 *Samuel Slater and the Origins of the American Textile Industry 1790-1860* (Cornell University Press, Ithaca, NY) as well as George S. White's 1836 *Memoir of Samuel*

Slater, the Father of American Manufacturers (Philadelphia, PA), published a year after Slater's death.

Research on John Brown's mansion and lifestyle appears in Susan G. Ferguson's 1975 "Eighteenth Century Wall Decoration in the John Brown House in Providence, RI," *Antiques Magazine*, 122-129; in Wendy Cooper's two-part 1973 "The Purchase of Furniture and Furnishings by John Brown (part 1)," *Antiques Magazine,* February and March; in Florence M. Montgomery's 1972 "Furnishing and Textiles at the John Brown House," *Antiques Magazine*, 101:3, 496-502; in Frank H. Goodyear's 1972 "Paintings in the John Brown House," *Rhode Island History*, 31:4, 35-52; in Clarkson F. Collins III, 1965 "Early Rhode Island Trade" in *The John Brown House Loan Exhibition Catalogue of Rhode Island Furniture* (The Rhode Island Historical Society, Providence, RI); in Eleanor Bradford Monahon's 1953 "John Brown's Dinner Set," *Rhode Island History*, 12:71, 67-71; in Martha W. Appleton's "Mrs. Vice President Adams Dines with Mr. John Brown and lady," *Rhode Island History*, 1:4, 97-104; and in Harrison S. Taft's 1946 monograph "John Brown's Mansion House on the Hill" at the RIHSL.

There exist numerous sources for background on the China trade. I found particularly useful Patrick Conner's 2009 *The Hongs of Canton: Western Merchants in South China 1700-1900 as Seen in Chinese Export Paintings* (English Art Books, London, UK); Carl I. Crossman's 1991 *The Decorative Arts of the China Trade* (Antique Collectors Club, Woodbridge, UK) which includes a photo of furniture made in China for Nicholas Brown III; James Kirker's 1978 *Adventures in China: Americans in the Southern Oceans, 1796-1826* (Oxford University Press, New York, NY). The quote by the Chinese emperor is taken from Doug Stewart's 2004 "Salem Sets Sail," *Smithsonian Magazine*, available on line at www. smithsonianmag.com/history/salem-sets-sail-2682502/.

Biographical information on John Francis, particularly his trip to France, can be found in *The Journal of John Francis: Oct 9-17, 1786* (pamphlet, privately printed by The Rhode Island Historical Society Library but available at the RIHSL), and in Glenn B. Skillin's 1970 "In Search of Cahoone, the 1790 Diary of John Francis," *Old Time New England*, 60:218, 55-71.

John Brown's activities at India Point are described in Caroline Frank's 2003 "John Brown's India Point," *Rhode Island History*, 61:10, 51-69. Background information on his banking activities can be found in *The One Hundred and Fiftieth Anniversary of the Providence National Bank, 1791-1941* (The Providence National Bank, Private Printing, 1941– but available at the RIHSL); in The Providence Institute for Savings 1931*Vignettes* and in William G. Roelker's 1941 *Rhode Island History* article "The Founding of the Providence Bank." John Brown's dust-up with Alexander Hamilton can be found in Harold Syrett, ed.'s 1977 *The Papers of Alexander Hamilton, Vol 25 (1800-1802)* (Columbia University Press, New York, NY) on pages 30 to 37. John Brown's forays into insurance are told in *The Providence Mutual Fire Insurance Company, A Century and A Half of Service, 1800-1950* (The Providence Mutual Fire Insurance Company); and in William G. Roelker and A. Clarkson's 1949 *One Hundred Fifty Years of Providence Washington Insurance Company, 1799-1949* (privately printed by the Providence Washington Insurance Company). The woeful tale of John Brown's tract in the Adirondacks is the subject of Henry A. Brown and R. Walton's 1988 *John Brown's Tract*, op. cit.

Manuscript Sources: In a hand-written manuscript "Reminiscences of Old Providence People," Zachariah Allen gives some pithy and sometimes caustic insights into the personalities of various characters in this book – Moses Brown was "a shrewd and grasping man," John Brown Francis was "an exemplary worthy man" despite the scandalous behavior of his alcoholic father, James B. Mason was "undisciplined and fraudulent" (Zachariah Allen Papers, RIHSL).

Correspondence between Nick and his uncle Moses is primarily in the RIHSL, Moses Brown archive (in microfilm as part of the Papers of the Slave Trade) and includes the letter of May 19th, 1790 offering advice on Nick's first trip to Philadelphia, numerous examples of Nick's interest in abolition and support of Freed Blacks ("Undated" 1792, December

21st, 1792, January 27th, 1794 (Nick to Moses about his attempt to convince Congress to ban the slave trade and a reference to George Benson's anti-slavery views), April 3th, 1811 (refers to the DeWolf family's "disgraceful traffic of slaves for Africa"), April 19th, 1819, "Tuesday 11 o'clock 1807)

CHAPTER 6—BROWN & IVES

In addition to the sources used to describe the growth and development of Providence in Chapters 1 and 2, I also found information on the city's transformation in the early nineteenth century in Russell B. Nye's 1960 *The Cultural Life of the New Nation, 1776-1830* (Harper Brothers, New York, NY); in Robert G. Workman's 1986 *The Eden of America, Rhode Island Landscapes 1820-1920* (The Museum of Art of the Rhode Island School of Design, Providence, RI); in Joseph K. Ott's 1973 "John Innes Clark and his Family – Beautiful People of Providence," 32:10, 123-133; and in Margaret Stillwell's 1943 *The Pageant of Benefit Street* and *While Benefit Street was Young* (both privately printed with the Akerman Standard Press, Providence, RI).

Further information on Ann Carter's father and family can be found in the Providence Preservation Society's pamphlet "Shakespeare's Head-21 Meeting Street, Providence, RI-A pre-Revolutionary landmark linking the city with colonial days" (PPS, Providence, RI). The story of Hope Brown Ives's quest to marry Thomas Ives is told in Isaac P. Noyes's 1905 *Reminiscences of Rhode Island and Ye Providence Plantations,* Op. Cit.

An example of furniture purchased by Nick and Ann at the time of their marriage can be found on page 321 in Patricia Kane's 2016 *Art & Industry in Earl America: Rhode Island Furniture 1650-1830* (Yale University Press, New Haven, CT).

In its *Vignettes* series, the Providence Institute for Savings published "Brown & Ives" in 1931. General background on maritime trade in the days of the Early Republic can be found in Laura S. Saunders's 1976 "Early Nineteenth Century Merchant Sail in Rhode Island," *Rhode Island History,* 35:2, 63-67; and in Stuart Bruchey's1958 "Success or Failure Factors - American merchants in Foreign Trade in the Eighteenth and

Early Nineteenth Centuries," *Business History Review*, 32, 272-292. More specific information on Brown & Ives's Java trade is in Robert W. Kenny's 1958 "The Maiden Voyage of the Ann & Hope of Providence to Botany Bay and Canton 1798-99," *American Neptune* 18:2, 105-136; in James B. Hedges and Jeanette D. Black's 1963 "Disaster in the South Seas: The Wreck of the Brigantine Eliza and The Subsequent Adventures of Captain Correy," *American Neptune*, 23:4, 233-254; and in Sharom Ahmat's 1965 "The Rhode Island Java Trade 1799-1836," *Rhode Island History*, 28:2, 34-48. Background on the firm's South American trade is in Earl C. Tanner's 1965 "Early 19th Century Providence Imports from the Caribbean and Brazil," *Rhode Island History*, 42:10, 116-128; his 1960 "Early 19th Century Providence Exports to Brazil," *Rhode Island History*, 19:7, 89-94; and in his 1957 "South American Ports in the Commerce of Providence (1800-1830)," *Rhode Island History*, 16:7, 65-78.

Manuscript Sources: Evidence of a long courtship between Nick and Ann Carter is in a receipt for Nick from Benjamin Bowen for attending Ann in the five years before their marriage, July 16th, 1802 (Carter-Danforth papers, RIHSL). Nick's letter to Benjamin Carter about his happiness at marrying Ann Carter, November 1791 (JHL). Information on the gifts made by Hope to the First Baptist Meeting House in order to placate negative public opinion about her marriage to Tom Ives are found in a June 27th, 1791 resolution of the First Baptist Society, in the JCBL, Brown Family Archive, Library Correspondence, 1767-1865, Folder 5. The poem quoted "On a young lady who gave a generous Donation" is in Folder 6 (February 7th, 1792). Descriptions of the furnishings bought by Nick and Tom Ives after their respective weddings are in the JCBL, Box 370, Folders 7-9, especially a letter by George Harrison of Philadelphia about order a carriage, June 30th, 1792 (Folder 8) and Box 371, Folders 1-4. Further information can be found in the Ives-Gammell-Safe Papers at the RIHSL, Box 1, including an inventory from the Newport silversmith Joseph Anthony, Jr. dated April 21st, 1792. The birth of Tom Ives's first child is described in a letter from his sister, Elizabeth, December 21th, 1792 (Box 370, Folder 9).

Correspondence regarding George Benson is in the JCBL, Box 44, Folders 9 (description of Newport during a bombardment by the British) and 11 (friction between Benson and his partners, Nick and Tom Ives, notably letters of September 17th, 1796). Further venomous correspondence is in Box 372, Folder 7, including the December 23th, 1795 "George Benson Terms for Closing Partnerhsip." Benson's expulsion from the First Baptist Church is recounted in the *Minutes of Church Meetings* (Charitable Baptist Society) May 27th, 1999, June 27th, 1799, July 25th, 1999, and August 23th, 1799 (my thanks to Dr. J. Stanley Lemons for pointing this out). Much later, Benson corresponded extensively with Moses Brown about the Peace Society and in one letter, November 9th, 1830, reminisced about his childhood and early relationship with the Brown family (in the JCBL, Brown Family Archive, Library Correspondence, 1767-1865, Folder 10).

CHAPTER 7—THE END OF AN ERA

Rhodc Island Federalist politics are covered in John P. Kaminsky's 1983 "Anti-federalism and the Perils of Homogenized History: A Review Essay," *Rhode Island History*, 42:1, 30-37. John Brown's speech to Congress can be found in full in the Annals of Congress X:686-89 and 699.

Further information on the DeWolf family can be found in Cynthia M. Johnson's 2014 *James DeWolfe and the Rhode Island Slave Trade* (The History Press, Charleston, SC); in Thomas N. DeWolf's 2008 *Inheriting the Trade: A Northern Family Confronts Its Legacy as the Largest Slave Trading Dynasty in US History* (Beacon Press, Boston, MA); and in Christy M. Nadalin's 1996 "The Last Years of the Rhode Island Slave Trade," *Rhode Island History*, 54:2, 35-49. The anecdote about Nicholas Brown II's attempting to borrow funds from James DeWolf comes from Rappleye's *Sons of Providence,* op. cit. 303.

In its 1944 *Vignettes* The Providence Institute for Savings covered "The year 1819" and "Jonathan Maxcy" (available at the RIHSL).

Manuscript Sources: Evidence of a long-standing relationship between Nick and Mary Stelle can be found in a bill for repairing Mary's shoe dated April 10th, 1793 (JCBL, Box 371, Folder 1). Letters among John Brown's daughters, Abby Francis and Sally Herreshoff, about Nick's re-marriage to Mary Stelle are at the RIHSL (Abby Brown Francis Papers, July 22nd, July 31st, and September 13th, 1801). John Brown Francis's re-mark about "Brown, Nicholas II (Nick) appears happy-&increases in corpulency" is in the same collection (November 7th, 1801). Elizabeth Fisher's letter to Sally Herreshoff on "the lamented death of our dear John's much beloved wife [Ann Brown Francis]," May 7th, 1828 is in the Herreshoff papers. President Maxcy's letter presenting "a heart glowing with gratitude" for the gift to the College of Rhode Island-November 29th, 1804 is in the JCBL, Brown Family Archive-Library Correspondence 1767-1865, Folder 6.

CHAPTER 8—A NATION TRANSFORMED

Beyond the extensive explanations of the dawn of American industry to be found in Hedges's *The Browns of Rhode Island and Providence Plantations*, op. cit., in McLoughlin's *Rhode Island: A History*, op. cit., and in Coleman's *The Transformation of Rhode Island*, op. cit. (in the list above of fundamental works used in researching this book), Alejandra Irigoin's 2009 "The End of a Silver Era: The Consequences of the Breakdown of the Spanish Peso Standard in China and the United States, 1780s-1850s," *Journal of World History*, 20:2, 207-243 discusses the end of the mari-time era.

Brown & Ives's real estate investments are covered in detail in Hedges's *The Browns of Rhode Island and Providence Plantations*. The growth of manufacturing in Rhode Island is well covered in Brendan F. Gilbane's 1975 "Pawtucket Village Mechanic—Iron, Ingenuity, and the Cotton Revolution," *Rhode Island History*, 34:2, 3-12; in Peter J. Coleman's 1975 "British Immigrants in Rhode Island during the War of 1812," *Rhode Island History* 34:8, 66-76; and in his 1964 "Rhode Island Cotton Manufacturing—A Study in Economic Conservatism," *Rhode Island History*, 23:3, 65-80.

Infrastructure investment is covered in Stewart Schneider's 2003

"Railroad Development in nineteenth Century Rhode Island," *Rhode Island History*, 61:7, 37-48; in The Providence Institute for Savings's 1939 *Vignettes* "The Turnpike Era" and "Washington Bridge" (available at the RIHSL). More specifically, the Blackstone Canal debacle is analyzed in Robert P. Bellrose's 1998 pamphlet *The Blackstone Canal* (Robert P. Bellrose, Bookseller, Slatersville, RI), available at the RIHSL; in Richard E. Greenwood's 1991 "Natural Run and Artificial Falls: Waterpower and the Blackstone Canal," *Rhode Island History*, 49:5, 51-62; and in The Providence Institute for Savings 1939 *Vignettes* "The Blackstone Canal."

Banking in the early Republic is covered in Naomi R. Lamoreaux and Christopher Glaiseka's 1991 "Vehicles of Privilege or Mobility? Banks in Providence, Rhode Island, during the Age of Jackson" *Business History Review,* 65:03, 502-507.

Manuscript Sources: Evidence of Brown & Ives's plans to pursue cotton manufacturing are found in a letter to Peleg Aborn, April 14th, 1825 at the JCBL, Brown Family Archive, Box 403, Folder 8.

CHAPTER 9–JACKSON'S AMERICA

Dr. Patrick J. Conley kindly told me about several Master's theses and PhD dissertations on the politics of nineteenth century Rhode Island, a topic he covers in his 1977 *Democracy in Decline: Rhode Island's Constitutional Development, 1776-1841* (Rhode Island Historical Society, Providence, RI). These most useful manuscripts are Thomas S. Allen's 1994 *Commerce, Credit and Community: The Transformation of Economic Relationships in Rhode Island, 1771-1850*, PhD Dissertation, Brown University; Michael B. Zuckerman's 1981 *The Political Economy of Industrial Rhode Island, 1790-1860*, PhD Dissertation, Brown University; Joseph M. Norton's 1975 California State University Master's Thesis *The Rhode Island Federalist Party: 1785-1815*; and James L. Conrad's 1973 *The Evolution of Industrial Capitalism in Rhode Island, 1790-1830*, PhD Dissertation, University of Connecticut.

Other rich sources on the topic include Ronald P. Formisano's 2008

For the People–American Populist Movements from the Revolution to the 1850s (The University of North Carolina Press, Chapel Hill, NC), Edward F. Sweet's 1971 Fordham University PhD dissertation *The Origins of Rhode Island's Democratic Party*, William N. Chambers's 1963 *Political Parties in the New Nation* (Oxford University Press, New York, NY), as well as other works edited by Patrick T. Conley: *Constitution Day–Reflections by Respected Scholars* (Rhode Island Publications Society, Providence, RI, 2010), and *Rhode Island in Rhetoric and Reflection* (RI Publications Society, Providence, RI, 2002).

Among the many books available on the Jacksonian era, I found most useful Jon Meacham's 2008 *American Lion: Andrew Jackson in the White House* (Random House, New York, NY), H.W. Brands's 2005 *Andrew Jackson: His Life and Times* (Doubleday (Random House), New York, NY), and Daniel Feller's 1995 *The Jacksonian Promise: America 1815-1840* (Johns Hopkins University Press, Baltimore, MD).

Thomas Wilson Dorr and the "Dorr War" are the subjects of Erik J. Chaput's 2013 *The People's Martyr: Thomas Wilson Dorr and his 1824 Rebellion* (University Press of Kansas, Lawrence, KS), and of William M. Wiecek's 2005 "A Peculiar Conservatism and the Dorr Rebellion: Constitutional Clash in Jacksonian America," *The American Journal of Legal History*, 22, 237-253.

Manuscript Sources: Correspondence relating to the Brown family's political involvement in the Jacksonian years is found at the JCBL in Box 408 (the state election of 1831, folder 7), Box 409 (views on the Tariff and Nullification, Folders 4 and 5), JCB in Washington reporting on speeches in Congress by Webster and Clay (Folder 6). Further correspondence on political issues is in the Ives-Gammell-Safe Papers at the RIHSL, Box 1, notably letters between Tom Ives and Benjamin Hazard regarding the 1831 state election and the candidacy of John Brown Francis. There is also extensive correspondence on the 1833 state election in the Henry A. Brown deposit, Folder 23, notably a March 20th, 1833 letter from Tom Ives to John Brown Francis in which he writes "As for the report that the Rich men of Providence will all go against you – if true, it will aid you in the country..."

In addition to the works by Russel B. Nye–*The Cultural Life of the New Nation, 1776-1830* op. cit. under Chapter 6, and his 1974 *Society and Culture in America, 1820-1860* (Harper & Row, New York, NY), the following sources cover in great detail social conditions in early nineteenth century Rhode Island: Mark S. Schantz's 2000 *Piety in Providence: Class Dimensions of Religious Experience in Antibellum Rhode Island* (Cornell University Press, Ithaca, NY); Charles C. Cole Jr.'s 1954 *The Social Ideas of the Northern Evangelists, 1826-1860* (Columbia University Press, New York, NY; Jan de Vries's 1994 "The Industrial Revolution and the Industrious Revolution," *Journal of Economic History*, 54:2, 249-270; John Gilkenson's 1986 *Middle Class Providence, 1820-1940* (Princeton University Press, Princeton, NJ); William M. Pillbury's 1972 "Earning a Living 1788-1818-Job Danforth Cabinetmaker," *Rhode Island* History 31:4, 81-93. and Brother Joseph Brennan's 1940 PhD dissertation *Social Conditions in Industrial Rhode Island - 1820-1860* (Catholic University of America).

There are also numerous sources on the topic of child labor in early textile mills. However, William Moran's 2002 *The Belles of New England, The Women of the Textile Mills and the Families Whose Wealth They Wove* (St Martin's Press, New York, NY) was of particular interest.

All of the books mentioned previously on the evolution of Providence were used in this chapter, as well as Robert P. Emlen's 1984 "A View of Providence: The Explication of a Landscape Painting," *Rhode Island History*, 43:5, 51-62.

Observations on New York City come from Sean Wilentz's 1984 *Chants Democratic: New York City and the Rise of the American Working Class, 1788-1850* (Oxford University Press, New York, NY).

The anecdote about Moses Brown's fighting the great fire of 1801 comes from Robert M. Hazelton's 1945 "Moses Brown on Fire Fighting," *Rhode Island History*, 4:3, 80-83.

The autobiography of William J. Brown was originally published in 1883 as *The Life of William J Brown of Providence, RI—With Personal*

Recollections of Incidents in Rhode Island by Angell and Co, Printer, Providence, RI, and I am fortunate to have a copy of this edition. It was reprinted in 2006 as a paperback by the University of New Hampshire Press, Durham, NH, with a preface by Joan Pope Melish entitled "The Diary of a Free Black Man."

The situation of African-Americans in Providence in the first half of the nineteenth century is covered by John W. Sweet's 2003 *Bodies Politics—Negotiating Race in the American North 1730-1830* (University of Pennsylvania Press, Philadelphia, PA); by Robert J. Cottrol's 1982 *Afro-Yankees: The Providence Black Community in the Antibellum Era* (Greenwood Press, Westport, CT); by Seth Rockman's 2009 "Slavery and Abolition along the Blackstone," in *Landscapes of Industry, An Industrial History of the Blackstone Valley* (Worcester History Museum, University of New England Press, Lebanon, NH); and in Julian Rammelkamp's 1948 "The Providence Negro Community, *Rhode Island History*, 7:1, 20-33.

Details on the Nightingale-Brown House come from Demian Hess's 1988 Master's Thesis *A Review of the Nightingale-Brown Estate* (The John Nicholas Brown Center for Public Humanities, Brown University). The registration form for the National Registry of Historical Places is NPS Form 10-900 OMB No. 102418 R.v. e-6 United States Department of the Interior National Park Service (1988).

CHAPTER 11—A BENEVOLENT EMPIRE

Further works on the evolution of Providence specifically used for this chapter include John H. Cady's 1942 *Walks Around Providence* (privately printed, Ackerman Standard Press, Providence, RI–available at the RIHSL), and William H. Jordy and Christopher Monkhouse's catalogue to the 1982 exhibition *Buildings on Paper - Rhode Island Architectural Drawings 1825-1945* (Bell Gallery, List Art Center - Brown University and Rhode Island Historical Society, Providence, RI).

Background on daily life in the early nineteenth century can be found in Marc McCutchen's 1993 *Everyday Life in the 1800s–A Guide for Writers, Students and Historians* (Writer's Digest Books); in Jack

Larkin's 1988 *The Reshaping of Everyday Life, 1790-1840* (Harper & Row, New York, NY); and in Meyer Reinhold's 1984 *Classica Americana: The Greek and Roman Heritage in the United States* (Wayne University Press, Detroit, MI).

More detail on the Second Great Awakening is in C. Allyn Russell's 1969 "Rhode Island Baptists 1825-1931," *Rhode Island History*, 28:4, 35-48, and in Clifford S. Griffin's 1960 *Their Brother's Keeper: Moral Stewardship in the US, 1800-1860* (Rutgers University Press, New Brunswick, NJ). A fascinating study of the charities and voluntary associations of the "Redeemer Nation," pertaining specifically to Providence (of which there are not many!) is John Gilkeson's 1981 Brown University PhD Dissertation *A City of Joiners: Voluntary Associations in the Formation of the Middle Class in Providence 1830-1920.* The topic is also covered in Conrad E. Wright's 1992 *The Transformation of Charity in Post-Revolutionary New England* (Northeastern University Press, Boston, MA). The story of the Society to Promote Faithful Domestic Servants is told in Jane Lancaster's 1993 "Encouraging Faithful Domestic Servants -- Face, Deviance and Social Control in Providence 1820-1850," *Rhode Island History,* 51:8,71-88.

An excellent history of the British anti-slavery movement is Adam Hochschild's 2005 *Bury the Chains: The British Struggle to Abolish Slavery* (Houghton Mifflin, New York, NY). Anti-abolitionist views come from Frances W. Goddard's three-volume 1870 *The Political and Miscellaneous Writing of William S. Goddard* (Sidney S. Rider & Brother, Providence, RI).

Biographical information on Garrison comes from Henry Mayer's 1998 *All On Fire–William Lloyd Garrison and the Abolition of Slavery* (W.W. Norton & Co, New York, NY).

CHAPTER 12—FATHERS AND SONS

The quote about James Brown (John Brown's son) having "the great gift of being well" comes from Jane Lancaster's article, "By The Pens of Females -- Girls' Diaries from Rhode Island 1788-1821," op. cit. The diary of James Brown is transcribed and annotated by Clarkson A. Collins 3rd in his three-part 1947-48 "James Brown's Diary (1787-1789)," *Rhode Island History Rhode Island History*, 7:1, 9-11; 6:10, 59-105; and 7:4, 51-56. Similarly, the letters of John Brown to his son are at the RIHSL but are also analyzed in Frank H. Brown's 1941 article in *Rhode Island History,* "A Colonial Merchant to His Son (John Brown to James Brown -- 1782/83)." However, the letters of Benjamin Carter are in the Rush Hawkins papers at the JHL but they are compiled in Robert W. Kenny's 1957 "Benjamin Carter, Physician Extraordinary," *Rhode Island History*, 16:10, 97-113. Benjamin Carter's 1816/17 diary of his travels with Nicholas III is also at the JHL..

The young John Carter Brown's travel diaries were painstakingly analyzed by Donald G. Rohr who published his findings in 2005 in *The Young JCB in Europe:Travel Diaries 1823-24* (The John Carter Brown Library, Providence, RI). Later diaries of John Carter Brown are still in family hands. Rohr also gave a talk which was reprinted in 2006 by the JCBL: "The Adventures of John Carter Brown, 1822-24" (talk given at the "Lefty Lewis Cabal," October 9th, 1996).

More on the Francis family and its descendants can be found in Maryalice Huggins's 2009 *Aesop's Mirror*: *A Love Story* (Sarah Crichton Books, Farrar Strauss Giroux, New York, NY).

Manuscript sources: The correspondence among Anne Willing Francis, her son John, and her daughter-in-law Abby Brown is at the RIHSL in the Francis family papers and in the Henry A. Brown repository.

Correspondence between Nick and his brother-in-law Crawford Carter showing his concern for the young man is in the Carter-Danforth Papers at the RIHSL (July 21st, 1806, January 5th, 1807, January 20th, 1808, April 25th, 1809). Correspondence between Crawford Carter and his nephew, JCB, is in the same collection (March 1826). His distaste for Nicholas III is evident in his letter of February 11th, 1826 to his sister Huldah. His observations about New York City are also found in the same letter. Observations on the death of his nieces, Ann Brown Francis, are in a letter to Huldah of May 7th, 1828. The undertaker's bill for Benjamin Carter's coffin, sent to Nicholas III April 25th, 1831, are also in this collection.

Further proof of Nick's attachment to his Carter relatives is in the Benjamin Carter collection at the JHL that includes letters from William R. Danforth (married to Carter's sister Elizabeth) in March 1823 relating financial troubles and thanking Nick for his support.

The letters of Benjamin Carter are in his archive at the JHL. Included is his travel diary from 1816. His sister, Elizabeth Carter, sent news on October 1st, 1809 about the Carter family and mentioned that "Mr. Brown's children are well – John has got to be quite a large boy & is preparing for College." The letter of protest from Huldah Carter about the way Brown & Ives treated her brother is dated December 4th, 1833 in the JCBL, Library Correspondence, 1767-1865 with a reply by Brown & Ives on December 17th.

There are several items in the Carter-Danforth Papers at the RIHSL that pertain to Nicholas III's sojourn in England with his uncle Benjamin Carter, including the shipping receipt for the trunk of books that would one day form the start of JCB's collection. The bill for Nicholas III's purchase of two gold watches while in London, August 18th, 1817 is at the JHL in the Benjamin Carter papers at the JHL.

Letters of Thomas P. Ives to his children are in Box 1 of the Ives-Gammell-Safe Papers at the RIHSL, notably the sentence "the children must be near & taught to love each other" (May 24th, 1808). The letter from Eliza Ives to her sister Charlotte, to which Tom Ives added a postscript, is also in this box. In Folder 3 is the letter from JCB to his uncle Tom Ives, thanking him for advice and admitting that he is torn between living in New York or Providence is dated May 31st, 1825.

A letter from Ann Brown Francis to her stepmother, Mary Stelle Brown, is in the Ives-Gammell-Safe Papers at the RIHSL (Miscellaneous Manuscripts). Ann's diary is in the JCBL, Brown Family Archive-Library Correspondence, 1767-1865, Folder 8 (also includes examples of JCB's penmanship). The heartbreaking letters between Nick and his sister Hope about the death of Ann Brown Francis are also in this box (including a note that Nicholas III came for the funeral, appearing "quite sympathetic &c.")

JCB's diary from his Western trip, December 2nd to December 28th, 1819 is in the JCBL, Library Correspondence, 1767-1865 – Folder 9. The letter from JCB to his father from London, July 20th, 1824, in which he notes "in Europe it is customary for young men to purchase (or their parents for them) a share in an established house and to partake in proportion of the loss and gain," is in the JCBL, Brown Family Archive, Miscellaneous Papers. The letter from JCB to Robert Hale Ives saying it is a pity their fathers did not invest in Manhattan real estate, July 24th, 1835 (JCBL-Library Correspondence 1767-1865, Folder 10).

Letters received by Abby and Anne Francis (daughters of Ann Carter Brown and John Brown Francis) from the Goddard and Herreshoff families are still in family hands.

The February 9th, 1833 "lunatic letter," in which Nicholas Brown III writes that his father should be locked up for giving so much money away to Brown University and other causes–one of the most important pieces of correspondence I found in researching this book–is in the JCBL, Brown Family Archive, Box 52. Other letters from the 1820s (when he was living in New York City) and 1830s (when he was living in Rockland County, NY, in which Nicholas III complains bitterly about his father are in Box 379, Folder 9, Box 412, Box 413, Folder 9, Box 414, Folder 5. The correspondence between Nicholas Brown III and John Brown Francis is still in family hands.

Broadsides covering the deaths of Rhoda Jenckes Brown, Ann Carter Brown, Mary Brown Vandelight, and Ann Brown Francis, are all at the JCBL in the Brown Family Archive, Library Correspondence, 1767-1865.

CHAPTER 13- FROM CHARITY TO PHILANTHROPY

I am extremely indebted to the eminent British art dealer and portrait specialist Philip Mould for his assistance in analyzing the Chester Harding and Thomas Sully portraits of Nick. The costume historian Dr. Ann Poulson provided me with further valuable insights on these portraits.

There is little information available on Nick's personality. I was extremely fortunate to come across a yellowed but undated newspaper clipping in a family scrapbook—probably from the late nineteenth century—which contained the many anecdotes to which I refer. Otherwise, the only other sources are "Sketches of Distinguished Merchants: The Life and Character of the Late Nicholas Brown," *Hunts Merchants Magazine*, December 1841; Francis Wayland's 1841 eulogy of Nick, "Discourse on the Life and Character of the Hon. Nicholas Brown" (Brown University Archive, Hay Library); and William Gammell's "Sketch of the Educational and Other Benefactions of the Late Hon. Nicholas Brown," *Barnard's American Journal of Education*, June, 1857 (available at the JCBL), which are all fine examples of nineteenth century prose floridity.

The story of the African Union Meeting House was first told in an 1821 pamphlet published by Brown & Danforth, republished by Ray Rickman in 2003, and available at the RIHSL. Further information can be found in Robert Rherer, Jr.'s 1965 "Negro Churches in Rhode Island," *Rhode Island History*, 25:1, 9-24. Nick's antislavery sentiment and his desire to assist freed blacks come through clearly in his letters to his uncle, Moses Brown, in the Moses Brown papers, 1790-1823, at the RIHSL, and in "Undated Correspondence with Close Family Members."

The founding of Butler Hospital is told in *A Century of Butler Hospital – 1844-1944*, privately printed by the Board of Trustees of The Butler Hospital in1944.

Manuscript Sources: A letter dated September 23rd, 1824 from Asa Messer introducing young JCB to Reverend Islington in London describes Nick: "There is no Baptist here, if any where, whose liberality is comparable to his and there are not may whose property is greater. It is certainly a pleasing consideration that his liberality is always directed to religious or charitable or literary objects." 1823 (JCBL-Library Correspondence 1767-1865, Folder 9). Nick pays for church pews, December 10th, 1831 (JCBL-Library Correspondence 1767-1865, Folder 10).

Correspondence between Nick and Ebenezer Thresher (1798-1886) about educating young men are revealing of his views and ideals. These are at the JHL, Special Collections. Other letters in this repository show

Nick's approach to philanthropy (supporting endowments, known as "sinking funds,") and his focus on religion and science. See in particular letters December 5th, 1831 and April 5th, 1833. Letters of September 22nd, 1838 and July 5th, 1838 refer to the number of demands made on his purse and his "heavy doings on the Hill [Brown University]."

Nick's desire to found a hospital for the insane is mentioned in a letter of May 11th, 1840 in the same repository.

CHAPTER 14–BROWN UNIVERSITY

My theory about the reasons for Nick's extraordinary generosity to Brown University was first described in Ben Schreckinger's 2012 Brown University term paper "Guided By Green: Brown and its relationship with outside sources of money" which he kindly shared with me.

There exist numerous sources on the life and philosophy of Francis Wayland, mostly from the nineteenth and early twentieth century (although he enjoyed a resurgence in the 1980s with the neo-liberal movement and the followers of the economist Friedrich Hayek). Among the most useful for my purposes, I found Francis Wayland, Jr. and H.L. Wayland's 1867 *A Memoir of the Life and Labors of Francis Wayland, D.D., LL.D., late president of Brown University, including selections from his personal reminiscences and correspondence, by his sons, Francis Wayland and H.L. Wayland* (2 volumes, Sheldon & Co, New York, NY); William G. Roelker's "Francis Wayland: A Neglected Pioneer of Higher Education," *Proceedings of the American Antiquarian Society*, Vol 53, 27-78, April 1943; Theodore R. Crane's 1959 Harvard PhD dissertation "Francis Wayland and Brown University," and his 1962 *Francis Wayland: Political Economist as Educator* (Brown University Press, Providence, RI); and Mark Y. Hamley's 1994 *Beyond a Christian Commonwealth: The Protestant Quarrel with the American Republic, 1830-1860* (University of North Carolina Press, Chapel Hill, NC).

In addition to the histories of Brown University cited under Chapter 2, the anecdote about "The War of the Greeks" comes from William Hastings's 1932 "The War of the Greeks at Brown," *New England Quarterly*, 5, 533-554.

Manuscript Sources: Most of the sources on the history of Brown University are kept at the JHL. These include 1826 correspondence between Nick and Francis Wayland (in particular letters of October 15th, 1826 and October 30th, 1826-in which Nick states "the best policy should be to hold out a liberal view & make the college a nursery of Science &c."

The Corporation minutes 1825-1841 show that Nick was present at every meeting; Nick's resignation from the Board of Trustees in 1828 in favor of his son JCB; the creation that year of a "Committee to consult with the President in relation to the affairs of the University" which included Tom Ives and Robert Hale Ives (thus Nick removed himself from any official position but played a huge role "behind the throne.")

Commentary on the actions taken by Francis Wayland can be found in the pages of *The Rhode Island American*, especially September 1st, 1830 ("… the rapid diminution of the graduating classes"); September 7th, 1830 (Letter to the Editor from "Anti-Croaker" which accuses Brown University of being "wholly inefficient and worthless as a *general* school. That institution belongs to a particular sect, is patronized by a single family, and must, in the nature of things, be directed by sectarian views and family influence.") Also editorials on September 10th, 11th, 12th, 21st, 24th, 28th, 1830. The Providence Journal chimed in with an article September 10th, 1830.

In the Brown University Archives at the JHL, there is a January 13th, 1823 letter to the University Corporation in which Nick states that "the dissemination of letters and knowledge is the great means of social happiness."

CHAPTER 15– LEGACIES

Nick's will is in the Brown University Archives, JHL.

Nicholas III's ill-fated adventures in Italy are told in Leo F. Stock's 1945 *Consular Relations Between the United States and the Papal States: Instructions and Dispatches*, (American Catholic Historical Association, Washington, DC). I was fortunate to hear Professor David Kertzner speak on the subject at the JCBL in Spring 2016.

The story of Rush Hawkins's memorial to his wife Annmary Brown is told in Margaret B. Sitwell's 1925 pamphlet *The Annmary Brown Memorial* (Privately Printed); that of Count Bajnotti's tributes to his wife Carrie Brown are told in Daniel F. Harrington's "A Romantic Tribute by a Famous Widower," *The Providence Journal* "My Turn," September 7th, 2016.

There are many sources on the uniquely American practice of generous private support for higher education, but I found particularly useful Merle Curti and Roderick Nash's 1965 *Philanthropy and the Shaping of American Higher Education* (Rutgers University Press, New Brunswick, NJ) and Julie A. Rueben's 1997 *The Making of the Modern University: Intellectual Transformation and the Marginalization of Morality* (University of Chicago Press, Chicago, IL). John Carter Brown's collection is described in Horatio Rogers's 1878 *Private Libraries of Providence with a Preliminary Essay on the Love of Books* (Sidney S. Rider, Providence, RI).

Manuscript Sources: Most materials relating to Nick's death, will and the ensuing legal battle pursued by his son, Nicholas II, can be found in the JCBL' Brown Family Archive, Box 52. The funeral procession is described in Folder 7. Nicholas III's vitriolic letters are in Folders 8-13.

JCB's views on money can be surmised from a February 1833 letter (JCBL, Box 409, Folder 6), referring to "young Buonaparte" driving a fine carriage in Baltimore: "he certainly has a right to drive a Coach & four." His views on Saratoga "The Comp'y at the Springs this season has been quite fashionable tho' many think not as much as in former years," August 10th, 1843, is in Box 420, Folder 10. The letter in which he writes "Only let me have a cool million…" was written on August 26th, 1834 to Robert Hale Ives. Crawford Carter's comments about his nephew Nicholas III's behavior in Italy are found in an April 1s, 1847 letter to H.H. Clements, Nicholas III's 1851 and 1852 letters from Europe after his exile from Italy (mentioning his commissioning of a portrait of his ancestor John Carter) are also in the Carter-Danforth Papers, RIHSL.

The gift of the John Carter Brown Library to Brown University is recounted in the *Brown Alumni Monthly*, "The John Carter Brown Library," November 1901 (when the collection was given to the university) and in May 1904 (when the building was completed).

Neil Harris's biography of John Carter Brown III is cited in the introduction to this chapter. Biographical information on the twentieth century Browns can be found in the RIAMCO finding aids on the papers of John Nicholas Brown, Harold Brown, Natalie Dresser Brown, John Nicholas Brown II, and Anne Kinsolving Brown (ASKB). Windshield House, my grandfather's modernist summer home on Fisher's Island is described in Dietrich Neumann, Ed.'s 2001 *Richard Neutra's Windshield House* (Yale University Press, New Haven, CT). More recently, J. Carter Brown's daughter Elissa Brown produced in 2016 the feature film "Windshield: A Vanished Vision." My father Nicholas Brown VI was interviewed in 2015 by historian George M. Goodwin, to whom I am indebted for sharing his unpublished manuscript "John Nicholas Brown: Architectural Advocate and Diplomat."

INDEX

I

J

Massachusetts Bay Colony, 2, 4, 15, 35

Massasoit Manufacturing Company, 167

Material culture; In the New Republic, 231, 232

Mather, Cotton, 35

Matteson, Frank, 350, 352, 354, 355

Matteson, George, 340, 341, 342, 350

Maxcy, Jonathan, 155, 156, 157, 279, 310

Maysville Road veto, 175

Mazzini, Giuseppe, 325

McCulloch v. Maryland, 184

Medieval Academy of America, 353

Meeting of Proprietors of the Providence Library, 34

Melish, Joanne Pope, xiv

Memorial Sloan Kettering Hospital, 364

Merchants, Emblems of wealth, 30

Messer, Asa, 155, 157, 158, 288, 297, 298, 299, 300, 305

Metacomet, Sachem. *See* King Philip

Methodist Church, 234

Metropolitan Museum of Art, New York, 363

Metropolitan Opera House, New York City, 342

Miantinomi, Sachem, 4

Mill Acts of 1832, 247

Miller& Hutchens, 221

Minott, Samuel, 30

Missouri Compromise, 152, 184, 244

Miss Searle's School, 270

Molasses Act, 24, 45

Monroe Doctrine, 151

Monroe, James, 151, 153, 164, 174, 183, 243

Montesquieu, Michel de, 152

Monuments Men, xvii, 358

Morris, Robert, 52, 55, 104, 108, 137, 138, 252, 254

Moses Brown School, 282

Mount Hope Insurance Company, 145

Mount Vernon Lodge, 256

Mr. Moody's Grammar School, 70

Mrs. Wilkinson's School, 71

Mr. Uptick's Tutorial, 70

Museum of Modern Art, New York, 356, 357

N

NAACP, 351

Napoleonic wars, 130, 147, 149, 150, 153, 199

Narragansett tribe, 4, 220

National Aquarium in Baltimore, 362

National Gallery of Art, Washington, DC, xvii, 362, 363

National Register of Historical Places, 218

National Republican Party, 185, 186, 190, 191, 192

National Urban League, 351

Netherlands Trading Company, 160

Neutra, Richard, 357

New England Anti-Slavery Society, 126, 246

New England Association of Farmers, Mechanics and Other Workingmen, 190

CPSIA information can be obtained
at www.ICGtesting.com
Printed in the USA
BVHW03*1256180918
527836BV00001B/1/P

9 781480 844162